Probably nowhere can you find the range of actual examples and keen insights offered by the spectrum of contributors to this landmark book. It is one to be pondered and treasured, and, although it is not the last word on the subject, it is certainly an impressive beginning. We are deeply indebted to both the contributors and the editors for so stout and comprehensive a set of documents, on so crucial and yet baffling a challenge. They are not interested in just any kind of business. Their focus is on what they define as *kingdom* enterprises.

—RALPH D. WINTER
President, William Carey International University

Forthright, practical, and compelling! *On Kingdom Business* addresses the tough questions surrounding profit making in the name of Christ, and convincingly validates the fact that authentic ministry can indeed take place within the context of authentic business. This book will bring welcomed confidence to many Christian entrepreneurs, as they realize that God's call to fulfill the Great Commission can be accomplished in and through business itself—seamlessly and legitimately.

—CHRISTIAN OVERMAN
Executive Director, Worldview Matters, Inc.

Kingdom entrepreneurship has come of age as global Christian businessmen and women unite to extol the virtues of investing in God's kingdom. *On Kingdom Business* is definitely recommended reading for discerning Christians committed to the Great Commission ministry.

—JOHN VONG
Research Director, Geneva Global, Inc.

Businessmen and women are fulfilling the Great Commission by more than giving money. *On Kingdom Business* tells their stories and reveals the methodologies that work in today's world. They are offering more pervasive and comprehensive impact than traditional missions. People interested in kingdom business will benefit by reading this remarkable book.

—JOHN H. WARTON, JR.
International Director, Business Professional Network

This book is going to make a good number of traditional missions supporters uncomfortable. Instead of upholding the model of the "full-time" missionary dependent on outside subsidy, these businesspeople with a heart for missions are practicing a full-time calling of establishing businesses that compete for capital and customers and create value. Business is not a necessary evil or a cover for the "real work" but a way to create investments, jobs, economic vitality, and a hearing for a credible gospel. It is hard work, but these pages are filled with the examples and learnings of extraordinary men and women—evangelistic entrepreneurs.

—FRED SMITH
President, The Gathering

Today's mission context demands the mobilization of tens of thousands of businessmen and women committed to spreading the gospel through genuine business. *On Kingdom Business* reveals several best practice models and discusses key issues related to kingdom entrepreneurship. It trumpets a clarion call for the church to recruit, train, and field its least utilized members and turn them into its most powerful asset for missions in the coming decades.

—CHUCK MADINGER
Missions Pastor, Southland Christian Church

ON KINGDOM BUSINESS

Transforming Missions Through Entrepreneurial Strategies

Tetsunao Yamamori
Kenneth A. Eldred

EDITORS

CROSSWAY BOOKS

A PUBLISHING MINISTRY OF
GOOD NEWS PUBLISHERS
WHEATON, ILLINOIS

On Kingdom Business: Transforming Missions Through Entrepreneurial Strategies

Copyright © 2003 by Tetsunao Yamamori and Kenneth A. Eldred

Published by Crossway Books
> A publishing ministry of Good News Publishers
> 1300 Crescent Street
> Wheaton, Illinois 60187

Cover design: David LaPlaca

Cover photo: Getty Images

First printing 2003

Printed in the United States of America

Unless otherwise indicated, all Scripture quotations are from The Holy Bible, English Standard Version, copyright © 2001 by Crossway Bibles, a division of Good News Publishers. Used by permission. All rights reserved.

Scripture references marked NASB are from the *New American Standard Bible®* Copyright © The Lockman Foundation 1960, 1962, 1963, 1968, 1971, 1972, 1973, 1975, 1977, 1995. Used by permission.

Scripture references marked NIV are from the *Holy Bible: New International Version.®* Copyright © 1973, 1978, 1984 by International Bible Society. Used by permission of Zondervan Publishing House. All rights reserved.

The "NIV" and "New International Version" trademarks are registered in the United States Patent and Trademark Office by International Bible Society. Use of either trademark requires the permission of International Bible Society.

Scripture references marked KJV are from the King James Version of the Bible.

Library of Congress Cataloging-in-Publication Data
On kingdom business : transforming missions through entrepreneurial
strategies / edited by Tetsunao Yamamori and Kenneth A. Eldred.
    p. cm.
    Papers from a conference held at Regent University, Virginia
Beach, Va. in October, 2002.
    ISBN 13: 978-1-58134-502-5
    ISBN 10: 1-58134-502-X (TPB : alk. paper)
    1. Business—Religious aspects—Congresses. 2. Entrepreneurship—
Religious aspects—Congresses. 3. Business—Cross-cultural studies—
Congresses. 4. Entrepreneurship—Cross-cultural studies—Congresses.
5. Missions—Congresses. I. Yamamori, Tetsunao, 1937-   .
II. Eldred, Kenneth A., 1943-   . III. Title.
HF5388.O5   2003
261.8'5—dc21   2003005162

ML		16	15	14	13	12	11	10	09	08	07	06
15	14	13	12	11	10	9	8	7	6	5	4	3	2

CONTENTS

PREFACE

We have come to the end of a remarkable century in global missions. Christians are present in every country on the face of the earth, and evangelical Christianity is the world's fastest growing major religion. In addition, Christians and missionaries in Asia, Africa, and Latin America outnumber their counterparts from the West, who so sacrificially brought them the gospel.

And yet, if our goal remains obeying Jesus' command to make disciples of all nations, then we have no room for complacency. According to David Barrett, about 1.6 billion of the world's 6.2 billion people have not heard the gospel and in fact have little or no opportunity to hear it. And despite all our hard work in the evangelical missions movement in reaching the "unreached," adherents of the other major world religions—Muslims, Hindus, and Buddhists—have been largely impervious to our evangelism. As my colleague Ralph Winter so cogently put it at the second Global Consultation on World Evangelization conference in Pretoria, South Africa, "More of the same will not be enough."

While many of these unreached people care little for Jesus Christ, they spend a lot of time thinking about Adam Smith, who wrote the "capitalist manifesto," *The Wealth of Nations*. To reach such people, we need to not only tell them about the gospel but also *show* it to them. How do we do this in the context of today's globalizing economy, in which people's felt needs center more on finding a job and attaining economic development than on investigating the claims of Christ? In a word, the answer is "business," or, to be more precise, "kingdom business." If the traditional Western missionary movement had some flaws this last century, surely one of the most obvious, in hindsight, was its failure to mobilize many Christian business professionals (beyond using their money) for the Great Commission. At the start of a new century and millennium, we can no longer afford this oversight.

In recent decades, of course, we have seen the strong emergence of tentmaking—working at a secular job while also working as a missionary—as an approach to gaining entry to so-called "restricted-access" nations. The church's interest in reaching the "10/40 Window"[1] has underscored the need for tentmaking of all types. In his book of world evangelization trends, *Missions in the Third Millennium,* Stan Guthrie writes, "Some of the strongest interest in the strategy comes from churches looking to unleash their laity for world missions in cost-effective and creative ways."[2] And indeed, tentmaking in recent years has evolved from a novelty to a respected tool, among churches and agencies. According to the *Mission Handbook*, the number of agency-supported tentmakers from the United States increased from 1,040 in 1992 to 3,220 in 1999. This dramatic jump occurred while the number of full-time traditional missionaries actually declined.

Tentmaking has borne some fruit, although there have been many failures along the way. Some tentmakers have been kicked out of the countries they were attempting to reach. Why? Because they were not doing the work their visa said they would do. Instead, their secular job was merely a cover for the "real" work of evangelism they hoped to do. Others have failed because they did not have access to spiritual support and fellowship in their busy or hostile environments. Another problem: Because most tentmakers are "job-takers," the flexibility and team cohesion so necessary for effective ministry are difficult. I would like to suggest a new model—or perhaps a return to the biblical paradigm: kingdom entrepreneurs.

In contrast to regular tentmakers, kingdom entrepreneurs are job *makers,* starting small to large for-profit businesses. These businesses are not fronts to get into closed countries (with the attendant ethical problems), but real enterprises that meet real human needs. As the former leader of a relief and development agency, I know that many restricted-access countries are seeking economic growth. They welcome entrepreneurs warmly, even when they shut their doors tightly to others.

Moreover, in churches worldwide there are increasing numbers of talented entrepreneurs who sense God's call to missions. These people want to use their unique skills and backgrounds for the kingdom. More and more are doing so, employing their business acumen as a means of ministry to the nations. Their goal is to share the gospel and make disciples across cultural divides while starting and maintaining for-profit businesses that produce tangible goods and services.

In recent years, various people have used different expressions to describe what I am calling "kingdom entrepreneurship": "kingdom business," "holistic business," "Great Commission companies," "kingdom companies," "entrepreneurial tentmaking," and "business as mission." All these nomenclatures point to doing ministry through business *ownership*. Such a business ministry can be carried out in a monocultural setting[3] as well as in a cross-cultural one. A cross-cultural setting requires additional training and added cultural sensitivity. Kingdom entrepreneurs are those who are engaged in kingdom entrepreneurship.

Kingdom entrepreneurs are business owners, called by God, to do ministry through business. They are business owners rather than business employees. They are entrepreneurs rather than salaried men and women. They are engaged full-time in business. They are more like Aquila and Priscilla than like Paul (Acts 18:1-5, 24-26).

If cross-cultural kingdom entrepreneurs wish to have a more precise self-definition as they work in the so-called "closed countries," I submit the following: Kingdom entrepreneurs are cross-cultural business owners, called by God, to do ministry through business in restricted-access countries.

In my research on successful models of kingdom business, I have identified three basic types of kingdom entrepreneurship.

1. *Cases of Strong Business and Weak Ministry.* On the extreme left of a continuum are Christian entrepreneurs who have successfully built their businesses, but whose ministry, for various reasons, has lagged behind. Building a business, especially in a cross-cultural setting, demands concentration and focus. It is not easy to survive and thrive in the business world. While a business may grow strong, ministry often remains weak.

2. *Cases of Strong Ministry and Weak Business.* On the extreme opposite end of the continuum are Christian entrepreneurs who have entered a restricted-access country on a business visa. While the ministry is well under way, the business does not receive much attention. After all, business is a "front" to secure entry into the country. Supporting churches and friends back home expect the ministry to succeed. But, after a while, the non-Christian local people who work in the company begin wondering where their salaries come from when obviously their company is not making a profit. They begin suspecting that something funny is going on. They may think, "Is this a CIA operation?" Rumors spread and the ministry is compromised. Some cases may be much less dramatic than this. Nevertheless, business does not receive adequate attention.

3. *Cases of Strong Business and Strong Ministry.* In the middle of the continuum are Christian entrepreneurs who do not lose sight of their original calling to do ministry through business—making disciples while making a profit through genuine business. Certain cultures revere and readily accept successful businessmen and women. However, businesses do not become successful overnight. There will be hardships and trials before kingdom entrepreneurs see any success. Integrating business and ministry is not an easy

assignment, but, by the grace of God, some kingdom entrepreneurs do succeed. While the cases in this volume come from this category, they are not all the same. They vary in degrees of success and scope.

This book reproduces in edited form most of the presentations made at the consultation on this topic held at Regent University (Virginia Beach, Virginia) in October 2002. As at the consultation, the material is divided into three main sections. The first, "Case Studies," looks at examples of kingdom business from around the world. These chapters provide many practical and hard-won insights for those considering this kind of ministry. The authors examine common barriers to such ministry, look at training issues, and share their own successes and failures in the Muslim world, across Asia, and in the Middle East. The second part of the book, "Essays," provides more conceptual undergirding for this approach. The third, "Conclusion," ties it all together with lessons learned and questions for the future.

We will need many kinds of missionaries and Christian workers in the coming decades. The task ahead of us is enormous. Christianity gained no "market share" in the twentieth century, while Islam grew by more than 50 percent. If we want to make a difference in our efforts to fulfill the Great Commission, we need to be willing to try new things. I believe kingdom business will be a strategy of choice for the twenty-first century. This book will help lay the conceptual groundwork.

I pray that this book will serve as a rallying point to further explore kingdom entrepreneurship. We need to awaken and deploy the underutilized army of Christian entrepreneurs around the world for the expansion of God's kingdom.

My coeditor Ken Eldred and I have many people to thank. Stan Guthrie of *Christianity Today* provided expert editorial assistance. Dr. Lane Dennis, president and CEO of Crossway Books, immediately agreed to publish this book, even when the consultation was no more than an idea. Dean John Mulford of the Regent University Graduate School of Business provided prompting and inspiration that were critical to the consultation becoming a reality. Rose Gilliana and Sarah Lane of Regent provided much-needed help in the day-to-day oversight leading up to the consultation. Living Stones Foundation, Fieldstead and Company, and Global HMR, Inc., provided the financial contributions to make the consultation and the publication of this book possible.

—Tetsunao Yamamori

EDITORS AND CONTRIBUTORS

Tetsunao Yamamori (book coeditor, preface) is president emeritus of Food for the Hungry International. He recently served as distinguished visiting professor at the Graduate School of Business, Regent University, and currently is Lausanne senior associate for holistic mission. He holds a Ph.D. from Duke University. He is author, coauthor, or editor of numerous books, including *Penetrating Missions' Final Frontier* (InterVarsity Press, 1993), *Holistic Entrepreneurs in China: A Handbook on the World Trade Organization and New Opportunities for Christians* (William Carey International University Press, 2002), *Exploring Religious Meaning*, 6th edn. (Prentice-Hall/Simon & Schuster, 2003), and *Progressive Pentecostalism: A Global Perspective* (University of California Press, 2003). He served as convenor of the Consultation for Holistic Entrepreneurs held at the Regent University Graduate School of Business, October 3-5, 2002.

Kenneth A. Eldred (book coeditor, introduction, chapter 18) is currently an investor and founder/CEO of Living Stones Foundation Charitable Trust. He has founded numerous successful companies, including Ariba Technologies, the leader in the Internet business-to-business industry, and Inmac, which went public in 1987 and later merged with MicroWarehouse. Internationally, he is cofounder and director of a call center based in India. He has also founded other ventures in Europe and China. He was named "Retail Entrepreneur of the Year" in 1988 by the Institute of American Entrepreneurs. He also serves on the Board of Advisors for Crosspoint Venture Partners. Crosspoint was named by *Forbes* as the most successful venture investment firm for three years in a row. He is also chairman of Parakletos Venture Capital. Eldred focuses his efforts primarily on charitable projects. He is in much demand as a speaker and an advisor to various ventures dedicated to kingdom entrepreneurship. He holds a B.A. and an M.B.A. from Stanford University.

Kim-kwong Chan (chapter 1) is executive secretary for mission and pastoral formation of the Hong Kong Christian Council. He holds a Ph.D. from the University of Ottawa and a Th.D. from St. Paul University. He has authored or coauthored nine books, including *Protestantism in Contemporary China* (Cambridge University Press, 1993), *Witnesses to Power: Stories of God's Quiet Work in a Changing China* (Paternoster, 2000), and *Holistic Entrepreneurs in China: A Handbook on the World Trade Organization and New Opportunities for Christians* (William Carey International University Press, 2003). The Hong Kong government recently appointed Chan as a Justice of the Peace.

Clem Schultz (chapter 2, with Sonia Chou) has twenty years' experience in doing business and missions simultaneously in East and Central Asia. He is president of AMI, a manufacturing and consulting company specializing in high-technology manufacturing and service start-ups. AMI starts an average of one new company a year. AMI facilitates church planting in the 10/40 Window through strategic and contractual alliances with more than fifteen mission agencies. Mr. Schultz was a divisional manager for two major multinational companies in East Asia. He has ten years of training in business and law.

Ken and Margie Crowell (chapter 3) have been married for forty-eight years and have three children and eight grandchildren. Ken served in the U.S. Army during the Korean War. He attended California State University/Northridge, Multnomah Bible College, and Western Seminary. He was an officer in the Los Angeles Police Department and has been an engineer at Areojet General, Tektronics, and Motorola in the United States and in Israel. Ken and Margie have formed the following companies in Israel: Galtronics (antennae), Galcom (radios), Galadon (communion products), Galilee Experience (multimedia), Galilee of the Nations (music), and Megavoice (voice storage).

Abiir William (chapter 4) was born in the Far East and received most of her education in the West. She then went to the Middle East to study Arabic. She has been engaged in kingdom business in the Arab world for the past thirteen years.

Patrick Lai (chapter 5 and appendix D) has a degree in business-marketing from the University of Oregon and an M.Div. from Trinity Evangelical Divinity School. He is completing a D.Miss. at the Asian Theological Seminary in Manila. Patrick has served in Asia for eighteen years: four in Hong Kong as a traditional missionary among Chinese under Overseas Missionary Fellowship, and the past fourteen as a tentmaker among Muslims with Frontiers. He and his team planted two churches and one fellowship group among Muslims while starting several businesses. He also is a consultant to businesses and nongovernmental organizations (NGOs) in Asia and North Africa.

Norman Teece (chapter 6) was born in Bedfordshire, England, in 1947, and worked for twenty-seven years as a mechanical engineer. Since 1993, he and his wife Fi have lived in Phnom Penh where they work among the very poor and disadvantaged in society, establishing business initiatives and community development projects. They have two grown sons in addition to their adopted son and family in Cambodia.

Daniel Batchelder (chapter 7) is the executive director of the International Foundation of Hope (IFHope). He has worked extensively in South Asia for the past five years. His work focuses on community and economic development in education, health care, small business development, and agriculture. Daniel is an entrepreneur who established a consulting firm that he directed for twenty-two years in northern Vermont. He has two grown sons and lives with his wife Anne in Colorado Springs.

Juerg Opprecht (chapter 8) is founder and president of Business Professional Network (BPN). He is married, has four children, and lives in Faoug, Vaud Canton, Switzerland. He finished his education in electrical engineering. He also received training in executive development at IMD Lausanne. After working in different management positions, he became the president of a family business with 1,000 employees. He now owns a real estate company and a five-star hotel in a well-known Swiss ski resort. He serves on the boards of several companies, including some Christian institutions.

Byung Ho Choi (chapter 9) is a South Korean businessman working in Central Asia. He is general director of Siroko and director of the Silk Road Chamber Choir.

Luke Watson (chapter 10) left a career as a research scientist in the West and began teaching at a university in South Asia as a means of evangelism. He later shifted to business and found better opportunities to pursue his calling. He holds a Ph.D. in a scientific field.

Joe Suozzo (chapter 11) and a Christar team established a network of house churches among the Chamar people of North India from 1989 to 1999. He completed a graduate thesis at Columbia International University on the characteristics of entrepreneurial tentmaking. He is currently serving as an interim pastor in one of his supporting churches in New Jersey. Joe and his family hope to return to Asia as tentmaking entrepreneurs to continue church planting among the unreached.

Peter Tsukahira (chapter 12) attended Bible school and seminary in the United States, then moved with his wife Rita to Tokyo, where they led a growing international fellowship of Christians. Peter also worked in the Japanese computer industry. In 1987, he was hired by an Israeli high-technology firm, and the family moved to Haifa. After the Gulf War in 1991, they assisted in the founding of Kehilat HaCarmel (Carmel Assembly) on Mount Carmel, and Peter became one of the pastors. Now an Israeli citizen, he is the founder of Carmel Communications, a ministry to Christians of many nations. Peter is ordained by World Challenge International Ministers' Fellowship, founded by David Wilkerson, and serves on the Board of Directors of Church Growth International, founded by David Yonggi Cho.

Wayne Grudem (chapter 13) is research professor of Bible and theology at Phoenix Seminary in Scottsdale, Arizona. He taught for twenty years at Trinity Evangelical Divinity School, Deerfield, Illinois, where he was chairman of the Department of Biblical and Systematic Theology. He received a B.A. from Harvard University, an M.Div. from Westminster Seminary, and a Ph.D. in New Testament from Cambridge University. He has published eight books, including *Systematic Theology* (IVP-U.K. and Zondervan). He is a past president of the Council on Biblical Manhood and Womanhood and a member of the Translation Oversight Committee for the *English Standard Version* of the Bible. He and his wife Margaret are members of the FamilyLife speaker team (a division of Campus Crusade for Christ).

Thomas Sudyk (chapter 14) is founder and CEO of Evangelistic Commerce (EC), which mobilizes professionals to start and operate for-profit companies in restricted-access countries. Enterprises include medical transcription, computer-aided design, software development, and exports to customers primarily in the West. EC offers extensive training programs interfacing business skills with mission purpose.

John Cragin (chapter 15) is professor of business at Oklahoma Baptist University. Among his many business positions held, he was director of international operations and president and CEO of a large company. He has started and run businesses and worked as a consultant to businesses and governments while working closely with a dozen missions organizations. John has lectured and supervised business-missions interns around the world. He holds a Ph.D. in management from the University of Oklahoma.

Heinz Suter (chapter 16) is a graduate of the Swiss Mercantile School and holds an M.A. in intercultural studies. He worked in banking before becoming involved in international missions through Operation Mobilization in Latin America. From 1984 to 1996 he lived with his family in Spain, where he helped found PM International. He was involved in tentmaking business projects in North Africa. Presently, he is promoting business involvement in missions through the "SALT Foundation" and the kingdom company in Basel, Switzerland, that he assists.

Michael R. Baer (chapter 17) is a pastor turned businessman. He is the founder and president of a small business consulting company based in Atlanta, Georgia. He is the executive director of IMED (International Micro Enterprise Development, Inc.). He lives in North Carolina with his wife and has two grown daughters.

John D. Beckett (chapter 19) is chairman and CEO of R. W. Beckett Corporation. After graduating from MIT with a B.S. in economics and mechanical engineering, he was an engineer in the aerospace industry. He joined his father in a small family-owned manufacturing business and turned it into a company with sales of nearly $100 million and more than 500 employees. He helped found Intercessors for America, is a founding board member of the International Leadership University, and is on the boards of Henry Blackaby Ministries and Concerts of Prayer International. His first book, *Loving Monday: Succeeding in Business Without Selling Your Soul,* was published in 1998 by InterVarsity Press. Spring Arbor University recently conferred on him an honorary Doctor of Law degree.

Steven L. Rundle (chapter 20 and appendix D) is associate professor of economics at Biola University, where he also teaches a "Business as Mission" course. He is cofounder of the Strategic Capital Group, a venture capital fund that assists companies bringing spiritual and economic blessing to the least-evangelized and least-developed parts of the world. Rundle is also coauthor of *Business as Mission: Globalization and the Emerging Role of Great Commission Companies* (InterVarsity Press, 2003). He holds a Ph.D. from Claremont Graduate University.

Thuan-seng Tan (chapter 21), an accountant by training, spent twenty years working with multinational corporations including Shell, British Petroleum, and Norcros, rising to the position of regional CEO. After becoming a Christian in 1982, he became a management consultant. In 1991 he set up Bright Arrows as a business platform for World Horizons, a Welsh-based missions organization. Bright Arrows has evolved into a holistic mission agency through kingdom business enterprise, with operations in six Asian countries.

Howard Norrish (chapter 22) was born in India to parents who were in the British army. Howard's early life was spent on the Indian subcontinent and in South Africa. He joined Operation Mobilization in 1963 and is based in London with OM's International Coordinating Team. Howard earned B.Sc. and M.Sc. degrees from the American University in Beirut, Lebanon, and a Ph.D. in biochemistry from Cambridge University. He taught for seven years in the medical school of King Saud University in Riyadh, Saudi Arabia.

Randolph Case (chapter 23) is an associate professor in the school of business at Regent University. His teaching and research focus on entrepreneurial strategy and the dynamics of personal change. He was the primary investigator in two broad studies of entrepreneurial management funded by the Pharmaceutical Education and Research Institute and Pricewaterhouse-Coopers. Case holds a B.S. in mechanical engineering from the University of Virginia, an M.B.A. from Columbia University, and a Ph.D. in management from the Wharton School of the University of Pennsylvania. Before earning his Ph.D., Case was chief financial officer of IMG Ltd., an information services company with subsidiaries in Europe and the United States.

Ralph A. Miller (chapter 24) is entrepreneur-in-residence at the Regent University Graduate School of Business. He teaches entrepreneurship, international business, and Christian values in business. A former Navy fighter pilot, Miller spent the past forty years in executive or board positions in industries such as aviation, banking, electronics, and travel, as well as in non-profit ministries. With a graduate degree in divinity, he focuses his teaching and mentoring on integrating Christian faith and biblical wisdom into the daily decision making process of Christian executives.

René Padilla (author of the three devotionals in appendix B) was born in Quito, Ecuador, and was reared in Bogota, Colombia. Since 1967 he has lived in Buenos Aires, Argentina. He received a Ph.D. in New Testament from the University of Manchester and an honorary D.D. from Wheaton College. He has served as a visiting professor at various universities, theological seminaries, and missiological centers around the world. He is currently president of the Kairos Foundation and editor-in-chief of *Ediciones Kairos* and of *Iglesia y Mision* magazines. He is also the international president of Tear Fund, United Kingdom and Ireland.

Kenell J. Touryan (author of "Dynamics of Faith" in appendix C) is chief technology analyst at the National Renewable Energy Laboratory of the U.S. Department of Energy. He uses his training and skills in science and technology working as a tentmaker to advance God's kingdom. He holds a Ph.D. in nuclear science from Princeton University.

INTRODUCTION

For several years now the Lord has shown me that business can be a powerful tool in mission work. Four years ago, I had a conversation with General Paul Cerjan, then president of Regent University, about the very subject. I was unaware of most of what was going on for the gospel's sake through business. We felt that much could be done with business, but exactly who was doing what, and where could we get a handle on what the Lord was doing around the world through business? John Mulford, dean of the business school at Regent University, and Ted Yamamori, distinguished visiting professor of holistic entrepreneurship at the Graduate School of Business, Regent University, picked up the challenge. Thanks to their energy and persistence, the first Consultation for Holistic Entrepreneurs was convened October 3-5, 2002.

The concept of business as a tool for spreading the gospel is not new. Starting with the apostle Paul and going right through the centuries, business has played a key role in missions. When Marco Polo first followed the trade route to China, he reported back that the Silk Road was dotted with Nestorian chapels. These chapels were a part of the business/mission outreach of these industrious people as early as the fifth century. They dominated the silk trade routes for hundreds of years (chapter 16). But, over the last century, we lost the concept of business and the gospel being partners in preaching. The connection was lost and the responsibility for missions fell to trained evangelists and missionaries. When business was rediscovered as a potential tool, it was more often than not seen as a way to enter closed access countries and even as a "front" for the true activity, which was building the kingdom.

When business is used as a front, the local people get suspicious. They wonder what the real reason is for the business to be in the country. When they don't know the answer and they don't see any visible means of support, they naturally begin to ask questions. At first, people hear that the strangers in their midst are students or tourists or even businessmen and women. This works for a while, but these "fronts" become meaningless with time: A ten-year "student" who has not yet received a degree but now has children? A "tourist" who has stayed for ten years? A "businessperson" whose business has not grown and who does not have any business hours or apparent business? Then they wonder: for whom do these people really work? Naturally, human nature assumes the worst. These missionaries must either be spies for the CIA, or drug dealers. What a poor basis for developing opportunities to share the gospel (chapters 5 and 14).

While there has been some success for business as a mission tool, it is not yet accepted as a mainstream option (chapter 14) and therefore is rarely provided for in our curriculum or thought process. Books are just now coming out that attempt to legitimize business as having an important role in spreading the gospel. In the fall of 2002, Ed Silvoso released his book *Anointed for Business* (Gospel Light), recognizing and encouraging the role of business in missions. There is a widespread feeling in the Christian world that business is actually a second-class citizen to a higher calling of pure ministry (chapters 1 and 20). It is often said that we need to leave our business world and "enter into the ministry." Many aspects of business, including ownership, it was argued, are not good. Years ago, I wrestled with this concept when I was struggling with what I should do with my life: ministry or business. In the final analysis, God put me in a business where I could minister to my employees and the business community in general. I was able to accomplish both. (Refer to chapters 12, 13, and 20.) I learned that business and ministry are symbiotic.

Business can be and should be an integral part of missions. For the adventurous, business is viewed as a ministry. Businesspeople see their role as a way to demonstrate their faith to those around them. Business also may be seen as a way to help Christians who need to have a job and are in a market where employment for Christians is almost impossible because of their faith (chapter 18). For years, smuggling was a way to bring the Bible into closed countries. At that time it was the only way in some countries. This approach must not be carried on into business for the gospel. We often hear how we must hide our faith and attempt to manage or start business outside of government approval. As a result, some people have gone to great lengths to obfuscate their business activities. In one case, an individual smuggled out production illegally for the cause of Christ and thereby nullified his testimony (chapter 2). Such are the efforts of some fledgling approaches to business as a mission.

Rarely do we have the confidence to do the outrageous, which is the realm in which the Holy Spirit works best—since we ourselves cannot accomplish it alone without him. But for the outrageous among us, business may be seen as an opportunity to win many to Christ, reach an entire city, and possibly influence the thought process and views of those who lead the country! I think of the company that built a church on the factory grounds as an integral part of the operations. Although the government was against it, those in power let it stand because they wanted the company in their country. Or, consider the first private government-sponsored Christian website in China (chapter 1).

It appears that business as a mission tool fell into disuse over the last eighty years or so because we entered into a period where capitalism was not seen by the developing nations as useful to them. Many developing nations were moving toward communism or certainly socialism as an economic model. India, China, and the Eastern bloc nations are cases in point. Certainly, in a socialist-leaning country, the idea of business and capitalism is like a sore thumb. Who needs it? It became essentially irrelevant—and worse, without nobility. Capitalism to the socialist mind is anathema. As a mission tool it was no longer useful. Since both socialism and capitalism are biblical concepts, there was no reason for the missionary to carry excess baggage, and the business avenue to missions was summarily dropped.

With the fall of the Soviet Union and the end of the Cold War, a very amazing but not surprising decision was made around the globe. One by one, nations began to realize that socialism as an economic and philosophic basis for self-development was a dead end. If it did not work in the Soviet Union, more than likely it would not work anywhere else. All countries have not reached this conclusion at the same time, but many around the globe are beginning to rethink their economic and philosophic basis of development. The decision to abandon socialism as a way to economic improvement in developing nations has come without a clear demarcation of the end of an era or the beginning of the next. Leaders of developing nations are realizing more and more that the old philosophy of socialism as a means to self-development has no future, and they are moving with faltering steps toward capitalism. Both India and China have shifted their thinking toward capitalism. As you study these two countries, it is pretty obvious, from their actions, which economic system won the economic battle and therefore the Cold War. Clearly, the capitalists won.

For the Christian, the economic system is not a relevant issue. We see in the Scriptures both capitalism and socialism at work. With Christ as our base, either one can and will work. I contend that neither one will work without the fundamental base of Christian principles in the equation. That is another chapter. What is relevant to the Christian is that capitalism and therefore business is back with a vengeance. For the last eighty years, the developing nations were saying, "Send us teachers and doctors because they will have the greatest effect on improving the conditions of our country." And we have obliged them. Yes, we did want to train and heal the people of developing nations, but we also wanted to bring the gospel.

Today, these nations are saying, "We are glad to have teachers and doctors, but also send us people who can teach us the art of business." Now, doctors and teachers can come from many countries, but businesspeople are preferred from those nations who have been successful as capitalists. The door is open, and we must adapt our methods and bring to the party the people and skills that these nations want. Imagine, developing nations are actually asking for Westerners, from all capitalist nations, to come and to develop business in their countries!

When we sent them doctors and teachers, we did not send them fake doctors or unknowledgeable teachers. We can do no less in this case. Here we need to catch up with the developing nations, who may be ahead of us. We can't send folks who are gospel-trained but have only a smattering of business knowledge (chapter 20) or we will find ourselves on the outside looking in. We must have adequate preparation for the task at hand. We need to send or provide practitioners who can honestly give these nations what they need, but with a twist: I believe that we can make the case that capitalism does not work without some cultural changes, including the open reception of some basic business principles which also happen to be scriptural principles. In this way, we lay the foundation for introducing the gospel. We must use tact in introducing these principles, but nonetheless, they are an important part of business.

We are on the edge of something really big, but we need to be wise in delivering our help to a needy world or we could fail. How could such a thing happen? We need to be appropriately prepared as professional missionaries and businesspeople. Such a person or group must be just as well prepared for the one as for the other. A strong suit in one and not the other will not be enough. Case study after case study in this book will attest to this conclusion.

A number of deficiencies generally exist for people who have mission skills but lack qualifications as businesspeople. These areas need to be recognized before they can be addressed. The missionary who wants to operate or develop a business must know that taking on business is not something one does lightly. The well-known and accepted data on business failure indicates that the odds are stacked against the would-be businessperson, but this failure rate can be mitigated significantly by being properly prepared.

It is like gravity. If one jumps off a fifty-story building and prays for the Lord to save him, he will be saved and continue his life that very day—in heaven! The Lord Jesus, tempted by that very prospect, answered Satan thusly: "You shall not put the Lord your God to the test" (Matt. 4:7). In Hosea, the Lord says: "My people are destroyed for lack of knowledge" (Hos. 4:6). Why do we think that we can do business in a foreign land and not know the business rules that must and do apply? It is better to spend some money on an education than spend a lot of money on a business idea only to lose a lot of money while at best learning one or two business concepts from our failure.

As you read this book, many areas will come to life with respect to successes and failures in business as mission. Stories in the first part of this book chronicle a number of successes but they also chronicle a number of mistakes that would have been more obvious to the experienced businessperson. I don't want to dwell on the successes (they will take care of themselves), but I would like to pull out some of the trends that I see in the failures so that we can all learn from them.

Basic business techniques are critical to founding a successful kingdom business. In many cases, a business plan was never developed. Many business activities are started without clear goals, objectives, and market analysis. Who would buy the product? What does the competition look like? How is the product going to be distributed and sold? What is the government climate? How can these problems be resolved? Although our desire is to help others, we must start with very clear-cut business objectives, a business model, and a plan designed to anticipate the issues that will arise. Clearly not all of the issues can be seen in advance, but the more the plan is thought through, the better the chance the business has of success. Venture capitalists who are at the front end of businesses are looking for one type of company: The Sure Thing, Inc. Some of the brightest minds spend days or months analyzing a business plan before they invest. Oftentimes the success or failure can be recognized long before we get to the money expenditure stage. But we need people to help us who have experience in building a solid business plan. We need to recruit the help and support of businesspeople from all areas of business to guide us in developing business opportunities so that we can be successful in presenting the gospel through successful businesses. Fortunately, such people are out there. How to tap into them will be the question we must think through.

To be successful, we also need to teach some basic business norms in cultures where they do not exist. Capitalism by itself, which is based on self-motivation, is not always enough. The good news is that basic business principles and norms are also good scriptural principles. We can teach these principles openly as we train people in the basic concepts of how business works. Business will not be successful without such attributes as honesty, the golden rule, quality, servant leadership, personal responsibility, respect for others, and so forth. A properly developed curriculum based on biblical principles is the key to training. We can openly proclaim these truths because they are the basis of successful business development, process, management, relations, and decision making. While capitalism is the system, scriptural truths and moral values are the glue that holds it all together. As we provide such knowledge, it is a shorter step to the gospel from there (chapter 14).

Successful business ventures require that people learn how to work together for a common purpose. The Lone Ranger approach to doing business is rarely effective. A single individual cannot ride into town, solve the people's problems, and go on from there. A business success has many fathers. No one builds a business alone. It takes many partners to reach a successful conclusion. Yet many have attempted to develop businesses in countries without having found ready marketing partners (chapter 15), or developing the appropriate technology partners or adequate process partners to bring a project to completion in the open market. Fortunately, for almost every industrial endeavor there are Christian businessmen and women around the world who have or can obtain the answer and complete the development of a mission business. I have found them eager to help and open to providing often simple but valuable advice and support. We need to be able to plug in to these extremely valuable resources on a real-time basis. The issue once again is how to find them and get them in the loop. This type of networking is a big challenge but is not insurmountable.

Many would-be venture developers view local governments as hindrances rather than as partners to the business development process. Indeed, in many developing countries, the governments themselves, while attempting to modernize their nations, have knee-jerk reactions to change that tend to hinder rather than foster the growth of business. Too often, because we are attempting to operate under the radar, we feel that we are unable to go to the leaders of various countries let alone ask them to make changes. If and when we do, they often are slow to react and leave us with frustration. In a small business setting it is often difficult to get their attention or to go high enough to get the results we need. Often, they don't trust us because we have gone so far in trying to develop our business without having involved them. We need to work with the governments and involve them from the beginning (chapter 8).

I know that many countries are not yet ready for business; however, more *are* ready every day. The change is happening rapidly, and we need to be aware of the telltale signs. We also need to know how to package our venture in such a way that the leaders can buy into the effort and not be embarrassed by local partisans with whom they must contend. Packaging is everything. If we think through what the leaders' problems are and whom they have to sell on the idea, we may be able to get them to ignore our plans to bring the gospel to them, or even to encourage our efforts. Many parts of China are a case in point. After a recent three-month study trip to China, David Aikman, former *Time* magazine foreign correspondent and senior fellow at the Ethics and Public Policy Center in Washington, D.C., reported on the EPPC website that there is much more tolerance for foreigners, such as the English Language in China group that brings in hundreds of teachers every year. The authorities know that they are Christian but since they obey the rules about evangelism *in class,* the authorities accept them. We need to learn how to work with governments, recognizing their needs without compromising our responsibilities to the Lord.

We need to develop basic management skills in both missionary businesspeople and those who will work for them. We need to be able to manage individuals above and within the organization to accomplish the objectives as set out by the business plan. We need to learn how to accomplish and monitor tasks that may involve people several layers removed from them in order to keep all of the parts of the business operating properly and thus deliver the results. Business is management; mission experience is often one-on-one. Business requires folks to rally around a new and different set of objectives for specific results under the overarching banner of Christ. The culture in the company, different from the culture at church or in the community, must be developed and nurtured. Multiple cultures must be managed at one time. When the business is small, this may not appear difficult, but that is when the seeds of the company culture are sown. What seeds get sown then will continue to get stronger as the company grows. But the culture must reflect the nature of the business. A high-service attitude must come up in a high-service business, while a quality-oriented, cost-conscious, work culture must grow up in a manufacturing operation. Ultimately, the quality of the company's business culture and its ability to stand the test will only show up over time.

We need to have the skill to assess risk in the marketplace and learn techniques to "manage risk down," to improve the odds of success. Some businesses have small risk and work well but can only reach a certain size, while others can become larger players and demand work in advance to reduce risk before additional capital can be brought in. Risk management comes with training and experience. Often, we are slow in seeing the need to manage risk and end up at a dead end because we cannot get the capital we need—because we have not managed down the risk beforehand. It is always best to start with small amounts of capital to get the business off the ground, and then learn what is necessary to reduce risk and increase the probability of success.

So does this mean that the missionary-businessperson must start over and go back to school? Not necessarily. In all the steps along the way, I believe that such a person can get help and make a lot of progress without a business background—if we can get the critical support of a board of advisors and adequate consulting help. We need to raise up such people; every year, extremely capable people are retiring from the business world who, if tapped, could offer enormous help. But we also need to start training young people as soon as possible to come into these marketplace opportunities and ply their business and missions training. It means preparing them at our schools (chapter 20).

Finally, we need to use our business opportunities to strengthen the indigenous church and encourage the sending church. As we begin to provide meaningful jobs to local believers, we need to teach them the importance of tithing and the significance of church financial development. The local church must become a giving body that can share back and help those in need. While this seems obvious, many in the Third World have never learned the art of giving to the church financially because they have never had money. I have spoken to a number of local pastors who believe that the money for the church must come from outside the country. In part they are correct but only because local members often have been under- or unemployed. As businesses develop and pay salaries and profits, the local members must feel the importance of giving for advancing the gospel. Teaching the concept of giving is hard when the missionary from afar makes many times the income of the local church members. It is hard to ask them to give. But the future of the church is dependent upon giving. If this were not so, I am sure Jesus and certainly Paul would not have spent so much time on it in the New Testament.

The local church in the sending country must also be involved. We need to bring the church along and encourage it to provide spiritual support and direction to its members so that we can get help to those who are out in the field bringing the business mission along (chapter 4). The church needs to see that sending business missionaries can be both successful and effective financially (chapters 15 and 20) and spiritually (chapter 13). This will require all who have an interest in business as a mission to help many pastors in the sending nations to learn the value of such work by elevating the value of business as a mission tool.

With the doors open, a new era is coming that can give missions an even brighter future. Kingdom business can have a huge impact. Business can provide much-needed jobs to local Christians. It can provide profit for the sustainability and growth of jobs in the country. It will then improve the income and therefore the GDP of the entire country and provide desperately needed hard currency through trade to Third World nations. With these results we can say to the developing nations, as Ken Crowell did, that we want to bless the entire nation in which we desire to work (chapter 3). With the successes we have seen in many cases, we will influence the direction of country leaders to open new and greater opportunities for the gospel. The impact for the gospel can be enormous. Of course, we need to resolve many issues that block our path, but as kingdom entrepreneurs we believe that all things are possible, above and beyond what we ask or think. The Lord has promised us the nations, and business can and will be one of the effective tools for the work as we prepare for the coming of the King.

—Kenneth A. Eldred

PART ONE

CASE
STUDIES

1

Esther Hui and Infosail

Kim-kwong Chan

Esther Hui is cofounder and president of Shenzhen Infosail Electronics Co., Ltd. Infosail provides support services in website management, e-commerce, and Internet-related software development. Although Infosail is a small company, recently it outbid eight big-league players to win a major contract to build and to maintain one of the most important official Chinese government news websites—Dragon News (21dnn.com). Newspapers and magazines have interviewed Esther because of her success as a businesswoman, and a national television documentary about her is in the works. Her biography is about much more than business, however. A native of Ningpo in Zhejiang Province, Esther has been a choir member for the Shenzhen Church since the mid-1980s.

THE CALL

Esther was born into a non-Christian family in Shanghai. Her grandfather was a rather wealthy businessman who lost everything when the communists took power. Both her father and mother were senior government cadres who divorced when Esther was a teenager. Her mother took Esther to Ningpo, her mother's hometown, where the family had run a business before 1949. Esther attended high school back in Shanghai in the early 1980s because she still retained her residential registration there. In Shanghai, however, she had neither relatives nor friends. Students in school bullied this rural girl.

One day, passing by a church, Esther heard the beautiful hymn-singing. Soon she began attending the services. During this time, Esther's mother moved to a new area without telling her. Esther struck up a friendship with an old man and his wife, Mr. and Mrs. Chu, in the church. The friendship quickly deepened, and this childless couple took Esther as their foster daughter. The man saw something in Esther—a special talent in business—even before Esther had a chance to demonstrate it. While Esther lived with the Chus, they formed her in the strict disciplines of daily Bible reading and prayer.

The man, Chu Chunen, came from an extremely wealthy background. His father-in-law had been an oil magnate in the 1920s and 30s. At some point the couple had experienced a miraculous healing, and they converted to the Christian faith. Mr. Chu, using his family wealth, then built a success-ful banking business. However, the Sino-Japanese war and later the Civil War destroyed most of his wealth. In the late 1940s, Mr. Chu decided to fold his business and study theology. Then the communists came, and the couple lost all that they had managed to hold onto. Mr. Chu had to work as a teacher in a factory school. Finally, they retired in the late 1970s. In a period of reform, the government later compensated them for wealth it had confiscated from them years before.

Her foster father told Esther, "If you have talent in a field, excel in it." She did. After high school, Esther got a job as a sales clerk at a government retailer. This was in the early 1980s, when the government was taking its first tentative steps in the transition from a planned to a market economy. In the company training program, Esther scored the highest among 500 people. Although the company sent her to study bookkeeping, she was soon trans-ferred to the accounting department and given more responsibility. Within a month, Esther made a suggestion to increase the sales volume fourfold. In fact, her division's weekly sales jumped from 40,000 to 160,000 RMB. Soon, the salary of people in her division jumped even higher, from 40 to 200 RMB per month, with overtime—rather attractive when the average worker's salary was around 60 RMB. Esther quickly became a rising star, attracting both admiration and jealousy.

In 1985, Esther convinced her boss to start doing business in Shenzhen, the newly designated Special Economic Zone next to Hong Kong. After a couple of successful deals, the company promoted her to sales manager. Within a year, she had netted 1 million RMB in profits for her division. Esther's monthly salary was now 1,500 RMB. Soon the company sent her to Hong Kong to solicit more international trade. Before she left, Mr. Chu gave her two biblical passages—Psalms 1 and 23—for comfort and inspiration. Evidently, they provided both.

After a couple years of success in Hong Kong, Esther went to Shenzhen to start her own business with just a couple thousand RMB in her pocket. She saw an opportunity in commodity trading, taking advantage of price dif-ferences between Hong Kong and Shenzhen, and between Shenzhen and the rest of China. Soon she made her first million and was well-known in business circles. Esther also became involved in trade, real estate, stock markets, and even black market currency exchanges and currency remittances, in which illegal private banks respond to market needs in place of the notoriously inefficient official banks.

Esther made enough money to enjoy a comfortable living from the interest on her wealth. Flush with success, Esther thought she might show her gratitude for God's blessings by going into "full-time ministry." Her foster father—who by then had started a church in his home village in Jiangsu and had received his ordination as a pastor—told her, "Your talent is more than just becoming a preacher. It is not realistic for you to become a pastor. Your heart is not there. Do not make the decision in a rush. Your talent is in business, and your call is to be a good Christian entrepreneur to witness to Christ in the business world." (Mr. Chu himself had grown a church from fewer than a dozen believers to several hundred people within just a few years. The church had constructed a new building with seating for 500 people.)

THE ENTREPRENEURIAL LAUNCH

Esther had never attended college, had never studied economics, business, or management. Although Shenzhen is a very commercialized city, few, if any, church members were businesspeople in the mid-1990s. She had virtually no guidance from the church. Few in the church even knew her as a businessperson.

As Esther pondered her future, she began to formulate her business philosophy. After much reflection, she came to three conclusions. First, people need to strive for a meaningful existence in life with a higher goal than simply making money. Second, entrepreneurs do not only work for themselves, but for all those who work under them; they have a moral obligation toward their employees. Third, businesses can create jobs and provide livelihoods for many people in society.

As she explored her options, in 1997 Esther took some courses in Internet and information technology (IT) and encountered a Mr. Ma, a computer engineer and brilliant IT instructor. Together seeing a future in Internet-related businesses, they launched Infosail. They spent almost the entire first year getting a feel for the market, facing competition from thousands of similar enterprises. They had many cash flow problems and near collapses of the business. However, during each crisis, Esther prayed and saw a series of unexpected eleventh-hour events that rescued Infosail. Esther took this as a sign from God to continue.

THE BUSINESS PLAN

Infosail specializes in building and maintaining news websites in China. It has a special competitive advantage by linking its human resources with several regional universities. Infosail provides scholarships to students who take their summer internships there and promise to work for the company for two years after graduation with below-market salaries but high projected bonuses. In this way, Infosail gets a constant supply of high quality graduates at a bargain rate. These workers are full of ideas and are aware of the latest Internet technology.

Infosail has secured several big projects. One of the most important coups was its successful bid, in March 2001, to build and maintain a major government news site (21dnn.com). The Propaganda Department of the Chinese Communist Party sponsors this site, which will be the official news site of the government (hence named 21dnn, to rival with CNN in the twenty-first century). Infosail prevailed over eight larger companies, including Yahoo, to secure the contract. Remarkably, Infosail did not pay a single cent in bribes or in entertainment expenses. Mr. Ma heads the newly established Beijing office and Esther is stationed at company headquarters in Shenzhen. Infosail has already produced a software package for provincial governments to establish their news websites. Some provincial governments are already lining up to use Infosail's products and services.

GROWTH OF BUSINESS

Most of Infosail's thirty-five employees work in Shenzhen. Yet it needs to hire five more staff and open a new office to respond to growing demands. It also plans an internal restructuring with specialized divisions and teams to sustain current projects. Infosail has some cash flow problems that can be alarming at times, although probably not fatal.

Other than Esther, there is only one Christian in the company. Mr. Ma shows some interest in Christianity but has not made a commitment. However, Esther finds outlets for her ministry impulses in other ways. She has created the only government-sanctioned private Christian website in China (which is not related to the official sanctioned church)—Chinachurch.com. After initial skepticism, both the Shenzhen municipal and the Guangdong provincial governments welcomed this site. Esther is now linking with Christian groups outside of China to improve it. Chinachurch.com provides devotional, evangelistic, and pastoral training materials on the Web. Eventually, Esther wants to build the first virtual reality church in China, as well as an on-line pastoral training school.

Esther upholds Christian principles of justice and compassion in her personal management. Admitting that some staffers have abused her Christian charity, she often sets the example for the kinds of behavior required. After sealing business agreements, Esther sends small gifts, making a distinction between gift giving—an Eastern way of cultivating relationships—and bribery. She expects nothing in return.

However, Esther will take business that may not be strictly legal. Some laws in China are simply irrelevant, contradictory, or unreasonable. For example, some prohibit freedom of worship or evangelizing others in public. Others demand that you take the government exchange rate, which is far lower than the real (or black) market rates. To follow these rules would make tasks such as purchasing needed equipment nearly impossible. Still other laws require you to get approval from twenty-seven ministries just to put up a small factory—a task that takes several years if you follow the letter of the law.

On the other hand, Esther stays out of businesses that may be profitable and legal but which she believes are unethical. For example, she turned down an opportunity to make huge profits exporting weapons to tyrannical regimes in Southeast Asia. Esther holds Christian principles above the law of the nation.

EVALUATION

Esther's business is rather ethical from a Christian standpoint. She successfully navigates through the gray seas of relationships and gifts. She maximizes her strength to compete with other firms in the market. She cares for her staff and sets a good example. Her integrity as an honest and trustworthy businessperson is well-known in the corporate circles of Shenzhen.

Infosail has established itself as a rising star in the field, with much potential in related areas such as e-commerce. Infosail is experiencing some healthy growing pains. It is a lean and effective enterprise, flexible enough to compete in the market.

Chinachurch.com may become a powerful tool to empower the tens of millions of Chinese Christians who lack information to help them become solid disciples of Christ. With a doubling in the number of Internet users every six months in China, this site can be a powerful means to reach not only these people but Web surfers as well.

However, Esther lacks relevant models integrating faith and business practices in China. She laments that the church in China not only fails to provide her with spiritual direction but at times openly condemns business practices as worldly. Yet given the right support, Esther can be a powerful witness for Christian faith in the emerging business community in China. She knows that businesses can be both profitable and ethical—for the advancement of the kingdom of God in China.

2

AMI AND GREAT COMMISSION COMPANIES

Clem Schultz with Sonia Chou

I was called to be a missionary at age 11, but it was not until college that God called me to work alongside East Asian Christians. In 1989 I left the multinational corporate world to focus on developing what are called Great Commission companies. I wanted to do world-class business while facilitating church planting work in the 10/40 Window.[1]

In 1989, I joined and bought controlling interest in a company called AMI, a consulting and manufacturing firm specializing in the technology sector. Business took off quickly. Initially, AMI did some small consulting jobs with a sister Great Commission company with two offices in East Asia. Within a few months, we had four employees plus our first management intern. The following year, we landed a $3 million-plus lighting equipment and technology deal, which allowed us to open additional offices in East and Central Asia.

From 1991 to 1993, AMI averaged sales of over $10 million per year in turnkey technologies in lighting and other high-automation manufacturing. In the early 1990s, we made our first equity investment in East Asia. We have helped start, and have an equity stake in, numerous factories in the region. We currently have equity in nine operations in East Asia. They produce medical devices, telecommunication parts, energy-efficient lamps and related products, and so on.

We have also managed new factories in East Asia on behalf of publicly traded American companies. One of them, a telecommunications start-up, made a profit of more than $10 million during its first twelve months from start of manufacturing. We also have had small manufacturing and representative offices in the Middle East and North Africa since the early 1990s. While the capitalization for each of these manufacturing ventures varies, in general it is somewhere in the range of the high six to the low eight figures. AMI's percentage normally falls somewhere between 15 and 100 percent.

Our large dollar and high-technology amounts of investment provide us with strong political leverage with governments. East Asian governments generally welcome foreign manufacturers, especially those with fairly large capitalization. As long as a company makes money and provides jobs for the local people, the governments will not interfere—unless it is rather openly breaking the law.

From that position of strength, AMI has established strategic alliances with more than fifteen nonprofit agencies to do education, development, and church planting work among local East Asian and Muslim communities. AMI does not directly receive any money from these organizations.

The following is a list of "best practices" for Great Commission companies which AMI has experientially learned working in the 10/40 Window. Each guideline provides a negative and a positive example to illustrate it. A commitment to "best practices" means that Great Commission companies will do these things:

1. . . . *have strategy coordinators.* This person focuses on the specific unreached city or group where the factory or company is located. He or she needs to be on the local company's board of directors to ensure the presence of annual Great Commission plans that are ambitious but culturally achievable. The strategy coordinator is a spiritual entrepreneur. He or she networks with local church leaders and creates strategies or methods related to evangelism, discipleship, and church planting so the business can do kingdom entrepreneurship. This person also serves as a spiritual consultant to help the business have maximum kingdom impact.

> *Negative Example:* AMI assisted the Widget Company, a telecommunication components manufacturer, to establish a factory in East Asia by completing a business plan and recruiting a general manager and a manufacturing engineer. Although the factory was in a Hui Muslim neighborhood, fewer than five of its first 4,500 employees were Muslims. The company initially had a strategy coordinator on its board, but it had no annual Great Commission plan to help the general manager balance work and faith.
>
> A family emergency forced the strategy coordinator to take a leave of absence. Then the Widget company's general manager failed in his spiritual accountability. He neglected the integration of faith in business. From a business perspective, the company was very suc-

cessful. It had a better than 40 percent return on investment. However, without either a plan or a strategy coordinator, Widget failed to plant a church among Hui Muslims.

Positive Example: When AMI set up a representative office in one East Asian city, a strategy coordinator was on the board of directors to ensure that there was an achievable Great Commission plan for the company. This person has been integral in helping AMI capitalize spiritually on its business success.

2. . . . *make sure that expatriates are spiritually accountable to a church or mission agency.* The company and the spiritual accountability groups should have contracts specifically addressing each expatriate's situation. Contracts are essential because they describe and specify the employee's job description and working terms. They should be updated in accordance with changes in employee duties.

Negative Example: In the early 1990s, AMI won a $1.5 million contract to source and install East Asia's first high-speed assembly equipment for a certain consumer product. AMI subcontracted installation of this equipment to a sister Great Commission company. This company in turn hired an engineer to oversee the installation. This engineer was on full support from nonprofit sources in the United States. He had no written contract concerning his "tent-making" role, so he saw an opportunity to simply do evangelism, which distracted him from his engineering duties. He spent most of his time outside of the factory, evangelizing non-Christians. He did not understand the expectations of the company, which caused a disjunction between work and faith. This man became very frustrated and while on the job site actually hit an East Asian employee and knocked him out. Had there been a contract to specify his job description, this disaster might have been avoided, and he might have contributed greatly to the company.

Positive Example: AMI helped a high-technology electronics company to establish a factory in East Asia. At the start of the operation, company people interviewed 120 applicants weekly and hired as many as 20 or more each week. During this process, the leaders learned to their sorrow that the marketing director, an expatriate, had had a sexual encounter with another employee. They decided to send the marketing director back to the States for a leave of absence to get some counseling, and they informed his accountability group, which agreed. Eventually the marketing director and his wife asked to return, affirming that their relationship had improved. However, by contract the spiritual accountability group had to approve the request. It did not. While it was a difficult and painful process for the company's general manager, the contract made her decision much easier.

3. . . . *emphasize church planting or ministry teams, focused on cities or people groups.* Normally the team leader is not the general manager. Stand-alone kingdom entrepreneurs are limited in terms of both finances and effectiveness. They need to be part of a team for accountability and encouragement.

> *Negative Example:* One tentmaker has been smuggling Bibles into East Asian countries since the mid-1980s. Whenever he left a particular East Asian country, he would also illegally smuggle out a commercial product that needed an export license. Unfortunately, there was no accountability group to confront him about his illegal actions. He tried to justify his illegal exporting by claiming that since this particular government would not allow Bibles to be imported, he was under no obligation to obey it in the matter of acquiring an export license for a commercial product. He actually earned his living this way. Without an accountability team, tentmakers can compromise their faith.

> *Positive Example:* So far, AMI has not had any major problems with "Lone Rangers" in our company. We have always worked with teams from mission agencies as we establish factories in East Asia and in other parts of the 10/40 Window. When AMI started working in a certain Central Asian country during the early 1990s, the number of Muslims who were followers of Christ was fewer than 10. Within a few years, however, AMI employees were meeting for discipleship on a weekly basis with more than 80 Muslims who are now followers of Jesus. The growth of these Muslim converts is one piece of evidence demonstrating the effectiveness of a team of kingdom professionals instead of stand-alone kingdom entrepreneurs.

4. . . . *have multiethnic or multinational management teams.* Three or more ethnicities/cultures are an ideal mix. Not all managers have to be Christians,

but most should be Christians committed to the Great Commission. Also, no key managers should be antagonistic toward Great Commission goals. We have found that ethnic and/or cultural diversity allows the company to be more effective in achieving its business goals while having fewer cultural and language limitations.

> *Negative Example:* When a sister Great Commission company first began in East Asia in the 1980s, the tentmakers were all Americans, and primarily from the same mission agency and similar cultures. It was difficult for them to interact with East Asians without understanding their culture or language. Despite their good intentions, these barriers prevented them from becoming effective.

> *Positive Example:* As mentioned previously, in the early 1990s, AMI launched a team in Central Asia consisting of more than 20 nonnationals from over 5 different countries with almost 10 different mission agencies. This diverse group has a broader impact in both business and ministry. With different skills and backgrounds, team members contribute to the growth of the company and a real people movement among a Muslim group.

5. . . . *have not only written business plans but annual Great Commission plans.* Such a plan sets goals, defines a purpose, and creates synergy for maximum kingdom effectiveness. It enumerates a company's goals not only in its business operation but also in its mission service. Without this plan, dissonance between business and faith may occur, blocking the growth of spiritual fruit and making the business unsustainable from a Great Commission perspective.

> *Negative Example:* AMI helped establish a company in East Asia that designs and manufactures high-end electronic circuits. The vice president, whom AMI recruited, was an American citizen from the ethnic background of the country he was working in. However, a secular East Asian company had a controlling equity interest in the factory. Thus, there was never an agreed-upon Great Commission plan. The vice president focused his ministry on the surrounding neighborhoods but neglected the non-believing workers within the factory. Because there was no synergy from the company itself, the ministry was not multiplying. In the end, the company had to let him

go. Without a Great Commission plan, a Great Commission company can quickly overlook its ministry responsibilities.

Positive Example: AMI's annual plan has proven to be very effective in a major unreached city in East Asia. It has laid out strategies for evangelism, discipleship, and church planting that have been in harmony with AMI's business type. We have been blessed with both business and ministry success.

6. . . . *base employee compensation primarily on performance (not donor support).* While it may be acceptable to employ some people who are on full support, it is crucial that the core management, non-national team be either fully or partly compensated according to performance. It is difficult for a manager to make good decisions not tied to the money that he or she is receiving. Conversely, managers are more likely to make careful decisions that are best for the company when their salaries are based upon performance. AMI does, however, allow non-nationals who work fewer than twenty hours per week to receive some or most of their compensation via nonprofit groups.

Negative Example: A successful tentmaker came to East Asia fully supported by donors, according to firm agency policy. This man brought in over $3 million in sales. However, he started making many poor business decisions, and became burned out, as the realization that his income was not based on his performance started to sink in. To break the logjam, he decided to resign from both the company and the mission agency and instead be a stand-alone entrepreneur.

Positive Example: A few years ago, AMI hired a facilities and site manager with more than ten years of work experience at a major transportation construction group in the United States. We wanted him to oversee the start of construction for a new manufacturing operation. During that time, we did not have enough money to pay him at market rates. In fact, he took a 40 percent pay cut to work with us. But he was very effective, and eventually the start-up company increased his salary.

7. . . . *must have significant export markets.* The export market provides two benefits: (1) political leverage, as the government recognizes that the company is bringing profits from outside sources, which stimulate the growth of the

local economy; and (2) insulation against local corruption. The goal for any Great Commission company is not to localize or nationalize its business. Many companies can easily capture the national market, but they must advance their professional standards to enter the international market. Having a significant export market allows the company to keep up with international expertise, resources, and standards. Fierce competition in the local market will not squeeze the international company so intensely. It is also less vulnerable to the threat of being closed down.

Ethnic and/or cultural diversity (mentioned earlier) reinforces this point. It allows the company to have a broader network and provides more specialization in skills that will expand a company's targets. In a company with only national employees, workers struggle to communicate with multinational companies and have very limited perspectives on business.

> *Negative Example:* One of AMI's factories in East Asia, although laden with excellent technology, constantly struggled because it lacked a significant export market. Although it represented a $3 million investment, its market was limited to its location. Soon AMI's local partner tried to squeeze AMI out of the business. Its leaders did not think they needed our knowledge of international markets. Although we stayed involved at a low level with the factory for over a decade, the company's initial technology lead continued to slip year after year. There were no major international customers to push the company to new levels of quality and technology.

> *Positive Example:* A multimillion-dollar investment in a factory producing a certain consumer product in East Asia has done very well over the last five-plus years. Thirty percent of the products are for the local market, while 70 percent go to North and South America and Europe. We believe that the large foreign market share has helped the company continue to innovate and improve in quality.

8. . . . *have formal employee training programs on business ethics.* Ensuring good work ethics and integrity is a must. The company should have written guidelines. AMI has a required four-step process whenever there is a possibility of bribery, corruption, or kickbacks. Employees and others related to AMI must thoroughly analyze each step in order. A "No" answer to any of the four questions will kill any proposed action. We teach this process at least annually at all AMI-related operations:

1. Does proposed action not violate the U.S. "FCPA" law?
2. Does your AMI associate have any uncomfortable feeling concerning the proposed action?
3. Is the proposed action transparent to all directly related parties?
4. Does the proposed action reflect the "Golden Rule," "Do unto others as you want them to do unto you" (note: a teaching of Jesus).

Recently AMI encountered an ethical dilemma regarding two companies entering into an expensive joint venture—Mercury, Inc., and Yangming. Disputes occurred between them, and the joint venture failed. Yangming held Mercury responsible for the failure. Mercury, denying the accusation, hired us to help them reach a compromise.

We consulted an East Asian law firm and estimated that Mercury had a 60 percent chance of winning the dispute by retaining this firm. If they did, they would save $2.5 million. However, during the consultation, we sensed that the firm might bend the law to win the dispute for Mercury, although we had no direct evidence that this would happen. In this case, the guidelines prevented the company from having any involvement in immoral work ethics.

9. . . . *screen their leadership teams before starting or expanding their businesses.* We think the Centre for Entrepreneurship and Economic Development (CEED) provides the best training for this. For more information, check out www.ceed-uofn.org. Sharon Swarr is the manager.

These guidelines give kingdom entrepreneurs an outline of what a Great Commission company should be like and how it should function effectively for the kingdom. But we always must keep in mind that we are God's fellow workers. We plant the seeds through business, but God causes the growth.

3

GALTRONICS:
A CASE STUDY IN ISRAEL

Ken and Margie Crowell

We were enjoying life to the fullest in the beautiful Sierra Nevada Mountains of California. Living in the lovely home Ken had built onto the Placerville Bible Book Store allowed Margie to do Christian ministry while staying at home with our two young children. Ken, an engineer with Aerojet General, served as Sunday school superintendent and youth leader at Calvary Bible Church. Fishing, water sports, and outdoor living filled our extra hours.

CONCERN FOR ISRAEL

Yet a challenge by a visiting missionary was the catalyst that prompted us to follow the Lord wherever he would lead. The "wherever" was first to Multnomah School of the Bible in Portland, Oregon, where we studied for five years. During this time we began to feel a special concern for Israel. The call became so real that our Christmas letter of 1968 told our friends and family that we were going to Israel after graduation, even though we did not know how. Israel had not accepted missionary visas for two decades.

Just before graduation, Ken received an offer from Motorola to work in Israel for three years doing research and development for new products. After a time of deep soul-searching, we saw the world of business as an open door to Israel. Over the next three years, the Lord confirmed our call with countless opportunities to share the gospel in the marketplace. We began to ask, "If this could take place with one believer in a secular company, what would happen if there was a 'Christian' company filled with believers?" Five years later, this simple vision brought forth a company known as Galtronics.

FIRM FOUNDATIONS

Over those five years, Ken continued to work for Motorola in Florida while preparing to launch a small company, with the intent of moving it to Israel.

Ken noted a lack of manufacturers of two-way antennas in Israel. With the approval of Motorola, Ken began to develop and produce UHF-VHF antennas. He also launched his new enterprise. The employees were Christians with a desire to bless Israel.

After resigning from Motorola, Ken approached the Israeli Consulate in Atlanta about the possibility of relocating in Israel. During the presentation, Ken told Israeli officials about the employees' faith in Jesus as Messiah and their desire to bless and help the emerging nation by providing employment and exporting product. Two hours into the presentation, the consulate director said, "I am not so concerned about your Christian involvement as I am about our need to strengthen our economy by establishing new businesses within Israel. We will welcome and assist you in Israel."

The Crowell family returned to Israel in November 1977 and settled in Tiberias, a city in Galilee that needed industry. Many people assume that the *Gal* in Galtronics stands for the Galilee region where we work. However, there is a much deeper meaning. *Gal* is the Hebrew word for "wave/roll," as in "to wave/roll over your trust onto" or to "commit oneself." Psalm 37:5 says, "Commit thy way unto the Lord [*Gal L'Adonai*]; trust also in him; and he shall bring it to pass" (KJV). This is a moment-by-moment waving or committing all onto the Lord.

The government appointed an officer from the Investment Authority to help establish the new company. He introduced Ken to each government office in order to cut the usual red tape new ventures routinely encountered in the process of obtaining "Government Approved" status. This man became a good friend for many years. The mayor of Tiberias helped us secure a suitable manufacturing building. Within eight months, Galtronics became a "Government Approved Enterprise," a feat that normally took three years.

OPPOSITION GROWS

After the initial warm welcome, however, opposition began to grow. A militant Jewish group known as Yad L'Achim, known for its hatred of all "missionaries," started spreading lies about Galtronics using posters, newspaper articles, and so on. Their attempts to discredit us would fill a book, but we thank the Lord for his protection and faithfulness. Under the Lord's guidance, a church, called Peniel Fellowship, began. The figurative stones of persecution strengthened and matured the group. Beginning with seven people, Peniel grew alongside Galtronics. Today it is a thriving fellowship of more than 250 members.

Overcoming the opposition took several years. We accomplished this slowly by becoming known personally in the city, entering into the local sports competitions (including winning the basketball tournament), and daily living out our faith in a nonthreatening manner.

LIVING OUT OUR PRINCIPLES

In 1978, we set forth the threefold purpose of Galtronics:

1. To establish a witness in areas where there is none, and to support the building of the local church.
2. To provide work for believers who cannot hold steady employment because of their faith, and to provide for an open witness, one to one, in a natural work environment.
3. To bless the nation of Israel by exporting high quality "Made in Israel" products, which will result in a strengthened economy.

We fully understood from the beginning that the business must be self-supporting and profitable. The government expected Galtronics to provide employment and export product to bring dollars into the country. Not only have we been able to do so, the prime minister's office and members of the Knesset gave Galtronics the nation's highest industrial award, the Praz Kaplan. The national newspapers carried headlines stating that this award was given "to Galtronics for blessing the Nation of Israel."

We started a summer volunteer program in 1981. The program, which continued for ten years, offered students from LeTourneau University an opportunity to use their professional training to be tentmakers in Israel. Students from John Brown University also came to share their talents and faith on a daily basis. Some of these young people have returned to Galtronics, have married, and have begun their own families in the land.

Our vision has expanded to include the following companies:

Galadon (1985): Believers distribute communion juice from Israel to bless the church worldwide.

Galcom (1987): This business manufactures radios tuned to specific Christian radio stations for missions use around the world.

Gal Group (1987): This is our administrative arm; it provides the other businesses with expertise in management, government interface, and marketing.

Galilee Experience (1990): This is a multimedia theater for tourists and Israelis. It includes a gift shop, an art gallery, and a cafe over-looking the Sea of Galilee. The presentation, thirty-four minutes long, covers 4,000 years of Galilean history, focusing on those who have shaped it the most—from Abraham to Jesus to Moshe Dayan.

Galilee of the Nations Music (1999): This venture provides music from Israel. It has become the largest producer of messianic music in the world. It pays royalties to local believing musicians, enabling them to support their families and ministries.

MegaVoice (reestablished 2000): This provides audio products with life-giving messages.

During Operation Desert Storm in 1991, the customers of Galtronics requested a backup production facility. We expanded with factories in Scotland and China. These moves gave our company international status, with 700 employees worldwide. By 1998 the company had reached a value of $70 million.

New Challenges

Several Christian advisors thought we should sell shares in the company and use the money to start other industries. After much thought and prayer, however, we decided not to enter into an initial public offering, as this would distract us from our original tentmaking purposes. Through the years we have had many offers from secular companies to buy Galtronics. However, we knew that the vision to bless Israel would not continue under new ownership, so we have chosen not to join in any such ventures.

When we needed more capital to grow, we accepted a group of Christian investors. But over two years of trying to make this arrangement work, we could not overcome some basic philosophical differences. The investors wanted to make the business profitable as quickly as possible. Then the company would distribute the profits through shareholders, who in turn would give to charitable organizations. Our vision, as always, is to run a kingdom business on biblical principles. The business helps develop tentmaking enterprises to support local believers.

Neither vision was any more right than the other, but they were incompatible. So both sides reached an amicable agreement to discontinue the second round of investment. We are currently reestablishing the business as a tentmaking ministry that remains in Israel, doing business according to our original vision.

4

BUSINESS IN THE MIDDLE EAST

Abiir William

I did not receive any business training before I launched out into the Middle East fourteen years ago to be a traditional missionary. Yet for all these years I have been involved in the business world. I want to present my own experiences and involvement in running private businesses in the Middle East.

When I arrived, I had to learn to answer questions from my curious neighbors. "Why are you here," they would ask me, "and what you are doing?" Frankly, I had almost as much trouble giving an answer I was comfortable with as one that would convince them. I was not alone. Many overseas workers struggle with this identity problem, especially those working in closed countries that prohibit "traditional" endeavors. Most unreached people live in nations that totally restrict traditional "overseas workers." Yes, these people can start as language students or as tourists, but these options do not allow them to stay in restricted countries for the long haul.

Sooner or later, such workers must leave sensitive areas to serve elsewhere. I have known many "overseas workers" serving in the Middle East who felt very frustrated and insecure because of this identity and status problem. At the same time, sending agencies find it difficult to recruit people for these areas. While doing business in such contexts is no panacea, it definitely can remove some barriers that traditional missionaries face. It can also provide a solid foundation for long-term tentmakers.

THE ESSENTIALS

In 1981, I felt called to serve the Lord cross-culturally. Then in 1988 I began to have a special desire to serve a certain majority people group. Everything I did from that point on reflected that commitment. Learning the language was the first priority, so that I could communicate and understand the people and their culture. At first our team's approach was to go door to door as booksellers. We offered cookbooks, educational books, and, of course, our book of Truth. Later, I enrolled at a local sewing center, which gave me many opportunities to build friendships. I offered to teach English to some girls in their homes. With these approaches, I built trust with local people. I was beginning to see how business could provide natural opportunities to share the gospel.

Mats Tunehag of Interdev says, "If we want to preach a full gospel, meeting real needs and influencing the whole of society, we will increasingly need to emphasize economic and business development."[1] The usual organizations are often already in place, providing Bible translations, literature and radio ministries, church planting, and development projects. As someone of Chinese origin, many people automatically pegged me as a businessperson, which helped me immensely. In fact, business platforms are a very good means of providing economic development and are welcomed almost everywhere. Business platforms also enable a demonstration of God's righteousness, in that they show that biblical ethics are realistic and enhance the dignity of human life.

Business has provided me with a tremendous opportunity to enter the lives of local people. It allows me to build the trust necessary for these people to listen to and accept the truth. Through business there is also a tremendous opportunity to enable believers in developing local churches to become self-sufficient and self-supporting in their ministries.

Of course, this kind of ministry has had no shortage of challenges. Almost three years ago, I faced a lot of pressure as a single woman running a business in the Middle East. At the same time, many of my supporters back home were having trouble understanding what I was doing. Many of them thought that running a business was not a "spiritual" activity. I also lacked capital or a supporting partner to back me up in running the business. At that point I felt very lonely and wanted to give up.

At the time I was helping a large Chinese television factory with marketing, and so I helped display its products during a fair. On the opening day, participants were not allowed to enter the exhibition hall before the president of Egypt. But God opened the gate for me, and our firm was the sole company to welcome him. When I shook hands with the president, a small voice told me, "Mary, I am your business partner. Even the president has to shake hands with you!" This small incident gave me great confidence for the challenges ahead.

I have faced many difficult choices. Once I was asked to accompany an Arab businessman to China as a translator. This contact might have made us a lot of money. But I was scheduled to speak with some Chinese churches in the States about my ministry.

I finally decided that my sharing with the Chinese churches was far more important than money. No, I did not raise a lot of money with them, but the mission of the Chinese churches was forever changed. I am convinced I made the right choice.

People who want to start any business need to have a certain degree of *knowledge*. So often mission-minded people just want to use business as a cover to get into a country but have no real interest in running the business. I have many reservations about this mentality. Christians need to be people of integrity in dealing with local governments. When we submit the official papers to set up a business, we have to be honest. When governments find out that companies are not involved in real businesses, they close them down. Would-be entrepreneurs need to do more research on the laws and policies of setting up a business in various countries. Then we can intelligently choose what kind of business will fit according to each situation. In my case, starting a business in the Arab world was not easy. It is time-consuming to go through all the procedures, and taxes are high. I opened a limited company many years ago, but the high taxation forced me to close. However, I have begun setting up a consulting business. While there will probably be limits in how much profit I can make, I expect this to be a great platform with which to minister to people.

TIME AND MONEY

The Christian tentmaker must have *time*. If you are not prepared to put time into a venture, then forget about business. You will also need a lot of energy and effort to set up and run a business. Yes, you can employ local people to help you run it, but it still takes effort to train them to do the job well. I have seen many businesses have to sail through rough waters because their local colleagues received much responsibility but little training. Most locals have not received proper business training, so you must put more effort into training them.

Another essential is *money*. No business can start without capital. Should the money come from the church, from the mission organization, or from other investments? A good business plan might attract a Christian businessperson who would like to make a good investment. In my case, my father, who owned a Chinese restaurant, gave me the capital to start my business.

I will not accept money from either mission agencies or churches. They almost always look at the business as a means to get into a country rather than as a ministry in itself. Their financial involvement might be more a hindrance than a blessing.

However, after my fourteen years attempting to do this kind of work, I can gratefully say that people back home are now becoming more realistic, understanding, and supportive of my business calling in this part of the world.

In running a business, however, you need to consider the possibility that you might actually lose money. In our idealistic enthusiasm with this approach, we often assume we will make money. This is not always the case, unfortunately.

When I first started as an entrepreneur, I took many risks. I found there were times to earn and there were times to lose. One of my objectives became maximizing the former and minimizing the latter. We cannot guarantee that there will always be profits in our business. We face definite additional risks in doing business in the non-Western world.

Remember, the church and the mission agency often consider profit-making to be unspiritual. We need to show those who object that money can be a vital resource for assisting the extension of the kingdom in developing countries.

BUSINESS OPTIONS

Start small. Create income-generating projects, such as Bible verses on papyrus bookmarks, Sudanese handicraft, bamboo crosses, a Christian video club, running a bazaar for the foreign community. This approach helps train people to be creative and work hard to earn their own living. Let me describe some of the businesses I tried.

My ability to communicate in Chinese, Arabic, and English gave me access to open doors between the Middle East and the Far East (mainly China). This venture was not related to any development or humanitarian projects. It was just pure business.

Now I am launching into the consulting business for those from the Far East or Chinese from overseas who would like to invest in the Middle East. To recruit Christian businessmen, I have established a company back in Hong Kong, and I am establishing a representative office in Egypt. I am also trying to recruit investors for this part of the world.

I also provide consulting to both Middle Eastern and Chinese people who are interested in doing business with one another.

I have been marketing the products and networking to distribute the products both locally and internationally. My market is not limited to the Chinese world. It links with the West, too. Good networking links the right people to make things happen and get the business done.

KINGDOM PERSPECTIVE

We need to create job opportunities for God's people. When I started a handicraft project among Sudanese and Egyptian people, I was able to provide them jobs to earn their own living. They became self-supporting, avoided the dependency syndrome, and were able to serve the Lord without worrying where their next meal would come from. All through the years of this project, many Christians became involved in full-time ministry. They proved themselves faithful in doing little things, and the Lord has entrusted them with bigger things for his kingdom.

My tentmaking ministry has resulted in a positive influence and witness among people in society. By God's grace, I have a tremendous opportunity to be part of the lives of local people, especially among the majority group. Most of my business contacts come from this group, in fact. Through these contacts, we can build deep relationships in which respect can be shown for different convictions. This is a great way to build the trust necessary for people to listen to and accept the Christian message. By making an economic contribution to the quality of people's lives, we have the opportunity to build trusting relationships.

Through the income from a small business, we have set up a fund to support some local ministry workers. Many people have been blessed through this fund. Ultimately, I want to establish a witness of integrity and holiness through the business.

CONCLUSION

There is a Chinese saying: "No needle is sharp on both ends." There are always pros and cons in running a real business in creative-access nations. My vision is to see more Asian businesspeople joining in my business, using their expertise to contribute to God's kingdom. After fourteen years in the Arab world, I can attest that Chinese and Asian people are well accepted in this part of the world, especially in light of the present political climate. Asian churches also have sufficient human and financial resources to make a big impact in business missions. We can do it. By God's grace, we will do it.

5

CHURCH PLANTING VIA SMALL BUSINESS IN ZAZALAND[1]

Patrick Lai

BACKGROUND

Until I read Christy Wilson's book *Today's Tentmakers*[2] in 1987, I had no idea what tentmaking was. I believed that people who were not in full-time professional Christian work were less than wholehearted about their faith. When I first embarked on missionary service, tentmaking was not an ambition, nor even a thought. I was only interested in reaching the lost. I had no desire to do business.

I attended the University of Oregon, where I studied business marketing. I did not begin to pursue a degree until my fourth year, when Overseas Missionary Fellowship (OMF) asked me to complete a degree. I chose marketing, in part because it seemed the closest discipline to evangelism. The Lord involved me in The Navigators for four years, and for two years I helped start and lead a church among the local Chinese community. These ministry efforts resulted in my "cramming four years of business studies into five."

After receiving an M.Div. at the suggestion of OMF and getting some valuable experience in a local church, my wife and I went to Hong Kong. We thought it would be our launchpad into an unreached area of China. However, we ended up as traditional missionaries. After two years of language study, our job was to disciple believers in a Baptist church. Dozens came to know the Lord, and we learned much about language-learning, living overseas, and working with Christians cross-culturally. But Hong Kong was our Samaria. We still had farther to go.

Next, we felt directed to a place in Asia I will call Zazaland, to plant churches among Zaza Muslims. Because OMF did not work there, we joined Frontiers, a mission agency that focuses exclusively on Muslims. Frontiers was new and disorganized, but it gave us opportunities to create and to risk.

Now there were no barriers and many new paradigms. God was free to take all he had invested into our lives and work through our gifts and abilities.

Making the transition from traditional missionary to tentmaker had its moments. The last thing a close friend and mission leader in Hong Kong told me was, "Tentmakers are not missionaries. You will not plant a church if you go into business!" I found this mentality interesting. When I went to seminary, not one person questioned my decision to lay aside my business background and degree to work in the church. Yet when I made it clear I was going to lay aside my seminary education to serve in the business community, many said I was wasting God's and others' investment in my life. I had lots of other discouraging moments, too. These forced me to check my heart and God's voice, ensuring that I was walking in his will and not my own. As you pursue tentmaking, many voices will cry out to you, all well-meaning. You must learn to recognize God's voice before going as a tentmaker. Also, be warned that if you are afraid to take risks, tentmaking may not be the best ministry for you.

In 1985, while serving in Hong Kong, a close American friend from our home church had offered my wife and me jobs working for his "widget company" in China. We had brushed aside his offer, but now that we wanted to get into Zazaland, we called him back. We asked if we could open a regional office and were thrilled when he agreed. After learning the business and building a plan for reaching the Zazas, we began recruiting a team and supporters. We also applied with the Zazaland government to open a regional office. We had our financial support from churches and individuals, so we decided to work on a commission basis, using the office primarily as an entry strategy rather than as a full-time enterprise.[3] This seemed to be the easiest and fastest method for getting a visa, learning the culture, and starting the ministry.

BEGINNINGS

During our first four years in Zazaland, this arrangement worked well. I was employed by the company on a project basis, which allowed me lots of free time. I probably worked only about thirty hours a month, leaving the majority of my time free to minister as I pleased. This seemed to be the perfect model. We had six other couples as team members. Each opened separate offices.

We were all wary of working for a business, fearful that we would "become entangled in civilian pursuits" (1 Tim. 2:4). We strove to be focused, keeping our eyes on God, not mammon. Our first five years in Zazaland were in a relatively poor area called Medina. Unemployment there was above 50 percent. It soon became clear that we needed to address the situation if we were to have credibility. The government was disorganized and only sporadically enforced the law. We decided that providing education and creating jobs would be helpful.

The team also chose to follow the Nevius model of church planting. We would strive to build a church that was self-instructing, self-governing, self-propagating, and self-supporting. We agreed to use Acts as our church planting manual. We invested time studying together to "adequately prepare ourselves for every good work" (see 2 Tim. 3:17). When the qualities of the Nevius model were instilled in the group of gathered believers, we would move on to another city.

Before we opened our first business, we wrote down two criteria. First, every business needed to be profitable within eighteen months. Second, every business needed to create witnessing opportunities. If a business failed at either point, we would shut it down.

We met with various new believers to learn their skills and experiences. We desired to create businesses they would want to operate and which would give them a good chance of success. With relatively little capital, we started six small businesses providing jobs for those who were out of work. No expatriates or team members worked in these businesses beyond the initial period of training the Zaza workers. No expatriate received an employment visa to work in these businesses. The initial investment for each was less than $10,000. In order, we began an English school, a kindergarten, a boat transport company, a taxi service, a thrift store, and a grocery store. To this day, the kindergarten and grocery store are doing very well. The English school is doing marginally well. The boat transport company, taxi service, and thrift store, however, have failed. The kindergarten employs six workers, the grocery store four, and the English school one—all from Zazaland.

Each of these three businesses has met our criteria of being profitable and creating witnessing opportunities. Today there is a thriving church in Medina of nearly eighty adult believers. From a business standpoint, the boat transport company and the taxi service were poorly managed. After two years, we shut them down and swallowed our losses. The thrift store was actually profitable. After three years, however, we had not seen even one person come to the Lord through it, so we shut it down, too.

After a few years, as Muslims began to believe and to be discipled, the government started taking a keen interest in our activities. Several times the police invited me to the station to talk about what we were "really" doing. By our fifth year, we had two groups of believers in two separate villages. The authorities soon realized we were doing very little business and a lot of evangelism and discipleship. Finally things came to a head. I was taken into custody and interrogated for two days. The authorities told my wife and me that we were a threat to the stability of the society, contributing nothing to the community. They gave us forty-eight hours to pack and leave. By God's grace, when we left Medina, the church was growing, and leaders were emerging. Fortunately, several of the team members were allowed to remain in the country and continue the work.

Being deported was very traumatic. With our two children we moved to a city on the other side of the border. We spent much of our time in soul-searching and seeking the Lord, trying to help from a distance. Nearly every month, we met with the team outside the country. Within a year, however, we came to realize that our work there was done. The churches reflected the Nevius model. National leaders were guiding the church and leading small groups. A pastor was appointed. The team signed the three successful businesses in Medina over to believers we trusted and had trained. The two groups we left behind have grown into solid churches.

We learned several basic lessons from our time in Medina. First, shortcuts, "the wide and easy path" (see Matt. 7:13), are not God's usual way of doing things. We came to realize that if we were to have a viable ministry, we needed a viable reason for being in the community. If we are adding value to a society in the form of education, creating jobs, bringing in capital, or enhancing people's lives, it is unlikely we will be deported for doing evangelism and church planting. (And if we are deported, we will most likely receive at least one clear warning first.) Residing as a student or having a "cover" job may work when starting out, but if we begin gathering believers into a church, sooner or later we will be found out. Then, if the government is hostile and we are not contributing anything of value to the society, authorities will deport us. After one year, we felt we understood God's will for a long-term entry strategy that would bless people in many ways, especially with the gospel.

After much prayer, some team members felt that the Lord would have them return to their home country. Others of us chose to move to the country of Rahat and the metropolitan city of Shahir, where there is a significant Zaza population. Whereas Zazaland is a typical Third World country, Rahat is more developed. Shahir is a wealthy, Westernized city. We knew the haphazard business approach we used in Medina would not work in Shahir.

STARTING OVER

Whereas the population of Medina was nearly 100 percent Zaza Muslim, Shahir was barely 20 percent Zaza. Our initial forays into Rahat showed us that the best businesses for meeting our two criteria would be in education and service. Building on what we already knew, and having two trained teachers on the team, we decided to register an English language school. However, we also had two couples with backgrounds in computers. They preferred to write or teach programming. So over two months we wrote up a thorough business plan, borrowing ideas from other tentmakers as well as our future competitors. We also met with some key Rahat government officials. By faith some of us moved into Shahir, living on tourist visas. The other team members took home leave while awaiting the go-ahead.

In addition to our church planting objectives and the two criteria for operating a business, we placed a high value on community. We believe Muslims need a community to move into when they choose to follow Jesus. Thus, we need to model for them what that community looks like. Living together would draw unwarranted attention to ourselves, so our community lifestyle would have to flow out of our work place. We prayerfully wrote a team manual, which clearly states our principles and practices. It also details our strategy and goals for both the business and the ministry. We emphasize accountability in character, family life, and devotional life, as well as work and ministry. We outlined our Zaza language objectives, contextualization and bonding strategies, defined what a team is, and the qualities desired in team members. Our doctrinal positions, standard of living, security procedures, and exit strategy, among other things, are also outlined in the manual. This manual has continued to serve as our guiding light in times of difficulty. In the past six years the team has grown to twenty adults; only one couple has been asked to leave because of character issues. No one has quit the team in Shahir.

Rather than see new team members trained by others back home, who do not understand our unique objectives, we train people ourselves. We also require each new team member to be commissioned by their home church and to raise at least 75 percent of their estimated financial support. All new team members are screened and hired by the team leader. New team members may join us only if they make a minimum five-year commitment. We agree that in hiring both expatriates and nationals, we place a higher value on character than on competence. We believe that competence flows out of character and that we can teach competence. Teaching character is much more difficult.

THE LAUNCH

We submitted our first draft of the business plan to several wealthy Christian friends and businessmen, making adjustments based on their feedback. Once the third draft was complete, we moved ahead, submitting the plans for the business to both venture capitalists (all Christians) and the Rahat government. Here we hit our first major roadblock. The Rahat government does not consider teaching software development to be education but business. This forced us to write another business plan for a trading and services company, which we named Titan. Titan's articles of incorporation are intentionally broad. Computer programming is just one of the services it provides.

Before we could get government approval for the private English school, all our facilities had to be in place, ready to operate. We also had to submit in advance the teaching curriculum for every course. These roadblocks naturally turned us to prayer. We obtained the money to buy the property from three sources. (1) My wife and I cashed in our retirement fund. (2) A silent partner invested $60,000. (3) We took out a bank loan of $80,000. Thus, we were able to purchase the property and remodel it, plus pay salaries and expenses for the first eight months of operations. Our business plan estimated that we would not make a profit until the eleventh month, but we trusted our income from the first eight months to be enough to carry us through the next three. Needless to say, we were on a very tight budget.

As I said, one of our key aims was community. To justify our relationships with one another, we decided to use adjacent office space for both businesses. When people asked why we knew each other, we had a logical answer.

We agreed that no new team members would be allowed to work for either business until they had completed at least eight months of full-time language study. That is enough for someone to engage in daily conversation and learn to share his or her testimony. After this initial period of full-time study, every team member continues language study under the supervision of a team language coordinator until able to read the daily newspaper and adequately share the faith in the Zaza language.

After the initial year of culture and language learning, each team member is expected during the second year to work forty to fifty hours a week. Each team member has a job contract and is paid a regular salary. The expatriate salaries are 5-10 percent above the market rate for national workers, rather than at expatriate salary levels. However, team members do raise financial support. This keeps them fully missionary in the eyes of their sending churches, and it keeps them accountable to ministry goals. It also provides a regular fixed income, enabling team members to have time for ministry and to keep their office hours within reasonable limits. Team members donate their salaries to a fund that they corporately manage. This fund can supplement the income of team members who are low on support. The fund also provides start-up capital for future businesses, as the team expands its sphere of ministry to other locations in Rahat. This fund also pays for team ministry expenses. Team members disburse at least a third of the fund for special ministry projects, including local and international charities.

Working full-time during this second year accomplishes four objectives. First, it brings new team members into the heart of the business. National coworkers see that the expatriates are not just learning the language but are integrally involved in the business. This period establishes their working identity in the community; it earns them respect. Team members set up a routine and become fully involved in the business.

Second, it allows team members to add value to the business or school, which we require. They add value by creating more services, or classes, which in turn increase our numbers of customers or students. We desire that each team member's contribution would increase revenue to the point matching a national's salary. When this happens, usually during the third year, we hire a qualified national to do most of the team member's job. We train the national to take over twenty to thirty hours of the team member's responsibilities, plus other tasks to make it a full-time job. The team member becomes the national employee's supervisor, and now his or her job requires only fifteen to thirty hours a week. At this point, team members may choose to continue working inside the office or to spend more time outside the office with people. Many become part-time employees, though some continue to work full-time and be paid a full salary. It is an individual decision. We realize that God has differing priorities for each member of the team.

Third, team members have high morale, which carries over into the lives and work of the national workers. When motivation runs low, we stimulate one another to try harder. We use a minimum of one-third of the profits for team vacations, team training, our children's education, and blessing other ministries. Such giving to Christian and local non-Christian agencies encourages our national workers, too. Coworkers know they are working for something more than just a paycheck.

Fourth, working full-time during the second year creates natural witnessing opportunities. When team members finish their language studies and begin working in the office, they become fully a part of "the community." The national workers are clearly watching and at times testing us and will often ask several team members the same question about our beliefs and practices. Hearing similar answers reinforces our witness. The nationals have told us they are encouraged to see us sacrificing for one another and for the community. Not once have we heard our collective Christian witness spoken of in a negative way.

We knew from experience that we could use the office to build relationships and live out the life of Christ. We also knew that we could openly share the gospel only outside the office, because the authorities have closed businesses that aggressively do so on-site. Thus each team member initiates verbal evangelism only outside the walls of the businesses. Of course, this takes time, but due to the flexibility of our schedules, we have the time.

Naturally, we located the school in Shahir's Zaza area. Nonetheless, we knew many of our students would not be Zaza. To attract Zaza students, we advertise in the Zaza language paper and nearby Zaza suburbs. To our joy, the students have been 30 to 50 percent Zaza, well above the demographic percentage for the city. On the other hand, as expected, the majority of Titan's customers (90 percent) have been non-Zaza. Still, team members working for Titan have established good Zaza friendships in their neighborhoods and by meeting people at clubs and coffee shops around town.

Both the English school and Titan have developed along the lines we projected in the business plan. The English school took about ten months longer than expected to reach profitability, while Titan was profitable nearly a year ahead of schedule. Thus, profits from Titan covered the small, temporary losses of the school (less than $700 a month). Further, Titan and the school share facilities as well as administrative support. Since Titan exceeded our revenue estimates, its funds have been available (as interest free loans) to help the school.

SURPRISES

Of course, as with any start-up, we encountered some unexpected problems. A big one involved money. While team members all agreed to accept salaries similar to what nationals are paid, most team members wanted to pay our nationals 5-10 percent above the national industry average. They felt this was a good testimony and would help us keep quality employees. However, this made it harder to get out of the red. One team member went without a salary for nearly six months. Team members also loaned the school approximately $8,000 to meet our additional expenses during the slow early months. Tentmaking involves a commitment of more than just the heart.

Further, team members with little business experience had what I call the "mission mentality" of doing business—meaning bigger is better. They were inclined to spend all their budgets quickly, believing that this was the way to get more money. Yes, you have to spend money to make money, but if there is little coming in, then little is able to go out. By the end of the fourth month, we held a meeting to correct this mentality. We gave the leaders their budgets for the rest of year, telling them that if they wanted to spend more, they would have to provide the money themselves. This greatly curtailed spending.

Our biggest surprise related to the English school was the interest shown by citizens from predominantly Muslim countries other than Rahat. These international students are very profitable for us, so we have altered our business plan to recruit them. We have set up a website using several languages and have hired recruiters to promote our programs abroad. We have also rented two nearby apartments, one to house men and the other for women. The rental money from these apartments is an additional source of income.

LIFE AND WORK

As the team leader and owner of the businesses, I have turned over the daily operations of the English school and Titan to two team members. I meet with each director weekly, or more frequently if necessary. Nationals now head some of the divisions within each business, meaning a few team members work under nationals. In the office we practice the policy of aggressively showing God's love to one another. We not only live out our faith, we talk about it. We daily seek opportunities to give credit to God, whether for the weather, a new client, or the healing of a headache. This has led many staff to ask questions about our beliefs. As I said, we cannot legally initiate evangelistic discussions, but there is no law against loving people and answering their questions. Our Zaza staff has learned that we will pray at the start of meetings and meals. We visit our staff in their homes and invite them to ours. We give bonuses as often as appropriate. We stress to everyone, both staff and clients, that our bottom line is their success and happiness, not simply making money. We involve our local staff in giving to charitable projects, even encouraging them to suggest worthy charities. We believe money is a tool for witnessing, nothing more. One slogan we promote is "We Bless Others Because God Has Blessed Us." We stress professionalism and value character while promoting a family mentality that gives responsibility and ownership to hard workers. We set the example in service. I have a smaller office than my national division heads. Team members and I wash the floor or clean the furniture as often as we ask others to do so. When a national staffer has to go home for an emergency, it is natural for one of the team members to cover for him or her.

We have many ways to let our lights shine in the office. Most opportunities are unplanned. For example, after discussing the concept of grace with our office manager over lunch, I could tell she did not understand. At the end of the month, I gave her a $100 bonus. While I had given her bonuses before, the amount this time was more than normal, and—unlike previous times—she had done nothing special to deserve this one. As I expected, she said, "I cannot think what I did to deserve this." I smiled and readily agreed she did not deserve this bonus, even as we do not deserve the gift of eternal life God so freely gives us by his grace. She now has a better understanding of grace.

We regularly have opportunities to talk about Christian holidays while teaching English. One day, two students asked to know more about Easter. Knowing our policy of not witnessing in the classroom, the teacher directed them to another team member who was free. This team member invited them for a cup of coffee and shared the gospel with them. We regularly have parties for the staff and use these times to share some aspect of our personal relationships with God.

Having a solid, mature, committed team is essential for our work and ministry. Therefore, I invest a lot of time with potential team members before they come to the field. Once on the field, team members meet weekly for worship or Bible study. The men meet biweekly for training. The women meet monthly. We have group social outings approximately once a month. Sometimes we bring Zaza friends to these socials. My wife and I attempt to meet with each couple or single person on the team once a month. These accountability times are opportunities to pray and discuss frankly both personal and ministry issues.

BENEFITS AND BLESSINGS

God has greatly blessed both the English school and Titan. These two businesses have created eight full-time and sixteen part-time jobs for nationals. In addition, we have created seven paid positions and three volunteer positions for team members.

The English school has made a profit six of the past twelve months. Student registration, as we had anticipated, is seasonal. Over the past year, the school recorded a net income of just over $1,000. Needless to say, this is not the kind of revenue that attracts major investors. Our objectives, of course, have always been broader than financial, and we are satisfied.

Titan has been profitable since its third month, averaging a net of more than $2,000 every month, or $25,000 annually. We are currently expanding Titan's portfolio of services to create more jobs for nationals and visas for expatriate team members.

To help keep our eyes fixed on Jesus, we strive to keep the profits in circulation. This not only blesses others; it minimizes our taxes. There is nothing wrong with working to make money, but this is not the primary reason Jesus brought us overseas. By giving generously to bless others, we believe we are not only obeying him in giving (Acts 20:35), but also exalting him in seeking his heavenly reward before earthly luxuries (Matthew 6:24; Luke 8:14; Proverbs 30:7-8) while providing a witness to others (Matthew 10:8; Luke 6:30).

The businesses have created many opportunities for us to share with both co-workers and clients. So far, just one Zaza in Shahir has believed, but many of our Zaza friends have moved from -6 or -5 on the Engel Scale to -3 or even -2[4]. We are keeping our eyes focused on the Perfecter of our faith, expecting a breakthrough any day now. The businesses provide the credibility, viability, and respect we need to maintain a consistent, long-term presence. To date we have not received any government warnings about our evangelism. Other than one time when a team member received some Christian materials in the mail, we have not had any problems with the government.

Team members who lead each business contact key government officials at least twice a year to update them on our business activities. We send these officials appropriate cards, pictures of their visits to our facilities, and government-approved gifts during festive seasons. These are open and legal efforts to build good and godly relationships with the authorities. On two occasions we have shared our beliefs with these officials.

EVALUATION

In evaluating any tentmaking venture, we must never emphasize either financial profits or evangelistic fruits at the expense of the other. We are now a full two years into the English school and three years into Titan. According to our initial financial objectives, the English school is barely profitable. We are making adjustments in both marketing and advertising, as well as altering our staff hours, in the hope of increasing both our cash flow and our profitability. From an evangelistic perspective, staffers have created numerous opportunities through both their works and their words. Thus, I would rate the English school a mild success.

Titan is a financially profitable business. Titan played a role in bringing one Zaza to faith and is continuing to provide other opportunities to witness. Titan has recently committed itself to expanding into nearby countries. To date, I would rate Titan a success. However, success is a process, not an achievement. Thus, we cannot remain still nor bask in the limelight. We acknowledge and thank our Savior and Master for his grace and provision.

INVESTING IN PEOPLE

Striving for balance in working and ministering both inside and outside the office is a constant struggle. Every person has different opinions and callings. Though all team members who have visas through the businesses receive a salary, we strive gradually to reduce the actual hours they have to be in the office. Our plan, including home church support, gives team members the flexibility to choose how much time they spend in the office.

I interview each potential team member extensively so that I understand his or her calling, goals, and expectations. I want to help each person achieve God's calling overseas. Naturally, I want the candidate to understand us better, too. The traditional missionary approach is for one set of laborers to recruit candidates back home, another set to provide training, still someone else to serve as field supervisor. Each of these groups has only very limited knowledge of what is actually happening on the field where the person will be assigned. Many times candidates get information that is out of date or just plain wrong. Many businesses that work in teams, however, involve team leaders in the selection of team members. That is how we approach it. By clarifying potential team members' expectations about work and ministry before they arrive, we enhance their—and our—chances of success. The best way is to bring potential workers to meet with those they will be actually working with on the field.

Research being done by the OPEN Network[5] shows that most future tentmakers expect to invest more time doing evangelism and disciple-making than in their actual job. However, once they arrive overseas, most spend more time at their job than in doing evangelism and discipleship. We can talk about balance and doing evangelism within business, or through business, or business as evangelism, but the real issue is the quality of the tentmaker's life. As leaders, we are accountable to God for those we lead (Heb. 13:17). We need to ask hard questions of both others and ourselves. We need to ensure that the tentmaker is maturing in Christ and is productive in both the job and the ministry.

My role as team leader is to minimize adverse conditions so that each team member can live and work under as favorable circumstances as possible. I want team members working as many hours as *they* want to and not as much as I want them to work. We find it difficult to limit team members' working hours during their first two years on the field. However, by their third year, team members who wish to reduce their hours in the office usually may do so, as I have discussed. Some team members want to work full-time, while some wish to work only a few hours a week. Clearly there are differing views on credibility and integrity in tentmaking. I don't choose between these options but allow team members to do as they feel led. This means I must come alongside them to hear what the Lord is telling them to do, and then hold them accountable. This flexibility helps produce high morale. Team members need little encouragement to develop relationships and do evangelism.

The Bible tells us, and good businesses show us, that it is wise to invest in people. I believe the investments we have made in ours will produce eternal returns, both in team members and in the Zaza community.

6

BUSINESS IN CAMBODIA

Norman Teece

A native of southern England, I spent twenty-seven years in industry, mainly in automotive design engineering. I left Ford Motor Company in eastern Essex in December 1990 and joined a small mission movement in South Wales. My wife and I knew after two years that our call was to Cambodia, but there were mountain-sized obstacles to overcome. Our preparation was a painful time of breaking and humbling, stripping away our English pride to enable us to go to the Khmer people with listening hearts—to go to a hurt and lost nation, not with a bag full of ready answers and solutions based on our Western thinking, but to go and listen and learn and simply make ourselves available to help in whatever way the Lord had prepared for us.

We relocated to Phnom Penh in November 1993 and quickly saw that the young Cambodian church seemed to be doing an effective job of evangelizing and church planting. But we saw a big lack in the discipling of new believers. Many new converts stayed in the church for only a few weeks before drifting away, never to return. No one seemed to follow them up, encourage them, or help them to persevere in the Christian life. There were many young people with great potential, but most had no job and daily faced a struggle to live, surrounded by lots of temptation to crime.

Slowly we began to see that our path was going to be different from the normal approach taken by missionaries and workers with NGOs. We perceived that God was telling us to create wholesome employment and business ventures, which would provide proper work and also the environment in which effective Christian discipling could take place. An old Essex friend used to regularly remind me, "Nothing is ever wasted in God's Kingdom." Instead of leaving behind all my work experience, I could see it was suddenly becoming freshly relevant.

WORKPLACE DISCIPLESHIP

In mid-1994, David, an English Christian businessman, imparted his vision to see craft production not only provide employment for local craftsmen and their families, but also as a means to reach out to their communities with the gospel in action. During a whirlwind few days, David started buying local goods such as delicate terracotta pots to fill a twenty-foot container. Then he returned home, leaving me with the job of getting the container organized, packed, and shipped. How would these crafts survive the five-hour truck journey over potholed roads to the port city?

During the following days of visits to various government departments, shippers, and customs offices, I learned that there were no clear procedures for export, no guidelines for beginners, no rules. No one was exporting anything. Coming in were massive amounts of international aid and a growing avalanche of foreign goods. On my second visit to a government agency controlling all goods into or out of the country, I was taken to meet the director and had to explain all over again how we wanted to send all these Cambodian crafts to the United Kingdom to sell, and how some of the profits would help poor people in Cambodia build better lives. He asked lots of questions, such as how much was I making; how much had we paid for certain items; why had I come to Cambodia; did we think we could help people in the villages? Finally, he grinned and said he liked what he had heard and would do everything he could to help. The man then took me through the warren of dirty, dark offices to collect all the signatures required, ensuring that no one tried to get money out of me. He waived all the charges he could have imposed and sent me on my way. I had paid only about 75 cents to photocopy the handwritten letters and notes. It had taken three hours, but I had all the papers in hand with the required signatures and stamps. I had even been able to share with this man God's love for the poor and oppressed.

Eventually, with a great deal of help from a team of Cambodian youngsters, the container was packed, cleared, and sent to the docks. Just three days later, the only road through the mountains became impassable for weeks when a bridge collapsed. The sale of these goods and the money we received for community development convinced us that this kind of business activity could be highly effective. It had opened up key relationships in several rural areas and brought financial blessing, too. Local people started asking us questions, and we began to share the gospel.

In 1995, we began the process of registering our company, which we called Bright Arrows, with the government. Forming a company was the only way we could legally export Cambodian goods. Through the jungle of documentation required, we obtained full approval in January 1996 for our company to invest in various kinds of business.

On a personal note, in 1995, we found ourselves "adopted" by a young man, Khemera, who had prayed for a mother and father since becoming a believer. Our adoption of Khemera—which translates as "all the Khmer people"—enabled our roots in the nation to go deep. It has enabled us to buy land and in innumerable ways has helped our cultural adaptation and understanding.

However, our business ventures did not meet with immediate success and we had many early setbacks. One example was a project that involved helping fine-arts students pay their tuition fees (and get some income) by producing hand painted watercolor greeting cards. Unfortunately, we could not compete with cheaper cards from Thailand and Indonesia.

Another venture involved negotiations to retool a large, disused cross-ply tire plant just outside Phnom Penh to produce radial tires. It all looked very promising, until a Chinese company was granted all production rights. Six years later, the factory is still closed and looking more derelict than ever. An opportunity to re-employ the local workforce and reduce foreign imports had been lost.

Over the last five years, the Bright Arrows team has grown and with it the variety and style of the projects that we handle. We have sought to avoid a hierarchical, pyramid-type organization and instead have adopted the flattest, most minimal structure to support our ventures. We are held together by relationship and all our activities share certain goals:

- provide genuine employment
- ensure quality discipleship where people grow in maturity
- give righteous pay and conditions
- provide an environment of faith and fellowship

The expatriate team comprises a core of one American and two English couples, plus eight associates drawn from the United States, the United Kingdom, Japan, and Canada (two of these on one-year assignments).

CURRENT PROJECTS

The Craft Project

Care for Cambodia (CfC) is a recently registered NGO, based in the outskirts of Phnom Penh and working in five provinces. CfC grew out of the craft project from the vision of the young man named Khemera whom we adopted.

He wanted to see Cambodians themselves helping other Cambodians, especially widows and orphans. CfC is the prime ministry arm of Bright Arrows, concerned with the lives and spiritual development of all the people connected with the company. CfC comprises around 120 people. Twelve are orphans (or children in crisis), and the rest are either part-time or full-time members. The project has attempted from the first to help rural workers balance their craftwork with their farming. We want to employ them where they live, not add to the number of people displaced by seeking work in the city. The craftwork itself has developed into hundreds of items, from basketware, pottery, leathercraft, beadwork, coconut shell, bamboo, sugar palm, and reed weaving. Chicken and turkey raising has also started, with the first batch of turkeys reaching the market for Thanksgiving 2001.

The Care for Cambodia craft exports, however, have suffered some real financial and government policy setbacks in recent years. Since our 1997–1998 fiscal year, we have been unable to get approval to export "forestry products." Without the numerous craft items from wood, bamboo, and rattan, the value of our containers plunged and has become unsustainable. In 2001, no containers went out at all. We are praying for new outlets and contacts and a change in the corrupt bureaucracy, which prevents fair trade.

The Sewing Project

Based in a village about forty miles north of Phnom Penh, our sewing project was originally set up by World Vision as a training course to help young women and girls. By mid-1995, World Vision was ready to take the machines and equipment and establish another course in a different location. Our local pastor, however, became concerned about the future of the ten trainees. After meeting with the World Vision team, Bright Arrows agreed to buy all the assets and to establish an export market for the sports shirts they made. The vision was to:

- further develop skills and quality
- establish overseas markets and export
- build a sustainable Cambodian business owned by the women
- continue discipling the women involved
- bring blessing to the community

Initially response was good, but quality and design input were inconsistent. The arrival of large, foreign-owned garment companies and new government legislation made the position of small producers untenable. Facing bias in export procedures and the establishment of a Garment Manufacturers' Association with expensive membership fees, we switched our focus to accessories (handbags, etc.) and home products. Now in a diminished form, the project has been handed over to the Cambodian staff with Bright Arrows maintaining help in marketing and other areas. We have also investigated establishing an embryonic company to conduct quality control inspection for overseas clients prior to shipment.

The Tile Project

Following the loss of a market for traditional cooking and water pots, we have trained local pot makers in a village on the banks of the Mekong River northwest of Phnom Penh to produce terracotta floor tiles. We knew of a potential market for high-value, handmade tiles, currently being supplied from Spain or Mexico.

We set up a kiln and compared our results with those obtained from traditional brushwood firing techniques. There was some initial success in producing a variety of tiles. However, financial problems at the U.K. end have discouraged both us and the local people. The business has not provided for the families, but the relational aspects of the project have continued. To help the participating families make a living, we arranged for small loans to help them grow vegetables and salad produce. Just as the first harvest was being taken to market in January 2001, tragedy struck. The key person died in a horrific road accident. Now, a United Kingdom-based company has expressed strong interest in importing Cambodian tiles for their 500 outlets nationwide.

"Jars of Clay"

Near the busy "Russian Market" in Phnom Penh, we also started a coffee shop selling homemade cakes. The venture, called Jars of Clay, provides meaningful employment to girls traumatized by prostitution. Working alongside World Vision, which provides them with most of the initial rehabilitation programs and counseling, we ensure that the girls have good and safe employment. Our vision is to reproduce this model. An English lady, who founded this work, currently employs five girls.

Vocational Training Center

In 1997, Bright Arrows and an international NGO called Harvest International Services (HIS) set up a joint venture to establish a vocational training center (VTC) for orphans and other disadvantaged children. The project was established under HIS's existing agreement with the Ministry of Social Affairs, Labor, Vocational Training and Youth Rehabilitation (MOS-ALVY), and it covered orphan and street children ministry as well as vocational training. Between 1997 and 1999, most of my time and energy went into this project. I was the principal and also the curriculum designer and instructor for the basic engineering course. Initially, we also offered courses in art and design as well as sewing.

Many applicants, who were referred to us by churches and other groups, had received only a year or two of primary education. Thus, we included literacy teaching and instructions in basic hygiene. Most of our first students came from squatter communities. It was hard to teach them concepts such as discipline and perseverance. From the outset, our objective was to keep class sizes small to ensure lots of personal contact, and to give help in finding jobs for those who satisfactorily completed the course so that they could help their families. Training that does not lead to proper employment is useless in Cambodia, and only serves to discourage the very people we attempt to help.

Placing those students in a job at the end of year one, however, presented a big challenge. Cambodia had almost no commercial infrastructure, and the few existing companies were only interested in taking the cream of the university crop. It became apparent that jobs would have to be created, and this increasingly was my burden. By March 1999, we placed the VTC under the full responsibility of HIS. The center moved to larger premises in the northern district of the city, while the engineering students from the 1998–1999 academic year formed the basis of a new venture called Ironworks. The VTC continues today, with a range of courses expanded to include computer information technology skills and computer repairs. Fifty students are currently attending, and to date about 130 have successfully completed their training and gained certificates validated by MOSALVY. Planned new courses include secretarial/office skills and motor vehicle maintenance and repair.

Ironworks

From a shaky beginning making craft and gift products for tourists, Ironworks has grown in strength, reputation, and product range. Because nearly all the resources of the VTC went to the new location, we began Ironworks with little more than the change in my pocket, an electric welder, and a collection of hand tools sent from the United Kingdom.

Ironworks is a cooperative of artisans working together and growing together, building a small business they own and a future that provides hope.

We aim to provide apprentice-type training, leading to full-time work in a safe and clean environment where they can grow in confidence and faith. Pay and conditions are higher than normal. The average Ironworks craftsman receives around $60 per month, including his food allowance and a savings plan. This compares to $23-25 per month for teachers, police officers, and government employees.

Until June 2001, the business struggled to break even and regularly needed cash injections to keep going. Revenue in 2000 totaled only around $12,000, of which almost 40 percent came in as donations. We have tried to make the business more sustainable by increasing productivity, but sales have been sluggish. In 2001, however, we saw a 30 percent-plus increase in income. The last two quarters of business actually generated a small profit for the first time. We had been praying that God would bless the work of our hands and bring in the customers. That happened, almost dramatically, especially for furniture and fittings for homes and gardens. We have won substantial orders for bunk beds and furniture for local orphanages, too. We often get surprised by inquiries for such things as canoe transporters, and we continue to sell small, eye-catching gifts for the tourist market.

Normally we employ nine young men, but occasionally one moves on to another job or to further training. Our relationship with the VTC enables us to take on new trainees. If the higher workload continues, no doubt we will recruit more.

Sadly, death visited this enterprise as it had the tile project. In August 2001, Seng Vichet, the gifted and capable young man being prepared to take a leading role, died instantly in a motorbike crash with a truck. Yet good has come even out of something so heartrending. The other young men, who relied heavily on either Vichet or me for many tricky jobs, have stepped up their efforts and are working with new vigor. Quality and productivity have risen appreciably. Others are rising up to take up the responsibilities that Vichet carried. We see that his untimely death will only delay the handing over of this business to the remaining young men.

FUTURE PLANS

I believe that our next project will focus on horticulture or agriculture and food processing. Eight years since our arrival, virtually no one processes food or drink from local fruit and vegetables. One reason is because seasonal harvests are short. Added to that is the fact that Cambodia has poor transport and distribution systems. I think we should take a closer look at how the ancient Khmers built their empire from the wealth of the land. Somehow, they managed to produce two or three harvests each year. Perhaps, in time, this fertile land will again produce abundant harvests, and Cambodia will become a garden for Southeast Asia.

But beyond the logistical difficulties, it will take a monumental and determined spiritual battle to overthrow the forces of evil that have controlled Cambodia for generations. High levels of corruption, high prices of raw materials, a dollar-based economy, and institutional indifference to the cause of small businesses continue to make this a challenging environment. Galatians 6:9, however, says, "And let us not grow weary of doing good." It is easy to become weary through discouragement, lack of success, and the feeling that what we do is small and insignificant. Much of our work so far has not produced the results we had hoped for, but we are pressing on, having learned much. We continue to pray and to watch for new opportunities.

How do we prepare for the new opportunity, the unexpected opening? We listen to the Spirit and remain pliable and open. We constantly look for the approaching cloud that is only the size of a man's hand (see 1 Kings 18:44).

In all our work and whatever the results, as in Abraham's case, we have found that in being faithful, God blesses us as much as, if not more than, we can bless others.

7

Business Among South Asian Refugees

Daniel Batchelder

The first time I visited the main shopping district of a war-torn nation in South Asia, women swarmed around me, carrying small babies and begging for anything I might give them. Every time I got out of my vehicle I would be suddenly surrounded. Weeping mothers, doe-eyed children on their shoulders, were grabbing, pulling, pleading with me for something, anything to help them take care of their families.

Twenty-three years of unrelenting military conflict, widespread human rights abuses, and, more recently, a four-year drought have created devastating humanitarian conditions for many families. Millions of refugees have fled their homelands in the past two decades. Military conflict has forced many to flee to neighboring countries for safety and for food, clothing, and shelter.

These families reportedly have the world's highest infant, child, and maternal mortality rates. They also have the lowest literacy rate and life expectancy and lowest level of food per capita. Twenty-five percent of newborns die before age 5.

We are not members of a relief agency, but the condition of the people is so desperate that we had to do something. Rather than provide direct relief, we looked for ways to stimulate economic and community development projects. While not ignoring the immediate needs of hurting families, we try to find creative solutions that bring hope and are economically sustainable for the future—not just providing a fish, but also teaching them how to fish. These people are like most of us. They would much rather have meaningful jobs than handouts.

One time a group of women approached me as I walked to my vehicle. One by one they showed me official documents certifying that they are widows. They were asking me for a job in a program we had created, the Widows Quilting Project.

WIDOWS QUILTING PROJECT

The treatment of women in this area has been appalling. A United Nations report estimated there are 30,000 widows in one city alone. These women were forbidden to go out in public by themselves, they were denied an opportunity to go to school, they could not visit a male doctor, and they were not allowed to work outside the home. How were they to feed their children and take care of themselves?

Meanwhile, fifty refugee camps surrounded one city. During the cold winter nights, children died simply because their mothers could not find a way to keep them warm. We began looking for a creative solution that would address both needs. The answer we came up with was the Widows Quilting Project. This is a business employing widows to make quilts for the families living in the camps.

There were several hurdles, of course. First, it was illegal for women to work outside of their homes. Therefore, we decided to bring material to the widows in their homes. A young man had his wife conduct a survey of widows who might want to participate. After an overwhelming 300 eager widows surfaced, we stopped the survey. It became clear that finding workers would not be our problem. A second hurdle was that we needed to find a way to market the quilts. Who would buy them?

The quilts are simple but durable. We deliver fabric, needles, thread, and more than seven pounds of raw cotton to each widow for each quilt. The two pieces of fabric are sewn together and the cotton evenly distributed in between. The "quilting" is all done by hand, with big needles and strong thread creating individual pockets to keep the cotton from shifting. The widows are paid by the piece. One widow set a record of producing seven quilts in one day. She made three times what a manual laborer can make in a day.

At first it was difficult to get orders for these quilts. Four women from Canada, California, Colorado, and Maryland provided the seed money to launch four individual projects employing twenty widows each. Soon we had more quilts than we had places to store them. Then orders began to come in. Individuals, families, businesses, churches, and other organizations started purchasing these quilts and asking us to distribute them to the refugee families who were in need. People were realizing that the same $5 used to bring relief to a child in a refugee camp also provided a job, dignity, and hope to a widow caring for her own children.

One recent winter, the project provided more than 30,000 day jobs for widows. Orders for 5,000 and 10,000 quilts from aid organizations have enabled this project to grow. At first we worried that we might not be able to meet such large orders in a timely manner. We soon found out, however, that for every widow working for this project, five more were waiting in the wings, hoping for an opportunity to work. This ability to quickly expand the work force has enabled us to keep up with very large orders, even on short notice.

Another hurdle was the seasonal nature of the work. While blankets and quilts were in demand during the winter, the need plunged during the summer. We soon found ourselves with an oversupply of quilts during the summer and little work for the widows. We decided to diversify and are now making the traditional bed mat and pillow set, called a *tow shak*. People use it both as a chair (while sitting cross-legged on the floor, with the pillow as a back rest) and as a bed. *Tow shaks* are in every home. They make a practical gift to a returning refugee family and are much less seasonally affected than quilts. We expect them to provide a more stable form of employment.

Yet another challenge was our response to the wildly fluctuating prices of cotton, needles and thread, and fabric. To hedge ourselves against such price swings, we set aside a few pennies from the sale of each quilt. We use this money to purchase more material to make more quilts. Thus, we measure the value of the project by how many quilts we have in inventory. Today we have more than three times the number of quilts that the initial investment produced.

We want these widows as well as many other families to find meaningful employment that offers a living wage and the dignity and hope that come from productive employment. We are exploring whether we can produce a line of women's clothing as well as other furnishings and accessories to be sold in the West.

CARPET WEAVING

This war-torn nation has experienced hundreds of thousands of Internally Displaced Persons. They are not refugees in the official sense because they have not left their country, but they are families on the run just the same. Thousands of these people have poured into neighboring cities to escape the fighting. The unemployment rate in these areas can exceed 80 to 90 percent.

One day I met with a representative of 9,000 families. Hamid was a young man in his early 30s who was quiet, thin, calm, and determined. He had been waiting for several days to meet with me. After listening to the story of how the members of his village had fled the fighting, I asked how we could help. He said that a little food would be a big help. I replied, "How about a job?" His eyes lit up and a big smile crossed his face.

His people all knew how to make traditional carpets. This was the genesis of our carpet-weaving project. We bought several looms and set them up in our project building. Natural dyed, hand-spun wool was soon being woven into beautiful handmade carpets. These families were becoming self-sufficient again.

Obtaining orders for carpets was difficult at best, however. Traditionally, refugee families prefer to employ younger children because they have small and very quick hands and can out-produce adults. But we try to instill some of the values many in the West have learned concerning child labor. Women also wanted to work, so we placed some of the looms in people's homes.

Eventually, we found a group that could produce carpets under a fairly predictable contract. Soon we had over fifty people working in the project. However, with recurring unrest, many of the people involved had to flee for their personal safety, including the group we had contracted with to produce carpets.

Today, we are in the rebuilding process. Several families continue to gain meaningful employment from carpet weaving, and recent new orders will allow us to expand this project once again.

We believe that, instead of starting something unfamiliar, you should build a foundation employing traditional skills.

TAILORING PROJECT

I remember the day I was introduced to Najib. I had asked our staff to be looking for entrepreneurs who needed some help getting started. Najib had run a tailoring shop making uniforms for the various militias. His situation mirrored that of many of the residents of the area at the time.

The country's economy was in a shambles. Most families, including Najib's, were barely making it. He struggled just to feed his wife and seven children. But we thought he showed much potential.

Najib agreed to set up a tailoring project that would be run according to the business principles we would teach him. We purchased the sewing machines and hired experienced workers. We started making clothes for men, women, and children, and offered them for sale in the local markets. We tried to make better clothes out of durable material.

As with most small business start-ups, the first few months were slow. We coached our staff on how to reach out to the marketplace so potential customers knew who we were and what products we had available. We set monthly quotas, took samples around to various shops, and did what we could to drum up business. Soon we found a niche making wedding dresses for local brides. Sometimes the bride wears two or three dresses during the extended wedding ceremonies in this culture. Soon we had to hire more workers. Since much of the work included beadwork and embroidering, we hired women to work in their homes. Often one family did the beadwork, another did the embroidering, and someone else did the final stitching back in the shop. At one point, the project was supporting more than 110 families.

Because of the restrictions on women working outside of their homes, visitors to our tailoring shop in 2001 could see a turban-wearing man with a two-foot-long gray beard sewing lovebirds and other frilly things on a pink wedding dress. Everyone was grateful for a chance to work.

In one area, our tailoring project produced five sample school uniforms for boys and five for girls. Ten students from a local elementary school donned these uniforms and visited the Ministry of Education. We hope officials will ask us to produce uniforms for students.

I knew we were beginning to make a difference the day our staff informed me that we were shipping clothes to neighboring countries. People can buy a set of durable clothes for refugee children for $6. Orders for clothing are coming from the local shops as well.

CHICKEN PROJECT

The nation where we work, with the size and population of Texas, has lost the ability to feed itself. The United Nations reports a looming 2.3-millon-metric-ton food deficit. Without significant help from the international community, many people will starve to death in this once proud nation. What could we do in the face of such need? We needed a food source that could renew itself quickly. We decided to think small—as small as a chicken egg.

Chicken eggs hatch in twenty-one days. Both the chicken and the egg are edible. Even more promising, the chicken is a traditional food source for many families.

It seemed like a good fit, so we launched our Chicken Project with three incubators, managed by a family that has its own small operation. Chickens are hatched and raised until they are one month or three months old. Then we sell them as potential laying hens or as meat birds to needy families.

Orders are really starting to flock in, so to speak. An aid agency may order several thousand chicks from us to give to families who are leaving the refugee camps and returning to their villages to start over.

DIRECT SEEDING AGRICULTURAL PROJECT

Beginning in the mid-1980s, a revolution occurred in dryland (non-irrigated) farming throughout North America. Dryland wheat farmers were seeing significant increases in yield by employing direct seeding/no till methods, and they had a near total conversion to these methods.

Obviously, with the food deficits and an ever-increasing flow of wheat and other cereal grains into our country, this looked like an attractive alternative. If the increases experienced in North America could be duplicated elsewhere, it would have a very positive impact not only on their local agricultural economy but also on their food supply.

We did extensive research to compare sites in North America with a certain area needing assistance. We selected sites with similar soil types, annual rainfall, and growing seasons. Our research predicted very conservatively that we should expect to double the amount of wheat grown per acre using traditional methods.

We purchased a John Deere Direct Seeder and other equipment, loaded a forty-foot container, and shipped it. We also purchased a tractor, and the United Nations Food and Agriculture Organization supplied the seed.

In January, amid a three-year drought, we planted some winter wheat. Several curious local farmers planted wheat using traditional methods next to our site. With only 40 percent of normal rainfall that year, the harvest was very light. The farmers had nothing, but our yield at least allowed us to recover the seed we had planted. This was quite a success, given the lack of moisture.

Unrest in the country kept us from planting in the fall, but we were able to resume our project in January. Although drought conditions still linger, this wheat crop should produce, as predicted, a notable increase in yield.

This project has significant implications for the entire nation. Helping farmers catch up with some of the agricultural advances of the past quarter century is one way to express our concern as they put the pieces of their lives, their families, and their communities back together. Instead of giving them a bag of flour, we are teaching them how to double their yield.

WHAT WE ARE LEARNING

We have made our share of mistakes, but we have also picked up a number of valuable lessons along the way:

> Several organizations working together, instead of competing with each other, can have a significant impact. Too often we see organi-

zations carving out their territory or setting up only their own projects. What we end up with is a patchwork of projects that fall well short of their potential. We need to find ways to work together (Psalm 133).

If entrepreneurs use their gifts to meet people's felt needs, everyone wins. International business interests often show up in impoverished areas of the world simply to exploit opportunities. If you come with the same gifts and abilities but use them to help, the results are life-changing (Phil. 2:4).

If my partners are successful, then I am successful. If we are all on the same team, then it makes sense to see others prosper (Phil. 2:3).

The basic principles underlying a successful business enterprise are the same in other countries as they are in my hometown: vision, planning, implementation, tenacity, and accountability (Eccles. 1:9).

Seek out the implementers. Most of us have the ability to come up with good ideas. Certain people, however, are gifted at implementation. Find them, make them part of your team, and empower them to implement. Give them the tools they need and take away as many obstacles as you can (1 Cor. 12:21).

8

Business in Kyrgyzstan

Juerg Opprecht

In 1998, I was surprised by the tremendous level of interest among church leaders in Bishkek, Kyrgyzstan, to a presentation I gave on starting small businesses. Afterwards, they pleaded with me, saying, "Please help us to provide work for our people."

I was reminded of Matthew 25:35 (NIV): "For I was hungry and you gave me something to eat, I was thirsty and you gave me something to drink, I was a stranger and you invited me in, I needed clothes and you clothed me, I was sick and you looked after me, I was in prison and you came to visit me."

I might also add: "I was unemployed and you gave me a job."

Profile of Kyrgyzstan

Kyrgyzstan has many challenges and opportunities. An eastern Central Asian state, it was founded in 1991 following the collapse of the Soviet Union. Kyrgyzstan has had basic democratic structures and a trustworthy president. Although about eighty ethnic groups live in Kyrgyzstan, the country is known for its comparatively high social stability, respect for human rights, and advanced process of democratization. Thus, Kyrgyzstan is a promising place to invest in aid projects.

Much of the economy, however, is based on bartering, and the old Soviet infrastructure is in decay. Sixty-five percent of the potential workforce is unemployed, creating poverty and robbing young people of a vision for the future. The country's seventy-year experience with Soviet communism has also robbed people of practical knowledge concerning business management. In spite of their poor social conditions, however, many of Kyrgyzstan's people have had good educations, though influenced by the communist system. By and large, they don't know how to take advantage of the new economic environment.

The annual inflation rate is nearly 19 percent, and the average wage is not keeping up. Worse, high tax rates make it hard for fledgling entrepreneurs to get businesses going. The government also is little help when it comes to providing access to start-up capital. State loans are available only for a short time and with unrealistically high interest rates. It is not surprising, then, that Kyrgyz entrepreneurs often get involved with elements of the mafia. Thankfully, inconspicuous small businesses are not usually targets of interest for the underworld.

THE BUSINESS PROFESSIONAL NETWORK

It is in this milieu of opportunities and challenges that the Business Professional Network has been trying to make a difference. So far, we have been encouraged. What is the BPN?

> Our Mandate:
> In July 1997 at the Global Consultation on World Evangelism (GCOWE '97) in Pretoria, South Africa, more than 4,000 church leaders challenged business leaders from around the world to engage business in the fulfillment of the Great Commission. Some of us decided to form the BPN so that we could begin the process.

> Our Vision:
> Our vision is to demonstrate God's love in action, primarily in the economically depressed and developing areas of the world, through developing new and existing businesses and creating jobs through business and professional people.

> Our Mission:
> We want to facilitate, stimulate, and empower the organized effort of individuals, existing businesses, marketplace ministries, churches, parachurch organizations, missionary societies, and service groups of all kinds to provide self-sustaining business development and job creation. As catalysts and unifiers, we seek to match the resources of the business community with the needs of the poor and unreached.

In a nutshell, we seek to provide loans to new entrepreneurs, so that they can start their own businesses and provide for their families so they can strengthen their churches. We also seek to provide training in business management as well as Christian business ethics. The appendixes at the end of this chapter provide more details about our structure and how Westerners can get involved.

OUR WORK IN KYRGYZSTAN

The goal of BPN in Kyrgyzstan, our first country of operation, is to establish sixty to eighty small businesses in the first three years and then to multiply the project in other countries.

Participants do not receive cash. We loan them equipment worth no more than $20,000 and expect them to pay back the amount, with interest, within four to five years.

But participants receive more than the loans. They get training in management, business ethics, and technical assistance. They attend SERVUS business management training courses for four years. On a regular basis, specialists who work with us teach them the basics:

1. how to make a basic business plan
2. how to make a basic marketing concept
3. basic accountancy
4. how to lead employees and how to negotiate successfully

Furthermore, the participants receive individual counseling and coaching on-site.

The project contributes to the economic development of the country by addressing the following issues:

1. promotion of businesses
2. promotion of home-produced goods and services
3. battle against unemployment, including the secondary effects of unemployment
4. rebuilding and supporting the middle-class structure of the country

WITNESSING THROUGH BUSINESS

Of course, helping entrepreneurs involves much more than imparting our skills. Those of us who help must first witness to our faith, because most participants have no more than a limited understanding of Christ. When we first started in Kyrgyzstan, many people asked, "Why are you doing this? What do you get out of this?" I answered, "The Holy Spirit led me to do this, and I am just obedient." Needless to say, they stood there with eyes and mouths wide open. Yet we must serve with a humble attitude, a heart of love, and hands to help. These will ignite hope, trust, and passion.

Having worked in this country for more than three years, I have no doubt that action must come before words. As Matthew 5:16 (NIV) says, "In the same way, let your light shine before men, that they may see your good deeds and praise your Father in heaven." In a country full of poverty and corruption, living the gospel comes before preaching it. A person's actions must confirm his preaching.

However, this is not as easy as we might think. What if judges, tax collectors, customers, and suppliers are corrupt? We must teach them, teach them, and teach them. We must change a mindset. Second, we must provide help. As a community of businessmen and women, they are able people, but they need to be brought together. To achieve this, we have made available the following:

1. We have translated *La Red,* an excellent small-group teaching program. This curriculum allows them to address specific business problems from a Christian perspective and encourages them to pray together.
2. We are laying the groundwork for a Christian trade association.
3. We make available local Christian lawyers and tax advisors.

By God's grace, most of our participants are developing big hearts to reach their nation with the gospel. As this is a Muslim country—albeit a rather liberal one—they do it mainly through establishing personal relationships.

CASE STUDIES

1. Veronika

After disappointment with disloyal business partners, Veronika, a trained dressmaker, decided to set up her own studio. Her loyal customers, for the most part, provide the sewing materials. Starting with 20 employees, Veronika's goal is to produce her own line of clothes in a business with 100 workers.

Despite four other similar enterprises in the market, Veronika is convinced that the quality of her work will give her a competitive advantage. But she needs $20,000 to purchase additional sewing machines and other equipment. She also needs instruction in basic business economics, and so she is grateful for training provided by our Business Professional Network.

However, Veronika faces more business uncertainty than does the average entrepreneur in the West. Seeking to buy a building to house her production facilities, Veronika's best efforts have come up short. Once she lost out on a building to someone who offered slightly more than she did—despite the seller's previous verbal commitment in her lawyer's presence to sell it to her. A guarantee in Kyrgyzstan means nothing if someone else makes a better offer. Another problem is that production volume greatly fluctuates. Often Veronika has fewer orders in winter than in the summer. This poses a challenge to her desire to keep her workers fully employed throughout the year, which is unusual in Kyrgyzstan.

Yet by trusting in God and persisting, this petite lady eventually found a suitable building. Veronika quickly learned how to totally trust in Jesus despite being a relatively new Christian. She has committed her life to Jesus and is constantly surprised at what Jesus does for her. Formerly an object of discrimination because of her small frame and "insignificant" profession, Veronika has developed a healthy self-image. Difficult situations and setbacks do not stop her.

Responding to the seasonal nature of the work, she of course employs additional temporary staff during summers. However, Veronika, like the patriarch Joseph, collects excess funds during these months in order to pay salaries during the sparser months. She also helps welfare cases from these funds.

2. Olga

With 62 employees at two locations, Olga and her son make men's pants and uniforms. They export some of the 60,000 trousers produced annually to Russia. Because of contacts they have made at trade fairs and exhibitions, they also have open doors to sell to Europe.

First, however, they need to unite both production locations, modernize and obtain more machinery, expand the product line into ladies' wear, and increase the number of employees to 100. To do all that, they received a loan of $20,000 from BPN in June 2000. Since that time, the number of employees has grown from 64 to 80.

However, this business, too, faces many obstacles. Corruption is an ever-present problem. The business exports many of its products to Russia. On route through Kyrgyzstan, Kazakhstan, and Russia, company representatives face blackmailing and harassment by customs officers and police. They also must pay protective duties on transit goods.

Olga has joined forces with other participants who face similar situations. Together they have written an open letter to the government describing the situation and asking that the nation's customs laws be enforced. Despite fears of a backlash, they also want to speak with customs department leaders.

Seeing how corruption has harmed their country, this group is facing it squarely according to the ethical instruction they have received through the Network. They seek to bring injustice into the open and make it a subject for discussion. Olga and the other BPN participants have already taken their injustices to a daily newspaper several times.

Meanwhile, Russian Kyrgyz are strongly discriminated against in Kyrgyzstan, due to a reaction against Russian conduct during the domination of the Soviet Union. Most Russian Kyrgyz have emigrated to Russia. As a Russian Kyrgyz, Olga suffers under the current discriminatory conditions. However, she remains in Kyrgyzstan (which she regards as her home) so that she can use her business to help the country's economy and to be a witness for Christ through her lifestyle.

Another obstacle is the presence in the market of cheap clothes from China. Although the homemade products are of better quality, they are also more expensive. However, BPN participants are beginning to see that customer satisfaction is an important key to success and that they do not have to measure success by price alone. However, there is much to be done in addressing the subject of quality.

Their business success is a result of God's grace as well as their perseverance and determination. They have learned that when they walk in God's ways, God will always be with them.

3. Nurlan

For several years, Nurlan led a state-owned business that registered and circulated economic data. His goal was to build up an independent printing and photocopying center. As part of the business plan, one of his employees completed an apprenticeship with a printer in Bishkek. With plenty of orders, the business developed very well. He started in November 1999 with two employees; now he has six. However, he needed a loan of $18,000 for the photocopier/printing machine.

One of the Network's conditions for participation is that businesses have their own premises. This was difficult for Nurlan, but through determination and hard work, he turned a dilapidated house into a sizeable production plant. He and his family did without personal comforts to raise the necessary funds. Nurlan is one of those people who lives for his goal and is totally absorbed in his assignment.

Of course, building in Kyrgyzstan is always difficult, requiring permission from ten to twenty different government departments. Not surprisingly, corruption is a problem. Officials look not only to the state's requirements but to their own as well. Therefore, it can take months or years to receive approval. The process goes considerably faster when the officials are "appeased" in some way.

Nurlan, however, knows that although corruption may produce results in the short term, in the long term it is destructive. As a Christian, he also seeks to be a good example to others. He takes deliberate steps against corruption. One is to hold open discussions with employees and officials while holding to his convictions. This approach does not eliminate the problem, but it certainly helps him cope better.

LESSONS LEARNED

1. *The strategy of small steps.* The greatest challenge is to change a mindset. One legacy of the Soviet heritage in Kyrgyzstan is that people are very quick to recognize problems but they do not quickly proceed to solutions.

In our seminars, we give participants extended time to express their concerns and to discuss problems. They write them all out on flip charts. Just looking at these charts, usually we have one thought: Hopeless. But then we have good discussions over lunch, and by the time we return, these entrepreneurs see that there are no problems—only solutions. And they start coming up with some amazing answers to what had, hours before, seemed hopeless problems.

2. *Seek and maintain contact with the government and with the public.* Explain what you are doing. Explain what you mean by "Christian ethics" in business. Don't preach; communicate. Everyone understands that societies need values. Show those with whom you come into contact that Christian values work.

3. *Establish tools for long-term continuity.* As mentioned previously, we are preparing to establish a local Christian BPN trade association. This will allow entrepreneurs not only to have fellowship and to pursue mutual interests but also to have a voice before the government. One day, participants will leave the program, and a trade association will help give them some continuity.

4. *Teach them. Encourage them. Love them.* While kingdom principles come first, be sure to teach excellence and help people to strive for it in their businesses. We are a blessing to this nation if we help establish successful enterprises.

5. *The blessing must be multiplied.* Network participants believe we are a blessing to them, which is good. But we tell them again and again, "Now, you must bless your church and your family. As a child of God, it is good to

have a successful business. But this is not enough. Create eternal values by helping the poor and needy, by standing up against unrighteousness, and by establishing social justice."

Nurlan, who runs a printing facility, wanted to impact the public schools. His marketing manager happens to be the niece of a famous Kyrgyz writer. This opened the door to the Ministry of Education. Eventually our participant received permission to print and distribute a special edition of the book of Proverbs in all the public schools of Kyrgyzstan as part of an ethics study program. This is the kind of massive influence we can have if we are patient in doing the small things, such as providing someone a job.

APPENDIX 1 TO CHAPTER 8

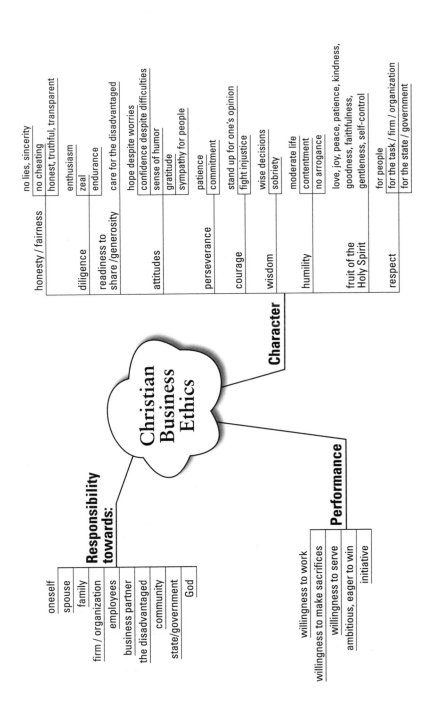

APPENDIX 2 TO CHAPTER 8
PROJECT PARTNERS

BPN AG, based in Switzerland, is the principal organization and carries the main responsibility. It supervises and raises funds for the projects. BPN brings together donors, investors, consultants, trainers, and participants qualified to receive financial and technical aid.

SERVUS Business Development, located in Switzerland, is in charge of the general project management on a day-to-day basis.

BPN CA is in charge of project management in Kyrgyzstan and answers to management in Switzerland. BPN CA directs all the on-site activities and keeps in touch with participants, local organizations, and the authorities in Kyrgyzstan.

DEZA, an organization of the Swiss Department of Foreign Affairs, has paid for part of the project management and infrastructure costs since the beginning of the project in 1999. Kyrgyzstan is currently one of the ten priority countries for cooperation listed by DEZA. The mission of DEZA is to build businesses in the developing countries by providing financial support.

APPENDIX 3 TO CHAPTER 8
SUPPORTING THESE PROJECTS

We believe in the special value of Western businesspeople sharing their expertise and financial capacities with the young entrepreneurs of this developing country. There are several ways for Western businesspeople to support our project in Kyrgyzstan:

As a Donor

You entrust us with a donation to support our work and help further development.

As an Investor

Your money, in U.S. dollars, will be invested in various projects as needed, or you may sponsor a specific business in Kyrgyzstan whose activities relate to your own business. You may provide one participant with a loan, possibly at no interest, for five years. If you want to participate for a longer period, we will support another participant. You may choose one of the participants presented by the board of BPN AG and finance the project fully or partially. Please ask for detailed descriptions of projects. BPN AG acts as trustee. Therefore, BPN AG will issue you with a trust deed and a letter of credit with the participant concerned.

As an Ambassador

You can make a project known within your circles, with the aim to find new donors, investors, and ambassadors. However, ambassadors must take a one-week trip to Kyrgyzstan. There they will meet with new Network participants and receive updates concerning the project.

9

Business in Central Asia

Byung Ho Choi

Although I have been a churchgoing Christian since childhood, my ambition has never been tentmaking. I came to Central Asia for business.

After graduating from college and fulfilling my military service in South Korea, I worked in the government's international currency exchange programs for a year and half. Then I worked at a British bank for ten years. At that point I was in my mid-30s, and I began to wonder whether I should stay at the bank or start my own business. One of my friends who lived in Germany told me that the Central Asian countries of the former Soviet Union had great entrepreneurial opportunity. I agreed.

Central Asia received its independence in 1991. While most of the people in this region consider themselves Muslims, for seventy years they were under the control of the communists. Communism and Islam have ruined the people psychologically and spiritually. Even now, the governments do not allow others to bring the gospel to the Muslim majorities. Those who do are expelled. Local former Muslim believers often go to prison. The minority groups, including Russians, Koreans, Azerbaijanis, and so on, have more freedom.

Thus, most missionaries work underground. They take on roles such as teachers and professors. Turkmenistan does not even allow NGOs to operate, believing that many of them are missionary organizations. The authorities do, however, allow companies to run businesses. Most of the other countries on the Silk Road do so as well.

TRIALS

Using my ingenuity and energy, I was sure I could be successful in business. First I sent a number of containers to a big distributor in Central Asia for trading on consignment. To minimize my company's risk, we made this other company sign a contract specifying that it would pay our money within one month of receiving the consignment. Despite the contract, however, this firm did not send the money as promised. Officials said they had no hard currency to make the transfer, only the local currency, which was no good to me. I could not convert it at the bank, where the exchange rate was about one-third of the market rate, so I had to wait.

After a year, a colleague of mine who was an advisor to the prime minister helped me bring this matter before the arbitration court, the nation's highest legal body. We won the case completely, but my company was no better off. The distribution company said the government did not allow it to convert the money. Since there was no way to enforce the decision, the result was meaningless.

So I went back to the drawing board and tried a different strategy. I established my own company in the country. I had to import the goods before I could register the company. Then officials issued me a patent, which meant I could convert currency. After a long time and a lot of money, I was finally ready to do business. This time I distributed the goods to small businessmen. I was even able to convert their payments at the bank. However, a new problem cropped up. The bank could only supply me with $200 to $300 per week in hard currency—in a good week, perhaps $500. The problem went beyond simply waiting for my money. As I waited, inflation ate up whatever profit I had made on paper. The official inflation rate was 36 percent, but actually it was about 150 percent. By the time my money was converted, I could not even cover the cost of the goods I had imported.

So I tried to send my goods to a private vendor, hoping that this company would pay me back promptly. As you may have guessed, my goods just disappeared, and I had no way to retrieve them or my money.

After these first three attempts failed, I looked for a different way. I wanted a business that did not depend on converting currency. Because I had been somewhat involved in my brother's construction company in South Korea, I decided to launch a business in trading construction materials. Mine was the only Korean company at the first Central Asian Construction Exhibition International in 1996. We won fourteen contracts for both big ($2 million) and small ($400,000) jobs. Not only had we won the contracts, but also overnight we had become one of the major contractors in our city. In the past only a few Turkish contractors had won these kinds of contracts. We were excited and worked hard.

Normally we signed two contracts, one for the local currency and one for hard currency. The former gave us the formal legal basis to do the project. The latter, called an offshore contract, allows businesses and investors to actually make money. All companies handled contracts in this manner.

However, large companies and government agencies could not convert currency, so we had to use intermediary companies to convert the currency for us. We did not want to have to do this, because of our previous experiences trying to convert currency, but we felt we had no choice.

Although these companies guaranteed they would compensate our company in dollars whenever the local currency contract fell short, they were not able to supply the hard currency to pay for the goods we imported from South Korea. The only way they could get hard currency was through the official rate. This meant that they would only pay my company about 30 percent of the actual cost of the work we performed. Despite my previous experiences, at the time I believed the problem was solvable, so I finished the job using my own money and also borrowing some. That was another mistake. At the end of the job we could not collect the money.

I had failed again. My creditor came to my office demanding money. The mafia types were outside my house day and night. All my jobs ground to a halt, and my workers quit. Some, however, returned to our warehouse and took everything.

At the same time, my church was experiencing problems. The church had been established in 1992. It was now 1997, and the government would not extend our pastor's visa. Worse, he had not trained anyone to take his place. I was the only person in the church from South Korea, so he asked me to take care of it. Complicating matters, our supporting churches stopped sending financial aid, thinking the ministry was over. Indeed, the church became much smaller, slimming down to fifteen people at a service. There was no preacher, nor any teachers. Facing the problems of my company and my church, I could see no way out. I simply fell on my knees and prayed. I had tried to do it my way but had failed.

MY NEW MISSION

At my church, some young members and I began to pray and study the Bible. The youth began to teach and tell people about Christ in their college. We began a prayer meeting on Wednesday and a youth gathering on Friday. We still did not have a pastor, but our church began to grow, and soon we had one hundred members.

About this same time, our company had three workers left. I said to them, "I don't know what to do. Let's pray." So we decided to come to work one hour early each day to pray.

God answered our prayers one by one, not all at once. He first would give us a small project. When that was almost finished, he would give us another job. This continued, and soon we turned a profit and began to pay our creditors and workers. God had answered our prayers. But more than that, I met him; I felt him. So did those with whom we interacted. Customarily our creditors would shout at us and force us to pay. As we began to willingly pay them, however, they began to change. As they saw what God was doing for us and in us, they began to understand and to help us. Some even came to faith.

I came to Central Asia for business. What I found during this time of trials was solid hope. I now recognize God's true calling for me, which is to devote myself to his kingdom business.

More than one hundred people work for my company now, and most of them go to the prayer meetings, entirely on their own. While many of them come because they do not want to feel like outsiders, I believe there is some genuine spiritual interest as well. The meetings begin with stretching and other exercises. Then someone reads the Bible and gives a message. Then we pray.

I had thought it would be very difficult to share Christ with the people, who are Muslims. But I found that they just have not had the opportunity to hear the gospel. Many listen very carefully, and some have received Christ into their hearts. I invite these people to join Bible study groups, of which we have two. These people will become leaders of the Bible study groups, and also of the company. The government sees the prayer and Bible study times as company meetings, and so it does not interfere.

Practical Ministry

My business is known by many as a "Christian company." One of the challenges I face now is that many of the church members in our city come to us looking for a job. Some of them are leaders who have completed seminary courses at the underground schools or in Moscow. Many of them cannot do the missions work they feel called to do because the churches cannot support them.

We are trying to address this dilemma by giving these local leaders opportunities to do spiritual ministry on the job. They lead the morning Bible study and prayer times and also work on the construction sites. However, this prominent role for them brought about a new problem. Their working colleagues would tell them, "You teach us a good message in the morning, but during the work day we don't see this teaching in action in your life." Talk about brutal honesty! Our company decided that we must do something to address this gaping hole in their Christian lives. We launched a practical training time for all our Christian workers, emphasizing that their beliefs must be evident in their lives. We provide our workers with both practical employment skills and spiritual skills.

Of course, this is not easy. During the decades of Communist Party control, people had no professional goals. When they finished school or college, the government would simply provide them with jobs. These jobs were secure, and workers did not have to meet any deadlines. If the work was not finished, there was no owner to take responsibility. Workers also were in the habit of taking things from their employers.

So when people began to work for my company, I had to teach them that they would not have a job if we did not meet our professional goals. They could not understand this idea. For many, it took years to adjust their way of thinking. Some of the Christian workers, however, understood this and began to take leadership positions in the company.

FUTURE GOALS

My vision is to be able to hand over the company to the Christian leaders to manage themselves. I hope some will start other companies elsewhere in the region. This kind of work has other implications for society beyond providing jobs and work skills, as important as these are.

When the Soviet Union controlled this country, and in the decade afterwards, the divorce rate hit 85 percent. Under the communist system, people's morals were destroyed. The family was destroyed and most children of those families experienced all kinds of social and psychological problems. But if people's character changes because of Christ and they have workplace skills, then many things will change in their lives. When the family becomes strong, then the country can become healthy and strong.

God gave me the vision to provide work and training to people, along with spiritual skills. I will continue to do this until God tells me to stop. We hope to continue these activities in other cities on the Silk Road.

We also have a vision to use our musical gifts and interests for the kingdom of God. My wife and I once were members of the Korea Oratorio Choir, the oldest choir in South Korea. My two daughters are studying music. One plays the piano, the other the violin. When we moved to our Central Asian country, we were thrilled to be in a city filled with quality music schools and an excellent musical tradition. Yet musicians here struggle financially, either from lack of work or lack of payment for their work. The national choir has shrunk from 60 members to 38.

I wanted to give unemployed choir members the opportunity to continue their musical careers through a choir. Because of finances, we have limited it to sixteen of our country's best vocalists, whom I support financially. We held our first concert in 1991. Because we registered as a professional choir, we may sing all kinds of songs, including those with spiritual messages (which incidentally are some of the best choir pieces). We sang the "Hallelujah Chorus" to a standing ovation and encore at our first concert. We have traveled to South Korea and hope to perform in China, Mongolia, Turkey, and the United States.

No longer do I do business alone. The concert tour has several ministry-related purposes. Not only can audiences hear the gospel through song, but it allows people who want to do mission work on the Silk Road (signifying the ancient trade routes) to join us. Then they can look for opportunities in these countries to make contacts, conduct market research, and find ways to start businesses. I hope that Christian companies set up branches in these countries.

My goal is that the companies and the choir become self-supporting, owned and managed by local Christians. My vision is that they become places where Christian faith is evident not only in theory but through action as well. In this way, business and missions can work together to extend God's kingdom.

10

BUSINESS IN SOUTH ASIA

Luke Watson

My only experience in business had been when my brother and I sold a box of persimmons from my grandmother's trees to the local fruit vendor in a nearby country town. Rather, I was a trained academic. Using my research background in a branch of science, I taught for several years as a professor at a postgraduate university in a major Asian city of a restricted-access country. I was there as a self-supporting tentmaker and worked with a few other Christians. Our goal was to plant churches among the unreached. In what little spare time I had, I studied the national language and a local language. I befriended some local men and began to share the gospel with them.

Eventually, several other Christians, including families, joined us, and we focused on one major unreached group. Several other teams as well began to focus on different aspects of Christian outreach to the same people group, such as Scripture translation and radio broadcasts. Many on these teams were officially either students of language and culture or missionaries. But since we often met for prayer and discussion, we were able to coordinate some of our efforts.

Unfortunately, my busy job did not give me much time to learn the language and develop relationships with the people we wanted to reach. When my contract ended after several years, I shifted to an official student status and found more time for ministry.

During all this time, two young men from the people group we adopted had placed their faith in Christ. Others were reading the Scriptures with us. As we focused on the spiritual lives of these young men and led them to trust in Christ, we were drawn into the concerns and difficulties of their lives in this impoverished country. The extreme poverty there is devastating for the majority of citizens; many basic needs of life, such as education, jobs, medical help, and so on, are not as readily available as in developed countries. While still teaching, I helped these young believers get training in order to improve their employability. While they never did land the jobs we hoped that they would, I decided to focus more time and energy on this crucial issue.

After several years, when my teaching job and language studies were finished, our team returned to the States to take a break, and I married a coworker from our field. We prayerfully reconsidered some basic premises of our work and decided that something was missing.

MAKING DISCIPLES

In developing countries, poverty, unemployment, poor medical systems, lack of education, oppression, injustice, and so on are much more severe than in developed countries. Thus, sins learned from the surrounding culture and environment are often quite different from those in developed nations. Making faithful disciples in developing countries involves a different process, requiring not only obedience-oriented teaching of the Word of God and prayer but also problem resolution. We have a commission from Christ to go and make disciples of all peoples (Matt. 28:18-20). We not only must baptize them in the name of the Father, Son, and Holy Spirit, but also teach them to obey all that Christ commanded us.

Of course, we must *be* disciples to make disciples. This involves action on physical as well as spiritual needs. The good Samaritan stopped to help the helpless man and thus fulfilled the law of love. Christ said, "Go and do likewise" (Luke 10:37). The Levite and the priest, who did not stop to help, seemed to think their responsibility was only with religious or spiritual problems. If we want to teach disciples to obey Christ's teachings, we must do it by obedience—not in token gestures but in a complete lifestyle. Church planting among the remaining unreached people groups is definitely an important step forward in completing the Great Commission, but we are not done until our disciples have been taught to obey all that Christ commanded us.

NEW APPROACH

So, despite my inexperience, we thought business would give us the best chance of having a long-term ministry with our people group. It would be not only the activity most acceptable to the government but also the best way to fulfill our goals of widespread natural contacts for evangelism and provision of jobs for believers and impoverished people. In fact, a secular expatriate businessman in our target country suggested this option to us.

We felt that to make disciples, we must first become involved in the problems of believers and seekers. We wanted to provide jobs, training, and education in order to introduce both the gospel and economic growth into the country. We also decided that secondary vehicles such as literacy and vocational training, as well as relief and development work, could follow the primary thrust of business. Our long-term vision for the business was to empower believers from the target group to become economically self-sufficient.

Profitability was a real but secondary goal designed to complement the primary goal. Accordingly, we could not simply respond to market demands with appropriate products and services. But we did need to evaluate the potential of a business for fulfilling our priority goals.

STARTING THE BUSINESS

After easily obtaining a business visa, we reentered, relocated, and prayerfully continued our business research. Unfortunately, the government wanted our business to be a large-scale exporter. This approach increases foreign reserves, which the country desperately needs to keep its economy afloat. Our initial efforts to fulfill this ideal, however, distracted us from our own goals for the business to provide contacts with the people we wanted to reach and to enable believers and people living in poverty to become economically self-sufficient. Therefore, we stopped trying to export general quality items and narrowed our focus to the production and marketing of specific craft items made by the local folks from among the peoples we wanted to reach. Although we knew these items to be generally in low demand, we decided to do it for ministry reasons. Since my wife and I were inexperienced, the challenges of product design work, quality control, management, and marketing were enough to keep us scrambling for the first few years.

Initially, we sought to market our goods to dealers in many developed countries, but because of extreme competition, we found markets in only two countries. We also market to expatriates inside our country. Our markets are primarily among Christians for two reasons. (1) They tend to be major buyers because they want to help the poor in developing countries. (2) Our sales transactions usually depend on mutual trust for both delivery and payment, and Christians are generally trustworthy. Because we are not a big business, we have to use noncommercial mailing techniques such as mail parcel or special courier. This restriction does have advantages. So far we have escaped confrontation with the major bribery and corruption systems that enter into big business.

Our eight years working with these local products have brought many ups and downs. Quality control and markets have steadily improved as we have gained experience in working with the local people, their products, and the markets. Over the last fifteen months, sales hit $25,000, our highest level. Until 2001, we operated continually at an annual loss. Whether we can maintain a level of profitability or even self-sustainability is questionable, however.

TURNING DIFFICULTIES INTO OPPORTUNITIES

Nonetheless, we are committed to trying. We face continual problems common to developing countries: (1) political and economic instability; (2) poor infrastructure, including faulty communication and transport systems, and frequent power outages; (3) inconsistent availability of supplies and materials; (4) poor-quality materials, equipment, and facilities; (5) corruption, deception, and lack of trust. Since quality control is also a major problem, we must check everything we produce to eliminate quick, shoddy work.

Deception and distrust are widespread in the land where we work. Numerous conflicts arise, sometimes intense ones, and we have had our share. While it is not easy to continue long term under such circumstances, if we can persevere through the difficulties and conduct business honestly and fairly, the effect on the local people is very positive. We have seen this among our workers, neighbors, and friends.

In a corruption-ridden society, simply paying honest wages and conducting business ethically may open some hearts to the light of Christ. One young man was doing a certain type of work for us that was in demand at many other businesses in the area. But he pestered us for a full-time salaried position in our office doing any work we could find for him. We found out that other employers took advantage of him because he had a speech impediment. Eventually, we hired him. After several months, he proclaimed us "great people" simply because we paid him an honest wage for good work, according to our word. This man loved to watch the "Jesus" movie in his own language and once had a dream that Jesus was putting rice in his hands. We think he may have already put his faith in Christ but is too fearful to tell us or anyone else. Within a year he had lost his speech impediment.

MANAGEMENT PRACTICES

Office workers, who are paid by salary, have increased to six. Home craft workers, who are paid by the piece, have fluctuated from 200 to our current 60; the latter are our consistent, high quality workers. Most of these are ethnically among our target people but are linguistically different. In fact, we eventually discovered that most of the target peoples indigenous to our city and area speak that different language.

Multiplicity of languages and dialects is a never-ending problem. Because of the interaction of many tribal, language, and ethnic groups, people of our group may speak one of about five different languages as their mother tongue, depending on exactly where they live. Initially, we focused on the largest of these five but often found it necessary to use the national language and learn portions of other languages as well.

We learned to adapt our management policies to the circumstances. For example, we initially paid all salaries at the end of each month. However, because of poverty, lack of planning, high unemployment, and the prevalent cultural tradition of extended family dependence on only one or two employed breadwinners, needs of workers would arise long before the end of each month. So we reset our policy to allow advance salary payment on current earnings. Deceit was so prevalent in the society that it sometimes clung to the life of a new believer, however. Since our better economic circumstances made us prime targets, we learned to avoid giving loans or advances on unearned income. In an emergency we would give help. But we almost always administered the gift ourselves, such as paying a trusted doctor directly for medical services.

INTEGRATING BUSINESS WITH MINISTRY

Numerous young men among our language group who worked for us appeared to be keenly interested in the Bible. Unfortunately, they were all from other geographic areas and came to our city only for jobs and education. We studied the Word of God together for several years, both in our city and in their own areas as we obtained permission from the government to travel in their areas. Many of them made commitments of faith in the Lord Jesus Christ.

However, none of them continued long-term with the business. Their reasons for departure included homesickness, dissatisfaction with the work, climate maladjustments, and so on. Unfortunately, we also observed a turning away from Christ or a general spiritual malaise in many professing believers. Needless to say, this was a great disappointment. Only two of the professing believers who were with us in those early days can still be identified as disciples of Christ. Thankfully, they have become effective ministers for Christ among their own people.

As we studied the experiences of others and looked to the Lord for peace, joy, and direction, we decided to become more flexible. Despite the possible fallout it might have on our business status in the country, we became more intentional and aggressive in our evangelism. I worked for several years to complete a detailed, contextualized, illustrated, evangelistic book in the local language of the unreached people group we were focused on. It uses eighty local proverbs to introduce scriptural counsel and then the gospel. Wide distribution of this book allows us to extend our gospel witness far beyond our personal presence and limitations.

Additionally, we conducted rather extensive relief work following a natural disaster in the area. This opened up natural opportunities for sharing the gospel personally in remote, unreached areas and for distributing evangelistic materials widely. Eventually, opposition to our evangelistic work became quite strong, however. But it did not seem to hurt our business status in the country, which confirms to us that our business status was the wisest strategic choice for our situation.

MINISTRY SHIFT

Because our workers showed little response to the gospel, eventually I started studying the language of yet another people group in our area, some of whom showed great responsiveness. As they grew in their faith, they became actively but wisely involved in ministry and discipling of others in their people group. I began employing these disciples for varying periods of time until they could find better long-term employment. Together we translated and adapted the evangelistic book for their group. This integration of business and discipling was more effective than our earlier efforts, probably for several reasons: (1) the believers were older and more mature, with families; (2) the believers had been prepared by God; (3) we were more experienced in both ministry and management; (4) products and markets were better developed, allowing us to create more job positions; (5) translation of our extensive evangelistic materials was integrated into both discipling and business, allowing more employment.

HEALTH AND LITERACY

From the beginning, my wife and I have given medical advice to our workers and the poor around us, using the book *Where There Is No Doctor* (Hesperion Foundation, 1992). We also refer people to doctors as appropriate. Since our workers have had little access to vitamins, calcium, and iron supplements, we have supplied those things, along with skim milk powder for protein. My wife, however, went a step further and began tracking body weight in a follow-up program for workers' infants under age 5. Since all infants were malnourished, some severely, and many died of infections, my wife decided to teach infant feeding and general health principles to the women, who expressed keen interest.

During the last three years, while continuing her heavy load of product design and business management, my wife designed and conducted daily literacy and education classes with an emphasis on basic health education. Along with a local Christian lady, she taught twenty of our workers and their teenage daughters, with preference given to the latter. Prayer was a daily part of each class. As my wife arbitrated conflicts between individuals and families, she had numerous natural opportunities to share Scripture verses, particularly those regarding forgiveness and reconciliation.

This entire literacy and education program required much planning, effort, and time. While it was a tremendous success in its own right, its primary importance was the way it integrated employee benefits with poverty alleviation. Because of the extremely low literacy rates in our areas of service, we want to greatly expand this kind of outreach. We hope to do so by training and employing local Christians to teach and manage these programs.

EFFECTIVENESS

As we have cared for needy people through business, literacy, health, and relief work, the resulting bonds of appreciation have allowed us to share the gospel and the Word of God freely, without opposition from a people who otherwise would have opposed us strongly. While preparing people's hearts to be spiritually receptive is God's business, without a doubt the business and mercy ministries were still necessary ingredients.

By God's grace, I have come a long way from my boyhood business experience selling persimmons. Although our business in South Asia has not yet fulfilled our initial vision for empowering local believers to become economically self-sufficient over the long term, it has still served beyond our expectations. It has: (1) been a primary vehicle for introducing the gospel to several unreached people groups; (2) provided temporary employment for local believers and seekers of those groups during periods of discipling; (3) provided a means for developing discipline and responsibility in the workers in societies governed more by bribery, influence-peddling, and hopelessness; and (4) provided a protective shield from opposition to our ministry by granting us favor with government authorities and local peoples through our small but positive effect on the local economy. As our Lord Jesus Christ showed us so vividly, the spoken gospel must be accompanied by deeds of compassion. When it is, great things can happen.

11

BUSINESS IN INDIA

Joe Suozzo

After graduating from Leicester Polytechnic in 1990 with a B.A. in Fashion and
Textile Design and Technology, Jessica Sanders worked for four years with a
clothing design company in the United Kingdom. During her years at the university and in London working for a secular employer, Jessica was deeply
involved in teaching the Alpha Course and in Sunday school at her local church.
She believes that her education, work experience, and previous lay ministries
uniquely prepared her for her current entrepreneurial responsibilities in Bhopal,
a slum-ridden area in India, eager for Western business partners.

In 1994, Jessica left England to join Renewal India, a nonprofit established
to reach out with the gospel to the urban poor via community development.
It works in close partnership with local evangelical churches in Bhopal.

Jessica was part of a team of entrepreneurs who launched Living Springs,
a high fashion clothing export company. Other partners in the venture were
a second Englishwoman, Cathy Rarig, and two Indians, Rakesh Singh and
Jyoti Parwar. Living Springs is a separately registered company working in
partnership with Renewal India.

Living Springs was established to train women from the slums of Bhopal
as seamstresses, and then produce export quality products through their
labors. The money earned subsidizes the women's training, covers operating
costs, and provides seed-capital for new microenterprises among the urban
poor. By 1998, Living Springs launched two new export companies, which
produce silkscreen cards and papier-mâché products.

CHARACTERISTICS OF THE BUSINESS

Two key factors contributed to the start-up of Living Springs. Jessica and her
team all had backgrounds in business, manufacturing, and high fashion
design. Cathy Rarig also had a B.A. in fashion design. Jessica's national partners both had previous experience in business and tailoring.

The second factor was the decision to run a venture that would make money. The vision from the beginning was to establish a community development project that would not need outside subsidies for its operating costs. The profits would be used exclusively to cover the costs of training, employment, and business operations.

Start-up capital for Living Springs was approximately $9,000, which came through a grant from Renewal U.K. By 1997, Living Springs was breaking even, with a gross income over $42,500. In 1998, Living Springs grossed nearly $68,500. Jessica and her team provided vision, solid management, design, and aggressive marketing in the United Kingdom. Renewal U.K. covered her personal and ministry expenses.

BUSINESS OPERATIONS

A nonprofit, Living Springs established its general procedures of operation by mutual agreement with its four partners and the Renewal India board. In Bhopal, Jessica and the Living Springs director provide oversight for the finances, implementation of design, inventory, and export of products. Jyoti Parwar manages the office, training programs, workers, and production. In the United Kingdom, Cathy Rarig handles the marketing and sales. Rakesh Singh networks the workers of Living Springs with the local church in various ministries.

Living Springs encountered few obstacles in legally establishing itself with the Indian government. It helped that Renewal India had already existed for several years and had a legal team and a diversified board of local pastors and Christian businesspeople in Bhopal. Second, the legal work was done in Bangalore, which is known for good government and less corruption. Third, India has a favorable business climate for export and nonprofit companies. The liberalization of the economy has created helpful tax laws for exporters. Living Springs exports products four times a year according to a quota agreement between the United Kingdom and India.

The company's initial struggles had to do with quality control. New workers had trouble producing export-quality cloth products during the first three years. Nonetheless, through a flat style of management and direct financial compensation for production, Living Springs was able to solve its quality control problems.

Living Springs offers a wide range of high fashion men's and women's clothing, travel bags, cushion covers, and kitchen-related items such as table cloths, napkins, teapot covers, pot holders, and so on. These generally sell for the equivalent of $10 to $75. After manufacturing the items, the markup is roughly 125 percent. When salaries, shipping, and other miscellaneous costs are accounted for, Living Springs is able to produce a healthy profit margin of 16 percent.

Cathy Rarig markets and sells the products by partnering with member companies of Fair Trade, a cooperative of nonprofit companies that seeks to promote goods produced by the poor in the developing world. Fair Trade has a number of expositions each year in the United Kingdom, where companies such as Living Springs can market their goods to the private sector.

Rarig also tries to penetrate smaller boutiques and to sell through catalogs and mail order. However, competition in the United Kingdom has become increasingly intense, and Living Springs is seeking new markets in the United States and in Bhopal.

Personnel and Public Relations

Living Springs employs twenty-five Indian workers at a time and trains ten workers annually. Six work in the office with responsibilities for accounting, inventory upkeep, and final packaging for export. Nineteen workers work in manufacturing. All salaries are linked to how much these people produce. All of the workers come from the slums of Bhopal, where they were previously beggars or prostitutes. Living Springs selects employees in partnership with Bhopal's local churches. It also trains others in the area, giving them needed job skills.

Because of management constraints, however, Living Springs can only hire six to ten workers each year. Therefore, one goal is to help the women who are trained find work in the manufacturing sector in Bhopal or as seamstresses in their local communities.

The Living Springs public relations strategy in India is to link its activities with the local church. Rakesh Singh is the son of a prominent pastor in the city, which has opened doors with the believing community. The business has also sponsored high fashion shows in the city. While the local church has been very critical of this approach, it has provided Living Springs with the publicity needed to penetrate the local market. In the United Kingdom, the business uses evangelical publications, conferences, and the Fair Trade Foundation to get the word out.

Characteristics of the Ministry

Jessica Sanders has a long-term goal of seeing impoverished women receive both practical vocational training and discipleship through the local evangelical church. She encourages personal discipleship with key employees.

The business invites local pastors to share Scripture on a weekly basis at the office.

Jessica's spiritual gifts are teaching, encouragement, and mercy. She believes that all her gifts are being used as she interacts with needy women through discipleship and vocational training. Her gifts of mercy and encouragement help create a positive work environment for the management and workers of Living Springs.

But Jessica has experienced some of the struggles common to tentmakers. Her responsibilities in starting and managing this venture have not provided her enough time to learn the local language, Hindi. Because so many people in Bhopal already speak English, Jessica spent only the first three months in language learning and cultural adaptation. Her goal has been to reach a functional level of Hindi usage for living and business. She believes that her current ability is sufficient, although she would like to go deeper. Despite the constant time pressures, she disciples some workers in English. Over the past several years, she has seen more than twenty ladies integrated into local churches from the slums of Bhopal.

However, her own devotional life has suffered since coming to India. She believes this has been due to the pressures of running her own business, the stresses of Indian culture, and the lack of structure for her life in Bhopal. She describes her relationship with God as "the backbone and center of all I do." Although she never experiences depression, her greatest spiritual struggle is her lack of intimacy with God.

Cultural and Family Issues

Nevertheless, Jessica has adjusted well to Bhopal culture. Although she does not plan to settle in India, her ministry has made life enjoyable. Jessica's greatest difficulties came during her first two years, when she was single. She felt that "people were always suspicious of those who lived alone with another single woman." After she married her partner, Rakesh Singh, barriers with local people started to come down.

"Being married in India makes life a lot easier, since people are more understanding of your role," Jessica notes. She enjoys the greater intensity and depth in relationships that an Indian extended family provides. She and Rakesh have a long-range goal of returning to the United Kingdom and raising a family.

Jessica does not see a conflict between her business responsibilities and ministry. Since Living Springs provides a platform for women to receive both vocational training and discipleship, she believes that her business activities and ministry are synonymous.

However, the business aspect of her work can be extremely hectic. Jessica must devote heavy hours each quarter to meet the demands for orders from the United Kingdom and to ship according to the quota system.

RELATIONSHIPS WITH CHRISTIANS

Understanding Jessica's relationships is essential to understanding her tent-making enterprise. Her home church meets all of her living and ministry expenses, and she has several dozen prayer partners and supporters. Though she describes her relationship with her supporters as positive, she feels a lack of accountability.

The same goes for her sending agency, Renewal U.K. Jessica says that while Renewal U.K. has done well in administrating the financial aspects of the work, it provides little accountability and emotional support. These come through the Renewal India team.

Renewal India provides a strong framework of accountability, ministry support, and counsel. The ministry has sixty community development workers in Bhopal in medical care, education, and drug rehabilitation. They are divided into teams by region and type of work. These teams meet weekly in small groups for prayer. Living Springs constitutes one working team.

Monthly, the project leaders pray and discuss their struggles and goals, guided by the directors of Renewal India. On a quarterly basis, workers with the three vocational training projects of Renewal India meet for planning and spiritual retreats. Twice a year all Renewal India workers meet to discuss struggles, victories, and crucial issues. Jessica is satisfied with the fellowship and accountability Renewal India provides. She says someone is always available for counsel and prayer.

RELATIONSHIPS IN THE COMMUNITY

The Bhopal community is generally sympathetic to the Living Springs goal of providing vocational training for impoverished women. This is not surprising. Traditionally, Hindus have been very tolerant of and benevolent toward community development projects. Living Springs courts favor with many Hindus in the city. Nonetheless, there is a militant Hindu presence, and Living Springs has to use much caution when it comes to the spiritual aspects of the work.

Despite some misgivings over the fashion shows, the Christian community is very supportive. Living Springs has worked hard to forge strong church relationships. It has successfully integrated trained women into the local church. Living Springs works with a small network of pastors, who regularly visit the work and minister to employees.

CONCLUSION

Living Springs has integrated community development principles with the forces of the marketplace. Jessica's approach to ministry is holistic and touches many facets of the women's lives. By partnering with Bhopal's local churches, she has seen a number of impoverished women trained and touched with the love of Jesus Christ.

PART TWO

ESSAYS

The Integration of Business and Ministry

Peter Tsukahira

Everyone seems to understand that Satan is alive and well in the world of business. Trade and commerce have been his domains for ages. Many scholars believe that the description of the "king of Tyre" in Ezekiel's prophecy is really a description of the devil himself:

> You were blameless in your ways from the day you were created until unrighteousness was found in you. By the abundance of your trade you were internally filled with violence, and you sinned; therefore I have cast you as profane from the mountain of God. And I have destroyed you, O covering cherub, from the midst of the stones of fire (Ezek. 28:15-16, NASB).

When Jesus was tempted by the devil, he did not dispute the Evil One's claim to have authority over "all the kingdoms of the world" (Matt. 4:8-9). According to the book of Revelation, at the time of the end, Satan's representative will have authority over the world's financial system, and no one will be able to do business without his sign of approval:

> And he causes all, the small and the great, and the rich and the poor, and the free men and the slaves, to be given a mark on their right hand or on their forehead, and he provides that no one will be able to buy or to sell, except the one who has the mark, either the name of the beast or the number of his name (Rev. 13:16-17, NASB).

Addressing the Dichotomy

How then are believers, the children of God's kingdom, to survive and advance in the world of business? Is this world redeemable according to God's plan? In past centuries, the church has retreated from the spiritual battle over the soul of business. Many ministers decry the unrighteousness of mammon from the safety of their church sanctuaries. Others, also skirting the battle, shamelessly peddle the gospel to the highest bidder. The purpose of this book is to bring clarity to some of the issues facing Christians in business, and to help mobilize them for ministry and world evangelization.

People in many churches believe that only full-time, fully supported ministers are truly qualified for spiritual ministry. One result of this deep but often unspoken belief is a cultural gap between businesspeople and the pastors who serve them. Believers who are in business often feel misunderstood by congregational leadership. In spite of his or her usefulness in administration or releasing funds for ministry, a businessperson's potential for ministry may be underestimated and underutilized. Yet believers who are businesspeople are powerful resources for the kingdom of God.

We need to help businesspeople find their spiritual calling and train them creatively for the Great Commission (Matt. 28:18-20). I believe God may call an individual into business while also calling him or her to ministry at home or on the mission field. But is it really possible for a Christian to succeed in business and ministry concurrently? Business and ministry may indeed require distinct skill sets, but proper training and discipleship can integrate them.

Personal Story

I am an Asian American Israeli. I have an Asian face, an American voice, and an Israeli passport. God has planted me and my family on Mount Carmel in Israel. Because my wife, Rita, is from a Jewish family, we were invited to come as *olim hadashim*—new immigrants. So we moved to Israel in 1987, became Israeli citizens, and began the difficult process of growing into a new culture. Our daughter, who was 2 when we moved, has grown up in Israel and is in the Israeli school system. Our son was born on Mount Carmel, in Haifa. Although few who first see me think I am an Israeli, I write as someone who has made a lifetime commitment to this nation. Israel is our home. We expect to live in Israel until we die, or until the Lord returns.

Rita and I came to the Lord in the early 1970s. At the time we were a part of the American "hippie" counterculture. She is from the suburbs of New York, and I was born in Boston. While I was growing up, my father taught Asian history at the university level and later worked as a diplomat for the U.S. government in Japan and Thailand. I spent my teenage years attending an international school in Japan and came back to Boston for college. In the chaotic years of the late 1960s and early 70s, the Lord brought us to himself. Because we came to see Jesus as the Messiah and Savior of the world, we simply dropped whatever hopes and dreams that we may have had about our own lives and said, "What is it that you want us to do? We are ready to go anywhere you want and do whatever you want us to do! We will speak whatever you give us to say. Here we are. Send us!"

Our lives have not followed a conventional pattern, largely because Rita is a Jewish believer in Jesus. Since the creation of the modern state of Israel in 1948, many Christians have had increased interest in biblical prophecy. Then, in the 1960s, a worldwide movement emerged of Jewish people who believe in Jesus as the Messiah, much like the early New Testament community. The challenge for messianic Jews today is to define in modern terms what it means to be both Jewish and a believer in Jesus the Messiah.

Both Rita and I knew that becoming believers in Jesus meant our whole lives would have to change. We grappled with our new identity as believers. As we prayed and fasted, the Lord said, "First of all, get married." So we got married, and later enrolled in Bible school at Christ for the Nations in Dallas, Texas. There the Lord said, "I am calling you to serve me in my ministry, but you will not minister in the United States. You will serve me in Japan and in Israel!" We finished our two years of Bible training and headed to California. I began studying for a Master of Divinity degree.

One Fourth of July while we drove to my uncle's home, our car broke down and began spewing clouds of smoke. I knew the repairs would be expensive, and I had no money. I was working as a bank teller to support the two of us and pay my tuition. I simply did not have the money, so I borrowed from a family member. It was embarrassing, and I asked the Lord for a better job.

A fellow student named Don in one of my counseling classes had worked for IBM before his calling to study the Bible. Later he found a job with another computer company. There had been a revolution in the computer industry, and this firm was making state-of-the-art "minicomputers." In the mid-1970s, minicomputers were being installed in many key industries. Because I had no experience, Don arranged for me to be hired provisionally. He said, "Peter, we'll give you ten weeks of training, and then you have six months. If you can prove you belong here, you can stay." I started learning to design and write programs in computer languages with odd names such as COBOL and FORTRAN.

Don, now my regional manager, came to me one day and said, "Peter, I have had a vision of you. You were sitting at a computer terminal, and everyone was crowding around you as you were showing them what you were doing." At the time I barely knew enough about computers to keep my job. But I discovered that I loved the technology and the clean, unrelenting logic of computers. My first COBOL program, a billing application for Coca Cola of Los Angeles, actually worked! Within two years, I was beginning to teach computer programming languages and to design courses. Don's vision had become reality.

The company began to send me overseas to conduct training courses. After that, I became a very junior marketing manager, starting projects for new software products in different parts of the world. These activities continued to develop as my seminary studies were finishing. I received my Master of Divinity degree and was ordained by the church. Rita finished her master's degree in communication and began teaching at California State University at Fullerton. I was on the staff of the church as a pastoral intern.

MOVING TO JAPAN

In 1981, doors were beginning to open for ministry in Japan. Rather than raise support money from different congregations, however, I realized that I had a valuable asset in my computer knowledge. I had worked in the industry for five years and had experience in a number of different departments. So I sent my resume to about ten Japanese companies. A Japanese electronics giant called NEC Corporation gave me a two-year contract in Tokyo.

After our move, I went to work in the heart of a very Japanese company among some 16,000 employees, designing and teaching software courses. I introduced Rita to the city, where I had lived as a teenager. It was a wonderful and challenging time.

At NEC, we sat crammed into large open offices without partitions. I had a lapel pin that identified me as an NEC man among the thousands of blue- and gray-suited men on the Tokyo subways. In the office, we listened to the company song in the morning, took a break for calisthenics at our desks in the afternoon, and lived a more or less typical "salaryman" existence. Rita taught in an international university.

Meanwhile, I became acquainted with a pastor who had just started a small international fellowship in the city center. He brought me alongside, and we began to lead this fellowship together. Bob had a vision for a large international congregation in the downtown that would serve as an example of growth to Japanese pastors. However, his responsibilities were regional, and he traveled a lot. I ended up pastoring the congregation alone for weeks and sometimes months at a time. The number of people began to grow and grow, and, in time, we went from about 15 people to more than 200. Part of the attraction was our worship singing. I had introduced choruses from the charismatic renewal of the time.

At first we tried to find the new believers Japanese-language congregations near their homes, but eventually most of them just stayed with us. These were exciting years of vibrant growth. People of many nationalities came into the congregation and were getting healed and saved. I took no salary from the congregation and remember it as a challenging and joyful time.

TWO PATHS

After two years, my NEC contract was completed, and I worked for an American computer company as national marketing manager. As my responsibilities grew, I began to feel that my life was moving along two very different paths—business and ministry. There were times when it was exciting and even exhilarating. But there were other times when it seemed like the rails of my life diverged, when one side began to pull against the other side.

Our weekly pastors' meetings were held during breakfast at a hotel restaurant close to my office. I would meet people for pastoral counseling on my lunch hour. If people had to see me urgently, I would take a short break from my work and meet them in a local coffee shop. We would talk and pray, and then I would go back to my office.

My company's regional headquarters were in Hong Kong. One time I was there for a marketing meeting with the national managers from Asia. A yacht was rented for us, and we spent a leisurely day sailing. By evening, we had docked at an outlying island for a sumptuous seafood dinner. The next night, the regional vice president invited me for some tennis. We played under the lights at his yacht club in Aberdeen. Afterwards he said, "Why don't you move down here to Hong Kong for six months and see how we do things in the regional office?" It was clearly an offer that would advance my career. I remembered a book on business success that said you had to have a good relationship with your boss's boss. This vice president could make me a country manager.

I thought of my own boss's beautiful home, his club memberships, and the company car with a driver that took him to work. As I was thinking of these possibilities, I knew that the answer had to be no. As the pastor of a congregation, it was impossible for me to leave Tokyo for six months. It was hard to say no. As a young pastor and businessman I went through great frustration and a painful tearing process in my heart. Sometimes I prayed, "Lord, are you ever going to allow me to really succeed in either one of these callings?" Sometimes I even asked God, "Would you please take me out of one or the other of these professions?" I would say, "Lord, why can't I be like this minister?" or, "Why can't I be like that businessman? Why am I stuck between these two worlds?"

BRIDGING THE DIVIDE

Is it really possible to fully integrate the two worlds of business and ministry? Does Scripture affirm this integration as God's will? Many believing businesspeople experience the personal stretching that I have felt, and wonder as I did how to find and stay on the "narrow way."

First of all, we must admit that, in the perceptions of many Christians, a dichotomy exists between business and ministry. A deep division is found at the level of culture. Culture contains values and expectations that lie beneath our conscious thoughts. Although church culture and business culture coexist in the believing community, they seem to have different values and goals, speak different languages, and have entirely different customs. While there are variations from country to country and from congregation to congregation, in general, business and ministry are like oil and water. They just do not mix easily.

As a pastor I recognize that businessmen have an important role in the congregation. They know how organizations work and they understand finance. It is good to have successful businessmen serving God and supporting the church. But there seems to be an unwritten understanding that while believing businessmen support the work of the ministry, they are not to *do* the work of the ministry. On the other hand, ministers who preach the gospel are expected to remain "unstained by the world" and out of the business environment. We try to keep these two vocations separate to prevent confusion, and, as a result, end up with a double standard in God's kingdom. Rather than preventing confusion, this creates an artificial situation where Christians may be forced to forsake one of their callings in order not to be torn apart by the opposing demands of two divergent identities.

From the church's point of view, businessmen tend to have a lower spiritual status. In certain countries this is more noticeable than in others. Christians do not see businessmen on the same spiritual level as ordained ministers. At the same time, they see businessmen as having more freedom, and they do not expect them to maintain the high level of sanctification required of ministers.

They say in some parts of Asia that Christian businessmen have two pairs of shoes. When they get up on Sunday morning to go to church, they put on their Christian shoes. But when Monday morning comes, they put on their business shoes. It is understood that these are two completely separate worlds with different sets of rules.

In South Korea a leading Christian businessman who built some of the largest buildings in the country also built a church and a Christian convention center. His name is a household word. However, he went to jail because of financial irregularities the government discovered in his business. The Christian community is still feeling the reverberations of his arrest and imprisonment.

This kind of double standard does not exist in Scripture. I believe the Lord wants to break down this false dichotomy in the kingdom of God.

JESUS THE BUILDER

Jesus worked in the business world. Most say he was a carpenter, but the Greek word is *tekton,* which simply means builder. Recent studies indicate that he may have been a worker in stone rather than in wood. He worked with his father, Joseph, in the family business, which we could call the construction industry. We know from the New Testament that he worked longer as a builder than he did as a minister. He spent eighteen years working under his father in and around Nazareth, and his public ministry lasted only about three-and-a-half years.

Many of Jesus' teachings and parables come right out of the working world. He knew the lives of the people to whom he ministered. He knew what it was like for them to buy and sell. He knew the pressures and the temptations to compromise that faced them. He knew their hearts and their habits. He had dealt with them in his trade for most of his life. So in Jesus' case, business was his preparation for ministry. He labored patiently for many long years until the day came when he left the family business and never went back.

PAUL THE TENTMAKER

Paul also worked in the business world. His work was concurrent with his ministry. Business was his vehicle for ministry. He was a skilled professional, an expert in his field. You never get the impression that Paul had trouble finding a job. Paul was a professional tentmaker. In those days, tents were not made in factories out of canvas or nylon but out of individual goat hairs woven together. In wet weather, goat hair swells up, creating an effective shield against wind and rain. In hot and dry weather, the goat hair weave breathes, letting air and some sunlight through, making the tent cool and pleasant. Weaving tents, therefore, was exacting manual labor. It took a long time to master the proper technique, which was usually passed down from father to son.

Paul's tentmaking trade was highly mobile. Many people used tents in those days, so he was able to find employment wherever he went. Income from the marketplace meant that Paul did not need support from local congregations. In fact, he boasted of this to the Corinthians:

> Do you not know that those who perform sacred services eat the food of the temple, and those who attend regularly to the altar have their share from the altar? So also the Lord directed those who proclaim the gospel to get their living from the gospel. But I have used none of these things. And I am not writing these things so that it will be done so in my case; for it would be better for me to die than have any man make my boast an empty one (1 Cor. 9:13-15, NASB).

Paul was able to say to the congregation he planted, "I never burdened you financially, because the Lord gave me this tentmaking work and has led me to work with my own hands among you." Paul's profession augmented and enabled his ministry.

AQUILA AND PRISCILLA: KINGDOM PROFESSIONALS

Jesus and Paul provide two good models of ministry with business. A third model, however, suits most believers in business: the "kingdom professional" model. A kingdom professional is someone who has integrated business with ministry and lives in both worlds simultaneously. Aquila and Priscilla represent this model.

During Paul's second missionary journey, he came to Corinth, a city built on an isthmus with two sea ports. Corinth was an important commercial center because its ports controlled the trade on both the Ionian and Aegean Seas:

> After these things Paul left Athens and went to Corinth. And he found a Jew named Aquila, a native of Pontus, having recently come from Italy with his wife Priscilla, because Claudius had commanded all the Jews to leave Rome. He came to them, and because he was of the same trade, he stayed with them and they were working, for by trade they were tent-makers. And he was reasoning in the synagogue every Sabbath and trying to persuade Jews and Greeks (Acts 18:1-4, NASB).

Paul first met Aquila and Priscilla in Corinth, where they ran a business. They are a biblical example of businesspeople who launched successfully into international ministry. Aquila and Priscilla hired Paul, and they began working together in the marketplace. Paul went out on every Sabbath to evangelize, and eventually he planted a congregation in that busy metropolis:

> Paul, having remained many days longer, took leave of the brethren and put out to sea for Syria, and with him were Priscilla and Aquila. In

Cenchrea he had his hair cut, for he was keeping a vow. They came to
Ephesus, and he left them there. Now he himself entered the synagogue and
reasoned with the Jews (Acts 18:18-19, NASB).

Paul stayed in Corinth for a while working with Aquila and Priscilla in
their established business. When he returned to his ministry base in Ephesus,
Aquila and Priscilla went with him. If they were not believers when Paul first
met them and began working with them, they obviously were by the time he
was ready to leave their city. They had caught his vision for missions, too. So
they uprooted their business and moved. We do not know if they were able
to transplant their client base from Greece to what is now Turkey, but they
relocated to Ephesus and became part of the church there:

> Now a Jew named Apollos, an Alexandrian by birth, an eloquent man,
> came to Ephesus; and he was mighty in the Scriptures. This man had been
> instructed in the way of the Lord; and being fervent in spirit, he was speak-
> ing and teaching accurately the things concerning Jesus, being acquainted
> only with the baptism of John; and he began to speak out boldly in the syn-
> agogue. But when Priscilla and Aquila heard him, they took him aside and
> explained to him the way of God more accurately (Acts 18:24-26, NASB).

Apollos was an Egyptian-born evangelist. He was a teacher, mighty in the
Word of God but not familiar with any baptism other than John's. Aquila and
Priscilla, however, had been discipled by Paul, so they took Apollos aside dis-
creetly. Apollos was not a lightweight in the ministry. Some scholars believe
that he was the writer of Hebrews. Aquila and Priscilla, this "kingdom professional" couple, were led by the Lord to speak into the life of one of the
leading ministers of their day. We can see their tact and sensitivity in not
rebuking him publicly, which would have hurt both his work and theirs. They
dealt with this well-known teacher privately and evidently influenced his life.
Aquila and Priscilla were a business-and-ministry couple who matured spiritually as they followed God's call.

The names of Aquila and Priscilla appear a number of times in the New
Testament, and notably among the salutations at the end of Romans, the
fullest exposition of Paul's theology and his understanding of God's purposes:

> Greet Prisca and Aquila, my fellow workers in Christ Jesus, who for my
> life risked their own necks, to whom not only do I give thanks, but also all
> the churches of the Gentiles; also greet the church that is in their house
> (Rom. 16:3-5a, NASB).

What became of this business-and-ministry couple? They moved their business from Corinth and followed Paul to Ephesus. They rubbed shoulders with the most anointed leaders of the early church in that spiritually dynamic environment. Then they moved to Rome, the great capital of the Empire, and probably set up shop again in their trade and became outstanding ministry leaders. Paul obviously regarded them as among his closest friends and most trusted associates.

As kingdom professionals, Aquila and Priscilla can be a model for us. We are not told that they left their profession in order to pursue the ministry. The Bible does not give us the sense that the early church saw a division between clergy and laity or between businesspeople and ministry leaders. All who believed were called to work out their salvation with fear and trembling. Because the church was more a movement than an institution, there was far less reliance on position and professional qualifications. Believers placed greater importance on calling and spiritual maturity. Anointed leaders exercised their gifts to edify the church, and the technicalities of their support were worked out in the most practical ways. Most of them worked in the marketplace.

Twenty centuries later, business is the predominant shaper of modern culture. Business in the global economy and ministry for the Lord may have different goals and require different skills. There may be tension between work for material gain and labor for "heavenly treasure," but the example of Jesus' life and death still connects these two worlds. Kingdom professionals must function in tension while maintaining the integrity of a focused life before God. By the Spirit and power of Jesus' self-sacrifice working in our lives, believers can do both business and ministry effectively.

The church today is on the verge of recovering the sense of God's presence in every area of human life. The Hebraic understanding of sacred and secular functioning together in dynamic unity is being restored to God's people. Believers called to bivocational ministry need not be compromised, fragmented, or financial failures. Finding the right personal balance between business and ministry is a matter of prayer and determined obedience to the Lord, who calls us all to himself.

13

HOW BUSINESS IN ITSELF CAN GLORIFY GOD

Wayne Grudem

A. INTRODUCTION: A NEGLECTED WAY TO GLORIFY GOD

When Christians hear the expression "glorifying God," we probably first think of *worship*—singing praise to God and giving thanks to him. Second, we think of *evangelism*—glorifying God by telling others about him, so that more people are brought into his kingdom. Third, we think of *giving*—glorifying God by contributing money to evangelism, to building up the church, and to the needs of the poor. Fourth, we might think of *faith*—glorifying God by depending on him in prayer and in our daily attitudes of heart. These four—worship, evangelism, giving, and faith—are excellent ways to glorify God, and working in a business provides many opportunities for glorifying God in these ways. But they are not my focus in this chapter because I think most Christians in business already understand how business can contribute to these ways of glorifying God.

In this chapter I want to look at business *in itself,* not just the good results that business can produce. Specifically, I want to look at the following aspects of business activity:

1. ownership
2. productivity
3. employment
4. commercial transactions
5. profit
6. money
7. inequality of possessions
8. competition
9. borrowing and lending

10. attitudes of heart

11. effect on world poverty

But before considering those things we need to consider two introductory points, the first dealing with the imitation of God, and the second dealing with sin.

1. Imitation: God enjoys seeing his character reflected in our lives.

There is another way to glorify God, one that we often overlook. This fifth way to glorify God is the key to understanding why God made the world the way he did. It is also the key to understanding why God gave us the moral commands he did. And it is the key to understanding why human beings have an instinctive drive to work, to be productive, to invent, to earn and save and give, and to do the thousands of specific activities that fill our days. It is the key to understanding why we take spontaneous delight in such activities. This fifth way to glorify God is *imitation*—imitation of the attributes of God.

God created us so that we would imitate him and so that he could look at us and see something of his wonderful attributes reflected in us. The first chapter of the Bible tells us, "So God created man in his own image, in the image of God he created him; male and female he created them" (Gen. 1:27). To be in God's image means to be *like* God and to *represent* God on the earth. This means that God created us to be more like him than anything else he made. He delights to look at us and see in us a reflection of his excellence. After God had created Adam and Eve, "God *saw* everything that he had made, and behold, it was *very good*" (Gen. 1:31).[1] He looked at his creation and took delight in it—yes, in all of it, but especially in human beings made in his image.

This is why Paul commands us, in Ephesians 5, *"Be imitators of God, as beloved children"* (Eph. 5:1). If you are a parent, you know that there is a special joy that comes when you see your children imitating some of your good qualities and following some of the moral standards that you have tried to model. When we feel that joy as parents, it is just a faint echo of what God feels when he sees us, as his children, imitating *his* excellent qualities. "Be imitators of God, as beloved children."

This idea of imitating God explains many of the commands in the Bible. For instance, "We love *because he first loved us*" (1 John 4:19). We imitate God's love when we act in love. Or, "You shall be holy, *for I am holy*" (1 Pet. 1:16, quoting Lev. 11:44). Similarly, Jesus taught, "Be merciful, *even as your*

Father is merciful" (Luke 6:36). And he also said, "You therefore must be perfect, *as your heavenly Father is perfect"* (Matt. 5:48). God wants us to be like him.

This idea of imitating God's character so that he will take delight in it explains other moral commands in the Bible as well. For example, God wants us to tell the truth and not lie because he is the God "who never lies" (Titus 1:2). He commands us not to commit adultery because he is a God who is faithful to his covenant commitments and he delights in seeing us be faithful to the covenant of marriage which we have entered into (see Mal. 2:14). And God commands children to "Honor your father and your mother" (Ex. 20:12; Eph. 6:2), as a reflection of the honor that the Son gives to the Father in the Trinity.

God created us in such a way that we would *want* to imitate his character and we would take spontaneous delight in seeing reflections of his character in our own actions and in the actions of others. Though this process is now marred by sin, we still see it happening to some extent. We feel a deep, fulfilling kind of joy and satisfaction in telling the truth (because God is truthful), treating others fairly (because God is fair and just), acting in love toward other people (because God is love), being faithful in our marriages and keeping our word in other commitments (because God is faithful), and so forth. We also enjoy seeing other people act in these ways, because in those actions we catch a glimpse of the character of God. In this way we can begin to understand how to fulfill the command, "So, whether you eat or drink, or whatever you do, do all to the glory of God" (1 Cor. 10:31).

2. But sin does not glorify God.

However, it is absolutely important to realize that we should never attempt to glorify God by acting in ways that disobey his Word. For example, if I were to speak the truth about my neighbor out of a malicious desire to harm him, I would not be glorifying God by imitating his truthfulness, because God's truthfulness is always consistent with all his other attributes, including his attribute of love. And when we read about a thief who robbed a bank through an intricate and skillful plan, we should not praise God for this thief's imitation of divine wisdom and skill, for God's wisdom is always manifested in ways that are consistent with his moral character, which cannot do evil, and consistent with his attributes of love and truthfulness. We must be careful never to try to imitate God's character in ways that contradict his moral law in the Bible.

B. SPECIFIC WAYS THAT BUSINESS CAN GLORIFY GOD

With this background we can now turn to consider specific aspects of business activity, and ask how they provide unique opportunities for glorifying God. We will find that in every aspect of business there are multiple layers of opportunities to give glory to God, as well as multiple temptations to sin.

1. Ownership: Owning possessions is fundamentally good and provides many opportunities for glorifying God, but also many temptations to sin.

When God gave the command, "You shall not steal" (Ex. 20:15), he affirmed the validity of personal ownership of possessions. I should not steal your car, because it *belongs* to you, not to me. Unless God intended us to own possessions, the command not to steal would make no sense. I believe the reason God gave the command, "You shall not steal," is that ownership of possessions is a fundamental way that we imitate God's sovereignty over the universe by our exercising "sovereignty" over a tiny portion of the universe, the things we own. When we take care of our possessions, we imitate God in his taking care of the whole universe, and he delights to see us imitate him in this way. In addition, when we care for our possessions, it gives us opportunity to imitate many other attributes of God, such as wisdom, knowledge, beauty, creativity, love for others, kindness, fairness, independence, freedom, exercise of will, blessedness (or joy), and so forth.

Now sometimes as Christians we refer to ownership as "stewardship," to remind us that what we "own" we do not own absolutely, but only as stewards taking care of what really belongs to God. This is because "the earth is the Lord's and the fullness thereof" (Ps. 24:1) and so ultimately it all belongs to him (see also Lev. 25:23; Ps. 50:10-12; Hag. 2:8; Luke 16:12; 1 Cor. 4:7).

Why do children from a very early age enjoy having toys that are their own, and why do they often want to have a pet that is their own, one they can care for? I realize that such "ownership" of toys and pets can be distorted by the sins of selfishness and laziness, but even if we lived in a sinless world children from a very young age would have a desire to have things that are their own. I think God has created us with a desire to own things because he wanted us to have a desire to imitate his sovereignty in this way. This desire in itself should not automatically be called "greed" because that word slanders something that is a good desire given to us by God.

When we are responsible stewards, whether taking care of our toys at age 4 or managing the entire factory at age 40, if we do this work "as unto the Lord," God looks at our imitation of his sovereignty and his other attributes, and he is pleased. In this way we are his image-bearers, people who are like God and who represent God on the earth, whether we own few possessions or many, and whether we own a small business or a large one.

So what should we do with the things we own? There are many good things to do, all of which can glorify God. A man who owns a tractor or a truck can use it to help "subdue" the earth (Gen. 1:28), that is, make it useful for us as human beings, whether through causing the earth to yield tomatoes and beans, or through extracting materials for plastics and silicon in order to make computers and Palm Pilots. Or we could use our possessions for our own enjoyment, with thanksgiving to God, "who richly provides us with everything to enjoy" (1 Tim. 6:17). On the other hand, we could give to the church some of what we own, to help evangelism and teaching, in order to build up the church. Or we could give some of our possessions to meet the needs of others, especially the poor: "Do not neglect to do good and to share what you have, for such sacrifices are pleasing to God" (Heb. 13:16). Or we could save some of our resources for future use, in order to enable us in the future to provide for our relatives, and especially for members of our own households (see 1 Tim. 5:8). We can glorify God through all of these uses of resources, if we have thanksgiving in our hearts to God.

On the other hand ownership of possessions provides many temptations to misuse the resources that God has entrusted to us. We can use our resources to pollute and destroy the earth, or to rob and oppress others, thereby disobeying Jesus' command to love our neighbors as ourselves (Matt. 22:39), and thereby dishonoring God by our actions. The author of Proverbs 30 knew that stealing is not imitating God but is showing to the world a picture of a God who is selfish and unjust: " . . . lest I be poor and steal *and profane the name of my God*" (Prov. 30:9). Or we could use our possessions to turn people away from the gospel and attack the church (see James 2:6-7). We could use our resources to advance our own pride, or we could become greedy and accumulate wealth for its own sake, or we could take wrongful security in riches (see Matt. 6:19; Luke 12:13-21; James 5:3). We could use our possessions foolishly and wastefully, abounding in luxury and self-indulgence while we neglect the needs of others (see James 5:5; 1 John 3:17). These things are rightly called "material*ism,*" and they are wrong.

But the distortions of something good must not cause us to think that the thing itself is evil. Possessions are not evil in themselves, and ownership of possessions is not wrong in itself. Nor is ownership something morally neutral. In itself, the ownership of possessions is something that is created by God, and is very good. Ownership provides multiple opportunities for glorifying God, and we should be thankful for it.

2. Productivity: Producing goods and services is fundamentally good and provides many opportunities for glorifying God, but also many temptations to sin.

We know that producing goods from the earth is fundamentally good in itself because it is part of the purpose for which God put us on the earth. Before there was sin in the world, God put Adam in the garden of Eden "to work it and keep it" (Gen. 2:15), and God told both Adam and Eve, before there was sin, "Be fruitful and multiply and fill the earth and *subdue it* and *have dominion* over the fish of the sea and over the birds of the heavens and over every living thing that moves on the earth" (Gen. 1:28). The word translated "subdue" (Heb. *kabash*) implies that Adam and Eve should make the resources of the earth useful for their own benefit, and this implies that God intended them to develop the earth so they could come to own agricultural products and animals, then housing and works of craftsmanship and beauty, and eventually buildings, means of transportation, cities, and inventions of all sorts.

Manufactured products give us opportunity to praise God for anything we look at in the world around us. Imagine what would happen if we were able somehow to transport Adam and Eve, before they had sinned, into a twenty-first-century American home. After giving them appropriate clothing, we would turn on the faucet to offer them a glass of water, and they would ask, "What's that?" When we explained that the pipes enabled us to have water whenever we wanted it, they would exclaim, "Do you mean to say that God has put in the earth materials that would enable you to make that water system?"

"Yes," we would reply.

"Then *praise God* for giving us such a great earth! And praise him for giving us the knowledge and skill to be able to make that water system!" They would have hearts sensitive to God's desire that he be honored in all things.

The refrigerator would elicit even more praise to God from their lips. And so would the electric lights and the newspaper and the oven and the telephone, and so forth. Their hearts would brim over with thankfulness to the Creator who had hidden such wonderful materials in the earth and had also given to human beings such skill in working with them. And as Adam and Eve's hearts were filled with overflowing thanksgiving to God, God would see it and be pleased. He would look with delight as the man and woman made in his image gave glory to their Creator and fulfilled the purpose for which they were made.

As we look at any manufactured item, no matter how common, can we not also discover hundreds of wonders of God's creation in the things that we have been able to make from the earth? Such richness and variety has not been found on any of the other planets known to us. "The whole earth is full of his glory" (Isa. 6:3).

God did not have to create us with a need for material things, and a need for the services of other people (think of the angels, who apparently do not have such needs), but in his wisdom he chose to do so. It may be that God created us with such needs because he knew that in the process of productive work we would have many opportunities to glorify him. When we work to produce (for example) pairs of shoes from the earth's resources, God sees us imitating his attributes of wisdom, knowledge, skill, strength, creativity, appreciation of beauty, sovereignty, planning for the future, and the use of language to communicate. In addition, when we produce pairs of shoes to be used by others, we demonstrate love for others, wisdom in understanding their needs, and interdependence and interpersonal cooperation (which are reflections of God's Trinitarian existence). If we do this, as Paul says, working heartily, "as for the Lord and not for men" (Col. 3:23), and if our hearts have joy and thanksgiving to God as we make this pair of shoes, then God delights to see his excellent character reflected in our lives, and others will see something of God's character in us as well. Our light will "shine before others, so that they may see [our] good works and give glory to [our] Father who is in heaven" (Matt. 5:16).

That is why God made us with a desire to be productive, to make or do something useful for other people. Therefore human desires to increase the production of goods and services are not in themselves greedy or materialistic or evil, but they represent God-given desires to accomplish and achieve and solve problems, desires to exercise dominion over the earth and exercise significant stewardship so that we and others may enjoy the resources of the earth that God made for our use and for our enjoyment.

Therefore, in contrast to some economic theories, *productive work* is not evil or undesirable in itself, or something to be avoided; nor does the Bible ever view positively the idea of retiring early and not working at anything again. Rather, work in itself is also something that is *fundamentally good* and God-given, for it was something that God commanded Adam and Eve to do before there was sin in the world. Although work since the Fall has aspects of pain and futility (Gen. 3:17-19), it is still not morally neutral but *fundamentally good* and pleasing to God.

Hindering and decreasing the earth's productivity is not good, however, because it simply allows the curse which God imposed in Genesis 3 to gain more and more influence in the world, and this is Satan's goal, not God's. After God imposed the curse that was required by his justice, the story of the

Bible is one of God working progressively to overcome the curse, and increasing the world's productivity is something we should do as one aspect of that task.

But significant temptations accompany all productions of goods and services. There is the temptation for our hearts to be turned from God so that we focus on material things for their own sake. There are also temptations to pride, and to turning our hearts away from love for our neighbor and turning toward selfishness, greed, and hard-heartedness. There are temptations to produce goods that bring monetary reward but that are harmful and destructive and evil (such as pornography and wrongful drugs).

But the distortions of something good must not cause us to think that the thing itself is evil. Increasing the production of goods and services is not morally neutral but is *fundamentally good* and pleasing to God.

3. Employment: Hiring people to do work is fundamentally good and provides many opportunities for glorifying God, but also many temptations to sin.

In contrast to Marxist theory, the Bible does not view it as evil for one person to hire another person and gain profit from that person's work. It is not necessarily "exploiting" the employee. Rather, Jesus said, "the laborer deserves his wages" (Luke 10:7), implicitly approving the idea of paying wages to employees. In fact, Jesus' parables often speak of servants and masters, and of people paying others for their work, with no hint that hiring people to work for wages is evil or wrong. (And John the Baptist told soldiers, "Be content with your wages" [Luke 3:14].)

For some occupations, employing someone else is necessary because some people sell services and not goods (in the ancient world, a maid or a messenger or the laborer in the field would work for someone else, and in the modern world a teacher or a baby-sitter or a painter or a plumber earns money when hired by another person). But the hiring of one person by another is also necessary for a greater production of goods. Many products can only be produced by a group of people working together (in the ancient world, we could think of shipbuilding and shipping, and in the modern world, the building of airplanes, ships, steel mills, and in most cases houses and computers, and many other consumer goods that are not made directly from raw materials). But working in groups requires the oversight of an owner or manager who pays the others for their work.

This is a wonderful ability that God has given us. Paying another person for his or her labor is an activity that is uniquely human. It is shared by no other creature. The ability to work for other people for pay, or to pay other people for their work, is another way that God has created us so that we would be able to glorify him more fully in such relationships.

Employer/employee relationships provide many opportunities for glorifying God. On both sides of the transaction, we can imitate God and he will take pleasure in us when he sees us showing honesty, fairness, trustworthiness, kindness, wisdom, and skill, and keeping our word regarding how much we promised to pay or what work we agreed to do. The employer/employee relationship also gives opportunity to demonstrate proper exercise of authority and proper responses to authority, in imitation of the authority that has eternally existed between the Father and Son in the Trinity.

When the arrangement is working properly, both parties benefit. This allows love for the other person to manifest itself, because if I am sewing shirts in someone else's shop, I can honestly seek the good of my employer, and seek to sew as many shirts as possible for him (cf. 1 Tim. 6:2), and he can seek my good, because he will pay me at the end of the day for a job well done. As in every good business transaction, both parties end up better off then they were before. In this case, I have more money at the end of the day than I did before, and my employer has more shirts ready to take to market than he did before. And so we have worked together to produce something that did not exist in the world before that day—the world is fifty shirts wealthier than it was when the day began. I have created some wealth in the world, and so there is also a slight imitation of God's attribute of creativity. So if you hire me to work in your business, you are doing good for me and you are providing many opportunities to glorify God.

However, employer/employee relationships carry many temptations to sin. An employer can exercise his authority with harshness and oppression and unfairness. He might withhold pay arbitrarily and unreasonably (contrary to Lev. 19:13) or might underpay his workers, keeping wages so low that workers have no opportunity to improve their standard of living (contrary to Deut. 24:1). He might also become puffed-up with pride. James writes about such sins of oppressive employers:

> Behold, the wages of the laborers who mowed your fields, which you kept back by fraud, are crying out against you, and the cries of the harvesters have reached the ears of the Lord of hosts (James 5:4).

Employees also have temptations to sin through carelessness in work (see Prov. 18:9), laziness, jealousy, bitterness, rebelliousness, dishonesty, or theft (see Titus 2:9-10).

But the distortions of something good must not cause us to think that the thing itself is evil. Employer/employee relationships, in themselves, are not morally neutral, but are fundamentally good and pleasing to God because they provide many opportunities to imitate God's character and so to glorify him.

4. Commercial transactions: Buying and selling are fundamentally good and provide many opportunities for glorifying God, but also many temptations to sin.

Several passages of Scripture assume that buying and selling are morally right. Regarding the sale of land in ancient Israel, God's law said, "If you make a sale to your neighbor or buy from your neighbor, you shall not wrong one another" (Lev. 25:14). This implies that it is *possible* and in fact is *expected* that people should buy and sell *without* wronging one another—that is, that both buyer and seller can *do right* in the transaction (see also Gen. 1:57; Lev. 19:35-36; Deut. 25:13-16; Prov. 11:26; 31:16; Jer. 32:25, 42-44).

In fact, buying and selling are necessary for anything beyond subsistence level living, and these activities are another part of what distinguishes us from the animal kingdom. No individual or family providing for all its own needs could produce more than a very low standard of living (that is, if it could buy and sell *absolutely nothing,* and had to live off only what it could produce itself, which would be a fairly simple range of foods and clothing). But when we can sell what we make and buy from others who specialize in producing milk or bread, orange juice or blueberries, bicycles or televisions, cars or computers, then, through the mechanism of buying and selling, we can all obtain a much higher standard of living, and thereby we fulfill God's purpose that we enjoy the resources of the earth with thanksgiving (1 Tim. 4:3-5; 6:17) while we "eat" and "drink" and "do all to the glory of God" (1 Cor. 10:31).

Therefore we should not look at commercial transactions as a necessary evil or as something just morally neutral. Rather, commercial transactions are in themselves good because through them we do good to other people. This is because of the amazing truth that in most voluntary commercial transactions, both parties benefit. If I sell you a copy of my book for $40, then I get something that I want more than that copy of the book—I get your $40. So I am better off than I was before, when I had too many copies of that book, copies that were useless to me. And I am happy. But you got something that you wanted more than your $40. You wanted a copy of my book, which you did not have. So you are better off than you were before, and you are happy. Thus by giving us the ability to buy and sell, God has given us a wonderful mechanism through which we can do good for each other, and we should be thankful for this process every time we buy or sell something. We can honestly see buying and selling as a means of loving our neighbor as ourselves.

Buying and selling are also activities unique to human beings out of all the creatures that God made. Rabbits and squirrels, dogs and cats, elephants and giraffes know nothing of this activity. Through buying and selling, God has given us a wonderful means to give glory to him.

We can imitate God's attributes each time we buy and sell, if we practice honesty, faithfulness to our commitments, fairness, and freedom of choice. Moreover, commercial transactions provide many opportunities for personal interaction, as when I realize that I am buying not just from a store but from a person, to whom I should show kindness and God's grace. In fact, every business transaction is an opportunity for us be fair and truthful and thus to obey Jesus' teaching, "So whatever you wish that others would do to you, do also to them, for this is the Law and the Prophets" (Matt. 7:12).

Because of the interpersonal nature of commercial transactions, business activity has significant stabilizing influence on a society. An individual farmer may not really like the auto mechanic in town very much, and the auto mechanic may not like the farmer very much, but the farmer *does* want his car to be fixed right the next time it breaks down, and the auto mechanic *does* love the sweet corn and tomatoes that the farmer sells, so it is to their mutual advantage to get along with each other, and their animosity is restrained. In fact, they may even seek the good of the other person for this reason! So it is with commercial transactions throughout the world and even between nations. This is an evidence of God's common grace, and so in this way God has provided among the human race a wonderful encouragement to love our neighbor because we seek not only our own welfare but the welfare of others. In buying and selling we also manifest interdependence and thus reflect the interdependence and interpersonal love among the members of the Trinity. Therefore, for those who have eyes to see it, commercial transactions provide another means of manifesting the glory of God in our lives.

However, commercial transactions provide many temptations to sin. Rather than seeking the good of our neighbors as well as ourselves, our hearts can be filled with greed, so that we seek only our own good, and give no thought for the good of others. Our hearts can be overcome with selfishness, an inordinate desire for wealth, and setting our hearts only on material gain. Paul says,

> Those who desire to be rich fall into temptation, into a snare, into many senseless and harmful desires that plunge people into ruin and destruction.

> For the love of money is a root of all kinds of evils. It is through this crav-
> ing that some have wandered away from the faith and pierced themselves
> with many pangs (1 Tim. 6:9-10).

Because of sin, we can also engage in dishonesty and in selling shoddy
materials whose defects are covered with glossy paint. Where there is excessive concentration of power or a huge imbalance in knowledge, there will
often be oppression of those who lack power or knowledge (as in government
sponsored monopolies where consumers are only allowed access to poor
quality, high-priced goods from one manufacturer for each product).

But the distortions of something good must not cause us to think that the
thing itself is evil. Commercial transactions in themselves are fundamentally
right and pleasing to God. They are a wonderful gift from him through which
he has enabled us to have many opportunities to glorify him.

5. Profit: Earning a profit is fundamentally good and provides many opportunities for glorifying God, but also many temptations to sin.

What is earning a profit? Fundamentally, it is using our resources to produce
more resources. In the parable of the minas (or pounds), Jesus tells of a nobleman calling ten of his servants and giving them one mina each (about three
months' wages), and telling them, "Engage in business until I come" (Luke
19:13). The servant who earned 1,000 percent profit was rewarded greatly,
for when he says, "Lord, your mina has made ten minas more," the nobleman responds, "Well done, good servant! Because you have been faithful in
a very little, you shall have authority over ten cities" (Luke 19:16-17). The
servant who made five more minas receives authority over five cities, and the
one who made no profit is rebuked for not at least putting the mina in the
bank to earn interest (v. 23).

The nobleman, of course, represents Jesus himself, who went to a far
country to receive a kingdom and then returned to reward his servants. The
parable has obvious applications to stewardship of spiritual gifts and ministries that Jesus entrusts to us, but in order for the parable to make sense, it
has to assume that good stewardship, in God's eyes, includes expanding and
multiplying whatever resources or stewardship God has entrusted to you.
Surely we cannot exclude money and material possessions from the application of the parable, for they are part of what God entrusts to each of us, and
our money and possessions can and should be used to glorify God. Seeking
profit, therefore, or seeking to multiply our resources, is seen as fundamentally good. Not to do so is condemned by the master when he returns.

The parable of the talents (Matt. 25:14-30) has a similar point, but the amounts are larger, for a talent was worth about twenty years' wages for a laborer, and different amounts are given at the outset.

Some people will object that earning a profit is "exploiting" other people. It might be, if there is a great disparity in power or knowledge between you and me and I cheat you or charge an exorbitant price when you have nowhere else to go and you need a pair of shoes. That is where earning a profit provides temptations to sin.

But the distortions of something good must not cause us to think that the thing itself is evil. If profit is made in a system of voluntary exchange not distorted by monopoly power, then when I earn a profit I also help you. You are better off because you have a pair of shoes that you wanted, and I am better off because I earned $4 profit, and that keeps me in business and makes me want to make more shoes to sell. Everybody wins, and nobody is exploited. Through this process, I glorify God by enlarging the possessions over which I am "sovereign" and over which I can exercise wise stewardship.

The ability to earn a profit is thus the ability to multiply our resources while helping other people. It is a wonderful ability that God gave us and it is not evil or morally neutral but fundamentally good. Through it we can reflect God's attributes of love for others, wisdom, sovereignty, planning for the future, and so forth.

6. Money: Money is fundamentally good and provides many opportunities for glorifying God, but also many temptations to sin.

People sometimes say that "money is the root of all evils," but the Bible does not say that. Paul says in 1 Timothy 6:10, "the *love of money* is a root of all kinds of evils," but that speaks of the love of money, not money itself.

In fact, money is fundamentally good because it is a human invention that sets us apart from the animal kingdom and enables us to subdue the earth by producing from the earth goods and services that bring benefit to others. Money enables us to be productive and enjoy the fruits of that productivity thousands of times more extensively than we could if no human being had money, and we just had to barter with each other.

Without money, I would have only one thing to trade with, and that is copies of my books. I would have hundreds of copies of *Systematic Theology*, but in a world with no money I would have no idea if one volume was worth a loaf of bread, or two shirts, or a bicycle, or a car. And the grocer might not be interested in reading my book, so he might not trade me a basket of groceries for even 100 books! Soon, even the merchants who did accept my book in trade would not want another one, or a third one, and I would end up with piles of books and no ability to find more people who wanted to trade something for them. Without money, I would soon be forced to revert to subsistence living by planting a garden and raising cows and chickens, and maybe bartering a few eggs from time to time. And so would you, with whatever you could produce.

But money is the one thing that *everybody* is willing to trade goods for, because it is the one thing that *everybody else* is willing to trade goods for. With a system of money, I suddenly know how much one volume of my book is worth. It is worth $40, because that is how much thousands of people have decided they are willing to pay for it. When I get the $40, that money temporarily holds the value of my book until I can go to the store and tell the grocer I would like to trade the $40 for some groceries. The same grocer who would not have traded *any* groceries for a theology book now eagerly accepts my $40 in money, because he knows that he can trade that money for *anything in the world* that he wants that costs $40.

So money is simply a tool for our use, and we can rightly thank God that in his wisdom he ordained that we would invent it and use it. It is simply a "medium of exchange," something that makes voluntary exchanges possible. It is, according to the *American Heritage Dictionary*, "a commodity . . . that is legally established as an exchangeable equivalent of all other commodities, such as goods and services, and is used as a measure of their comparative values on the market." Money makes voluntary exchanges more fair, less wasteful, and far more extensive. We need money to exist in order for us to be good stewards of the earth and to glorify God through using it wisely.

If money were evil in itself, then God would not have any. But he says, "The silver is mine, and the gold is mine, declares the Lord of hosts" (Hag. 2:8). It all belongs to him, and he entrusts it to us so that through it we would glorify him.

Money provides many opportunities to glorify God, through investing and expanding our stewardship and imitating God's sovereignty and wisdom, through meeting our own needs and thus imitating God's independence, through giving to others and imitating God's mercy and love, or through giving to the church and to evangelism and thus bringing others into the kingdom.

Yet because money carries so much power and so much value, it is a heavy responsibility, and it carries with it constant temptations to sin. We can become ensnared in the love of money (1 Tim. 6:10) and it can turn our hearts from God. Jesus warned, "You cannot serve God and money" (Matt. 6:24), and he warned against accumulating too much that we hoard and do not use for good:

> Do not lay up for yourselves treasures on earth, where moth and rust destroy and where thieves break in and steal, but lay up for yourselves treasures in heaven, where neither moth nor rust destroys and where thieves do not break in and steal. For where your treasure is, there your heart will be also (Matt. 6:19-21).

But the distortions of something good must not cause us to think that the thing itself is evil. Money is good in itself, and provides us many opportunities for glorifying God.

7. Inequality of possessions: Inequality of possessions is fundamentally good and provides many opportunities for glorifying God, but also many temptations to sin; and some kinds of inequalities are wrong in themselves.

It may seem surprising to us to think that inequalities of possessions in themselves can be good and pleasing to God. However, there is no sin or evil in heaven, and there are varying degrees of reward in heaven and various kinds of stewardships that God entrusts to different people. Jesus will say to one person, "You shall have authority over ten cities," and to another, "You are to be over five cities" (Luke 19:17, 19). Therefore the idea of inequality of stewardship must be given by God and must be good. Paul is not speaking to unbelievers but to the Corinthian believers when he says, "For we must all appear before the judgment seat of Christ, so that each one may receive what is due for what he has done in the body, whether good or evil" (2 Cor. 5:10), and this implies degrees of reward for what we have done in this life. Many other passages teach or imply degrees of reward for believers at the final judgment.[2] Even among the angels, there are differing levels of authority and stewardship established by God, and we cannot say that such a system is wrong or sinful in itself.

When we consider this, we realize that inequalities are necessary in a world that requires a great variety of tasks to be done. Some tasks require stewardship of large amounts of resources (such as ownership of a steel mill or manufacturing airplanes), and some tasks require stewardship of small amounts of resources. And God has given some people greater abilities than others: abilities in artistic or musical skills, abilities in mathematics or science, abilities in leadership, abilities in business skills and buying and selling, and so forth. Those with larger abilities in such areas will naturally gain larger rewards, if reward is given fairly, according to the value that each person produces.

The goal of God is never to produce equality of possessions among us. In the Year of Jubilee (Leviticus 25), agricultural land returned to its previous owner and debts were canceled, but there was no equalizing of money or jewels or cattle or sheep, and houses inside walled cities did not revert to the previous owner (Lev. 25:29-30). In 2 Corinthians, Paul did not say that God's goal was equality, for he did not tell the wealthy Corinthians to send money to the poor Macedonians mentioned in 2 Corinthians 8:1-5, but only that they should contribute their fair share in helping the famine-stricken Christians in Jerusalem: "as a matter of fairness your abundance at the present time should supply their need, so that their abundance may supply your need, that there may be fairness" (2 Cor. 8:13-14, ESV; the Greek word *isotes* also means "fairness" in Col. 4:1, where it cannot mean "equality").

Inequalities in possessions provide many opportunities for glorifying God. If God gives us a small stewardship with regard to material possessions or abilities and opportunities, then we can glorify him through being content in him, trusting in him for our needs, expecting reward from him, and being faithful to our commitments. In fact, those who are poor will often give more sacrificially than those who are rich. Jesus told his disciples that the poor widow who put a penny in the offering "has put in more than all those who are contributing to the offering box. For they all contributed out of their abundance, but she out of her poverty has put in everything she had, all she had to live on" (Mark 12:43-44). And James tells us,

> Has not God chosen those who are poor in the world to be rich in faith
> and heirs of the kingdom which he has promised to those who love him?
> (James 2:5).

Thus, the Bible does not teach a "health and wealth gospel" (at least not until heaven!). There are inequalities of gifts and abilities, and there are also evil, oppressive systems in the world, and many of God's most righteous people will not be rich in this life.

Those who have large resources are also to be content in God and trust in him, not in their riches, and both James and Paul suggest that they face greater temptations (see 1 Tim. 6:9-10; James 2:6-7; 5:1-6). Those who are rich have more opportunities and also more obligation to give generously to the poor (1 Tim. 6:17-19).

But inequalities in possessions and opportunities and abilities provide many temptations to sin. There are temptations, on the part of the wealthy or those who have large stewardships, to be proud, selfish, and think too highly of themselves, and not to trust in God. On the other hand, those to whom God has entrusted less have temptations to coveting and jealousy and not valuing their own calling, to which God has called them.

In addition to this, we must be very clear that there are some kinds of inequalities in possessions and opportunities that are wrong in themselves. Poverty will not exist in the age to come, and so Jesus' statement, "the poor you always have with you" (John 12:8), applies only to this age, not to the age to come. Poverty is one of the results of living in a world affected by sin and the Fall and by God's curse on the productivity on the earth (Gen. 3:17-19).

We are always to seek to help the poor overcome their poverty. John says, "If anyone has the world's goods and sees his brother in need, yet closes his heart against him, how does God's love abide in him?" (1 John 3:17). And when Paul went to Jerusalem to confirm the validity of his teaching in conversation with the apostles who were there, he found that they were in agreement, and then added, "they asked us to remember the poor, the very thing I was eager to do" (Gal. 2:10; see also Matt. 25:39-40; Acts 2:45; 4:35; Rom. 12:13; 15:25-27; Eph. 4:28; Titus 3:14; Heb. 13:16).

The emphasis in the New Testament is on helping poor Christians, especially those who are near us or who come to our attention (see 1 John 3:17; Matt. 25:39-40; Rom. 15:25-27; 2 Cor. 8-9), but it is also right to help non-Christians who are poor and needy, as we see in the parable of the good Samaritan (Luke 10:25-37), and in Jesus' teaching, where he told us, "love your enemies, and do good, and lend, expecting nothing in return, and your reward will be great, and you will be sons of the Most High, for he is kind to the ungrateful and the evil" (Luke 6:35; compare also Jesus' practice of healing all who came to him, not just those who believed in him as the Messiah).

On the other hand when James condemns the rich, he seems to imply that there is a level of luxury and spending on one's own self that is excessive and that is not pleasing to God:

> Come now, you rich, weep and howl for the miseries that are coming upon you. . . . Your gold and silver have corroded, and their corrosion will be evidence against you and will eat your flesh like fire. You have laid up treasure in the last days. . . . You have lived on the earth in luxury and in self-indulgence. You have fattened your hearts in a day of slaughter (James 5:1-5).

He does not here imply that all those who are rich are evil, for in this passage he speaks of the fraud and murder committed by these rich people

(James 5:4, 6), and Paul says that Timothy should tell "the rich in this present age" that they are "not to be haughty, nor to set their hopes on the uncertainty of riches, but on God, who richly provides us with everything to enjoy." Paul does not say that the rich are to give away all their wealth, but that they are "to do good, to be rich in good works, to be generous and ready to share, thus storing up treasure for themselves as a good foundation for the future, so that they may take hold of that which is truly life" (1 Tim. 6:17-19).

Yet it is hard to escape the conclusion that James believes there is a level of luxury and self-indulgence that is wrong in itself, and this would be the wrongful counterpart to the excessive inequality of poverty.

But the distortions of something good must not cause us to think that the thing itself is evil. The evils of poverty and excessive, self-indulgent wealth must not cause us to think that God's goal is total equality of possessions, or that all inequalities are wrong. Inequalities in abilities and opportunities and possessions will be part of our life in heaven forever, and are in themselves good and pleasing to God, and provide many opportunities for glorifying him.

8. Competition: Competition is fundamentally good and provides many opportunities for glorifying God, but also many temptations to sin.

As with other aspects of business that we have considered, so it is with competition: the evils and distortions that have sometimes accompanied competition have led people to the conclusion that competition is evil in itself. But this is not true. We can think of some examples from other areas of life. For example, most people think competition in sports is a good thing, whether in children's soccer leagues or Little League baseball or in professional sports. Although we can all think of bad examples of coaches who were overly competitive, for the most part we think competition in sports is a good system and we think it fair that the best teams receive some prize or award at the end.

Similarly, in our school system, the assigning of grades is a competitive activity in which the best math students, and the best English students, and the best art and music students, receive higher grades. The grading system provides guidance to help students find something they can do well, and the result is that when I fly in an airplane, I am glad that it has been designed by someone who got straight A's in mathematics and engineering. The grading system was "competitive" and it guided society in assigning jobs to those who were best suited to those jobs.

In the business world, competition does that as well. We hired a careless painter once for our house, and he only lasted a day. But then we found a good painter and we were willing to pay more for his high quality work. The bad painter needed to find another occupation, and we were helping him do that by asking him not to come back the next day. The world is so diverse, and the economic system has so many needs, that I am sure there is some area in which he can fulfill a need and do well. But it wasn't painting.

So a competitive system is one in which we test our abilities and find if we can do something better than others, and so be paid for it. The system works well when we reward better work and greater quantity of work with greater reward.

In fact, if you have ever shopped around for the lowest price on a shirt or a computer or a car, your actions show that you approve of competition in the economy, because you are making competition work. You are buying from the person who can produce and distribute a computer cheaper than someone else, and you are encouraging that more efficient manufacturer to stay in business, you are discouraging the less efficient, more expensive computer manufacturers from staying in business. It happens every day and we take it for granted. And the result is, because of competition, people keep getting better at making things, the real prices of consumer goods keep falling and falling over the course of decades, and in economic terms, the society continues to obtain a higher standard of living.

In addition, God has created us with a desire to do well, and to improve what we are able to do. Competition spurs us on to do better, because we see others doing better and we decide we can do that too. I may think I am teaching an excellent theology class, but when I see the assignments and projects my fellow theology professor gives his class, I see that his class is better, so I decide that I should try harder and assign better projects too. I glorify God more by striving for excellence and imitating God's excellence more fully.

Competition seems to be the system God intended when he gave some people greater talents in one area and gave other people greater talents in another area, and when he established a world where justice and fairness would require giving greater reward for better work.

Competition brings many opportunities to glorify God, as we try to use our talents to their full potential and thus manifest the God-like abilities that he has granted to us, with thankfulness in our hearts to him. Competition enables each person to find a role in which he or she can make a positive contribution to society and thus a role in which people can work in a way that serves others by doing good for them. Competition is thus a sort of societal functioning of God's attributes of wisdom and kindness, and it is a way society helps people discover God's will for their lives. Competition also enables us individually to demonstrate fairness and kindness toward others, even those with whom we compete.

On the other hand, competition brings many temptations to sin. There is a difference between trying to do a job better than others, on the one hand, and trying to harm others and prevent them from earning a living on the other hand. There is nothing wrong with trying to run a better car repair shop than the one down the street, but there is a lot wrong with lying about the other mechanic, or stealing his tools, or in my heart seeking to do him harm.

Competition also brings temptations to pride, and to excessive work that allows no rest or time with family or with God. And there is the temptation to a distortion of life values so that we become unable even to enjoy the fruits of our labor.

But the distortions of something good must not cause us to think that the thing itself is evil. These temptations to sin should not obscure the fact that competition in itself, within appropriate limits (some of which should be established by government), is good and pleasing to God, and provides many opportunities for glorifying God.

9. Borrowing and lending: Borrowing and lending are fundamentally good and provide many opportunities for glorifying God, but also many temptations to sin.

Sometimes Christians have read Old Testament passages that speak against lending money at interest (what the King James Version called "usury"), and they have had an uneasy conscience about borrowing or lending money at interest because of these passages. But if we look at these passages in detail, and understand them in their proper historical context, they seem only to prohibit taking advantage of the poor in their poverty (see Ex. 22:25; Lev. 25:35-37; Deut. 23:19; Ps. 15:5; Prov. 28:8; Neh. 5:7-10; Luke 6:34). There are other passages, even in the Old Testament, that assume that people will borrow some things (see Ex. 22:14; 2 Kings 4:3), and some verses regulate the process of lending (see Deut. 24:10). In fact, some verses encourage lending and commend the person who lends: "It is well with the man who deals generously and lends; who conducts his affairs with justice" (Ps. 112:5; cf. Ps. 37:26).

I do not think that Romans 13:8 ("owe no one anything") prohibits all borrowing or even discourages borrowing, for taken in context it simply says we should pay what we owe when we owe it. If we look at the statement in its proper context, translated to show the connection between verse 7 and verse 8 (as is done in the recently published *English Standard Version*), it reads as follows:

> For the same reason you also pay taxes, for the authorities are ministers of God, attending to this very thing. Pay to all *what is owed* to them: taxes to whom taxes are *owed*, revenue to whom revenue is *owed*, respect to whom respect is *owed*, honor to whom honor is *owed*. *Owe* no one anything, except to love each other, for the one who loves another has fulfilled the law (Rom. 13:6-8).

As is evident in this translation, the command "owe no one anything" is simply a summary of the obligations to pay what we owe that Paul has specified in the previous verses, whether taxes or respect or honor or so forth. Therefore, if I have a mortgage on my house, I should make the mortgage payments when they are "owed"; that is, I should make payments on time as I have agreed to do. I do not "owe" the entire balance of the mortgage to the lender until the date specified. Therefore I have borrowed money, and I am carrying a long-term debt, and I am completely obedient to Romans 13:8, "owe no one anything," because I have no past-due payments on my mortgage. Now borrowing may at times be unwise (see Prov. 22:7, "the borrower is the slave of the lender"; also Deut. 28:12), and the ability to borrow may be misused by those who incur excessive debt ("The wicked borrows but does not pay back," Psalm 37:21), and borrowing does carry some risk and some obligations that can be very hard to get out of (see Ex. 22:14), but the Bible does not say that borrowing in itself is wrong.

It seems to me, therefore, that borrowing and lending in themselves are not prohibited by God, but that many places in the Bible assume that these things will happen. Jesus even seems to approve lending money at interest, not to the poor who need it to live (as in the Old Testament passages quoted above), but to the bankers who borrow the money from us so they can use it to make more money: "Why then did you not put my money in the bank, and at my coming I might have collected it with interest?" (Luke 19:23; also Matt. 25:27).

In fact, the process of borrowing and lending is another wonderful gift that God has given to us as human beings. It is another activity that is unique among human beings, for animals don't borrow or lend or pay interest, nor could they even understand the process.

What are borrowing and lending? In itself, lending is the temporary transfer of the *control* of property but not of the *ownership* of property. This wonderful process allows the lender to have an infinite variety of choices with respect to the following factors:

(a) *Control.* I have an infinite variety of choices between keeping an item and giving it away. I can lend you my car and come with you while you run your errand, or I can lend it to you for one brief errand, or I can lend it to you without restrictions for a day or a week or a year.

(b) *Amount.* I can loan you a small item (such as my pocket knife) or a large item (such as my car or house), and there are all sorts of choices in between.

(c) *Risk.* There is very small risk in letting my wife borrow my car keys or my jacket, but there is very large risk in letting a total stranger borrow my car, and there are all sorts of choices in between.

Borrowing also allows the borrower to have an infinite variety of choices between no use of an item and owning the item. I can rent a car for a day, a week, or a month, thus allowing me to have little use, or some use, or much use of the car, without actually owning it.

Borrowing and lending multiplies the usefulness of all the wealth of a society. My local library may have only one copy of a reference book, but 300 people might use it in a year, thus giving my community as much value as 300 copies of that book if each person had to buy one. I only own one car, but because of the process of borrowing and lending, I can fly into any city in the United States and have the use of a rental car for a day, without having to own a car in that city. Without the existence of borrowing and lending, I would have to own thousands of cars in order to have the same ability.

And of course, when I borrow money to buy a house or start a business, I enjoy the usefulness of that money (just as I enjoy the usefulness of a rental car) for a period of time without actually having to own the money myself. I pay a fee for the use of that money (what is called interest), but that is far easier than obtaining all the money myself before I can gain the use of it. And so borrowing and lending multiplies the usefulness of money in a society as well.

In this way, borrowing and lending multiply phenomenally our God-given enjoyment of the material creation, and our potential for being thankful to God for all these things and glorifying him through our use of them.

In borrowing and lending, we can reflect many of God's attributes. We can demonstrate trustworthiness and faithful stewardship, honesty, wisdom, love, and mercy.

However, there are temptations to sin that accompany borrowing. As many Americans are now discovering, there is a great temptation to borrow more than is wise, or to borrow for things they cannot afford and do not need, and thus they become foolishly entangled in interest payments that reflect poor stewardship and wastefulness, and that entrap people in a downward spiral of more and more debt. In addition, lenders can be greedy or selfish, and can lend to people who have no reasonable expectation of repaying, and then take advantage of people in their poverty and distress.

But the distortions of something good must not cause us to think that the thing itself is evil. Borrowing and lending are wonderful, uniquely human abilities that are good in themselves and pleasing to God and bring many opportunities for glorifying him. In fact, I expect that there will be borrowing and lending, not to overcome poverty but to multiply our abilities to glorify God, even in heaven. (But I don't know what the interest rate will be!)

10. Attitudes of heart.

The Ten Commandments end with a reminder that God is concerned not only with our actions but also with our attitudes of heart, for God says, "You shall not covet . . . anything that is your neighbor's" (Ex. 20:17). Although I have touched on this at various points, it is appropriate that we end this discussion by remembering that in every aspect of business activity, God knows our hearts, and we glorify him by having attitudes of heart in which he delights. "Let the words of my mouth *and the meditation of my heart* be acceptable in your sight, O LORD, my rock and my redeemer" (Ps. 19:14). God "knows the secrets of the heart" (Ps. 44:21; cf. Luke 16:15; Acts 15:8).

Therefore in all our ownership of property, in all our stewardship, if we want to glorify God in business, we should seek to avoid pride and should have hearts full of thanksgiving toward God and love for others. In producing goods and services for others, and in using them for our own enjoyment, we should have hearts of thanksgiving to God for his goodness in providing these things to us. If we work for someone else, we should work as if we were working "for the Lord and not for men, knowing that from the Lord you will receive the inheritance as your reward" (Col. 3:23-24). And if others work for us, we need to think of them as equal in value as human beings made in the image of God, and our heart's desire should be that the job bring them good and not harm. We should be thankful to God for money and profit, but we should never love money or profit. We are to love God and our neighbor instead.

As we look at all of the business activities in the world around us, we will see evil mixed with good, and then our hearts should feel sorrow and grief when we see God's commands being disobeyed and his purposes violated. But our hearts should also be filled with joy and thanksgiving and praise to him for the wonders of his creation, and for his remarkable wisdom in designing so many amazing ways in which business activity in itself is fundamentally good and brings glory to God.

11. *Application to world poverty.*

I have been encouraging you to change your attitudes toward many of the components of business activity. I do not want you to feel vaguely guilty about business, and I do not want you even to feel that business is morally neutral but it does some good because at least it is a means of advancing the gospel. Now I agree that business is a wonderful means of advancing the gospel, and all the essays in this book are a testimony to that fact, and I rejoice in it and thank God that thousands of businesses around the world do advance the gospel.

But I have been aiming at something more. I want you not to feel vague guilt but rather to *rejoice* in the God-given goodness of business in itself pursued in obedience to God. I want you to *enjoy* and thank God for,

1. Ownership
2. Productivity
3. Employment
4. Commercial transactions
5. Profit
6. Money
7. Inequality of possessions
8. Competition
9. Borrowing and lending

Yet some will think, what about the poor? What about those who own almost nothing, who cannot buy and sell, cannot make a profit, have no money, and have no opportunity to compete?

We should always seek to help the poor to overcome their poverty. John says, "If anyone has the world's goods and sees his brother in need, yet closes his heart against him, how does God's love abide in him?" (1 John 3:17). And Paul says in Galatians 2:10, "they asked us to remember the poor, the very thing I was eager to do" (Gal. 2:10; see also Matt. 25:39-40; Acts 2:45; 4:35; Rom. 12:13; 15:25-27; Eph. 4:28; Titus 3:14; Heb. 13:16).

But *how* should we remember the poor? *How* should we open our heart to our brother in need? A short-term solution is to give food and clothing to the poor, and that is certainly right. But it is no long-term solution, for the food is soon eaten and the clothing wears out.

I believe the only long-term solution to world poverty is business. That is because businesses produce goods, and businesses produce jobs. And businesses continue producing goods year after year, and continue providing jobs and paying wages year after year. Therefore if we are ever going to see *long-term* solutions to world poverty, I believe it will come through starting and maintaining productive, profitable businesses.

But if that is true, if the solution to world poverty is business rightly pursued, then why hasn't business solved world poverty already? Of course, part of the reason is sinful misuse of business power to benefit only a tiny number of people. Another large reason is evil governments that hinder businesses from helping people overcome poverty. But I think the largest reason is negative attitudes toward business in the world community.

If people think business is evil, they will hesitate to start businesses, and they will never feel real freedom to enjoy working in business, because it will always be tainted with the faint cloud of false guilt. Who can enjoy being an evil materialist who works with evil money to earn evil profits by exploiting laborers and producing material goods that feed people's evil greed and enhance their evil pride and sustain their evil inequality of possessions and feed their evil competitiveness? Who wants to devote his life to such an evil pursuit as business? What government would ever want to establish laws and policies that would encourage such an evil thing as business? And so with the attitude that business is fundamentally evil in all its parts, business activity is hindered at every point, and poverty remains. (And I think that negative attitude toward business in itself—not toward distortions and abuses, but toward business activity in itself—is ultimately a lie of the enemy who wants to keep God's people from fulfilling his purposes.)

But what if Christians could change their attitudes toward business, and what if Christians could begin to change the attitudes of the world toward business?

If attitudes toward business change in the ways I have described, then who could resist being a God-pleasing subduer of the earth who uses materials from God's good creation and works with the God-given gift of money to earn morally good profits, and shows love to his neighbors by giving them jobs and by producing material goods that overcome world poverty, goods that enable people to glorify God for his goodness, that sustain just and fair differences in possessions, and that encourage morally good and beneficial competition? What a great career that would be! What a great activity for governments to favor and encourage! What a solution to world poverty! What a way to glorify God!

14

STRATEGIC CONSIDERATIONS IN BUSINESS AS MISSION

Thomas Sudyk

With all the enthusiasm about using the marketplace to reach lost people, why are so few people doing it? The main reason is that there is a vast chasm between the world of business and the mission community.

It is not unusual for corporate American Christians to ask, "What more can I do for God?" Some end up serving as deacons or elders. Others directly enter ministry as pastors, youth ministers, or other ministry leaders. Based on stories I have heard and my own observations, such transitions are rarely successful.

A businessperson relocated from the rigor and risk of a business into the culture of the typical church suffers a tremendous shock. Gone is the discipline of the marketplace, which keeps businesspeople constantly accountable for their decisions. Gone is aggressive pursuit of easily measured goals. Gone also is the healthy insistence that employees consistently contribute some tangible value to the organization. Often, feelings and "spiritual revelations" seem to replace analysis and strategy as the guideposts for decisions. Methods of successful businesspeople are suddenly considered harsh, insensitive, or, at a minimum, out of place. A new vocabulary must be mastered, different expectations adopted, and varying results tolerated.

Why do Christians expect businesspeople entering ministry to abandon their skills gained from years of education and hard work? Do we expect an extremely talented neurosurgeon to go to the mission field to teach vacation Bible school? Most of us would see it as a waste of his or her God-given talent. That same neurosurgeon going to the mission field to do neurosurgery would make more sense. In the same way, the time has come to reconsider how we respond to businesspeople who want to do more on God's behalf. It makes no sense to move a business professional away from his or her talents and calling just so the work can be labeled "spiritual."

We need to show business professionals that their business talents are compatible with, and even essential for, kingdom-enlarging work. God instills in businesspeople the giftedness necessary to succeed in the marketplace. Strategically employed people with these gifts can have a powerful, unique impact on evangelism, especially in cultures and countries closed to traditional missionary efforts.

UNLOCKING THEIR POTENTIAL

The time has come to unlock the business brain for evangelism. Such unlocking will reinvigorate seasoned business professionals who have grown bored with the daily operations of business. Having mastered their enterprises or their markets, many lack inspiration or challenge. They want a positive and lasting challenge. Questions arise such as, "How can I do something with eternal significance?" Or, "If I want to work for God, shouldn't my work be in the church? Where do I start?"

Learning to use business talents, experience, and connections to support God's work creates new excitement, a new sense of spiritual self-worth. The skills obtained through competitive battles fought, difficult contracts negotiated, and motivating employees are suddenly relevant to eternally significant matters.

Consider the young adult just embarking on a career. Facing many choices, he or she must decide whether to pursue a secular career or religious training. Unfortunately, in today's educational environment, the choices are exclusive—"secular" or "sacred." And the results are disproportionate.

In the 1997–1998 school year, schools conferred a total of 1,184,406 bachelor's degrees.[1] Of those, 5,903 (.5 percent) were in theological studies and religious vocations; 8,207 (.7 percent) were in philosophy and religion. Combined, these students represented just over 1 percent (.0119) of the degrees. In contrast, schools granted 233,119 business and marketing degrees in the same year, representing 19.7 percent of all degrees conferred. For master's degrees, the contrast is even greater. The combined percentage for religious degrees increases to 1.4 percent, but business degrees increase even more, to 23.8 percent.[2] Young adults are making decisions that are overwhelmingly in favor of secular careers, resulting in fewer young people becoming pastors and missionaries.

IMBALANCE OF RESOURCES

While the training may be secular, the educational choices are not necessarily indicative of the hearts of these individuals. If you estimate that 15 percent of the population is Christian and serious about the faith, it would be reasonable to assume this would be reflected in the educational system. Therefore, of the 1,184,406 graduates with bachelor's degrees, one might expect that 177,660 (15 percent) would want to use their skills for some sort of Christian endeavor. Remember that the 177,660 represent only one graduating class—a single year. In comparison, consider the fact that the United States has only 49,000 missionaries serving in other nations.

How then do we reach this large group of mission-minded people with secular training? How do we inspire them to take up the task of missions? How do we help them overcome obstacles? Where do we start?

First of all, we need to realize that getting a group of people focused and willing to act is not a new challenge. In the months leading up to World War II, while Hitler was overrunning Europe, the United States had just 170,000 men in its armed forces, thanks to a pacifist political climate that had begun spreading after World War I. We did not want to get involved in the affairs of Europe. We failed to maintain the resources required to do the job even if we had wanted to. I believe the mission situation in the church today is very similar. Only a small portion of our Christian resources is available for fulfilling the Great Commission, either at home or abroad.

While sharing the gospel is not the same as a military operation, the resources needed to effectively "go into all the world" are similar. Galvanized by the attack on Pearl Harbor, the country committed itself to the conflict; the U.S. army grew from 170,000 to 7.2 million. Not all of the 7.2 million were on the front lines. Some estimate that only 1 percent of military personnel were directly involved in combat. The rest were behind the lines delivering the ammunition, training pilots, commanding troop transport ships, cooking food, gathering intelligence, and doing all the things that made the combat soldiers' job possible. Not only were the ranks of the military expanded, but the nation shifted its ability and resources to meet the challenge. Automobile factories were converted to produce tanks, aircraft were manufactured in record numbers, and new weapons and tactics were developed. How do we create a similar passion within the church for sharing Christ? And if we create the passion, who will go?

Just as the energies of a nation were focused to reach a goal, the church must examine the resources it has available to reach the world for Christ. As the automobile factory was converted to produce tanks, our businesspeople should be challenged to see themselves as a critical part of fulfilling the Great Commission. They should understand that the same skills they use every day can and should be used for reaching into the farthest corners of the world. While sending missionaries from one country to another is not the sole determination of a country's commitment to evangelism, I do believe it is a significant indicator. One can draw a parallel between the 49,000 U.S. missionaries in the field to our army before World War II. We are commanded to reach out to all nations—more of our numbers need to go, if only to show the world our obedience and to return reports of how God is working throughout the world.

For additional perspective, consider that, according to *World Christian Encyclopedia,* of the $270 billion given in the United States for church and parachurch activities, only .02 percent ($54 million) goes to "World A," which is predominantly restricted-access countries. Most mission efforts are focused on countries that are open to missionaries. Men and women following the traditional paths to international mission service are welcome in these countries. By default, the countries that establish barriers to the gospel receive less attention. In these restricted countries, traditional mission methods are obsolete, but business channels are wide open.

Let us assume that the current system of recruiting missionaries is efficient and represents the recruitment of all available missionary candidates. To increase the number of missionaries you would need to expand the pool from which candidates are drawn. Based on the educational data presented earlier, I think the pool could be expanded exponentially by intentionally including business and professional students. But the current system excludes these Christians from consideration unless they are willing to abandon their secular aspirations.

In 1999 and early 2000 I interviewed numerous business professors at Christian colleges. I asked them how they advised a student in the business program who had a burning passion for missions. Shockingly, they nearly always said they would advise the student to change to the mission program. These are godly men and women who are committed to shaping the lives of their students spiritually, yet they knew that the chasm between missions and business was too wide. The students had to choose one or the other.

Changing the System

I believe it is possible to change the "system." We can inspire business students to consider using their careers for evangelism and in so doing effectively increase the potential workforce of the kingdom. This is a radical departure from the traditional perception of the businessperson's role of simply funding the "real" missionaries by writing a check.

Such radical change does not come easily. Meaningful change seldom does. After hearing about what we are doing, a seasoned businessman and founder of an international workplace ministry said to me, "That is really hard to do." The comment was sincere and spoken with an entrepreneurial undertone that seemed to say, "If only I were younger . . . what an exciting challenge." Yes, the challenge is intimidating, but the potential rewards are worth the effort. Businesspeople learn to accomplish such difficult goals in the marketplace.

Not everyone rising to the challenge of business as mission need move overseas—nor should he or she. No entrepreneur operates in a vacuum, not even a holistic entrepreneur. Most of us (99 percent) will provide vital support services here at home—similar to the factory workers and mess cooks who were critical to the war effort. We can find the customers who will buy from the business missionary. We can support the export process, provide capital, and feed new business ideas and opportunities into the network.

Reflecting on my own life, I often think of the parable of the sower. Jesus says of the seed that falls among the thorns, "but the worries of this life and the deceitfulness of wealth choke it, making it unfruitful" (Matt. 13:22, NIV). For forty-five years, this accurately described my life. I was busy getting my education, then getting my career in line, then raising a family and working hard. When the family was grown, I would need to prepare for retirement. Finally, when I retired, I would have time for the Lord. Fortunately, God sent me a wake-up call.

It is important to understand that the people represented by the parable of the sower are Christians, but they are unfruitful. How do those of us who are immersed in the secular world become fruitful? I do not suggest that we automatically run to the church or mission organization for the solution, but rather look to our talents and see what we are equipped to do now.

The debate over business as mission often concludes with lofty rhetoric but little action. This is unacceptable. To have value, the concept must result in action on a broad scale. But how do you change two hundred years of tradition?

REACHING YOUNG PEOPLE

I think reaching young people is key, which is why I spend a lot of time with them. "Why are you wasting your time with young people when they don't have any money?" one mission leader asked me. I reflected a long time on that thought. It was true that if my goal were simply to fund ministry, the students would be the last people I should seek; but if we are going to change the way the next generation views their responsibility for evangelism, it is the most critical audience to reach.

Young people see a global society that is connected electronically and able to be traversed easily and quickly by jet aircraft. They have not had to internalize the changes over the past fifty years, and more dramatically in the past ten years, with the explosion of telecommunications. The world has shrunk, driven by commerce and the thriving international trade of the postwar era. As trade grew and the expenses of travel and communication declined, new players entered the market. International business was no longer the sole domain of multinational corporations, and new markets and competitive forces emerged. This is the world in which young people have grown up, and they see that it is a world full of opportunity.

The world has changed rapidly, but often our missionary methods have not kept pace. Consider the following story:

> In a remote Indian village, a friend of mine inquired as to whether the people knew Jesus. A long discussion among the members of the village ensued. The leader then reported to the interpreter that they knew everyone in the village and the surrounding area, and there was no one by the name of Jesus. What made this answer seem so dramatic to my friend was that they had bottles of Pepsi in the village. Pepsi had penetrated this market—remote as it was—and yet nobody knew who Jesus was.

Who is to blame? Certainly we cannot market salvation as we would a soft drink, but the comparison is stark. Where were the missionaries, the church planters, the believers who could have given these people a chance to hear the Good News?

Another, more instructive example comes from China:

> A large Korean factory was being relocated to China for a more competitive labor market. The owners were believers. They insisted that a Christian church be built on the factory grounds. The government refused. The owners built it anyway. Today it stands with government approval—granted because the economic benefit of the factory outweighed the government's desire to restrict religion. If that had been a mission agency church, it would never have been tolerated.

In the first example, the bottle of Pepsi reached the remote village to meet a market need. If the suppliers had been believers, the message of Christ could have come to the village, too. And in the second example, the factory owners knew that their responsibility was to spread the truth of God in a hostile land—so they seized the opportunity and leveraged their position. Of course it would have been a "cleaner" transaction without the religious aspect. But what is the point of our existence if not to tell others of Christ, using the tools God has given us?

CHRIST IN PINSTRIPES

The message of Christ can legitimately hold a "business visa." It can be embodied in a profitable business, a business unashamedly pursuing profits. Business brings prosperity to a country. Most everyone wants to prosper, so businessmen are welcome to come and trade. Business itself is devoid of religion and ideology, but businesspeople are not. The distinction is significant. When countries welcome business, they understand that with it come businesspeople who may have religious and ideological beliefs different from those of the government.

This occurred to me on my first visit to an Arab country. In a land known for its persecution of Christianity, more than 300 of us worshiped openly in a state-sanctioned sanctuary and with a pastor who held a pastor's visa. I was astounded. But we were Western businesspeople. In their minds, of course, we were Christians, and as guests in their country, our worship was accommodated. It had nothing to do with their stance on religious freedom or on how they viewed Christianity—it was a cost of doing business with the West.

These accommodations do not create a license to evangelize in restricted countries, but they do create a foothold and a support structure for the local church. Depending on the particular country and situation, opportunities for evangelism can occur. And, as we saw in China, in proportion to the value the company has to the host country, the "envelope" can be pushed—the opportunity can be maximized. This is not for the faint-of-heart. The church in China required a firm hand and skillful negotiations—again, skills gained in the marketplace.

UNDER FALSE PRETENSES

Brother Andrew, the founder of Open Doors, encourages evangelism by "being there."[3] We should indeed "be there," but how we "get there" is also important. People want to know who is moving into the neighborhood—it is human nature. They are concerned for their safety, their children's safety, and the safety of their possessions. They are interested in their neighbors and the community they live in (in Eastern countries often much more than in Western ones). To wonder why a person is there is natural, and the question deserves a genuine answer. Unfortunately, some missionaries go to countries under false pretenses, claiming to be running businesses that are nothing more than a sham. As witnesses of Christ, to found our ministry on a lie is a violation of the foundations of our faith. We need to "be there," but legitimately.

Today's Western view of business and mission is that either you are a businessperson or you are a missionary. Or if you are a Christian on business in a country, people assume that your job duties will not allow you to be a "real" missionary; you are just a part-timer (interpreted: really, you are just a businessperson). Sometimes the lines are blurred—such as when a missionary is pretending to be a businessperson so he or she can sneak into a country.

When the local people ask, "Why are you here?" they already have some preconceived ideas and scenarios that they expect you to fit into. When we sold our business in Texas and moved to our home state, Michigan, a few years ago, people always asked if our jobs brought us to Michigan. When I explained that we sold a business and now God had called me into ministry doing international business to spread the gospel, their mouths usually dropped open. Most people would have expected me to have been transferred or at least moved to better my job situation. People on the mission field have their own expectations, and we need to have a legitimate answer to their questions.

Missionaries who enter countries under false pretenses are starting with a lie. People are not stupid. When a white couple with two small children arrives in a Muslim country to open a travel agency, they know something is wrong. They start to think, "Why are they really here?" They observe no meaningful business or employment; they see the couple spending beyond their apparent means. They don't work, but they live in a nice house and have an expensive car. It is easy to conclude that they must be doing something illegal. It is not just a matter of their lifestyle. The ministry is based on a lie, a lie that devalues the message and degrades the missionaries in the eyes of the very people they want to reach.

I believe the lies are tolerated because today's mission community has few alternatives in restricted countries. Justification of false entry platforms can be precariously balanced on the letter of the law where a "paper" business exists but no real business is done. The reason mission agencies resort to such tactics is that people with real business talent have been effectively stripped away from any strategic missions involvement.

No one is happy with this situation. Godly business professors want to equip their students to be strategic agents for kingdom work. Mission agencies want more "missionaries" in the field and understand that business is a key. Why is more progress not being made?

Progress is lacking because we have failed to see that we can be *both* a businessperson *and* a missionary. The Scriptures require us to represent Christ wherever we go, to be missionaries all the time. Paul was both an apostle (evangelist) and a tentmaker. The two roles were intertwined, each a significant part of the whole person. We need to internalize the responsibility of the Great Commission. It is a personal command for every Christian.

MOVING FROM THEORY TO ACTION

How does the businessperson move from theory to action? There is no simple formula. The courses of action are as diverse as the world of business. The real answer lies in the creative minds of businesspeople around the world.

Consider, for instance, the following "case study" involving the export of castor oil. Castor oil is used in a variety of products, including cosmetics. The higher the grade, the more translucent the oil is. Purchases are made in 40,000-pound increments (a volume equal to the capacity of a semi-trailer/ISO container). High-grade castor oil is a valuable commodity and is manufactured in India and South America.

As a businessman in Michigan, I purchased 120,000 pounds of castor oil a year. I used the oil as a main ingredient for a mole-repelling product that we marketed to large retailers. I purchase castor oil from a chemical broker in Chicago who purchases it from a broker in Bombay, India. The broker in India purchases the oil from a mill, and the mill purchases the raw seeds from local farmers.

Analysis indicated that a sufficient margin existed, after covering all the expenses related to transportation, duties and customs, to bypass the two brokers and export the oil myself. If I bought the oil at the same price that the Chicago broker paid, we would have a net profit of $6,000. This $6,000 could be effectively transferred toward kingdom work.

This was "new" money for the kingdom. It was not previously available for kingdom work. I produced it by the way I structured a business transaction—a skill not taught in seminary. This is also money that can appear in a restricted-access country as the byproduct of an international transaction free of U.S. income tax.

The project needed to meet expectation of price, quality, and delivery. Further, we wanted to establish a sufficient structure to fund evangelism and create an ongoing stream of transactions—sustainability. We were not experienced in international transactions, shipping, or customs. We had to draft and issue letters of credit, evaluate credit risks, and insure against risks of transport theft or loss.

We formed a U.S.-based company, Company One, to provide the capital to fund the letter of credit and to act as a seller of the oil to the end customer. This allowed the customer to avoid being involved in an international purchase and to receive credit terms from Company One. Company Two was formed in India to act as a purchaser from the processing mill. This company gave a concrete presence in India for a Western couple and also allowed for on-site negotiation of the product and pre-shipping inspections.

Company Two sold to Company One. Company One contracted with Company Two for the oil, Company Two arranged for the purchase of the oil based on a letter of credit from Company One, Company One sold the oil to the Midwest Company, which then repackaged the oil, selling it to a retailer. On a $24,000 sale to the Midwest Company, we realized a net profit of $6,000. We allocated this to support outreach missions in India.

The approach allows Christian businesspeople to have legitimate access to India, where they can be evangelists. Company One can sell oil and other products to U.S. customers. Company Two can explore other exports. Money from the profits can support ministries without being considered a foreign contribution.

Even a relatively small formulating and packaging company can impact missions internationally. Not only can it have a direct effect, but it can make business sense. And when it is profitable, it becomes sustainable, creating a new and renewing resource for missions.

Differences with Microenterprise

How is this different from microenterprise projects or economic development programs? These are the kinds of programs in which a village woman is given a sewing machine to earn money or where a man is given a small loan to make brooms.

Most of these programs are based on donations. If the donations ceased, so would the programs. By that standard, they are not self-sustaining but rather are an innovative way of giving. The businesses they create are generally small and have little impact on the country.

People generally assume that the community benefits because of the cash flow of the business. However, in many cases the individual who receives the loan or gift has a competitive advantage because he received free or discounted capital. This advantage simply moves money from one person in the community to another. The woman who gets the new sewing machine can now compete against the women who were already sewing clothes. The market for tailoring does not magically expand because a new resource is added to the community. The money that was in the community (often a slum) is redistributed—without a net gain. This is an over-simplification of the impact of many good programs, of course. But we need to realize that helping someone go into "business" does not provide an automatic uplift of the society.

Transformation of a community or a country comes with larger enterprises. When you consider that the United States imported $1,258,170,149,352 worth of products in 2000, it is easier to understand the proportional impact of a $100 microloan. These programs are not bad. They empower the individuals involved and are a good first step, but they are not "business" as we define it.

NEW INTEREST

When I look at the way business can impact missions, particularly missions to restricted-access countries, I get excited. As I have mentioned, of the $270 billion given in the United States for church and parachurch activities, only $54 million goes to restricted-access countries. The United States alone imports over $180 billion in products from these countries. If we could tap into only 1 percent of this trade and shift it to kingdom work, we would more than double the money going to these countries. Not only would we be able to direct more funds into kingdom work, we could do it more strategically and with more flexibility than traditional methods allow.

Exciting and refreshing interest in business as mission is building in the world of Christian education. Professors are inspiring students to use their skills strategically and to see business as a calling. Universities are including these concepts in their business curricula, where tangible applications of the theories can be developed.

But what can young college graduates really do? Do we have to wait twenty years before they are in a position to act? Who are the holistic entrepreneurs? Are they the smartest students? Are they young or old? Do they operate in a vacuum or as part of a team? Entrepreneurs, holistic or otherwise, are best defined by their desire to succeed. If we can inspire Christians with such drive to direct their energies toward combined business and kingdom purposes, we will create holistic entrepreneurs.

What does a young entrepreneur bring to a foreign field? Business professionals, particularly in Asia, are generally more educated and more driven than most Americans. Even the uneducated people in many countries are skilled traders who are well connected to suppliers, making them formidable competitors. Therefore, holistic entrepreneurs must have a skill that provides a distinct competitive advantage, or they need partners who can provide that advantage. Such partners will be the real backbone of the business as missions movement, just as the cooks, factory workers, and trainers of World War II were the real power behind our country's military success.

Viewed this way, success is not dependent upon twenty-year-olds who are willing to serve overseas. Business as mission is bigger than they are. Nor are we restricted to a local business. We can expand our horizons to create international businesses that leverage networks of believers. Governments often approve, because such international transactions bring hard currency to their impoverished countries. Such benefits strengthen the legitimacy of the holistic entrepreneur living aboard.

One ministry partner of our organization, Evangelistic Commerce, presented the gospel to 3 million children in India in a single year through vacation Bible schools. This took logistical presence in the country and frequent travel. Our business system provided a business reason for an executive to be in the country, a long-term business visa, and ongoing support and encouragement. Another ministry partner has 700-plus indigenous missionaries planting churches across the country. This partner had relied heavily on a traditional paper-and-pencil system to coordinate the ministry. One of our business enterprises, however, provided computer equipment.

A strategic partner of Evangelistic Commerce also hosts a secure e-mail service. Leveraging an existing software company's expertise, the system allows encrypted e-mail between mission agencies as well as technical support of the ministry's technology needs. This is a for-profit company doing kingdom work—under the radar of the government.

RELATIONSHIP WITH MISSIONS

It is unrealistic to expect that strategic business systems can be integral to traditional mission organizations. The obstacles are profit, process, and execution.

A successful business needs to be based on profit—a foreign principle to most mission and economic development programs. Without profit, a business is just another social program distributing money from shareholders (donors) to its customers or employees. To many people not in the business world, profit is paramount to exploitation.

Mission agencies often base their choice of what business to do in a closed country on (1) who wants to go; (2) their skills or training; (3) how will it help the poor; and (4) what they think the government will allow. Rarely do they consider the basic business question: "How are we going to make money?" From a business perspective, this should be the *first* question. I sometimes reduce the goal of Evangelistic Commerce to "making money to support the spread of the gospel." This is a gross oversimplification of what the company is about, but it helps me identify the perspective of the listener. Businesspeople commonly smile and start asking, "How do you do it?" They are interested in how it is done, why internationally, and what the payoffs are in evangelism. Non-businesspeople, on the other hand, are often taken aback that Evangelistic Commerce is about making money. Who is making the money, are you exploiting people, do you give all the money to the church? They miss the point. Business is about making money. How that money is made and how it is spent have significant moral, ethical, and religious implications, but making the money, in and of itself, is not bad.

I would expect that Paul was a small businessman, as were most of the craftsmen of his day. Large commercial enterprises were not common in biblical times. It was an economy similar to many developing areas today, where skilled individuals traded their abilities for other goods or services. I believe Paul had to bid jobs, buy raw materials, enlist coworkers, and market his wares. He was in business and was not just an employee. He is a role model for us. He made money.

What Paul did with the money was under his control. He earned it and he spent it. Scripture does not record any formal tie between his business and the church. As a man of God, he saw fit to spend the money as God directed, on his own support, possibly on the support of his coworkers, to buy new tools, to pay laborers, or to finance his missionary journeys. Paul took the talent that God had given him and used it to make money, applying that money to God's purposes.

THE ROLE OF BUSINESS IN MISSIONS

In the greater scheme of things, what is the role of business in spreading the gospel? I believe it is foundational. I recently read a mission agency's recruitment brochure describing mission work in the United Arab Emirates—a highly restricted country. A major problem, as the agency saw it, was the group of Western employees in the country who were chasing profit and living lifestyles that were a poor reflection on Christianity. The agency was seeking missionaries to reflect a true Christian lifestyle, although I am not sure how they expected to get in. They seemed to miss the point that businesspeople were already there, accepted and protected. Think how far they could "push the envelope" if they were part of the business community and not trying to sneak in.

I believe the answer is to send people who are bivocational—missionaries and businesspeople. The answer is *both/and,* not *either/or.*

A POWERFUL TOOL

Every businessman and businesswoman should prayerfully consider their roles in missions. How can God use your talents, experience, and abilities outside the constraints of traditional mission systems? Most who read this will probably want to go no farther than thinking about all this as an interesting theory. But some will take up the challenge; you will devote your talent and your experience to an eternal purpose—a purpose that you are uniquely prepared for.

If you want to go no farther than the "interesting theory" option but feel that God is nudging you, then pray. God has a way of reaching out to those who love him. Don't let "the worries of this life and the deceitfulness of wealth" (Matt. 13:22, NIV) keep you from exploring what God may have in store for you.

Be aware, however, that business is a powerful tool for the kingdom, and Satan will dramatically oppose your move toward action. I now count it as confirmation of a person's calling when he or she encounters obstacles getting started. I have seen it numerous times.

Looking to traditional mission agencies or the church for objective guidance may be disappointing. Neither tends to think from a business perspective. Workplace ministries can help you learn personal spiritual development, ethics, and spiritual leadership. But first do an honest personal inventory, in writing. This inventory should list your passions, your natural abilities (giftedness), your learned abilities, your educational qualifications, and your capacity to act.

My personal inventory (very simplified) might look like this:

Passion: I really want to see God glorified and the saving grace of Jesus demonstrated through business.

Natural ability: I am a good communicator, not afraid of risks and energized by a large goal.

Learned abilities: I have been the CEO of several companies, and I understand financial matters.

Educational qualifications: I hold an advanced college degree.

Capacity to act: I am able to spend 60 percent of my time pursuing God's call. I can commit some of my company's resources, I can contribute financially, and I can speak to young people.

Students may have more time but less experience than a senior business-man. Jot down the talents God has given you and every imaginable way you might use those talents.

However, I always question requests that ask me to do things outside my skill set and training. The classic example is the executive who goes to a Third World country to help build a church building. What is happening? The cost of traveling to the country far exceeds the equivalent labor costs for local people to do the work. (A donation would be more efficient.) The "skills" needed were not business skills. What was the purpose? I believe the primary purpose of such a project is to get people involved and show them the need while they do something tangible. But the trip represents a gross underutilization of the businessperson's talents. While we can serve where there is a need, we must always seek to use the talents God has given us to the greatest extent possible. Use the inventory to guide you in applying your talents to the fullest. Avoid less fruitful pursuits—even worthy ones.

In everything you do, remember the words of Jesus, which apply as well to business as they do to traditional missions: "Therefore go and make disciples of all nations, baptizing them in the name of the Father and of the Son and of the Holy Sprit, and teaching them to obey everything I have commanded you" (Matt. 28:19-20, NIV).

15

THE BUSINESS OF MISSIONS—
THE MISSIONS OF BUSINESS

John Cragin

Mike is a Christian businessman managing millions of investment dollars for a nonprofit foundation. Haddid is a third-generation Lebanese American businessman managing regional sales for an advertising company. They were in my office to strategize about how they could use their business interests and know-how to reach the world for Christ. During the two weeks before those meetings I had similar conversations with businesspeople from Ukraine, the Czech Republic, Chile, China, the Netherlands, Brazil, Turkey, England, India, Russia, Morocco, and Mozambique. And then there were the phone calls and e-mails from the American manufacturing firm's president, two company vice presidents, a Fortune 100 corporate lawyer, an investment banker, a major franchise owner, a successful headhunter, a business broker, and several university business students. All of these were independently seeking the Lord's direction, asking the same basic question: "How can I use my God-given business talents and interests to impact the world for Jesus Christ?"

Most were seriously looking for ways to maximize their lifetime impact for Christ. They had not the slightest doubt about their individual responsibilities to go to the uttermost parts of the world to share the power of the Cross and the hope of the Resurrection. It may be a new millennium, but the questions people ask about business missions are much the same as they were asking in the old millennium.

AVOID BIFURCATION

Starting a business of any kind without a good understanding of the causes of failure virtually guarantees failure. Most businesses fail in the first few years. The success rate is even lower for Christian companies doing kingdom business in foreign marketplaces. People often say that business missions fail so often because the wrong kinds of people are in charge. That may be a contributing factor, but the more likely reason is that people launch the enterprise without a good understanding of and commitment to basic success criteria. Building an enduring, high-impact business mission begins with the cornerstones.

Ultimately, every believer is accountable for how he uses *all* of his talents and resources in response to the Great Commission and the Great Commandment. This applies to the Christian who is a business owner, the Christian who is an employee of a secular business, and it certainly applies to all involved in business missions. Unfortunately, a *spare time, spare change* theology has become so prevalent in the church that few ever question it. In the same way that *spare time, spare change* has led to segmentation in the individual Christian's life and mission, it leads to *bifurcation* in business missions. Christians often see business missions as a special hybrid with two independent departments, which they evaluate in entirely separate ways. They measure one department (the "true" business) against business criteria, while they measure the other department (the "true" ministry) against missions criteria. Some Christians actually staff missions this way, with some people responsible for the business and others focusing on ministry. This kind of thinking inevitably leads to the idea that business and mission are in conflict, competing for resources.

Naturally, proponents who think this way believe that any effort that is "75 percent mission and 25 percent business" is better than one that is "25 percent mission and 75 percent business." The logical conclusion is occasionally stated, "Frankly, we wish we did not have to engage in business at all." The business is seen as an unfortunate but necessary evil, required to provide support for the ministry. It is either a source of revenue or a convenient "cover" for penetrating parts of the world not open to traditional missions.

Apart from the difficulty of constantly detouring around all those biblical passages that seem to say, "Thou shalt love the Lord with *all* your heart, mind, soul and strength," and "him only shalt thou serve" (see Mark 12:30; Matt. 4:10), a bifurcated business mission almost always ends up as Siamese twins, uncompetitive as a business and unimpressive as a mission—unworthy of investment as a business, unworthy of investment as a mission. Not only is this approach inconsistent with Scripture, it also makes no practical sense.

From a steward's point of view, a business mission can be a great investment. Business can be an effective and efficient way to impact the world for Christ, as a comparison of the following three "models" will show.

Model A: Average Evangelical Church

There are 800 members on the roll, with 300 in Sunday morning Bible study. Total annual contribution required to support the budget is $500,000. The church has one pastor, one education minister, one music minister, one youth minister, two office workers, and one custodian. Total hours worked by members to generate the income are 28,000. Hours worked by church staff are 12,000. Number of people baptized is 50. Number of people receiving witness by staff is 500 and by members is 500. Contribution dollar cost per gospel witness is $500,000 divided by 1,000, or $500. Hour cost per gospel witness is 40,000 divided by 1,000, or 40.

Model B: Average Overseas Mission

There is a team of four units in Oslo, Norway. It consists of one administrator and three church planters. Total annual contribution required to support budget (including salaries, operations, regional and national headquarters overhead) is $200,000. Total hours worked by home country church members to support the budget is 15,000. Hours worked by Oslo team totals 8,000. Hours worked by regional and national headquarters staff is 1,000. Number of people receiving witness through Oslo staff is 1,500. Contribution dollar cost per witness is $200,000 divided by 1,500 or $133. Hour cost per witness is 24,000 divided by 1,500, or 16.

Model C: Business Mission

Again, we will place a team of four units in Oslo, all of them "up to their eyebrows" in the business. Total annual contributions required to support budget are $0. Total hours worked by home country church members to support the budget are 0. Hours worked by Oslo team total 10,000. Number of people receiving gospel witness through Oslo staff is 1,000 (800 via team witness, 200 via investment in local evangelistic work). Contribution dollar cost per witness is 0. Hour cost per witness is 10,000 divided by 1000, or 10.

STRUCTURAL COMPONENTS

While business mission strategists can help reduce the risk of failure by ensuring that the effort is not bifurcated and that all those involved understand and reject the *spare time, spare change* mentality, the business mission architect must address structural components that help bring success.

Prayer and Fasting

Many factors contribute to business mission failure, but most of them are rooted in the misguided tendency to believe one's brilliant ideas and business or ministry skills will suffice to get the job done. Few Christians would publicly announce their intention to carry out a business mission in their own strength. Most would acknowledge the need for the Lord's guidance, but subsequent behaviors often belie these proclamations. No business mission should be attempted that is not, from the initial inspiration, brought before the Lord by *every* involved person with much prayer and fasting. If people are not prepared to fast and pray, they should stop before it is too late.

Sole Proprietorship

A kingdom company has one owner—Jesus Christ. The company works for his kingdom *only*. A business mission does not pursue profits for worldly purposes while providing money to fund a ministry. This is dangerously close to trying to serve God *and mammon* or God *through mammon*. The business mission seeks first the kingdom of God—doing God's work, God's way, for God's reasons.

While the Creator Christ is the kingdom company's sole proprietor, and all the subsidiary companies serve the purposes of his kingdom, in the United States and most other countries, temporal ownership must be delegated to one or more of his human creations. One individual, several individuals, a company or companies, a church or mission organization, a foundation or any combination may own a business mission company. What matters is that *every* owner and manager be totally and irrevocably committed to the mission and to the measures of performance, and that key operational staff have the professional and ministry skills needed. It is common to find this fundamental principle compromised in order to include a needed investor or staff with certain critical expertise.

Products, Markets, and Customers

Christians should never force-fit business missions into a target location where there is little or no opportunity to market a product competitively and profitably. A good product or service idea is good only if enough people are willing to pay for it. Far too many business mission efforts try to create demand when they should be trying to satisfy demand. They inevitably fail. A business mission will not secure its position and impact if it tries to sell a product or service for which there is no significant unmet demand. Therefore, the company's portfolio must consist of several products (rarely just one) that customers want and for which the supply is inadequate. A good reality check is this: If there is a market, there will be competitors. If there are no competitors, very likely there is no market.

Business missions require good market research. Business missionaries should spend significant energy in the target market area generating a list and description of potential customers, competitors, and suppliers. The company should send representatives to relevant industry trade shows in the country. It should do in-depth study of competitors' products and services, including market segmentation, pricing, features, distribution channels, advertising, and what the customers like and do not like about them.

The business mission company should have detailed knowledge of the regulations for setting up and registering a company office and for obtaining visas. It should document import and export regulations, channels, and costs. It should investigate local labor laws. It should make pre-planning inquiries with the American Chamber of Commerce, the Commercial Section of the U.S. Embassy, and other business organizations. The company should be aware of the work of other mission organizations in the area and, where appropriate, make contact.

Exactly the same warning applies to gaining an understanding of the peoples that will be targeted with the gospel. The business missionary must do enough research to identify the specific spheres of influence and the most effective approaches to reaching them. A business mission should never plan to enter the market and then, once there, try to determine how to present the gospel.

Measurable Results

All types of mission efforts must meet the financial efficiency criterion the Bible calls "stewardship." Since over the long run no mission effort can spend more than it takes in, every mission must measure and control revenues and costs. The business mission must set up accounting procedures and books before the company begins operations in foreign markets. It must research local regulations regarding income reporting, employee payroll withholding, and various kinds of taxes (VAT, profits, sales, import tariffs, etc.). It must carefully forecast income, cost of sales, operations costs, marketing and administrative costs, and foreign exchange rates to provide data for at least two years of supportable pro forma financials.

But a mission must do more than live within its budget. Most missions want to grow, to multiply, to extend their impact. This can only happen if the mission is successful enough to deserve additional revenues, beyond total costs. The kingdom company seeks to achieve a satisfactory profit margin. An unprofitable enterprise indicates that the products and services are not of a quality and price to be competitive.

Mission efforts must also meet the strategic effectiveness criterion the Bible calls fruitfulness, or what businesspeople call "relative yield." We should not waste time on fruitless efforts. The seed of the gospel should show a yield 30-, 60-, or 100-fold. If it does not, we are obliged to consider both the soil into which we are sowing and the power on which we are relying.

To achieve its purpose, the business mission company must develop and invest in Great Commission efforts that are synergistic with and leveraged by the company's presence in strategically selected markets. It must set standards for evangelism and discipleship, measure results, and evaluate results per dollar invested for every sphere of influence identified in the market analysis. Company spheres of influence and the spheres of influence of each team member are specific market segments targeted for impact. At the company level, this includes hundreds of people who work for suppliers, customers, competitors, banks, associated companies, civic and government organizations. For the team, this includes business contacts, friends and neighbors, shop owners and employees, classmates and teachers, and probably special segments such as hospitals, orphanages, hostels, and shelters. Any parts of the company that do not produce to standards are pruned. An axe is laid to the root of those that do not produce at all.

BUSINESS MISSIONS EXAMPLES

Now we come to examples of business missions. The purpose here is *not* to compare the relative performance of the examples, nor to suggest that any of these examples be copied. Rather, it is to highlight a wide variety of successful approaches to business missions in order to stimulate prayer and encourage faith and bold action. These examples include a wide spectrum of economies, cultures, and political systems in Asia, Europe, Africa, South America, and the Middle East. I have made no distinction between models that have been operating for many years in multiple locations and models preparing for their first launch. Each general category will indicate the approximate level of start-up capitalization required.

Manufacturing—$450,000

In one such business mission, approximately $5,000 was spent to contract an independent study of the target market. The analysis included market demand, growth, pricing, distribution channels, and competition. The product line consisted of a dozen similar, relatively low technology industrial products used in many parts of the economy. The production plant required a space of about 20,000 square feet, which allowed for inventory and planned expansion. The production line was taken out of mothballs in the United States, cut into parts, shipped to the target market in containers. Going with it was a starting supply of finished products, raw materials, samples, tools, and spare parts. The plant was then reassembled on-site in space secured by long-term lease. Sales objectives are now $1.5 million annually with net income of $200,000.

The primary focus of the team is evangelism in the company's spheres of influence, with an emphasis on training and multiplication in the individual spheres of influence. The company has a reasonably high profile in the community and is heavily involved in community service to the poor and needy. Potential exists to start sales and distribution offices in multiple locations in the target market and in several export markets, each becoming a mission point.

Private Schools—$25,000 to $1.5 million

Three private schools, over 7,000 miles apart, in four very different cultures and economies, have demonstrated business mission potential where certain types of education are in high demand and where supply is limited.

Over a year of careful research and planning went into the launch of a private school in a country where American-style education was suddenly in demand. With the vision of a new believer with local credibility and a handful of American educators, the school began in government-allocated facilities with 80 elementary-level children, all from influential local families, 10 local teachers, and 10 American teachers. Organizers obtained 100 percent financing from local sources, even though the economy was in ruins. Within a year, the school became preeminent, and enrollment jumped to 120. Three years later, a state-of-the-art campus was under construction in a prime location. The school now serves more than 300 students, including some nonlocals. Technically nonprofit, the school generates revenues well beyond its costs, which it reinvests in its own programs and in several community efforts.

The primary evangelistic target is the school's own strategic sphere of influence. Team members also planted what is now a large international church serving a dozen nationalities. Significant programs with orphanages and needy children have attracted national attention.

Another group has established a similar private school with far less initial capital—under $250,000—most of which came from local sources. It now hosts more than 300 children K-8 and will soon expand its facilities to accommodate 400 K-12 students. A significant percentage of the children come from Muslim families. School executives are now developing plans to double the size of the school to accommodate more than 800.

While many missions efforts are based on specialized areas of education (commonly English language teaching), most are funded by donations. However, in one important target market, a world away from the others described here, a for-profit English language school began in borrowed school facilities with $25,000, five local teachers, and five Americans certified in TESOL (Teaching English to Speakers of Other Languages). The program used advanced techniques and digital materials and immediately established itself as the premier school in the region. Within two years, it had 700 students and more than enough revenue to consider expansion. As in all of these four schools, every student and parent was a specific subject of prayer and personal witness.

Consulting and Training—$25,000 to $50,000

Supply and demand considerations often lead business missions strategists to the business-to-business markets. Many strategic target areas are only beginning to enter the world's competitive economic environment. Learning to compete is not easy. Learning the complexities of competing in a broad international market is frightening. Rapid globalization has created two basic consulting segments. Businesses and governments need help in attracting investment and in developing their own abilities to compete. Businesses and governments in countries outside the target market need help learning how to do business in new, strange, and potentially profitable markets.

In some important but economically poor target markets the demand for business consulting and training is relatively limited. Nonetheless, even in these areas there are opportunities for consulting and training in agriculture, mining, health care, infrastructure projects, and the like paid for by governments or major international development organizations. There is no reason why a carefully selected team of Christian experts could not be formed to compete for such projects.

In one large developing country, a team of highly credentialed Christian consultants submitted bids on five projects contracted by the U.S. International Trade Administration. The projects ranged in size from $10,000 to $25,000. The time needed to research the project and write the proposals (which must follow very specific protocols) ranged from 20 to 50 hours and totaled 150 hours for all five projects, or about $6,000 in time value. Competing against well-established names in the consulting business, the team was nevertheless able to win three of the contracts with a total value of $48,000. Because the results of the projects were published by the ITA, a certain credibility was established for the team, resulting in further consulting business. Though it is difficult to win enough consulting business in a single country to support even a small team, the opportunities created for highly leveraged witness are significant.

In another example where specific expertise and supply/demand imbalance led to a powerful consulting business, two young men with computer science training and less than a year of professional experience discovered their talents were sorely needed in a part of the world with a weak Christian witness. They contracted their services to a large Internet service provider and moved abroad. Retained for more than $90,000 per year each, they were not only able to have a clear witness inside the company spheres of influence but also to play a key role in the formation and growth of house churches.

Consulting often leads to training opportunities. A team of five business graduates with credentials in marketing, international business, and accounting set up a small consulting company in the former Soviet Union. For two years they ran a successful accountancy and market research consulting operation, building an impressive list of international and local clients. Eventually they discovered a very significant demand among local businesses for the skills they were providing as consultants. They developed three levels of training in accounting, in both English and the local language, one training program in building market share, and one in strategic planning. The accountancy series was in such demand that local people had to be added to the team.

In another part of the world, a team of four business graduates set up a consulting company whose primary client was a state commerce department from the United States. Many U.S. state commerce departments subcontract business research and development work in various parts of the world where their constituents have interests. The team presented a proposal to establish and run an office for the state in the target region. At the same time, they developed a working relationship with the largest national agency concerned with building business in the U.S. This allowed them to house their offices in a prestigious trade center and to be in constant communication and cooperation with this large agency. In addition to income from the state commerce department, they were able to contract for market research and development work with various American clients and with local companies wanting work done in the United States.

A consulting team in Asia was providing a wide variety of services in many industries for companies and governments. Through team members' consulting and a significant presence in the American Chamber, they learned of an unmet demand for professional training for executive secretaries and executive assistants. Taking advantage of a small cadre of highly trained American executive secretaries, they designed and marketed a program that became the benchmark in the market and have trained hundreds of local men and women. Every trainee hears the gospel. Several dozen small groups have been established to help the new Christians learn to use their company positions to introduce others to Christ.

Import and Export Outsourcing—$15,000 to $40,000

Trading is the business model many strategists consider when trying to develop a business mission for developing or impoverished countries. Import/export is very complex, high risk, and extremely competitive. There is a tendency among some naïve planners to believe they can find or create a consumer market for local crafts or artwork. Rarely do such schemes generate enough income to sustain the business mission. Nonetheless, there is potential.

Many U.S. companies are looking for sales representation in key foreign markets. In some cases, they see an advantage to having an American agent handling their products. A large heavy-equipment manufacturer was displeased with the service it was getting from its local agent in an important market. A team of three Americans offered to complete a thorough market research and then, on the basis of that work, to become the new agent for the U.S. firm. By selling similar services to a handful of companies in related industries, the group was able to generate enough commissions to sustain the business mission.

Other U.S. companies are looking for help sourcing (importing) components and raw materials from low-cost foreign markets. It is expensive to locate, qualify, and control foreign suppliers. Language and culture barriers can make communication and coordination a real nightmare.

In the same way that a U.S. exporter will pay a commission for sales to foreign markets, companies will pay fees and commissions to agents who act as their sourcing arms in supplier countries. One such team established a sourcing relationship with a large U.S. distributor of tractor parts, many of which could be sourced from Asia. The team provided search and qualification services and negotiated for the buyer. Then it coordinated quality inspections and shipping schedules. Within a year, the company was sourcing over

$2 million through the team, generating fees and commissions of $75,000 annually, most of it from relatively easy repeat business.

Services Outsourcing—$25,000 to $50,000

Many firms operating outside home borders find that services they routinely outsourced at home are less available abroad. This supply/demand imbalance can create significant opportunities for business missions.

Hospitality—$25,000 to $150,000

Expatriate individuals and families are hungry for modern services, even in many of the most underdeveloped parts of the world. There are relatively low-capital opportunities in such things as bed-and-breakfast accommodations, restaurants, convenience stores, and individual teachers and tutors for local and expatriate children.

One mission family entered a joint venture arrangement with a local restaurant owner, turning a modest facility into an extremely popular and profitable establishment serving hard-to-get Western food with home-cooked flavor in a family atmosphere.

The wife of a CPA involved in a business mission felt she had little to contribute to the enterprise until she realized she was the only professionally licensed Western hairdresser in a city of 7 million. Within a short time she was styling the hair of the wives of the leaders of government and industry, as well as foreign diplomats and visiting heads of state.

Franchising—$25,000 to $50,000

Some successful business models can be taught and then replicated by people without extensive business training, experience, or credentials. A successful American marketing services company has recently begun building a portfolio of three specific marketing consulting products with the intention of offering relatively low-cost franchise opportunities exclusively to small teams committed to business missions.

A second franchise model offers considerable promise for reaching influential college-age students who are seeking to complete undergraduate or graduate degrees in the United States. Most Christian universities are interested in attracting more foreign students. But many of these students have difficulty gaining admission, even when they have the funds. And, the limited duration of their visas and the cost of traveling to the States make that extra year extremely wasteful. The franchise proposes to establish small teams in target countries who will set up prep programs fully endorsed by cooperating universities. Successful completion of the program would guarantee nationals admission into any one of the cooperating universities and eliminate most, if not all, of the remedial studies. The schools would pay a screening and preparation fee equal to 5 percent of the four-year costs. For example, if the annual published cost was $15,000, the school would pay the franchise a one-time fee of $3,000 per qualified student. In addition, prospective students would pay a fee of $1,500 in local currency for the one-semester preparatory training (taking place in their home country, in rented facilities, in evening sessions of six hours per week, or a total of 90 hours).

CONCLUSION

As is evident from this very limited list of examples, individuals and organizations are gradually acquiring the experience they need to develop and sustain effective business missions. While traditional mission efforts, relief work, and contribution-funded services will likely continue to make up the bulk of global outreach efforts, it is already clear that much good work can be done for the kingdom using carefully planned and designed business models. Self-financed, high-impact missions are desirable, entirely possible, and in some cases may produce higher yield per dollar and hour invested than other strategies. Continuing advances in business missions are necessary if the body of Christ is going to catch up with its Great Commission responsibilities.

STARTING KINGDOM COMPANIES: A BIBLICAL AND HISTORICAL OVERVIEW

Heinz A. Suter

The kingdom company is not a new concept. It is older than the Hebrew Scriptures and as new as a high-tech start-up. In this chapter we will examine examples from the Bible and from missions history.

BIBLICAL EXAMPLES

In the Old Testament, besides priests, Levites, and temple servants (so-called "full-timers"), we encounter people earning their living and fulfilling God's calling and purpose in their everyday contexts. Some were holistic entrepreneurs. Some developed family businesses as "kingdom companies." Others were high-ranking civil servants.

Abraham was a wealthy sheep farmer (Genesis). Joseph was a steward and later a prime minister in Egypt (Genesis). Moses was a prince of Egypt (Exodus). Joshua was a military commander in Canaan (Joshua). Deborah was a judge in Canaan (Judges 4–5). Ezra was a scribe, teacher, and historian (Ezra). Esther was a queen of Persia (Esther). Job was the "greatest man of the East"—a farmer and rancher (Job). Amos was a shepherd and horticulturist (Amos).

In the New Testament, Acts 18:1-3 shows how God used normal holistic entrepreneurship to advance the kingdom of God. When Priscilla and Aquila opened a tentmaking shop in Corinth, Paul joined them, because he also was a tentmaker. Thus, Paul could earn his living, provide for others, and show Christlike character in the marketplace (Acts 20:31-35; 1 Thess. 2:9; 2 Thess. 3:8). Even so, this role did not keep Paul from receiving financial gifts at other times (2 Cor. 11:8-9; Phil. 4:10-19).

Since commerce and trade at that time were based on traveling, we assume that many of those who were scattered because of persecution (Acts 8:1-4; 11:19-24) set up their businesses elsewhere.

Acts 16:14 tells us about "Lydia, from the city of Thyatira, a seller of purple fabrics" (NASB). In her home in Philippi, Paul established the first church of Western Europe (Acts 16:15).

Thyatira, a city in Asia Minor, has a history as a center of trade and commerce and had links to major trading routes. It is one of the seven cities mentioned in Revelation 1:11. Ephesus was a great export center at the end of the Asiatic caravan route. Smyrna was a natural port for the ancient trade route. Thyatira itself was an important center of manufacture, dyeing, garment making, pottery, and brass working. It comes as no surprise, therefore, that among the first messengers of the gospel were small merchants and traders from Asia Minor who sold garments and spices in Marseilles and Lyons, in Alexandria and Carthage. One of them was Lydia in Philippi, some 100 miles south of her hometown.

This short look at some biblical examples shows that it is possible to advance the kingdom of God through one's business and professional skills. If it was possible to be a holistic entrepreneur in biblical times, should it not be possible today?

HISTORICAL OVERVIEW

Church historian Stephen Neill notes three characteristics that helped spread Christianity during its first few centuries:

1. *A great network of roads, spanning the Empire from north to south and east to west.* To a degree, one's relationship to the roads determined one's situation in the Empire, and the history of the roads was therefore the history of the regions they served. Historian Kenneth Scott Latourette observes, "This road-building, made possible by the *Pax Romana,* led to the growth of travel and commerce, facilitating not only political unity but cultural and religious exchange."[1]

Both the Christians and the Gentiles of that era praised this peaceful time, which lasted from the reign of Augustus (27 B.C.) to that of Marcus Aurelius (A.D. 180), or slightly more than 200 years. It was extremely helpful in the rise of business, craft, industry, agriculture, trade, and the formation of financial assets. By giving freedom from enemies without and from piracy within, and by improving all means of communication, the era fostered trade and commerce and promoted the well-being and happiness of citizens and subjects. No wonder M. P. Charlesworth concludes, "To the mercantile population it was an age of hope, the dawn of a new era . . . and of pushing far into unknown lands in the promotion of trade."[2] Nor should we forget the Mediterranean Sea, which Adalbert Hamman mentions as the "most important Roman trade route."[3]

2. *The Greek language as the main channel for communication within the Empire.* Greek became the *lingua franca* of the Empire and was spoken in most of its commercially active cities, such as the ones mentioned in Revelation 1 in Asia Minor. Ruth Tucker says, "Unlike most missionaries of later centuries, the early evangelists were not forced to endure years of grueling language study. Greek was the universal language of the Empire, and Christians could communicate the Gospel freely wherever they went."[4] Likewise, Christian and all other businesspeople, traders, and merchants could travel freely.

3. *A large Jewish expatriate community.* Neill speaks of Jews making up about 7 percent of the Empire's population at that time. Thus, short stops or long winter layovers at ports along the Mediterranean coast permitted believing Jewish passengers to visit their compatriots, establish new friendships, and share the gospel. No wonder, then, that Paul met "some brethren at Puteoli" (Acts 28:13-14), a trading port in southern Italy with "ironworks and factories."[5] Paul could arrive almost as a family member, enjoying the benefits of a powerful and highly privileged association. This Jewish network also had synagogues around the Roman Empire, which Jewish or Christian merchants and traders visited (Acts 13:14; 14:1; 17:1-2, etc.). Christians could share the Good News as they went.

The *Pax Romana* allowed a great network of roads to be built throughout the Empire. The commonly spoken Greek language helped Christians in business to communicate. The Jewish network throughout the Roman Empire gave believers a platform of contacts.

We can see how God used this historical context for the spread of the gospel. Roland Allen stated that "tradesmen knew how to give some account of God and did not believe without evidence."[6]

Churches were established during this time in several commercial cities of southern France, including Marseilles, Arles, Vienna, and Lyon. Many merchants resided in such towns in southern Gaul, selling flax, linen, wool, and clothing. During the early centuries, the church was a predominantly urban phenomenon that moved along the trade routes from city to city.[7] In

Lyons, where Irenaeus was bishop in the second century, many of the first church members were migrant traders from Asia Minor.

The Nestorians

The Nestorian church was founded after a schism concerning the divinity of Christ at the council in Ephesus in 432. It quickly expanded eastward as the silk roads developed.[8] For good or ill, these roads united the regions and empires all the way along the routes, beginning with the Roman Empire in the Mediterranean region, followed by the Byzantine Empire, through the Middle East, and into Central Asia and northern India, where the emergence of Islam provided a new unity. Interestingly, Voll concludes, "Muslim merchants carried both their trade goods and their faith."[9]

As in the times of the early church, the network of silk roads greatly facilitated not only commerce but also the spread of various religions all the way to China. Nestorian Kurd George M. Lamsa says:

> The coincidence of the opening up of the trade routes into Farther Asia—with the ascendancy of the Nestorian church—offered a ready outlet for missionary efforts.[10]

The missionaries of the Eastern churches, who brought the silk trade to the West, together with the Jews, dominated commerce along the silk roads. In the sixth and seventh centuries the caravan cities of Merv, Herat, and Samarkand built churches. Many Nestorians were traders. Others were carpenters, smiths, and weavers.[11] They carried Christianity to China, where they filled appointments as secretaries, physicians, or stewards in the households of nobles and princes. Nestorian Mar Sargis of Samarkand, whose forefathers were all famous court physicians, was appointed by the Mongol emperor Kublai Khan as assistant to the governor in the district of Xinjiang.

Traces of Christianity have been encountered on the road from Samarkand (today Uzbekistan) to Khotan (Xinjiang province of China), in the form of inscriptions of Christian Sogdian merchants.[12]

Nestorian missionary activity in Central Asia was at its peak between the fifth and the ninth centuries. Nestorian patriarch Timothy chose a metropolitan bishop from Samarkand to oversee the area of Turkistan and to appoint bishops for Bukhara and Tashkent; the church and missionary center in Samarkand existed until the twelfth century.

Christy Wilson, the "father of tentmaking," cites John Stewart, who notes, "there were more people in the eleventh century in Asia who called themselves Christians than there were in all of Europe."[13] There were

Christians among the Turkish merchants from Ing-lesia, capital of the Tangute kingdom (destroyed in 1225 by Genghis Khan).[14] Hans Haussig notes the existence of commercial lists dating from 1295, which prove the connection between Christian missions and Western enterprises.[15]

Even Marco Polo (1254–1323) says that the silk trade routes from Baghdad to Peking were lined with Nestorian chapels.[16]

History furnishes hard evidence that God used business, trade, and solid Christian professionalism to transmit the gospel along the silk routes, probably starting from as early as the day of Pentecost (Acts 2:9), where "Parthians, Medes and Elamites" were present in Jerusalem, and continuing up until the twelfth and thirteenth centuries.

Pre-Reformation, Reformation, and the Puritans

Thomas Aquinas (1224–1274) spearheaded a significant shift in the church's ethics of work.[17] Based on Luke 10:42, the *vita contemplativa* (of Mary) was given preference over the *vita activa* (of Martha). People viewed work as morally neutral, like eating or drinking. Praying, studying the Scriptures, and preaching became the only sacred activities. Working and eating were merely "secular." Thus we received a separation of the "sacred" from the "secular." People believed that the only genuine calling, or *vocatio Dei*, was the ecclesiastical calling. This work was "sanctified" and was seen to be of greater value than secular work.

Martin Luther (1483–1546), a former monk, recognized the problems of solitude, separation from family, and otherworldly living associated with monastic life. He realized that the Christian virtues could only be practiced within the world and its institutions of marriage, state, and profession.

He developed the thesis, based on 1 Corinthians 7:17-24, that every person has a "calling" (vocation) of God, which is the state of life (the "standing") to which God has appointed him or her. To put it another way, every person has a calling from God with regard to his worldly duties. Home life, the relationship that exists between parents and children, is a "calling" (*vocatio*), as are one's relationships and daily responsibilities at the workplace. Luther said that every profession or daily activity is a "calling" that—if executed properly—should in itself serve both man and God (Col. 3:17, 23; 1 Cor. 10:31). Luther said:

> Everyone should conduct his life so that it is pleasing to God, even if in the eyes of the world it is humble or despised. A servant, a maid, a father, or a mother, all these are forms of life given by His Godly word and sanctified to please God.[18]

So whatever state of life in which one finds himself—whether preparing for exams, filling out invoices, selling clothing, bargaining for better prices, or developing better management strategies—should be regarded as God's calling. Every sort of activity constitutes worship and service to God.

Luther was thus the first theologian in the Middle Ages to apply the term "calling" (*vocatio*) to earthly activities. Luther understood that not only religious representatives but also farmers, princes, traders, and every other sort of person were to understand their works as gifts and callings of God.

Another great Reformer, John Calvin (1506–1564) of Geneva, saw work as a sign of the fellowship and solidarity of humanity under God. Since man does not depend on the church, priesthood, or any other aid to salvation, but solely on the sovereign elective will of God, he stands as an individual before God. Therefore, he must "work out his election" (salvation) in and through his everyday work. By this means, he glorifies God. In this context, every aspect of economic or social activity becomes a tool *ad majorem gloriam Dei*—for the greater glory of God. "Whatever you do, do all to the glory of God" (1 Cor. 10:31).

So "work" becomes a means of persevering in faith, obedience, and the calling of God. The "secular" and "sacred" are no longer divided, but integrated. Each individual's work is to be done unto God and is therefore spiritual. Idleness and enjoyment do not unfold God's will and multiply his glory. Active work does.

Essentially, this was the motivation behind the individualism, industriousness, and self-discipline that undergirded the Protestant work ethic and the future industrialization of the predominantly Protestant countries.

The Counter-Reformation of the 1560s saw around 100,000 Protestants fleeing their countries. They settled primarily in important trading centers such as Frankfurt, Nuremberg, Cologne, Hamburg, and Aachen (in Germany); in London, Colchester, and Norwich (in England); and at Leiden and Haarlem (in Holland). This migration established a pan-European network of Calvinistic merchants, guided by the principle of election and the new emerging work ethic, and united by their shared experience of displacement and minority existence.

The British Puritans were the true heirs of Protestant business ethics. They integrated these principles in their seventeenth- and eighteenth-century churches. "Labor" became in itself a kind of spiritual discipline, imposed by the will of God. It is not merely an economic means, to be laid aside when physical needs have been satisfied. It is a spiritual activity, for in it alone can the soul find health. Work continues as an ethical duty long after it has ceased to be a material necessity. It should be no surprise that godly discipline became indeed the very ark of the Puritan covenant. "Discipline" included all questions of moral conduct, of which economic conduct was a natural part. A strong individualism emerged, which was congenial to the world of business. Puritan Richard Baxter (1615–1691) wrote in his *Christian Directory:*

> Be wholly taken up in the diligent business of your lawful callings, when you are not exercised in the more immediate service of God. . . . The truly godly servant will do all the service in obedience to God, as if God himself had bid him do it.[19]

The Puritans' godly ideal—hard work, frugality, humbleness, integrity, honesty—brought forth wealth. Success in business was in itself almost a sign of spiritual grace, for it was a proof that a man had labored faithfully in his vocation and God had blessed his trade. This Puritan approach to life, the spiritualization of every aspect and motive and economic activity, set in motion a potent workforce and a powerful source of self-reproducing capital, pouring its torrents into the development of Western industries. These founding fathers—Independents, Congregationalists, Baptists, Mennonites, Quakers of England, Holland, and Germany—went to America to lay the spiritual and economic foundations of that prosperous country. Their spiritual and ethical heritage also influenced the Moravians and later the Basel Mission.

The Moravians

Jan Hus, a priest who lived in Bohemia around the start of the fifteenth century, was greatly influenced by the writings of the English reformer John Wycliffe. Hus particularly attacked the abuses and disorders in the official church. Before his death (he was burned as a heretic), Hus established the Church of the Brotherhood. His followers felt themselves closely allied with the Waldensians. Together, in 1467, the two groups established the United Brethren. These Bohemian Brethren had also spread into neighboring Moravia, emphasizing "less the theoretical doctrine of the Gospel, but more and more the practice of Christianity—as seen in the lives of Paul, Augustine, Francis, Wycliffe and Hus" (the reference here being to Paul's model of self-support).[20]

At this time, the Bohemian-Moravian Brethren were self-supporting. A small remnant of them survived the many European religious wars of the sixteenth and seventeenth centuries. The remaining Brothers—now settled in Saxony—in 1722 obtained permission from the pious count of Zinzendorf to establish themselves on one of his estates, called Herrnhut.

Ludwig von Zinzendorf (1700–1760) was himself influenced by the example and teachings of the great Lutheran Pietist August Hermann Francke. Under this man's teaching, young Count Ludwig learned the operational unity of business and missions, seeing that "this Christian entrepreneur [Francke] managed to support his community of institutions not only through a widespread network of collections, but also by means of business enterprises."[21]

Missions was the top priority of every Moravian. Living sacrificially for the Savior was the highest calling of the Brethren, which again was a typical Protestant ethic of life and work.

Moravians viewed Paul as a kind of itinerant Christian tradesman who worked for his own living while being involved in counseling and preaching. Every member of the Moravian community was expected to be ready for a similar ministry. All of them were lay people who were trained not as theologians but as evangelists. As self-supporting laymen, they were expected to work alongside their prospective converts, witnessing their faith by the spoken word and by their living example. The first list of the inhabitants of Herrnhut, compiled by Otto Uttendörfer, mentions more than a dozen trades and professions, such as linen weavers, carpenters, bricklayers, shoemakers, smiths, potters, bakers, tailors, and tanners.[22]

Moravians were businesspeople in the marketplace who were committed to making disciples and modeling a lifestyle in which their work ethic was very prominent.

Abraham Dürninger (1706–1773), one of the Moravians, became the father of the first European house of commerce. Dürninger sold only with fixed prices and fixed wages.[23] He soon was called "the merchant blessed of God," who had audiences with the king of Saxony, who continued to consult him for commercial and personal reasons.[24] In 1821, the Dürningers' trading company maintained branches in twenty-six countries. Thus, Moravians gave traders and common people alike a demonstration of honest business methods. And, by the competition arising from their example, they also forced other traders to treat people more fairly. Alongside their commerce and crafts, the Moravian laymen also witnessed about their faith.

In 1740, a group of Moravian missionaries arrived in Paramaribo, Suriname, and quickly established the practical connections between "merchant" and "missions." The shoemaker and the carpenter immediately had enough to do. The missionaries established the forerunner of what was to become the support base for the Brethren congregation in Suriname: the C. Kersten trading company, founded in 1768. Sitting together on a tailor's bench, it was easy for people to converse about the gospel. Moravians gradually gained influence among the black slaves of Suriname, gave them work, and offered them a new way of life in Christ.

By 1862, the *Unitas Fraternum* could contemplate with joy that the missions in Suriname, South Africa, and Labrador were financially self-supporting. This was a true triumph of the Pauline practice. However, at the General Synod in 1869, delegates thoroughly discussed the distinction between merchant and mission, without reaching any clear decision.[25] Worse, at the General Synod of 1899, delegates decided to make a complete philosophical separation between "business" and "mission." Still, they held there was an unbreakable bond between the means and the purpose of ministry. To that extent they could not abandon the Pauline principle.

The missions of the tailors, the bakers, and the watchmakers to Paramaribo blossomed such that, by 1926, this became the largest Moravian congregation in the world, with 13,000 members worshiping in seven church buildings.

For nearly 200 years in the Moravian mission movement, business, crafts, and trade served as very useful tools in God's hands in order to spread the gospel holistically to various parts of the world.

The Basel Missions Trading Company

In 1999, the Welinvest company in Basel bought one of the largest Swiss trading companies for $130 million. This may sound like simply another lucrative financial deal, until you realize that the purchased firm, UTC (Union Trading Company Ltd.), began as the Basel Missions Trading Company. Founded in 1859, UTC has grown into a worldwide holding company, with a yearly gross turnover of more then 2 billion Swiss Francs and over 6,000 employees in seventeen countries.

But how did this happen?

1. *History and context of Basel.* Situated on the Rhine, between the French Alsace and southern Germany, Basel is still today a crossroads city. People from more than a hundred national backgrounds reside there.

In 1225–1226, the first and for many centuries the only bridge over the Rhine was built at Basel, making the city the single viable connection between the cities and seaports of Italy, middle Europe, the Rhinelands, and Holland. Quite naturally, Basel developed the art of hospitality toward the plethora of travelers, traders, and craftsmen who frequented the city, extending citizenship to many. It also attracted the philosophers and intellectuals of the time.

Not surprisingly, Basel opened the doors of the first university of

Switzerland in 1460, attracting leading freethinkers, intellectuals, artists, seekers for truth, humanists, and teachers such as Erasmus of Rotterdam (1469–1536). In their thirst for truth and for renewal of the established church, the Basel humanists searched the Scriptures and the works of the church fathers. In 1516, Erasmus—at the personal invitation of the printing master Johannes Frobe (who learned his business at the feet of Gutenberg himself)—translated the New Testament from the best Greek texts available.

Basel was Europe's book printing center. When Martin Luther (1483–1546) posted his famous Ninety-five Theses at Wittenberg in 1517, people in Basel eagerly received them. The printers set to work at once, thus helping to advance the Reformation, not only in Basel and in Switzerland, but also in southern Germany, France, England, and Spain.

In 1529, Basel turned Protestant, after Zurich (1525, with Ulrich Zwingli), and Berne (1528), and became an attractive harbor for many seeking the new faith from other European nations, like Marco Perez, a Spanish Jew of noble birth, who converted to Calvin's Protestant teachings. He established trading links from Basel to the Flemish port city of Antwerp.

Within a century—especially during the Thirty Years' War (1618–1648)—many of the Protestant Huguenots would come as refugees from neighboring France. Among them were the forefathers of Adolf Christ, who in 1859 became the first president of the Basel Missions Trading Company (later UTC); and the family of Matthias Preiswerk (1515–1592/93) of Colmar, France, who "had religious motives, since he presumably belonged to the secret adherents of the Reformation."[26] Generations later, his heirs were involved in the trading company.

In the next century, Basel opened its doors to 300 Moravians and 150 Pietists from Germany who were seeking more religious liberty. Many of these evangelical refugees brought their professional knowledge and insights. Those from Italy were skilled in weaving, spinning, and coloring. Those from France brought new techniques in trade and the weaving industry.

By the end of the seventeenth century, their legacy to Basel was more Christianity, more industry, more commerce, more social justice, and more prosperity. The Huguenots had a powerful influence. They owned all the larger trading companies in the southwest, southeast, and northwest of France, and their influence on matters of faith, commerce, and industry in Basel was decisive.[27]

In 1780, the Deutsche Christentumsgesellschaft (German Christian Society) was founded in Basel. The objective was "to mission the world over." By 1799, the movement had a total of more than thirty meeting places, even as far north as Holland and Denmark. It began to forge links between

Christians of every social stratum: aristocrats, ministers, generals, deputies, professors, doctors, merchants, traders, farmers, and Protestant pastors alike.[28]

Soon contacts were established with the recently founded British missions societies, such as the Baptist Mission Society (founded in 1792 and significantly influenced by a speech by William Carey) and the London Mission Society (founded in 1795).

Thus Basel was the ideal background, a mixture of faith, industriousness, open-mindedness, and expansion, for the founding of the first Swiss missions agency.

2. *The Basel Mission.* At the beginning of the nineteenth century, Carl Ferdinand Spittler became secretary of the German Christian Society and started the Basel Mission. Thus, on September 25, 1815—just a few days after the siege of the city of Basel by 100 French cannons, set up by Napoleon—seven men met together with a single divine purpose: to found a mission school which later became the Basel Mission. Pastor Blumhardt was appointed its first missions inspector.[29]

From the outset, Blumhardt's understanding was that the missionary, besides receiving theological training, should also be trained in craftsmanship and trade. His ideal was "the craftsman-theologian," an integrated model of human life in all its aspects.[30]

The movement grew quickly. In 1820, in connection with the Caucasus Mission, the Basel Mission committee went from six to 13 members, mainly from Basel. Most of them were burghers, merchants, and industrialists. Some were even members of the city council. By 1833, 73 "Basel missionaries" (mainly from southern Germany, but also from Switzerland) were serving the Lord around the globe. In 1834, the mission started a work on the southwest coast of India. By 1843, missionary activity had reached all the way to the Danish Gold Coast, now known as Ghana.

3. *The Basel Missions Trading Company.* Basel's spiritual, economic, and political background produced the kind of people who would become the Basel Mission's pioneers and create an ideal for the Basel Missions Trading Company.

The forerunner of the Trading Company was "the Industrial Commission," established on November 24, 1852. Inspector Joseph Josenhans observed during an overseer's trip to India[31] that the economic development offered by the Basel craftsmen-theologians to new Indian Christians (who had been rejected by their own people) was professionally inadequate. They needed more economic support and technical advice. As explained in an official letter sent on February 1, 1854, by Josenhans and Carl Sarasin, their understanding of the mission was as follows:

> As a mission itself, a mission not through preaching, but through the power of example, through a model of Christianity revealing itself in practical life situations . . . a mission doing everything possible to make it visible that godliness is profitable.[32]

Thus, in August 1853, the young missionary-merchant Gottlob Pfleiderer from Waiblingen, Germany, was sent to Mangalore, India. His job was to oversee the mission's weaving mills and to set up the provision of needed raw materials and the sale of the finished products on a professional basis. Soon Pfleiderer opened a little shop, which not only imported necessary items for the missionaries but also started to sell imported groceries and paper products to clients outside the missionary community.

In December 1854, Basel sent a young merchant, Ludwig Rottmann (also German), to the African Gold Coast as a forwarding agent. He also opened a small store, from which he imported and distributed European food, medicines, household appliances, tissues, tar, and tools. The initial venture capital of 5,000 Swiss Francs came from the pious silk manufacturer and city council member Daniel Burckhardt-Forcart (1805–1879). The venture also received 1,000 Pounds Sterling from the Basel Mission. The first year of operation ended with a profit of 2,148.40 Swiss Francs.[33]

So the little shop of Christiansborg grew naturally under mercantile principles. The national merchants and traders appeared and bought larger quantities of certain products, in order to sell them further inland. In exchange, they offered their palm oil, gold dust, and ivory.[34]

Slowly, the import of European goods increased. By mid-1857, 60,000 Swiss Francs had already been invested. At the same time, the spiritual dimension of the business was kept clear, as City Council member Sarasin wrote in May 1856:

> Our business should never be done on a temporary, secular basis, but our shop should be a spiritual oasis amongst the vast heathen desert and support the surrounding, growing Christian Church.[35]

Soon, more mission trading shops opened, and trade grew. In January 1859, the board approved the founding of a separate Mission Trading Company. The president of the company was Ulrich Zellweger, described as the "energetic and clearheaded Swiss banker who had dreamed up the whole idea of a missions-trading company."[36] The company's shareholders were recruited from a circle of friends sympathetic to the Basel Mission. Many were from the Protestant industrial-business families typical of Basel.

By 1862, a new trading post opened in Ado Fa, without a single mission station nearby, to act as "light in the darkness." As the missions committee stated on August 31, 1863: "Profits shall not be the main goal of the company—rather, the example of using Christian principles in Business."[37]

Not surprisingly, trade became one of the chief activities of the Basel commercial missionaries on the Gold Coast. They were among the first to introduce the cacao plant to that region, in 1857. It took more than thirty years of setbacks, restarts, growing, and planting. The breakthrough came in 1891, with the first shipment of cocoa to Europe.[38] In 1911, Ghana exported 40,000 tons and became a world leader in cocoa export for decades. As William Danker says, "In this way, the Missions Trading Company and its agricultural efforts helped to create and strengthen an independent class of African farmers as free children of God."[39]

Meanwhile, in India, the weaving industry of the Basel Mission developed in Tschombala. The tissue had such a high quality and their workers were so skillful that its products became known as "mission-cloth," and this became a synonym for quality. During a thanksgiving service in Kannanur on the business's twenty-fifth anniversary in India, one of the 186 converted weavers challenged the rest by stating, "We should influence the heathen through our faithfulness to the Lord in the marketplace and our lifestyle in general."[40]

John Haller, a German weaver-missionary, invented the cloth that could withstand the burning Indian sun. He gave his new color the name "khaki," which in the local Kanares language means "dusty." The police chief of Mangalore had his entire police force clothed in this color. On a visit of the Basel Mission weaving establishment at Balmatha, Lord Roberts of Kandahar, then commander-in-chief of Her Majesty's forces in India, was so impressed with the practicality of this cloth that he emphatically recommended its use in the British Army.[41] From a humble mission beginning, khaki began its march around the world.

Other types of mission factories were started, such as printing, roof tile production, and book binding. By 1913, they employed more than 6,000 workers. Amid corruption, the Basel Mission industries showed a better way. In addition, in 1867 the industrial commission in Basel introduced social health insurance, pensions, and worker savings plans long before such social concerns became law in Switzerland.

CONCLUSION

Expanding business ventures have been vehicles of Christian skill and pro-fessionalism, God-inspired farsightedness and faith, and ethical and social concern for centuries. They have been instrumental in impacting and trans-forming whole regions, societies, and countries to the glory of God and the advancement of his kingdom. Obviously, to continue in this long tradition, we need to keep our theological priorities in order. There cannot be any dis-junction between the sacred and the secular. Using business as a vehicle for missions is spiritual and holistic, as we have seen from biblical examples and missions history.

In our increasingly globalized world, kingdom entrepreneurship shall come to have even more importance. Starting kingdom companies will be a top priority in the decades to come.

17

INTERNATIONAL DEVELOPMENT SYSTEMS: A CASE STUDY

Michael R. Baer

We are entering the "kingdom company" era in world missions, especially in regard to unreached peoples in restricted-access countries. When the modern mission age began, most effort centered on the traditional missionary. An individual, totally devoted to evangelization, church planting, or humanitarian work, would relocate to the targeted country and do full-time mission work. For 200 years this model has changed very little. In the past two decades, however, it has been supplemented by the tentmaker strategy. Tentmakers either operate real businesses or work for real businesses in targeted areas. They use their spare time to build relationships, evangelize, make disciples, and plant evangelical churches.

Now, a new model is emerging—the "kingdom business." It is in some ways a hybrid of traditional missions and tentmaking. In other ways, it is entirely different. The main similarity is that it is focused *as an enterprise* on evangelical mission goals and that it uses business as a vehicle for ministry. The main difference, on the other hand, is that it is not a "shell business"[1] but rather a for-profit operation that ministers *through its operation* rather than in spare time *from it.*

Founded in 1998, International Development Systems[2] is *a real, for-profit company providing a real, for-profit service to its clients while simultaneously and seamlessly focusing on the support of church planting among unreached peoples.* Here we will look at the history, mission, methodology, and results of International Development Systems.

HISTORY

In 1994, the founder of International Development Systems, Michael Roberts, began traveling to Central Asia in the former Soviet Union in connection with a leadership curriculum for the state medical university. While on this visit, he sensed a great hunger for business training among nationals and thought that God could use this in evangelizing the area. Consequently, while maintaining his executive role in corporate America, Roberts began recruiting small teams of American businessmen and women to deliver training seminars. The response was overwhelming, and some attendees subsequently came to faith in Christ. Nevertheless, the effort was sporadic and had little cohesive strategy.

By 1997, there had been some church growth, but not much. The church among the target people group of the region had grown from approximately 50 in 1991 to 450 by the end of 1997. Evangelical workers in the country concluded that the extreme economic deprivation of the area was strangling church growth. These workers invited Roberts and his teams to design and deliver a microeconomic development (MED) program in February 1998.

All participants hailed the meeting as a success, and work began immediately to expand its influence and to refine its methodology. People realized that the work could not go on without greater support from the United States and greater involvement from Roberts. After months of prayer, Roberts left his corporate job and, in May 1998, founded International Development Systems, Inc., a for-profit, small business development firm focused on training, coaching, and funding small businesses and microenterprise development in the United States and elsewhere. Now a $1 million consulting firm, IDS operates in eight countries and employs ten people along with other affiliate professionals.

MISSION

The mission statement of International Development Systems illustrates the thinking behind a kingdom company: *to support church planting among unreached people groups, especially in the 10/40 Window, through the seamless marriage of business and ministry.* In other words, while operating a true, for-profit business (in this case, small business coaching), the company and all its employees and affiliates are ultimately focused on world evangelization *through* the activities of the company both in the United States and abroad.[3]

Reflecting this statement, the company not only provides cutting-edge services to its clients (resulting in exponential growth in revenues and profits since its founding) but also a sustainable income to its employees. Each member of the team, regardless of his or her denominational affiliation, also has substantial freedom to participate in the direct mission activity of the company or in his or her own ministry passions.

METHODOLOGY

By definition, the purposes of all kingdom companies will be virtually the same: to glorify God and directly engage in his purposes in the world. Moreover, all kingdom companies operate on the basis of biblical principles (e.g., honesty, quality, integrity, etc.) and attempt to influence individuals for Christ and to bring about societal transformation. Methodology, on the other hand, will be vastly different, dictated by the type of business.

In the case of International Development Systems, its method centers around the IDS Project, a microenterprise development effort focused on church planting and, in turn, spawning dozens of kingdom companies among unreached people groups.

The potential impact of kingdom business on church growth became readily apparent in 1998. Michael Roberts and others formulated the IDS Project to provide multi-phased microenterprise development training, consulting, and funding aimed at equipping national Christians to support their families, their local church, and ultimately national church planting and cross-cultural mission activity. The subsequent founding of International Development Systems as a small and microbusiness coaching firm only served to support, staff, and finance this program.

Reinvesting profits from U.S. operations in the IDS Project,[4] International Development Systems uses its staff and volunteers from American congregations to conduct training in holistic entrepreneurialism, biblical business practices, and market-driven economics. Profits, along with donations to a partner charity, provide the basis for microcredits to qualified graduates whose businesses are also focused on kingdom purposes within their people group or across ethnic barriers. Currently, in addition to time given to staff to participate, one full-time employee is devoted entirely to the coordination of the IDS Project.

RESULTS

The results of International Development Systems and the IDS Project among the unreached have shown the hand of God on this work. While the company has experienced strong revenue and profit growth in its U.S. operations and has more than twenty-five active clients in the American business community, the Project has come to take on a life of its own and has impacted the growth of the church in unforeseen ways. One veteran Christian worker said she has never seen the believers in her country "as excited about or encouraged by anything" as they are about this work. Since 1997, the church has grown from 450 to more than 6,000, with projections well in excess of

15,000 by 2004. Of course, there are many factors in this phenomenal growth. Nevertheless, many workers in the country attribute much of it to the empowering impact of the IDS Project—a strong testimony to the efficaciousness of microenterprise development.[5]

Since the Project's beginning in 1998, it has expanded (as the continued mission of International Development Systems) into five other pioneer mission fields. Nearly 1,000 believers have been trained, more than 75 businesses have been started (with only two failures), more than $150,000 in microcredits have been issued, and more than 100 American business professionals have been mobilized as volunteers with nearly 100 more slated to participate in 2002.

The following mini-case studies further illustrate the impact of International Development Systems. Each graduate of the IDS Project is required to consider his or her personal call to kingdom business and to include a "kingdom impact statement" in the business plan in order to qualify for funding.[6] In other words, the Project has become more than just an economic engine for church growth among unreached peoples. It has evolved into a "kingdom business incubator" of sorts, the full impact of which has yet to be seen.

Karl

Karl is one of the earliest believers among his people, converted before the fall of the Soviet Union. After a horrendous period of backsliding and a miraculous restoration, Karl emerged as a respected leader of the few Christians in his country. Karl has a tremendous passion for Christ and for reaching his people with the truth. In 1999, like most others in Central Asia, he was living in abject poverty and crippled in his ability to impact his community. However, after graduating from the IDS Project, Karl was enabled to launch a small cattle business in a village about an hour from the capital city. Blessed with an innate sense of business, Karl soon began to prosper.

Today, Karl operates three businesses and provides employment to a significant number of believers in his village. Karl has also become the pastor of a church in his village and the overseer for nearly twenty other cell groups in surrounding villages and hamlets. As an act of gratitude, Karl returns to address each convening class in the IDS Project to give real life counsel on the formation and operation of a "kingdom business."

Charles

Charles was forced to drop out of law school for financial reasons at age 22. After becoming a believer, he attended the IDS Project in 1999 and planned to start a cattle business. He wanted to operate his business as a witness to Christ and to reach out to unbelievers around him. However, God had other plans—illustrating that business is not everyone's calling. His dilemma was that, while attending his father's Muslim funeral in the totally unreached southern portion of the country, he had felt compelled by God to stand and preach the gospel. This would normally have been a death wish, but God blessed his words. Five nationals immediately came to Christ. Within a week, five others believed.

The small group of new believers asked Charles to be their "leader" (not knowing the concept of a pastor). This was the dilemma Charles presented to his American counselor in 1999. The answer was obvious and Charles prepared, with the blessing of IDS, to move his cattle business to the south and care for these new converts. Once more, God was to change his plans, for Charles soon found himself leading dozens to Christ and founding a church of more than 100 where there had previously been no believers at all. Faced with death threats, Charles continued to minister. Today, through the work of this evangelist, there are more than 1,000 Christians in this region. Charles is now preparing to venture into the final unreached province of his country where he will, no doubt, experience blessing and great danger.

Timothy and Anna

Timothy and Anna represent a classic husband and wife team in business. Both are relatively new believers with a heart to reach out to those around them. In 1999, Timothy attended the IDS Project while Anna served as an interpreter. Their vision was to start a copy center. Timothy had already formed a business relationship with Toshiba (Germany) and came to the training with a solid business plan. With some coaching and adjustment, he qualified for a micro-credit loan and began his copy business. From this single location, he now provides copies and printing for a variety of businesses in the capital city, continues to demonstrate godly living to his customers, and has recently joined the national Advisory Council for the IDS Project in his country.

Kenneth

Kenneth is a former banker whose vision for a kingdom business included employing his Christian brothers and sisters and witnessing through relationships. His retail flower business has been successful and has expanded into multiple locations and provided jobs to many needy believers. However, with a vision of his own, Kenneth came to the IDS Project requesting funding for a national credit union whose purpose would be to multiply kingdom companies through proper management of local funds. IDS became a member, made a significant "deposit," and the credit union is now funding other businesses. It will eventually expand throughout the country and handle the financial distributions of the IDS Project.

Kenneth has been invited to consult with Christians in another part of the former Soviet Union on launching their own church-based credit union.

Elizabeth

Elizabeth is one of thirty known believers among her people group. Young and outcast, Elizabeth possesses a great heart for God and a natural sense of business. Her vision is to use a food processing and delivery business to reach out to students in her city and to support the planting of a church in her area. She wrote her business plan as a part of the IDS Project in August 2001 and was funded within days. Time alone will demonstrate whether she will reach her goal.

Andre

Following a miraculous conversion from a Muslim background, Andre found himself outcast and unemployed. He brought experience in animal husbandry to the IDS Project and has recently begun a cattle business whose aim (in addition to providing for his family and a small local congregation) is to support his ministry to prisons and orphanages.

These brief case studies demonstrate the "ripple effect" any kingdom business can have. Doors continue to open and new people group representatives continue to request the launch of the IDS Project. As International Development Systems resources grow and as each international office (serving as a base for the IDS Project) reaches self-sustainability, expansion will continue.

CONCLUSION

International Development Systems exists as a kingdom company by the grace of God. Its mission is focused on the eternal purposes of God in the world. It is an example, not the model, of how a business can use its normal (or abnormal) course of operations to fulfill the Great Commission.

If God is pleased to awaken and mobilize the vast resources of American and international Christian business professionals, the results will be historic. No longer do businesspeople need to see themselves as merely "checkbooks," economic contributors to an enterprise in which they are otherwise uninvolved. Instead, men and women of faith and business can begin to view their calling as sacred and strategic—a vessel "fit for the Master's use" (see 2 Tim. 2:21).

Appendix 1 to Chapter 17
International Development Systems, Inc.

Statement of Vision

The purpose of International Development Systems, Inc., is to be fully and strategically involved in what God is doing in the world—at home and especially among unreached people groups.

To accomplish this we will . . .

- Build an organization that provides a base of operations for our associates so that they can support their lifestyles and at the same time have the freedom to pursue their God-given ministry passion;
- Provide immense and measurable value to our clients in the services we perform so that we grow in financial benefit and stability;
- Conduct ourselves internally so as to edify each other and externally so as to be a consistent witness to Christ in the world;
- Throw ourselves and our resources in obedience to Christ as he leads our involvement in local and international ministry.

Appendix 2 to Chapter 17
IDS Testimonial: Valeria

My name is Valeria. I have been a Christian for eight years. I live in a small town.

It was a blessing for me to attend a business conference and learn about the IDS Project. We have many different ethnic groups in our town, and it is a Muslim region. Now they have great interest in Christianity. Not long ago one lady became a Christian. She is the first lady from this people group to become a Christian.

It is important to have businessmen in our church. This helps us to make an impact for the kingdom through all the people groups in our town. Before this conference, we were praying about this in my church. It was very painful for us to see that most of the Christians are very poor. When we tell people about God, very often they tell us that they don't want to be Christians, because most Christians are poor.

Sometimes there is no work for people, because our economic situation is difficult. Sometimes people want to start new businesses but don't have the money; other times they lack knowledge about marketing and business plans. We want God to be glorified through business; this will be a strong testimony for all non-Christians. We must spend money for his kingdom.

Thank you for this Project. It encourages us, and we understand that God will do great work through us. Thank you for opening your hearts for Russians and other people who live all over Russia. God bless you.

APPENDIX 3 TO CHAPTER 17
SAMPLE BUSINESS PLAN OF AN IDS PROJECT GRADUATE

Business Description

S. is presently operating a successful retail business selling carbonated beverages to the general public from April to November. In his current business model, all sales come from a shop in K., a city of 80,000. Customers purchase the beverages by the glass or by the liter, (75 percent and 25 percent, respectively) from a stationary soda-dispensing machine.

S. wants to expand his business by purchasing two additional soda machines. He wants to purchase the machines with wheels, which he can easily move in his truck from location to location. Such mobility will allow S. to address the pent-up demand for cold refreshments at any two of the three daily bazaars that are held in K. He will also add incremental revenues by adding this additional capacity for bulk liter sales for carryout and to cater to large parties.

Kingdom Impact

S. feels that he will be able to help people, especially those who are doing God's work, from the fruits of his labor. A woman graduate of a Bible college who is doing missionary work will receive added support. He will also be employing two more employees, who will be affected by the Christian manner in which he conducts his business. In the event that they are believers, he hopes to strengthen their love of Christ. If they are not believers, S. hopes that they will grow to accept Jesus Christ through his Christian conduct of the business. S. will have more money to increase his tithe to his church. He will continue to provide free sodas at festivals for orphan children in his community.

Investment Required

The total investment required to purchase two new soda-dispensing machines is $1,325. S. will provide $175 in equity and is requesting a loan of $1,150.00 to be repaid over two seasons.

18

KINGDOM-BASED INVESTING

Kenneth A. Eldred

The case studies in this book contain a number of examples of believers who have taken their gifts in entrepreneurship to faraway lands in an effort both to build a successful business and to further the kingdom of God. My story is slightly different. I do not have day-to-day management responsibilities overseas. Rather, I serve as a strategic investor to a company in India, closely advising the local entrepreneur and advancing the church through the company's intentional hiring and training of Christian employees. It is a model we have termed "openness to kingdom-based investing."

THE LORD'S GROUNDWORK

God started planting the seeds for this new India company at a small Catholic college in California almost forty years ago. While attending Notre Dame College in Belmont, California, my wife, Roberta, became a friend of an Indian female student. They stayed in touch, even when we moved to New Jersey following my 1968 graduation from business school at Stanford University. This friend has a brother named Mr. V., who came to the United States to work in New Jersey. Mr. V. had recently been married, and it was natural for us to invite him over for frequent visits. Those visits continued for decades.

We were not yet committed believers. I left my firm in New York City in the early 1970s to look for a job in California. But during this time, we committed our lives to Christ.

I figured that a decision for Christ meant that I would need to become a pastor. My true desire, however, was to be a businessman. Eventually, I surrendered and agreed to follow him wherever that would lead me—even as a pastor in a poor area. But like Abraham, whom God asked to offer his precious son but then provided another way, I was not required to carry out the sacrifice. The Lord was more concerned with my demonstration of willingness.

As a new believer, I wanted to be a Christian full-time, not just a week-end warrior whose faith had no bearing on his weekday activities. Slowly, I began to understand what that meant. God began teaching me how to bring the two parts of my life together.

God also showed me more clearly the business opportunities before me like ducks in a shooting gallery. Since I struggled to see business opportunities, I asked God either to open my eyes or to remove the veil. He did.

I wanted to start a business. A friend said he had about a dozen ideas, so we went through them one by one. At one point, I felt God saying, "This is it!" We reviewed that particular business concept for ninety days, and with $5,000 and a grocery bag full of computer connector parts, we founded Inmac. God was teaching me that he could not only be a part of the business, but that he could guide me.

In those days there were no computer superstores stocking every conceivable component on their shelves. You could buy computer peripherals only with complete systems. The novel idea behind Inmac was to offer computer products, supplies, and accessories by direct mail. Through some early struggles, the company survived and then thrived. Inmac went public in 1987, and by the time we sold the company to MicroWarehouse in 1996, it had grown to $400 million in annual revenues.

After selling Inmac, I felt God telling me to extricate myself from all corporate boards, so I did. John Mumford, a Christian brother and a close friend since our days in business school, was a cofounder of Inmac and the founding director of Crosspoint Venture Partners. Together, we conceived Ariba Technologies, a supply chain management company that would facilitate procurement using the Internet. With the assistance of some folks at Benchmark Capital Partners, we cofounded Ariba in 1996.

THE BIRTH OF AN INDIA COMPANY

In March 1999, Mr. V. approached me with a business start-up concept and asked for my help. He wanted to take advantage of the relatively low cost and high quality of labor available in English-speaking India to establish a new company that would serve customers in the United States. I agreed to help my friend, under one condition—that he would give capable young Christians in India the opportunity to work for him. Mr. V. said, "Absolutely!" and a new company was born.

However, I was unsure about my level of involvement with this new company. Mr. V. asked me to serve on the board of the company, but I was extremely hesitant due to God's earlier leading to drop all board positions. I prayed about it. In May, the pastor of a local church said he had a word from God for me. He said, "You're wrestling with a decision regarding a company, and God wants you to know he's in it and wants you to take the role." Further, he said, "You are involved with another company that is going to take off like a rocket."

Our initial hopes were to price the public offering of Ariba at $8 per share. Two months later, Ariba went public at $23 per share. On opening day, however, the stock closed at $90 per share, corresponding to a company valuation of about $6 billion. (Over the next year, Ariba was valued as high as $40 billion.) That exceeded our wildest expectations and increased my confidence in the Lord's leading regarding this India-based company. I agreed to join the board of directors.

I felt that God really wanted me to use my position of influence to advance his kingdom in India. Here was my simple kingdom-based investing model:

- We could be intentional about hiring Christians.
- We could offer attractive wages to this India company's employees.
- Someone could equip and mentor the Christians in the company.
- Christians from the company could give to the local church.

However, this model for furthering the church in developing nations cannot be divorced from sound investing practices. Several key components were essential to my participation.

THE ENTREPRENEUR

First and foremost, I had absolute trust in the integrity and ability of Mr. V. Our twenty-five-year history as friends meant that I had observed him, his family, and his ethical decisions. I had seen him through good and bad times. I knew about the companies he was in and had visited the company he led before.

After graduating from one of the finest Indian universities, Mr. V. completed an MBA in Colorado and took a position with Public Services Electric and Gas in New Jersey. He then returned to India, where he purchased a semiconductor company that had in place a buyback agreement with a U.S. company. However, the president of the U.S. partner corporation swindled his own company, sending it into bankruptcy. Mr. V. eventually managed to sell his company without a serious loss, but it was a tense entrepreneurial learning experience.

For the next twelve years, Mr. V. was the India country manager for a major Western multimedia company. His education and experience in the United States and his management role at a Western company were all highly important to our common understanding of business concerns.

It was during his next post as CEO of a chemical company that I witnessed Mr. V.'s integrity in full force. Mr. V. had built it from a small Indian company to one with about $50 million in annual revenues. The company had a great year, and Mr. V. was offered a bonus. Mr. V. told the owners that his hard-working employees deserved one as well, but they flatly refused. Mr. V. then suggested distributing his own bonus to the employees, but they still refused. He insisted that the company should share its profits with the hard-working employees, but the message fell on deaf ears, and Mr. V. resigned.

During the last six months of his employment with the chemical company, Mr. V. traveled to Vietnam to negotiate a $10 million contract. Before settling the deal, he told the Vietnamese partners that he would be leaving the company. They said, "Here's the contract. There's no company name at the top. You put your name in there, and we'll do the deal with you." He said, "No, it's not my business—it's theirs," and he signed the deal for the company. That kind of character and integrity gave me confidence in Mr. V.

Everywhere he went, Mr. V. found success. Just before starting the new India company, he was CEO of one of the largest cellular phone companies in India. Despite the huge sums spent by AT&T and other companies in three second-tier states, Mr. V. acquired more subscribers than any other cell phone company in India, garnering a 67 percent market share. This cellular phone company grew to 3,000 employees.

About that time, some venture capitalists came to India, looking for good managers. They tried to convince Mr. V. to pursue a start-up venture, but he was not interested. However, when the owners of the cellular phone company refused to give him a piece of the business, he resigned and started the new India company.

Mr. V. discovered that the outsourcing of call centers provided a potentially enormous business opportunity. Once strictly proprietary and developed in-house by call center operations, the necessary software had become Web-based and commercially available. And the communication capabilities between India and the rest of the world had been greatly enhanced through fiber-optic telecommunications, enabling calls from the other side of the world to sound local, at very low cost.

Mr. V. developed a business plan that called for an $8 million investment. These American venture capitalists thought his proposal was too expensive, as they were hearing several other plans that proposed $1-2 million of funding. Convinced that the $8 million estimate was on the mark for the establishment of a world-class business, Mr. V. stuck to his plan. Ultimately, however, he failed to persuade them.

EVALUATING THE BUSINESS OPPORTUNITY

At this point Mr. V. asked me to participate financially, and I did. In addition to requiring absolute trust in the integrity and capabilities of the founders, I have a set of attributes that help me evaluate specific business opportunities. The following are mine, and they fit me. They may need to be modified to fit your needs, but there is a germ of an idea in each:

1. The individual at the top and his or her team are "A" players.
2. The business is part of or supporting a fast-growing market (at least 15-20 percent growth per year).
3. The market size is at least $100 million.
4. It is a new market opportunity as a result of trends and changes in the market.
5. There is an opportunity for technology to play a new role heretofore unavailable in order to improve the business.
6. A national or international market exists. It is not dependent on a local economy.
7. There is a fragmented market ownership with no clear leader or major players.
8. Obvious and natural competitors are committed in another direction.
9. Barriers to entry can be built behind you. It will be difficult for potential competitors to enter later.
10. The business is not dependent on government regulation for success.
11. It fills a need—perceived and actual—and preferably can be measured in economic value.
12. The business is capable of superior profits (at least 10-20 percent per year).
13. The venture does not require large amounts of capital, at least until the idea is proven.
14. The opportunity is capable of returns in excess of twenty times your investment.
15. Your skills and experience fit with the business opportunity.
16. The venture is a place where you can leverage yourself.

17. It is not a labor-intensive business. Labor should be a small component of the total value.

18. It represents an honest business that is morally acceptable before the Lord.

Not only was Mr. V. a long-time friend in whom I could have full confidence, but the business opportunity stacked up well against my evaluation criteria. The company was founded in January 2000.

India-based New Company Beginnings

The search for a suitable location initially focused on New Delhi, the capital of India, and on Bangalore, the Silicon Valley of India. Ultimately, we chose Bombay because the landing point for fiber-optic cables to the United States is at the Prabhadevi Exchange in Bombay. In fact, God provided a building only a hundred yards from the fiber-optic termination point, allowing the best possible telecommunications connection. (Additional space is available all around, vacated by failed software companies, and the India-based company has been able to leverage its equipment by running connections across to other buildings.)

Chosen for its proximity to the fiber-optic network, in God's providence Bombay is one of the few cosmopolitan cities in India with an open religious attitude. As a result, the company started with Hindus, Muslims, and Christians among its twenty-five people.

Mr. V. lost the first order because the company was not adequately staffed. In June 2000, he found another source of funding which assumed a 50 percent ownership stake.

The company's initial focus was on collections. Their clients have found that calling on customers who are 30 to 60 days delinquent in their payment is very effective in their collection efforts. By outsourcing the work to India, these U.S. companies can save more than 50 percent in their costs. Furthermore, Indian call center staff are far more qualified than their American counterparts, and the prospects of retention are much higher. A McKinsey and Company study in February 2000 stating that India would become a destination for such centers added momentum and some legitimacy to the business.

The Lord's Hand at Work

Throughout this venture, we have seen clear examples of God's blessing. Over a forty-eight-hour period in February 2001, Mr. V. assembled a sales proposal of several hundred pages to a well-known U.S. company. Although this was the first time he had submitted such a document, the officials were so impressed by the completeness of his work that they invited him to their headquarters to discuss it further. They informed Mr. V. that they already had a committed partner valued at nearly $1 billion at the time. However, taken by Mr. V. personally, the officers signed a contract, even though the India-based company was very small. "Thanks to Jesus, they chose us," Mr. V. says.

One of my business school classmates, Pat Gross, is the chairman of American Management Systems. He also serves on a number of boards, one of which is a well-known U.S. credit card company. I invited him to have lunch with Mr. V. and me. Realizing that in my years of knowing Pat I had never asked this question, I asked him what his father had done. "He was a professor who taught energy and power management," was Pat's reply.

Pat went on to say that one of his father's students, an Indian, had become a dear friend many years before. Pat had since lost touch with him, but he did have a treasured sculpture of the Taj Mahal the friend had given to his father. It turned out that Mr. V. was the son of this long-lost friend. "Your father was so important to my dad," said Pat, "tell me what I can do to help you." He opened doors for us at his company, which has become a major source of business.

We hired an Indian Christian in the Bay Area who happened to be a friend of the founder of Providian, another major company. The founder agreed to take a look at this India-based new company, but backed off after discovering that the company worked for Providian's competitors. There would be no competitive advantage to the U.S. client. Eventually, God changed his heart, and our company has secured a significant amount of business from them.

What was a very small company in February 2001 quickly grew. The company was adding about 150 agents per month as it grew to 900 people by March 2002.

QUALITY EMPLOYEES

Part of this India-based new company's success stems from its commitment to quality service. That quality starts with its employees. Unlike similar companies in the United States, 99 percent of this company's employees are college graduates, and more than half have consumer or finance backgrounds. A full 77 percent have had formal computer training.

The company is able to attract some of the best and brightest to this work because it offers a very generous—for India—compensation rate of $350 per month. (An Indian can probably afford to hire a servant at that salary.) As

Henry Ford did with his assembly line workers, the company is committed to raising the economic level of its employees. We are also passionate about making our employees shareholders in the success of the company by offering bonuses and a stock option plan, both relatively novel concepts in this industry.

This India-based company has been extremely successful in hiring capable Christians from some of the local Christian schools. Their performance level has proven to be so high that Mr. V. no longer needs my encouragement on this score. About 80 percent of the company's employees are Christians. In a society where Christians rank socially below any of the Hindu castes, that is no small feat. They can have a hard time finding jobs in India, but Mr. V. has embraced them.

In times of rapid expansion, a couple of Christian groups that know exactly what we are seeking pre-screen candidates for us. Once hired, they receive rigorous training before they ever start interfacing with customers. They understand we are providing a top-flight service that appears to originate in the United States.

To accomplish this, we teach them to speak American English. Agents spend a lot of time learning the idiosyncrasies of the language spoken in North America, studying the accent and speed at which we speak and the way we say words. They also read American magazines and books, learning our phrases and idioms. Finally, the agents watch CNN for thirty minutes a day to understand the country and its nuances: what the weather is like, who is in the news, and what businesses interest people.

As a result, agents can converse with customers as if they were their neighbors. Our dedicated fiber-optic connections make the conversations seem like local calls, and customers assume the person with whom they are speaking is nearby. They rarely ask for the caller's location. We make intelligent and friendly calls. On a quest for quality, this India-based company has achieved better results than anyone in the industry—including U.S. competitors.

Most customers want this India-based company to have multiple locations to manage the risk. If an earthquake or power outage were to strike in one location, the other sites could pick up the slack. This business need gives us the opportunity to hire Christians from other cities. It will also allow us to build the church throughout other major cities in India.

THE CHALLENGE OF DISCIPLESHIP

However, the faith of many of the company's Christian employees is more cultural than personal. While raised in Christian homes, they often do not understand what they believe. They tell about the cultural challenges of being a Christian in India, but they are not well versed in Scripture.

Thus, we have a huge opportunity to provide Christian education and discipling. We want to make all of the Christian employees so aware of their faith and so in love with Jesus that (1) they know they are saved, (2) they share their faith with others, (3) they begin to participate in their communities as middle-class individuals, and (4) they begin to tithe in the church.

I have asked Christian leaders in Bombay to work with our employees, but few have responded. While there may be several reasons for this, perhaps the caste system poses the most serious challenge. Castes are part of the Indian culture and persist informally even in the church. Someone, such as a pastor, who is likely earning considerably less than these recent graduates, has a hard time instructing them. The education and discipleship of the Christian employees at this India-based company remains one of our most pressing challenges. Bringing in a European or American Christian who is considered above the system might be one way around the problem.

ANALYZING THE MODEL

Kingdom-based investing allows us to help the church in areas where it is a distinct minority. Employed and upwardly mobile Christians provide more resources to the local church for evangelism and expansion.

The beauty of this model is that we can replicate it over and over. Selling a successful venture at a significant profit results in more money for future ventures. We get multiple bites from the same cherry as we recycle the same assets to build multiple enterprises.

Business success will also likely ensure the continuance of the attitudes and policies that have brought the success, even after you leave. A thriving venture established on Christian values will not be upset. No one wants to mess with success.

Companies such as this India-based company and others described in this book rely on customers and business relationships in the developed world. God has placed many believers in positions of influence to open doors and make introductions. Let me be clear: I am not advocating special breaks for such ventures. Rather, I am asking that Christians be willing to give these companies a chance to demonstrate their capabilities. In the end, the business decision should rightfully be made on the value of the products and services of such companies.

Recently I asked a senior executive at an American credit card company to consider introducing this India-based company to relevant decision makers. One man, in a position of influence and acting in the interest of his organization, made a simple phone call that could produce business that will affect hundreds of Indian Christians. Many people can assist foreign businesses and further the church without leaving their offices or investing a cent.

God may call others to a deeper involvement. Kingdom-based investing requires people who are willing to use their energy and experience to come alongside entrepreneurs. It does not require relocation to restricted-access countries. It does involve exerting your influence as a trusted advisor and investor for the advancement of the kingdom of God.

Clearly there are the typical risks associated with venture capital, which must be managed by people who have some venture experience. Critical differences have to be overcome. It is not a model for all nations. Some countries are not yet ready for this investing and are more suited to microenterprise development. But where it does make sense, the payoff for the kingdom can be enormous.

19

Taking Faith to Work

John D. Beckett

Introduction

We business leaders are an intriguing lot. We pride ourselves on grasping the big picture, maintaining a long-term view, thinking "out of the box," innovating for competitive advantage, and leading where no one has gone. We put in long hours and devote ourselves to building higher, faster, better. We succeed in creating vast and visible empires. We are powerful. We are admired.

Yet I wonder. How often are we chasing the wind? Is it possible that many of us, for all of our leadership abilities, are missing the big picture, thinking short term, "in the box," innovating in wrong ways? Could it be that the brightest minds and most esteemed leaders in business are missing it—climbing a ladder that is leaning against the wrong wall?

More are asking such questions after September 11, 2001. In one hour, New York office space equivalent to the total office space in Houston crumbled into a million-ton heap. Those business leaders who escaped were, for the moment, driven by one overwhelming impulse—to be home with family. Later, workers entering the ghostly buildings surrounding the World Trade Center described the surreal images from the day time stopped—abandoned Palm Pilots, memos interrupted in mid-sentence, jettisoned purses, all buried under inches of dust. In an instant, priorities were turned upside down. What seemed to matter most mattered least.

Like the aftershocks following an earthquake, the fall of Enron, Arthur Andersen, Global Crossing, Worldcom, and other bastions of commerce have further shaken the business community and our economy. A renewed and needed focus on ethics and integrity has ensued. The combined impact of these external and internal threats prompt tough questions. Perhaps the toughest is whether we will simply shake off the dust and return to former ways—perhaps wrong ways—or begin looking at work and life in a larger dimension.

I want to examine four ideas, each challenging us to understand our work in a larger context. Put another way, they can help us reach toward God's perspective. I'll pose these topics as questions:

1. How can a biblical view of work and occupations lift our vision, helping us take a large and redemptive approach to workplace issues?
2. What are the primary cultural and practical barriers to integrating faith with our work?
3. What indicators do we see today for a radical transformation that brings the workplace into alignment with God's agenda?
4. What are today's best practices to help guide the business leader who wants to serve Christ, taking his or her work to the next level and beyond?

1. HOW A BIBLICAL VIEW CAN LIFT OUR VISION

When I was in my late twenties, I made a life-changing decision to follow Christ. I took this step of faith in part because of a succession of workplace challenges that convinced me that my own wits and wisdom were not sufficient. I realized I needed to release myself to God. I knew he was there, but until then, I had only a distant and impersonal relationship with him. God graciously came to me, responding beyond my greatest expectations to my desire for a closer, more intimate bond.

Initially, I found myself in two worlds—a faith world and a work world. As I became acquainted with other believers who were also businesspeople, I found this was the norm. In fact, some were quite emphatic, saying faith and business just don't mix.

Soon, new sets of problems made me aware that work and faith indeed needed to mix. For example, there was a serious disagreement between two of our senior managers. It had become personal, with one accusing the other of deception and defamation of character.

While stewing over this problem one evening, my eyes fell on a previously unopened book in my study by a popular Christian author. As I scanned through the book, I realized spiritual warfare was raging between these two, and that, as a believer, I had authority in Christ to do something about it. The author asked us to imagine ourselves as a policeman standing in a busy intersection directing traffic, but without a uniform. Obviously, no one would obey such a policeman. To get results, he would need to put on his uniform. Likewise, as Christians, we need to "put on Christ."

I wondered, "Could Christ have an interest in this tinderbox of workplace emotions?" I had nothing to lose, so I "put on Christ" and ordered the devil to stop his intrusion. The next day I was stunned to see a totally changed atmosphere between these two—as if nothing had ever happened.

This incident brought me to a new and vital understanding: God cares about the workplace as much as he cares about other areas of life. I concluded it was legitimate to bring Christ into every aspect of work—not just interpersonal difficulties but hiring decisions, promotions, finances, planning, even technical innovation. I began to see how often biblical lessons come from workplace settings. Here are a few examples:

- From the beginning, God linked man's creation with work: " . . . and there was no man to work the ground . . . then the Lord God formed the man . . ." (Gen. 2:5, 7)
- The earliest descendants of Adam were identified by their professions. Abel raised livestock and his brother Cain was a farmer. Tubal-Cain was a metalworker.
- "Heroes of the faith" at some point in their lives were schooled in "secular" vocations where character and competencies were forged. Moses and David were shepherds. Nehemiah and Daniel were servants to kings. Peter and Andrew were fishermen, Matthew a tax collector. Jesus probably spent well over a decade as a carpenter.
- Most of Jesus' illustrations drew on the imagery of workplace settings: A sower went out to sow; there once was an owner of a vineyard; the kingdom of God is like a merchant who . . .

The Bible is a remarkable handbook for practical issues in business and the professions. We can have confidence that God wants to be actively involved in our work. We can pray to him for wisdom and understanding.

The Middle East oil embargo presented a severe challenge to our company, and a group of our company's management decided to pray about it. No, God didn't end the embargo. But he gave us confidence to not retrench or lay people off, but to be bold, to move ahead aggressively, one day at a time, and look to him and his provision. Our competitors became very cautious and drew back, only to find that when things returned to normal, they had lost significant market share to us. Far beyond the advantage we gained was the lesson we learned of turning to the Lord for guidance in every situation.

This understanding has radically changed my view of work. It enables me to see work as a high calling, of the same caliber as a more direct form of ministry. I can seek the Holy Spirit's guidance on work issues. I can invite him into problems large and small. I can look for his larger purposes and bring them to life in our company. Here are some of the ways he helps us reflect his purposes:

- To provide a work culture that gives dignity and meaning to all who work with us, where each person is profoundly valued as an individual, and is able to express his or her God-given abilities to the fullest.
- To serve customers with genuine care and thoroughgoing excellence.
- To make integrity the standard, not just a byword. No compromise is justifiable that would contradict basic values such as honesty, truthfulness, or honoring commitments.
- To see our work as part of a larger plan, an aspect of God's divine intent. In this context we can look for his glory and grace to be extended—right in the workplace.

Yet this view of the workplace is in the minority today. There are barriers, some formidable, to a fuller integration of faith and work.

2. CULTURAL AND PRACTICAL BARRIERS

Jesus loved the marketplace. He seemed more at home amid crowds of every-day folks than with the religious people of his day. If we were to encounter him today, would he not be in machine shops and on constructions jobs, in hospitals and classrooms and laboratories? I like to think of him this way—widely informed, interested in ideas, with many skills, a keen listener, an avid learner, an engaging conversationalist with a winsome personality. He would be a delight to be with, willing to give counsel, eager to reveal truth and provide understanding.

That his presence is not more evident in the business world reflects our resistance more than his reluctance. Some of our primary problems are: (1) immature faith; (2) an unbiblical worldview; (3) a hostile environment; and (4) the wrong bottom line.

1. *Immature faith.* Here is the person who has had an encounter with Christ, but who has not sought to become mature. The Scriptures admonish us to not remain spiritual infants, but to grow in Christ.

In the early church, the pattern for growth was focused in four areas. Christians continued in the Word, in fellowship, in the breaking of bread, and in prayer (Acts 2:42). They didn't need doctorates in theology to become solid Christians, but they did need diligence. God has provided "all things that pertain to life and godliness" (2 Pet. 1:3). The Christian life is both possible and practical.

In my forty-plus years in the workplace, I've seen the profound impact of people who actively pursued Christian growth—and they weren't always in leadership. I think of Mary, who worked on our plant floor. Though a diabetic and no stranger to family difficulties, Mary reflected joy and a quiet confidence in God that was transparent and contagious. Her sturdy faith manifested itself in a ready smile, a desire to sacrifice for others, and a capacity to encourage that made her both respected and loved.

2. *Unbiblical worldview.* Ideas have consequences. One particularly damaging idea, pervasive in Western thought, holds that the world is constructed with higher and lower realms. Socrates, Plato, and Aristotle espoused this worldview, always placing the more "noble" pursuits, such as learning, the arts, and philosophy, in the upper realm. More common endeavors, such as vocations, the trades—generally things we call "work"—were placed in the lower realm, and thus regarded as secondary in importance.

Ideas die hard, and this one not only survived ancient Greece but today profoundly influences modern culture. Most Christians I know in business see their work as a lesser calling than more direct forms of ministry. Most church leaders share that view, and do little to change it.

But the view is not valid. Francis Schaeffer responded to the dichotomy thusly:

> It is not only that true spirituality covers all of life, but it covers all parts of the spectrum of life equally. In this sense there is nothing concerning reality that is not spiritual.[1]

The biblical view holds that there is no "higher" and "lower." The issue is whether an activity or even a vocation is in accordance with God's ways. The Bible says that everything honorable can be viewed as holy if undertaken "as for the Lord" (Col. 3:23).

Imagine how those in business, the arts, and the professions could be unleashed if church leadership would come to them and say, "How can we in the church mobilize to make you more effective in your ministry in the marketplace?"

3. *Hostile environment.* We are never free from the influences of our culture. Some people in government would like to clinically separate matters of faith from everyday work. Not long ago the Equal Employment Opportunities Commission sought to restrict religious expression in the workplace. Only determined opposition by large numbers of concerned Christians, myself included, kept that from happening.

Those who seek to regulate and legislate God out of the workplace need to realize that most who have integrated their beliefs into their work make better employees. Better employees make better, more honorable companies, which, in turn, strengthen the entire nation.

4. *Inordinate focus on the "bottom line."* Wall Street is driven by financial results and little else. Of course, profits matter, but how they're achieved also matters. I believe it's time to focus *above* the bottom line—not just on numbers, but on people.

Among our business's core values is the need for a "profound respect for the individual." We value people for who they are, not just for what they can do. The atmosphere of any business is altered when people—people in their entirety—are put first. This means not just their brains and backs, but their personalities, their emotions, and, yes, their faith.

If business leaders will encourage the expression of individuals' personal beliefs and values, they'll be amazed at the "buy in" and, in the long run, the bottom-line results. Here's the message they need to communicate: Bring your whole person to work. Don't leave a precious and vital part of you behind.

If we can move beyond these barriers—immaturity, incorrect worldview, hostile environment, and the wrong bottom line—we will see an astounding and delightful awakening of the spiritual dimension in our workplaces.

3. SIGNS OF TRANSFORMATION

What indicators do we see today for a radical transformation to bring the workplace into alignment with God's agenda? This phenomenon became apparent to me in the mid-90s in an unusual way.

ABC News, hearing that our company was seeking to follow biblical principles, asked to do a feature story on us for "World News Tonight with Peter Jennings." We were reluctant at first, mindful of how the media can put its own spin on a story. But we agreed, and let ABC probe deeply into our business policies and practices. The network boiled down fifteen hours of video into a four-minute news feature.

Shortly after the broadcast, ABC's correspondent, Peggy Wehmeyer, called me to say that the number of positive comments about the story exceeded those for any other in the history of the evening news. People were hungry for a workplace where they didn't have to set aside deeply held spiritual beliefs and values.

My first book, *Loving Monday: Succeeding in Business Without Selling Your Soul* (InterVarsity Press, 1998), summarized what we had learned in our work. The book has gone through multiple printings and translations. But more significantly, *Loving Monday* has brought me in contact with thousands of Christians who are having a broad impact in their work.

Consider the CEO Forum. The vision of Mac McQuiston at Focus on the Family is to link Christian executives of large companies, to help them grow in their faith, and to find practical ways to influence the culture of their organizations with biblically based approaches. This Forum has now become an important source of encouragement to well over 100 top execs, many heading Fortune 500 companies. They have come to realize that God put them in these leadership positions, not just to be good business leaders— which they are—but to extend God's kingdom in the spheres to which they have been called. Each quarter, the majority of these execs are "together" in small groups on conference calls—sharing challenges, victories, needs for prayer. Several have said these calls fuel faith and encouragement for days.

Have you noticed the increase in articles in magazines and newspapers dealing with this topic? In the last few years, cover articles on faith in the workplace have appeared in *Business Week, Industry Week,* and *Fortune*— as well as many national and regional newspapers. Books on the subject are now steadily rolling off the presses, with titles such as *Jesus—CEO, Believers in Business, God Is My CEO,* and *Spiritual Leadership.*

Organizations, both national and international, provide additional networks for business and professional people who want to integrate their spiritual and work worlds. The Christian Business Men's Committee's 15,000 members have fellowship meetings, small and large, to encourage one another in their faith walk. Likewise, the successes of the Fellowship of Companies for Christ, the International Christian Chamber of Commerce, and many other similar groups provide further evidence that people in the marketplace are seriously trying to know and follow God's will for their endeavors.

The best indicator of what God is doing in the workplace, however, lies not with what is most publicly visible, but with the quiet, hidden works of faith and grace that spring naturally from the business leader who knows he or she is ultimately accountable to God, and is approaching work with utmost diligence and a sense of stewardship.

After September 11, Steve Reinemund, president of PepsiCo, invited employees at the company's headquarters in Purchase, New York, to attend a prayer gathering. To his surprise and delight, nearly all the headquarters staff—numbering more than 1,000—attended.

Archie Dunham, chairman and CEO of Conoco, is intent on seeing sustainable and worthy corporate values etched into the minds and hearts of the company's 20,000 employees. Maybe this is one reason Conoco was recently named the best large company to work for in Houston.

Ralph Larsen, chairman and CEO of Johnson and Johnson, expects his company's leadership to respond ethically to the inevitable crises that befall a huge, diversified pharmaceutical firm. During the Tylenol poisoning scare of the 1980s, the company pulled its entire inventory off the market, replacing it in tamper-proof packaging. This expensive act is still a model for corporate responsibility.

The evidence is mounting. God wants to be vitally involved in our work, and more and more of his children are saying they want to be involved with him, on and off the job. But we're seeing only the beginning.

4. BEST PRACTICES

What are today's "best practices" to help guide the business leader who wants to serve Christ, taking his work to the next level and beyond? I wish I could draw upon a solid body of research examining the best of what is happening as believers seek to practically integrate faith and work. To my knowledge, that kind of study has yet to be done. But there is a need. When one organization polled leaders of marketplace ministries to determine areas of primary interest, heading the list was "seeing and hearing about models of ministry in the workplace." Tied for second was "hearing what God is doing in the workplace today from a diverse perspective."

When ABC News did the story on our company, the correspondent asked, "John, what makes your business different from those down the street?" I believe this was, and is, the right question. The challenge to be distinctive is presented in the final book of the Old Testament. To paraphrase Malachi 3:18: "You will see a difference between those who serve the Lord, and those who don't."

Lacking more exhaustive data, I will present an informal list of several ways I have seen serious Christians approach business leadership.

1. *The Lordship of Christ in all endeavors.* When Christ is clearly placed at the top, we will be drawn to him for wisdom, understanding, and guidance. The Scriptures become relevant and provide practical direction. As one

conference speaker said, "If you want to know how to run a business, get a Bible and read the book of Proverbs."

Prayer becomes a life-source. I've been part of a small prayer group, some members of whom have been meeting weekly for nearly thirty years. It has been a tremendous forum in which to bring business challenges before the Lord. We have often seen direct answers to these prayers.

2. *A clear sense of direction.* Statements of vision, mission, and values have become mainstream business thinking—although I continue to be surprised at significant businesses that haven't specifically identified where they are going or the guidelines by which they will get there.

For the Christian business leader, working through statements of direction with others in senior leadership provides a wonderful opportunity to think through the distinctives of the organization. A desire for a spiritual dimension in the company can be reflected in these statements. Then the leader must integrate those distinctives into and throughout the enterprise. This provides the opportunity to teach what is most important. This kind of proactive approach shapes corporate culture. The result is an organization defined by choice, not by chance.

3. *Putting people first.* A biblically based approach affirms each person's high value as someone created in the image and likeness of God. This view of the individual profoundly affects self-worth and the strength of relationships in an organization. People are no longer "resources." Strong marriages and families are important. Individual development is encouraged. This helps each person find his or her gifts and callings.

We need not be caught in a trade-off between people and profits. We can take a redemptive approach that highly values the person, even during times of staff reductions or terminations. Some of the greatest opportunities to pull together and strengthen a business come in difficult times. We recently needed to boost our production to meet surging customer demand, and we asked our salaried employees to work on our plant floor. Nearly all said yes, and had a great time working a partial night shift alongside hourly employees to help meet the challenge.

4. *Living by uncompromising integrity.* A biblical approach requires very high standards for personal conduct and adherence to core values. One simply cannot follow the Lord and cut corners, play loose with the truth, disregard commitments, or be sloppy in work habits.

For some this may seem like a straitjacket. "After all, this is how business is run . . ." But I am convinced that businesspeople can succeed without selling their souls. We have found that customers far prefer dependability, honesty, truth (even when it hurts), and a willingness to admit mistakes.

This commitment to integrity is perhaps the clearest indicator of the difference between those who serve the Lord and those who don't. Our business, though far from perfect, has prospered and grown for more than six decades and has become the market leader in our product lines by taking a principled approach. When customers comment on our business, they often note that we are honorable people who can be trusted to do the right thing. Millions of dollars spent in public relations campaigns could not achieve a more rewarding assessment.

5. Stewardship—seeing our work as a trust. The Scriptures reveal that even our very lives are not our own, but we have been purchased as a prized possession by Jesus Christ (1 Cor. 6:19-20). If this is so with each person, then it follows that those things entrusted to us also belong to him. All we have, all we are, our talents, our capabilities are entrusted and on loan to us from God.

An attitude of stewardship has helped carry me through some challenging times. One time our company faced a union organization drive. I concluded that the work atmosphere would be permanently altered if our employees belonged to a union, interposing a third party between the company's employees and leadership. Direct relationships and accountability would be gone. The Bible teaches us that a steward is a good shepherd, one who cares for the sheep. On the other hand, a hireling, a hired hand, doesn't have the same care for the sheep, and he runs away at trouble (John 10:11-13). I took that analogy into the workplace and orchestrated an aggressive campaign to protect the rights of employees who didn't want to belong to a union. In due course, the organizers withdrew and we were able to retain and strengthen the direct relationship with our employees. Many came forward later to thank us for not yielding to this external pressure.

As ever, businesses today face pressures from outside groups and agencies that run counter to biblical truth. Examples include pressure to remove religious expression in the workplace, pressure to require abortion coverage in health plans, and pressure to provide benefits for same-sex marriages. Leaders who are stewards will perceive the larger issues involved in such challenges and will mount a defense.

6. Serving, rather than being served. In the West, we still live in the "me generation." Business jargon even includes the acronym, WIFM, or, "What's in it for me?" In contrast, Jesus came to serve, not to be served.

Jesus' example has direct application to the workplace via the concept of the customer. Every organization, for-profit or nonprofit, has customers. Organizations exist to serve customers. Beyond the "external customers" that we sell to, there are "internal customers" in every organization: a machinist making parts for an assembler, a secretary making flight reservations or typing a letter. Supervisors can be servants. They don't have to bark out orders for the work crew. They can come alongside to help people be successful by obtaining needed resources, removing roadblocks, training, encouraging, rewarding—serving.

Jesus' example of servanthood turns the traditional management-structure pyramid upside down. The whole organization focuses outward, on the customer. To work, the concept of serving must be deeply ingrained. Instead of a WIFM attitude, true servants want to see others succeed, and ask, "How can I help you?" "How can I serve you?" The organization oriented this way is beautiful.

7. *Innovation and growth*. The seventh, though by no means the final, distinguishing mark of those who serve the Lord is the expectation of expanding horizons. The popular petition featured in *The Prayer of Jabez* has helped millions to see that God delights in increase. In 1 Chronicles 4:9-10, Jabez is encouraged to pray that God would bless him and enlarge his territory. God is able, for he presides over an open, expanding universe of perhaps more than 100 billion galaxies. Our world, but a tiny speck, continues to be favored by God's creative energy.

God is poised to open creative floodgates for those who eagerly look to him for new ideas, new inventions, new solutions. Time and again we have encountered problems in our business that seemed to defy solution, but which, after a season of prayer, have given way to innovative, even eloquent solutions.

Lost in current biographies of many creative pioneers is the degree to which they looked to God for their creative impulses. Isaac Newton, George Frideric Handel, Johann Sebastian Bach, George Washington, William Wilberforce, and Albert Einstein come to mind. Shunning the norm, they expected the God of all creation to impart truth and wisdom, and indeed he did.

CONCLUSION

God has an agenda for the workplace. There, vast numbers invest enormous amounts of hours and energy. Many are searching for meaning beyond the paycheck. They have a sense of calling, wanting to know that they can serve the Lord right where they are.

God wants workplaces around the world to be populated with his people and saturated with his Spirit. The deepest needs of people can be met within the context of work. We can hope that through the obedience of God's people, small flames of progress that are now flickering will be fanned into bright flames of radical transformation in the workplaces of America and the world.

By understanding God's desire for the workplace, by addressing barriers to belief and practical integration, by objectively assessing the mounting evidence that God is at work, and by seeking to be distinctive in ways that demonstrate his presence, we can more fully experience what the Lord wants to do among us.

Let us continue to pray that his kingdom come, his will be done here on earth, including in our places of work.

20

PREPARING THE NEXT GENERATION OF KINGDOM ENTREPRENEURS

Steven L. Rundle

The blunderings of sanctified amateurism, impervious to the need to get qualified in the area where one hopes to function, are neither good Christianity nor good business.

—J. I. PACKER[1]

Most Christians recognize without difficulty the link between professionalism and impact in the workplace. Some, however, apparently believe there are exceptions to this rule. Specifically, some mission-minded Christians believe that when large numbers of people are at risk of dying without *ever* hearing the gospel message, it is acceptable in those cases for missionaries to masquerade as ordinary working professionals if that is the only way to gain access to the people they are trying to reach. Professionalism cannot be faked, however, and even the most zealous missionaries are recognizing that amateurism and deception, no matter how sanctified, is not a good model of Christian discipleship. This raises the question, Who else should be sent to tell these people about Jesus, and what qualifications should they have?

Globalization is turning missions on its head. Everything we once thought we knew about missions and missionaries is being challenged—for example, the belief that time spent at work leaves less time for ministry. Globalization is forcing us to revisit such issues.

Several years ago I created a course at Biola University called "Tentmaking Entrepreneurship." Aside from the slightly different name, the course—now renamed "Business as Mission"—is a study of many of the same topics being discussed in this book. Specifically, it is an exploration of the unique opportunities and problems associated with using business as a vehicle for missions in parts of the world that have been resistant to conventional missionary strategies. While preparing for the course, I looked far and wide for curriculum ideas and academically rigorous materials, and found very little. With the exception of Ralph Miller's courses at Regent University, and some fine programs in economic development, little was being done to expose business students to, much less prepare them for, a business career in less-evangelized parts of the world.

I have wondered about this for quite some time, and have come up with three likely explanations. First, most Christian business programs promote, or at least claim to promote, the "integration of faith and work," and therefore believe they are already equipping people to be effective missionaries. At best I would say students are being prepared for "near-neighbor" outreach within the context of a career in corporate America. But since fewer schools even require such basics as chapel attendance or Bible courses, even this may be a stretch. Second, missions departments and schools of world mission are naturally reluctant to start offering their own specialized business courses. A few seminaries have begun offering programs in "marketplace theology," a promising trend given the anti-capitalism bias that apparently still exists in many seminaries according to a recent study by the Acton Institute.[2] But we should not mistake these for business programs. Third, creating a degree program that integrates course work in business and cross-cultural missions is not a trivial matter. Business schools, especially those that are professionally accredited, cannot simply create degree programs with a stroke of a pen, but face significant constraints that tend to make innovation a slow, costly, and risky process. Like any business, schools must carefully consider the issues of demand, cost, potential competition, and so on.

A fair question someone might ask, then, is, Given the wide variety of good business and missionary training programs already out there, why bother creating something new? To that I would reply that kingdom entrepreneurship is a unique, highly specialized mission strategy that merits its own specialized curriculum. It is certainly possible for people to acquire the necessary training on their own, but if we are serious about mobilizing and equipping an entire generation of kingdom entrepreneurs, a more structured approach is required. Universities and colleges can provide the structure, consistency, and credibility that is lacking when people fashion their own training program. The most effective programs will be innovative and flexible, with multiple tracks to account for different backgrounds and career goals.

Before discussing the preparation of kingdom entrepreneurs in more detail, I want to elaborate on my claim about the uniqueness of this mission strategy. Then I will address the question of the adequacy of our existing approaches to screening and training people for cross-cultural work. As we will see, serious questions are being raised by both business and mission scholars about the way people are selected and trained for overseas assignments. On the bright side, their research also sheds light on the characteristics one should look for in people before sending them abroad. Finally, I will suggest steps that can be taken to better prepare the next generation of kingdom entrepreneurs.

THE UNIQUENESS OF KINGDOM ENTREPRENEURSHIP

We are told that kingdom entrepreneurs are men and women who "do business holistically." Therefore, I will be working from the assumption that we are talking about businesspeople in the broader sense—those who enjoy the daily operation of a business (management, accounting, human resource management, and so on) as well as those who are gifted at taking an idea and overcoming countless obstacles to make a successful business out of it (entrepreneurs). As any venture capitalist will tell you, entrepreneurs do not always make good managers or accountants, nor do good managers or accountants necessarily make good entrepreneurs. We certainly want to mobilize entrepreneurs, but a discussion focusing entirely on entrepreneurs would be overly narrow at this stage.

There are a variety of business models contained in this book. Some involve physically relocating a business and a missions-minded management team to a less-evangelized country. Other models promote the idea of tapping into the resources and transactions of businesses in this country and redirecting them for the benefit of the kingdom. Evangelistic Commerce and the business development groups of the Business Professional Network fall into this category. What all the models have in common is a specific interest in bringing the love of Christ to people who know little about him. The qualifications and training required will differ slightly for each model. For the purposes of this essay I will be focusing mainly on those who physically relocate their business in the less-developed and less-evangelized parts of the world. Much of what I have to say, however, can be generalized without much trouble.

Probably most of those reading this book agree that a Christian-managed business can be an effective way to reach people for Christ. Agreeing on what we mean by "effective," however, might be a problem. Ultimately it depends on one's views about the relative importance of social and spiritual ministry. When all is said and done, is the spiritual impact ultimately the only thing that matters, or can someone be considered effective if they merely improve the quality of people's lives? I have argued elsewhere that the most effective kingdom entrepreneurs are those who recognize without difficulty the importance of a *successful* business to their mission strategy.[3] Among the world's poorest and most oppressed peoples, a financially successful business is not only a legitimate ministry in itself but can support other kinds of ministry. An unsuccessful business fails on both counts.

In an ideal world, all Christian business professionals would be reflecting Christ in their workplaces. To help facilitate this, there is now a significant movement—let's call it the "marketplace ministries" movement—that promotes the idea of integrating our faith and work. Under the marketplace ministries umbrella are Christian business associations, conferences, and countless books that aim to help people glorify Christ in the workplace. For those who are interested in surveying this extensive literature, InterVarsity Press has just published an annotated bibliography on this topic—a book about all the books![4] Kingdom entrepreneurship is a relatively narrow field within this broader field of marketplace ministries. What sets it apart is the intentionally evangelistic and cross-cultural nature of the business.

Let me elaborate on this, because I know it raises many questions. First, let me address the cross-cultural nature of kingdom entrepreneurship. There is no question that the spiritual need in corporate America is great. Evangelism and discipleship in places that already have a strong Christian presence is certainly a good thing, and fits squarely within the Great Commission. However, unlike the unsaved in America, there are many parts of the world where the probability is quite high that a person will live and die without encountering a *single follower* of Jesus Christ, at least one who is able to explain the gospel in a culturally meaningful way. The kingdom entrepreneur is one who, like Paul, feels compelled to take the gospel first and foremost to those places where Christ has never been preached (Rom. 15:20). They desire to meet human need in the spiritually and economically most impoverished places. God does not call every Christian to work in this context, nor should those who are not called be made to feel like second-class Christians.

Next let me address the evangelistic nature of kingdom entrepreneurship. There is no question that, especially among the world's poorest and most oppressed peoples, a successful and socially responsible business is a legitimate ministry in itself. One way the kingdom entrepreneur touches the lives of others is by providing good jobs, encouraging the professional growth of employees, improving social welfare, and so on. But the impact does not stop there. What distinguishes the kingdom entrepreneur is that he or she not only models Christian discipleship but goes out of the way to create opportunities to *tell others* about the motivation behind his or her behavior. David Befus of Latin America Mission has a colorful way of making this point. He says that if we simply make people healthier or more prosperous without telling them about the ultimate source of human satisfaction, all we've done is make them more comfortable for their journey to hell.

The reason I think this is worth emphasizing is because one gets the impression from some of the things written on the theology of marketplace ministry that almost anything qualifies as missions. The distinction between the Creation Mandate and the Great Commission is being blurred, if not by the authors, at least by some of their readers. The problem happens this way: God is a worker, he is creative, and his mission includes the restoration of his physical and spiritual creation. As his children, we are co-creators and participants in his global plan. Our work therefore has intrinsic value. It is also an act of worship, and ultimately we serve God when we serve others through our work. Work is, in that sense, a form of ministry. Where I part company, however, is when it is concluded that all Christians are missionaries simply because they work! On one hand I appreciate the theological defense for ordinary work, and the reminder that the Great Commission applies to all Christians, not just those in professional ministry. But the danger here is that when taken to its logical limit, it can have the opposite of the desired effect by actually *absolving* us of any direct responsibility to tell others about Christ. Fulfilling the Creation Mandate is not the same thing as fulfilling the Great Commission. If I fulfill the Great Commission simply by making widgets, then telling others about Christ is merely an elective add-on, something better left for the zealots. Kingdom entrepreneurs are not merely "silent witnesses," but people who are ready and able to verbally give an account for the hope that is within them. Again, they go out of their way to create opportunities for this.

It is useful to have a label that captures the distinctiveness of what we are talking about here. Is the label "Kingdom Entrepreneur" an improvement over alternative labels? Only time will tell. But if we want to prevent it from becoming an innocuous, meaningless term, we need to clearly and forcefully define it at the outset. So let me propose the following as a definition:

> Kingdom entrepreneurs are *authentic* businesspeople with proven competence in at least one area of business administration. They are spiritually gifted much like traditional missionaries, but are called and equipped to use those gifts in a business context. Kingdom entrepreneurs have a genuine desire to see communities of faith spring up in the spiritually driest places, and are willing to live and work in these places to make that happen. Rather than perceiving

the business as a distraction from their ministry, kingdom entrepreneurs recognize it as the necessary context for their incarnational outreach. The daily struggles—meeting deadlines, satisfying customers, being victimized by corruption—are precisely the things that enable kingdom entrepreneurs to model Christian discipleship on a daily basis.

THE EFFECTIVENESS OF EXISTING TRAINING PROGRAMS

How do we know if someone is qualified for such sacrificial and difficult work? What preparation should be required? What characteristics, if any, do the most effective kingdom entrepreneurs have in common? Unfortunately, little research has been done specifically on kingdom entrepreneurs. The well-known study by Don Hamilton is certainly helpful,[5] but he looked at tentmakers more generally, not kingdom entrepreneurs specifically. Therefore the list of qualifications he produced is not occupation-specific. Appropriate training and experience is expected, but never specifically addressed in his book.

Someone who did specifically raise this issue was Derek Christensen in his address to the Tentmakers International Exchange Congress in Melbourne, Australia. He pointed out that while extensive training for missionaries is accepted as given, even required in most cases, in the case of tentmakers we are more willing to "throw in a couple weekend courses, pack a correspondence course in their bag and wave their plane goodbye."[6] Similarly, Ted Ward recently lamented that "[a]ppropriate background, experience, education, and motivation for [the least-evangelized countries] are sadly lacking" not just among tentmakers, but among American missionaries more generally.[7]

In the most extensive study of missionary attrition ever done, the World Evangelical Fellowship (WEF) found that 5.1 percent of the mission force leaves the field every year, an annual loss of 7,650 career missionaries.[8] Missionaries who return prematurely often struggle with post-attrition feelings of guilt, failure, and in some cases a deterioration in physical and mental health.[9] In addition to the obvious human toll, the financial cost is staggering. In 1983, Stanley Linquist of the Link Care Foundation estimated the cost of attrition per missionary to be between $35,000 and $60,000.[10] Assuming these costs have kept up with inflation, the figures would now be between $63,000 and $107,000 per missionary. Approximately 38 percent of the missionary force are Americans. That means approximately 2,907 American missionaries return prematurely each year (38 percent of 7,650), at an annual cost of somewhere between $181 million and $310 million. If we include the roughly 1,836 missionaries from other "Old Sending Countries"—Australia, Canada, Denmark, Germany, and the United Kingdom—who return early, the figure climbs to between $295 million and $506 million per year. To put this into perspective, the most recent *World Christian Encyclopedia* reports that an estimated $15 billion per year is spent on foreign missions. Of that, $490 million goes to evangelistic ministry in World B contexts (those countries that are evangelized but not Christian), and only $54 million goes to outreach in World A contexts (countries that are non-evangelized and non-Christian).

Yet missionaries are not the only ones struggling in these countries. Business professionals, and in particular Americans, are having a tough go at it. Somewhere between 10 and 40 percent of American business professionals return early from extended assignments abroad because of job dissatisfaction or difficulties with adjusting to a foreign country.[11] An unknown additional number endure their jobs but suffer from burnout, low motivation, inadequate skills, marriage difficulties, alcoholism, and other problems.[12] The estimated annual cost to American businesses is between $2 and $2.5 billion.[13] So both the business and missions literatures have identified this as a significant problem.

What causes people to leave these countries prematurely? First we need to recognize that not all attrition is preventable. War, marriage, and death are just a few of the unpreventable things that can force a person to leave the field prematurely. Similarly, most businesses fail even under the best of conditions. Starting a business in a foreign, less-developed country is infinitely more difficult. Nevertheless, deficiencies in cultural preparedness and training are widely considered to be a major cause of the problems among both missionaries and multinational corporations.[14]

The silver lining of the attrition research is the information it gives about successful expatriates. One thing is clear: cross-cultural knowledge alone is not a good predictor of success. Knowledge must be accompanied by a *satisfaction* with other cultures,[15] or, as Tetsunao Yamamori puts it, "a sense of wonder: a genuine desire to be immersed in a complex foreign culture and to learn as much as possible about it."[16] Black and Gregersen found that the American business professionals who are *least* likely to return early share the following characteristics.[17] They are people who:

- do not give up after initial embarrassment or failure in a cross-cultural environment;
- are willing to venture out into the local community, establish social ties, experiment with the different foods, games, and so on;

- have social ties with foreigners living in the U.S.

What a unique opportunity this presents Christian colleges! Many companies and mission agencies are putting this information to good use. Nearly half of all major U.S. companies, for example, now give some cross-cultural training to their employees before transferring them overseas, up from about 10 percent a decade ago.[18] More companies are using as one of their screens a demonstrated ability to handle cross-cultural situations. The strongest candidates have already worked or lived abroad or at the very least have traveled extensively. The most ideal candidate can also speak a foreign language.[19]

SCREENING AND SELECTING KINGDOM ENTREPRENEURS

Let me pull all of this together. Kingdom entrepreneurs are genuine business professionals who respond to God's call to live and work among those who have had little or no opportunity to hear the gospel. They have a sincere interest in other peoples and other ways of life. They are patient, flexible, and able to get by without the comforts of suburban America. As far as spiritual qualifications go, Hamilton's study found that the most effective ones are those who:

- actively share their faith at home as well as abroad;
- had prior experience leading evangelistic Bible studies at home;
- were responding to God's call to do the same thing cross-culturally, specifically in a workplace context; and
- had a strong relationship with their home church.

Most sending churches and mission agencies now look for these characteristics in their tentmaker candidates. The interesting follow-up question then is: Has the track record improved? If not, why not? I believe the reason we are still having problems is not because of a lack of screening, but rather because greater weight is given to things that are less critical to success, and less weight to those that are more critical. For example, I would argue that in the screening and selection process there is a natural bias in favor of those with formal Bible training, even though it is not listed above. The screening process is also too forgiving of deficiencies in the area of practical work experience. Take a look at the typical class of tentmaker candidates that passes through the established mission agencies and you will see what I mean. More often than not their primary work experience has been as a youth pastor, involvement in campus ministries, and the like. Not only do they have little experience in ordinary jobs, but frankly they don't care much about such jobs either, except for their usefulness as an entry strategy.

(By the way, it never fails to surprise me, and disturb me, when people ask for advice about what course [yes, usually singular] they can take, seminar they can attend, or book they can read that will teach them enough to pass themselves off as a business professional, because they will soon be leaving for some God-forsaken place as a supposedly Pauline-style "tentmaker." First of all, the less-developed, less-evangelized countries of the world are no place to send people for Business 101. Second, how easily some people overlook the fact that Paul was no amateur. How foolish it is to think that professional missionaries disguising themselves as ordinary workers can credibly do what Paul did, which was to model lay missions.)

Patrick Lai's forthcoming update and extension of Hamilton's study is likely to raise serious questions about this selection bias.[20] The preliminary results of his research indicate that the relationship between formal Bible training and tentmaker effectiveness is statistically insignificant. What does this mean? Should we quit encouraging people to take Bible classes? No, that is not what this research is telling us. What it does say is that a certificate or degree from a Bible school or seminary is not a good predictor of who will or will not make a good tentmaker. Frontiers president Rick Love apparently agrees. In a recent fundraising letter, he observed that "the skills involved in leading groups of believers in these locations *are not readily learned in Bible school or seminary*"[21] (emphasis added).

How can this be? How can something so absolutely central to our way of preparing missionaries not make for a more effective planter and discipler of churches? I would suggest the reason is that what initially draws people to Christ is not the Christian doctrines *per se* but the attractiveness of the lives of his followers. Rodney Stark, a sociologist who has spent the better part of his career studying how conversion works, makes the same point in his book *The Rise of Christianity*. He has found that at the time of conversion—whether it be to Christianity, Mormonism, the Unification Church, or whatever—most people understand very little about the doctrines. People are attracted by the communities, the relationships, that exist between the disciples.[22]

Don't get me wrong. I believe that all Christians in the marketplace should have a healthy understanding of the Bible and of Christian doctrines. But how foolish we have been to think that a degree in theology will necessarily make a person more effective in reaching people for Christ! By intellectualizing and professionalizing missions, we have effectively disarmed and disabled a great many ordinary Christians. Every study of church growth reveals that the gospel always spreads most quickly and naturally when the lay people are the primary agents of missions. For example, in Michael Green's study of evangelism in the early church, he observes that:

> Christianity was from its inception a lay movement, and so it continued for a remarkably long time. In a sense, the apostles inevitably became "professionals." But as early as Acts 8 we find that it is not the apostles but the "amateur" missionaries . . . who took the gospel with them wherever they went. . . . They went everywhere gossiping the gospel; they did it naturally, enthusiastically, and with the conviction of those who are not paid to say that sort of thing. Consequently, they were taken seriously, and the movement spread, notably among the lower classes.[23]

Does this mean then that all Christians are qualified to be kingdom entrepreneurs? No, that would be committing the opposite error of amateurism. Spiritual maturity, knowledge of Scripture, and the ability to share one's faith cross-culturally are still critically important, not to mention the appropriate professional training and experience.

THE TRAINING OF KINGDOM ENTREPRENEURS

How should someone prepare for service as a kingdom entrepreneur? Let me answer this by first sharing a story from William Danker's excellent book *Profit for the Lord*.[24] In 1752 the Moravians sent their first missionary team to the Eskimos of Labrador. Being unfamiliar with the political and cultural cross-currents of the region, the team leader made an innocent mistake that cost the lives of himself and six of his companions. The Moravians never gave up on this goal, however, and after *nineteen years* of additional preparation they returned and established a presence that lasted 170 years. When my students and I discuss this case in class, it never fails to stimulate a lively discussion about preparation and training in a rapidly changing and increasingly impatient society. On one hand, the need is great and the workers are few, so it is tempting to streamline the process as much as possible. On the other hand, as Patrick Lai has pointed out, the stakes are too high to be making too many mistakes at the outset.[25] Not only are people's lives and souls literally at risk, but in a business context substantial financial investments are at stake as well.

I see several lessons that can be learned from the Moravian experience. First, crossing cultures and building meaningful relationships require considerable preparation. Just because a person is effective in a monocultural context does not mean they will make good cross-cultural witnesses. Second, preparation is a life-long process. Along the way we may find it useful to earn a degree or two, but the learning process never ends. Moreover, in the individualized curriculum that God has prepared for each one of us, it may not always be obvious what skills are being developed. It does not disturb me if my students do not immediately go overseas. In fact, it would probably disturb me more if they did. The business degree is but one of many tools needed to be effective kingdom entrepreneurs. Third, an effective training program will strike a proper balance between formal education, on-the-job training, and other life experience. By "formal education" I do not mean an inflexible one-size-fits-all curriculum. An effective training program will integrate study-abroad components (preferably in a non-Western country), internships, seminars, and less formal methods of instruction, such as mentoring, apprenticeships, and so on. Excellent examples of U.S.-based internships designed to help a person with his or her cross-cultural ministry skills are the Livingstone Internship (Frontiers) and the Los Angeles Multicultural Internship (Paraclete). The internship by Evangelistic Commerce (EC) and the seminars by the Center for Entrepreneurship and Economic Development (CEED) are excellent examples of controlled, field-based programs that can be used to supplement the classroom teaching. Relationships could also be formed between schools and individual businesses. Not only would such a relationship allow students to rub shoulders with kingdom entrepreneurs, but it could free up the kingdom entrepreneurs from time to time for other forms of outreach and ministry.

What are some of the practical issues? At Biola the easiest first step was to create a single course, a survey course that is open to all majors. Single, elective courses can be created fairly easily so long as they fit within the overall mission of the school. I have included an abbreviated version of the course syllabus as an appendix. Because most of the students are business majors with little background in the topic of missions, unreached peoples, and so on, I spend the first few weeks going over these basic topics. Then we look at the various ways in which a for-profit business can impact the world for Christ. Later we examine some specific issues such as raising capital, business plan development, ethics, and so on, while always mindful to keep it accessible to the non-business majors. There is a group project that requires a combination of social, political, religious, and economic research. The first time I taught the course I required a business plan, but that puts the non-business students at an unfair disadvantage, and I believe this may have discouraged some from taking the course. If and when we develop this into a full degree program, I anticipate there will be follow-up courses that go into greater depth in each of these areas, as well as overseas components, internships, and so on.

A full degree program is more challenging, however, because in the process of creating a blend of business and missions courses, the marketability of the degree can be compromised. In the end you may end up graduating students who are only marginally qualified in either area. At the graduate level the problem becomes even more difficult because you have fewer units to work with. We ran into this problem at Biola with a Master of Arts degree that combined coursework in intercultural studies and international business. It was offered through the School of Intercultural Studies, had few if any entry standards, and attracted mainly students who could not get admitted into a regular MBA program. In the end the business faculty essentially walked away from the program and created their own graduate degree with stiffer entry requirements.

For professionally accredited schools of business, like ours at Biola, there are other constraints that I will not go into here. Suffice it to say that there are significant issues that must be carefully thought through before any new degree programs can be launched. For this reason, the path of least resistance for many schools is probably to create joint degree programs. This allows each degree-awarding school to stick to its primary area of specialty, which would result in a stronger, more complete program. The downside of course is the extra time required.

One final issue that might become a problem down the road is the matter of "open enrollment." That is, does the school admit non-Christians? Biola is one of the few remaining Christian schools that does not knowingly admit non-Christians. Generally speaking, I like the idea of open enrollment, but it raises some potential problems in the case of a program in kingdom entrepreneurship. An open university cannot exclude non-Christian students from certain classes. Or rather, this is legally untested territory. Such a school might be obliged to accept, say, a fundamentalist Muslim into the program. How many of you would be willing to create partnerships and internships with me if I could not guarantee the students would even be Christian? Kingdom entrepreneurs who are even remotely concerned about security would be reluctant to associate with such a program. Maybe I am being silly for even thinking a non-Christian would try to enroll in such a program. But in an age when people willingly blow themselves up for the sake of their religion, how can we be sure they would not also be willing to pay the price of tuition and a few years in school? Few schools have the resources to pursue such a court battle.

CONCLUDING THOUGHTS

Kingdom entrepreneurship is a missionary strategy that combines the skills of a businessperson and a missionary. It is more than an entry strategy for missionaries, and involves more than simply "integrating faith and work." Failure to recognize the uniqueness of the strategy, and the preparation required, is the single biggest reason why the track record for Kingdom entrepreneurs is not better than it is. Failure to recognize the uniqueness of this mission strategy is also the reason why Christian universities have not responded sooner. The good news is that many of the resources necessary to create such a program are already in place and merely have to be packaged in a way that makes sense.

In closing, let me make one more appeal. Creating effective training programs cannot happen in a vacuum. We need to know what works and what does not work. Since there has been so little research done in kingdom entrepreneurship, I have pulled together some threads from other closely related disciplines. That may be fine for getting us started, but there is a desperate need for more research specifically on kingdom entrepreneurs. For example, do kingdom entrepreneurs return prematurely more or less frequently than other expatriates? To what degree do the problems of ineffectiveness and attrition reflect a mismatch between spiritual gifts and the type of business? What are the benchmarks of effective kingdom entrepreneurship? What is the relationship, if any, between type of business, socioeconomic variables, and effectiveness? The field of kingdom entrepreneurship is an extremely rich one for academic research. My hope is that this book will inspire graduate students and faculty alike to start looking more closely at this as a source for future research ideas.

APPENDIX TO CHAPTER 20

SYLLABUS FOR BUSINESS 450: "BUSINESS AS MISSION"

FALL 2001, BIOLA UNIVERSITY, SCHOOL OF BUSINESS

Motivation for this Course: The end of colonialism in the 1960s, together with the collapse of the Soviet Union in the late 1980s, has rekindled a spirit of national and cultural pride. Most countries, particularly the newly liberated ones, are now fiercely protective of their political and economic independence and deeply suspicious of outsiders. One casualty of this heightened nationalism is the missionary visa. These countries are not interested, frankly, in allowing foreigners into the country for the sole purpose of converting others to their religion. On the other hand, these same countries encourage, and are in fact aggressively seeking entrepreneurship and capital from abroad.

The initial response by many missionaries to this new era of missions has been to disguise themselves as business professionals and use business mainly as an "entry strategy." The object has been to do the least amount of "work" possible, only enough to appear legitimate (at least in their own eyes—few others are fooled so easily). However, while there have been some successes, the results have been generally mixed, and many Christians now recognize that this "ends justify the means" approach to ministry is dishonest and a poor witness. When properly perceived, a job-creating, for-profit business can be a tremendously effective vehicle for ministry. In addition to meeting specific economic and social needs, it creates its own context, and resources, for spiritual ministry. A legitimate, profitable business can also provide long-term access to people who are difficult to reach by other, more traditional mission strategies.

The general themes covered in this course include: (1) the theologies of mission, business, and the integration of the two, (2) practical issues related to using business as a vehicle for cross-cultural missions, and (3) specific for-profit business models and case studies. The purpose of the course is to give the student a better understanding of the economic, cultural, and missiological issues involved in using business in missions, and an appreciation of the strengths and weaknesses of the various business models being used.

Required Textbooks:

Bryant Myers, *Walking with the Poor: Principles and Practices of Tranformational Development* (Maryknoll, N.Y.: Orbis, 1999).

R. Paul Stevens, *The Other Six Days: Vocation, Work, and Ministry in Biblical Perspective* (Grand Rapids, Mich.: Eerdmans, 1999).

Annual Editions: Entrepreneurship 01/02, 3rd edn. (Guilford, Conn.: McGraw-Hill/Dushkin, 2001).

Business as Mission Coursepack.

Coursework, Grading, and Deadlines: The course is comprised of both individual and group activities. Individually, the student will be expected to keep up with the required readings and contribute to the class discussion. Class preparation and participation will account for 30 percent of the course grade. Another 30 percent will be based on the (approximately) four quizzes that will be drawn from the material covered in the readings and class discussions. The balance of your grade will be based on two group activities. In one group you will be asked to be the discussion leaders for one class period. This assignment will be worth 10 percent of your grade. The remaining 30 percent of your grade will be based on a group research project and end-of-semester presentation that will be described in more detail in a separate handout.

Approximate Schedule of Topics and Readings: Below each date and topic is a list of the required readings for that day. The schedule is an approximation of the order in which the topics will be covered. Since some of the guest speakers have not yet been able to commit to an exact date, a certain amount of grace and flexibility will be required from the students throughout the semester.

Monday, Aug. 27: Introduction to the Course

Wednesday, Aug. 29: Setting the Context

> Steve Rundle and Tom Steffen, *Business as Mission: Globalization and the Emerging Role of Great Commission Companies* (Downers Grove, Ill.: InterVarsity Press, forthcoming), chapter 1.

Monday, Sept. 3: No Class—Labor Day

Wednesday, Sept. 5: Guest Lecture (Visiting Practitioner): The Opportunities and Pitfalls of Combining Business and Missions

Monday, Sept. 10: The Mandate for Global Mission, Part I

> Ralph Winter, "The New Macedonia: A Revolutionary New Era in Mission Begins," in R. D. Winter and S. C. Hawthorne, eds., *Perspectives on the World Christian Movement,* 3rd edn. (Pasadena, Calif.: William Carey Library, 1999), 339-353.

> Ralph Winter and Bruce Koch, "Finishing the Task: The Unreached Peoples Challenge," in R. D. Winter and S. C. Hawthorne, eds., *Perspectives on the World Christian Movement,* 3rd edn. (Pasadena, Calif.: William Carey Library, 1999), 509-524.

Wednesday, Sept. 12: The Mandate for Global Mission, Part II

> Myers, *Walking with the Poor,* chapters 1 and 2

Lesslie Newbigin, *The Gospel in a Pluralist Society* (Grand Rapids, Mich.: Eerdmans, 1989), 116-127.

Don Richardson, "Do Missionaries Destroy Cultures?" in R. D. Winter and S. C. Hawthorne (eds.), *Perspectives on the World Christian Movement,* 3rd edn. (Pasadena, Calif.: William Carey Library, 1999), 460-468.

Monday, Sept. 17: Guest Lecture (Missions Professor): The Current Status of World Mission

Tetsunao Yamamori, *God's New Envoys: A Bold Strategy for Penetrating "Closed Countries"* (Portland, Ore.: Multnomah, 1987), chapters 1 and 2.

Wednesday, Sept. 19: The Biblical Basis for Business as Mission

Michael McLoughlin, "Back to the Future of Missions: The Case for Marketplace Ministry," *Vocatio* (December 2000): 1-6.

Ruth E. Siemens, "Why Did Paul Make Tents? A Biblical Basis for Tentmaking," GO Paper A-1 (1996).

Monday, Sept. 24: Why the Interest in Holistic Approaches to World Mission?

David Hesselgrave, "Redefining Holism," *Evangelical Missions Quarterly* (1999): 278-284.

Bryant Myers, "Another Look at 'Holistic Mission,'" *Evangelical Missions Quarterly* (1999): 285-287.

Wednesday, Sept. 26: Perspectives on Great Commission Companies

Dwight Nordstrom and Jim Nielsen, "How Business Is Integral to Tentmaking," *International Journal of Frontier Missions* (January/March 1998): 15-18.

Steven Rundle, "Ministry, Profit and the Schizophrenic Tentmaker," *Evangelical Missions Quarterly* (July 2000): 292-300.

Monday, Oct. 1: Evaluating an Idea for a Great Commission Company

> Amar Bhide, "The Questions Every Entrepreneur Must Answer," *Harvard Business Review* (November/December 1996).

> Patrick Lai, "Starting a Business in a Restricted Access Nation," *International Journal of Frontier Missions* (January/March 1998): 41-46.

> *Annual Editions,* articles 4, 10, 11, and 34.

Wednesday, Oct. 3: The Historical Precedence for Business as Mission, Part I

> William Danker, *Profit for the Lord* (Grand Rapids, Mich.: Eerdmans, 1971), chapters 2-5.

Monday, Oct. 8: Historical Precedence, Part II

> William Danker, *Profit for the Lord* (Grand Rapids, Mich.: Eerdmans, 1971), chapters 6-10.

Wednesday, Oct. 10: The Theology of Work, Part I

> Stevens, *The Other Six Days,* chapters 2 and 3.

> Doug Sherman and William Hendricks, *Your Work Matters to God* (Colorado Springs: NavPress, 1987), 43-86.

Monday, Oct. 15: Guest Lecture (Seminary Professor): Theology of Work, Part II

> Stevens, *The Other Six Days,* chapters 4-6.

Wednesday, Oct. 17: No Class—Torey Conference

Monday, Oct. 22: Overview of Great Commission Business Models

Wednesday, Oct. 24: Case Study: Creating Businesses at Home that Advance the Kingdom Abroad

Monday, Oct. 29: Developing a Business Plan

Annual Editions, articles 22 and 23

Wednesday, Oct. 31: Preparing for a Business-Missions Career Abroad

Steven Rundle, "The Christian Business Scholar and the Great Commission: A Proposal for Expanding the Agenda," *Journal of Biblical Integration in Business* (Fall 2000): 94-108.

Monday, Nov. 5: Guest Lecture (Intercultural Studies Professor): Cross-cultural Communications and Adjustment

Eloise Meneses and John Stapleford, "Defeating the Baals: Balanced Christian Living in Different Cultural Systems," *Christian Scholar's Review* (Fall 2000): 83-106.

Judy Lingenfelter, "Why Do We Argue Over How to Help the Poor?" *Missiology* (April 1998): 155-166.

Paul Heibert, "Cultural Differences and the Communication of the Gospel," in R. D. Winter and S. C. Hawthorne, eds., *Perspectives on the World Christian Movement,* 3rd edn. (Pasadena, Calif.: William Carey Library, 1999), 373-383.

Charles Kraft, "Culture, Worldview and Contextualization," in R. D. Winter and S. C. Hawthorne, eds., *Perspectives on the World Christian Movement,* 3rd edn. (Pasadena, Calif.: William Carey Library, 1999), 384-391.

Wednesday, Nov. 7: Toward a Theology of Corporate Social Responsibility

Dennis Bakke, "Values Don't Work in Business," in M. Stackhouse et. al., eds., *On Moral Business: Classical and Contemporary Resources for Ethics in Economic Life* (Grand Rapids, Mich.: Eerdmans, 1995), 713-717.

Michael Novak, "Seven Corporate Responsibilities," in John Houck and Oliver Williams, eds., *Is the Good Corporation Dead? Social*

Responsibility in a Global Economy (Lanham, Md.: Rowman and Littlefield, 1996), 189-202.

Monday, Nov. 12: The Integrity of Business as Mission

Ruth E. Siemens, "Tentmaker Ethics: When Is It Right to Lie?" GO Paper A-4 (1997).

Robert Morris, "Shrewd Yet Innocent: Thoughts on Tentmaking Integrity," *International Journal of Frontier Missions* (1998): 5-8.

Michael Roemmele, "Cloak-and-Dagger Tentmakers Need Not Apply," *Evangelical Missions Quarterly* (1993): 164-169.

Gary Taylor, "Don't Call Me a Tentmaker," *International Journal of Frontier Missions* (January/March 1998): 23-26.

Wednesday, Nov. 14: International Business Ethics, Part I

Steven Falkiner, "Bribery: Where Are the Lines?" *Evangelical Missions Quarterly* (1999): 22-29.

Gregory Nichols, "A Case for Bribery: Giving Versus Taking," *Evangelical Missions Quarterly* (1999): 30-33.

Cathy Thornberg, "Bribery: Coming to Terms with a Moral Dilemma," *Evangelical Missions Quarterly* (1999): 34-37.

Monday, Nov. 19: Guest Lecture (Business Ethics Professor): Business Ethics in a Global Economy, Part II

Norman Bowie, "Business Ethics and Cultural Relativism," in Scott Rae and Kenman Wong, *Beyond Integrity: A Judeo-Christian Approach to Business Ethics* (Grand Rapids, Mich.: Zondervan, 1996), 90-97.

Thomas Donaldson, "Multinational Decision-Making: Reconciling International Norms," in Scott Rae and Kenman Wong, *Beyond Integrity: A Judeo-Christian Approach to Business Ethics* (Grand Rapids, Mich.: Zondervan, 1996), 97-104.

Scott Rae and Kenman Wong, "Cases," in Scott Rae and Kenman Wong, *Beyond Integrity: A Judeo-Christian Approach to Business Ethics* (Grand Rapids, Mich.: Zondervan, 1996), 105-108.

Scott Rae and Kenman Wong, "Commentary," in Scott Rae and Kenman Wong, *Beyond Integrity: A Judeo-Christian Approach to Business Ethics* (Grand Rapids, Mich.: Zondervan, 1996), 109-116.

Wednesday, Nov. 21: Raising Capital for a Kingdom Company

Mitchell Berlin, "That Thing Venture Capitalists Do," *Business Review* (January/February 1998): 15-26.

James Stancill, "How Much Money Does Your New Venture Need?" *Harvard Business Review* (May/June 1986).

Amar Bhide, "Bootstrap Finance: The Art of Start-ups," *Harvard Business Review* (November/December 1992).

Monday, Nov. 26: The Importance of Mentors and Accountability

Annual Editions, article 14.

Greg Livingstone, *Planting Churches in Muslim Cities: A Team Approach* (Grand Rapids, Mich.: Baker, 1993), 95-115.

Howard Norrish, "Lone Ranger: Yes or No?" *Evangelical Missions Quarterly* (1996): 6-14.

J. Christy Wilson, Jr., "Successful Tentmaking Depends on Mission Agencies," *International Journal of Frontier Missions* (1997): 141-143.

Wednesday, Nov. 28: Practical Problems with Business in Missions

Monday, Dec. 3: Presentation of Group Projects

Wednesday, Dec. 5: Presentation of Group Projects

PART THREE

CONCLUSION

21

REVIEW OF THE CASE STUDIES FROM A BUSINESS PERSPECTIVE

Thuan-seng Tan

The eleven case studies in this volume are but a very small sampling of the many Great Commission businesses that have sprung up over the past two decades, seemingly spontaneously. We serve a wonderfully creative God. As we study the relatively recent resurgence of business as a Great Commission instrument, we need to remember that our rules do not limit God. Consequently, our review of these case studies from a business perspective does not invalidate the following chapter, which analyzes them strictly from a kingdom standpoint. God can make fruitful what may seem illogical according to accepted business principles.

At the outset, it may be useful to differentiate between "tent-making" as a craft skill, which provided the apostle Paul with a source of itinerant income, and tentmaking as a business, such as that owned by Priscilla and Aquila, who used it effectively for Great Commission objectives. In current missiology, the term "tentmaker" usually refers to someone who is an employee rather than a business owner. In this chapter, I am focusing only on Great Commission businesses. This may be helpful when reviewing some of the case studies (such as in chapters 2, 4, 5, 7, 9, and 11), where the lines are somewhat blurred.

The well-documented challenges facing tentmakers usually involve balancing secular employment with evangelistic efforts. The Great Commission entrepreneur also faces acute challenges in balancing work and missions objectives. In addition, he or she has to contend with many other pressing concerns, such as finding capital, securing licenses, managing cash flow and employees, developing products, finding markets, meeting competition, securing foreign exchange, and so on.

Starting about two centuries ago, Moravian missionaries, Swiss missionaries under the Basel Trading Society, and, later, China Inland Mission workers from Great Britain successfully adopted both tentmaking and Great Commission business models alongside traditional missions. The Moravians gave their tentmakers and Great Commission entrepreneurs full missionary status. Those who went out with a craft or Great Commission business were often more successful in impacting target communities, despite the time they spent in "secular" activities.

The case studies in this book are all kingdom businesses on the mission field. However, there is also a growing number of kingdom businesses based in sending nations, initiated and owned by Christian entrepreneurs who are committed to using the resources generated in economically advanced home countries to start up and support projects in the 10/40 Window.

BRIGHT ARROWS

Bright Arrows is one such holistic kingdom business. Incorporated in 1991, its name is inspired by Isaiah 49:2:

> He made my mouth like a sharp sword;
>   in the shadow of his hand he hid me;
> he made me a polished arrow;
>   in his quiver he hid me away.

The "Bow," or sending, operations are in Singapore and Malaysia. They generate funds for investment into "Arrow" projects in 10/40 Window nations, including Cambodia, the People's Republic of China, and Malaysia. In addition to funds, the Bow operations also provide prayer and continuing professional support in planning, information technology, accounting, and export marketing, as well as coordination of missions training and oversight. Bright Arrows Cambodia was incorporated from the outset as an investment company and now provides employment for some fifteen expatriate professionals sent from six countries.

There has also been a merging of Bow and Arrow opportunities and functions in two significant ways:

1. In recent years, we have seen large population movements from 10/40 Window countries to sending nations. This redefines to some extent the mission field, which today may be in our immediate neighborhood.
2. We rejoice that some of our Bows have heeded the call to become Arrows and some of the very best consultants are now deployed on the front line.

COMPLEX CHALLENGES

Starting and sustaining a business in a foreign country, with its different political, legal, commercial, and cultural practices, is extremely complex and challenging. There is a common thread of struggles in nearly all the case studies. Usually underfunded, inadequately prepared to cope with the local bureaucracy and corrupt officials, and with limited market knowledge, Great Commission entrepreneurs and businesses often go through a baptism of fire. We see this particularly in case studies 2, 5, 6, 9, and 10.

In chapter 4, Abiir William touches on the scale of a Great Commission business. She correctly recommends that there is wisdom in starting small. Apart from the reality that seed capital is often hard to come by, this will allow time to build a solid foundation for your business. It is essential to find out whom you can trust and whom you would do well to avoid. Coming from a faster paced, industrialized society, it is easy to impatiently want to operate on a larger scale. That may be feasible only if you can find a missionary who is established in the local scene, or a trustworthy local believer. Either one could help shorten the learning curve. Another compelling reason to start small is to keep below the radar of the local mafia and corrupt officials.

The downside of starting small is that with most business activities, there is an optimum scale. If you do not attain such an economy of scale fairly quickly, the business may not be viable. However, some businesses, such as consulting, are not dependent on size. In consulting, you are essentially selling expertise. In trading, you are leveraging your network of international contacts. In education or professional translation, you may bring the advantage of overseas expertise and accreditation. These businesses, however, do not usually generate significant employment, which is often a high priority if you want to provide the kind of discipling environment illustrated in nearly all of the case studies. For these kinds of environments, labor-intensive production activities are often essential.

As national laws permit, you could set up several viable alternatives to manufacturing. You could start a chain of small food outlets catering as a domestic franchise system. Or you could launch a direct-selling organization to distribute basic commodities, such as milk powder, cooking oil, spices, detergents, and so on. Such projects can provide considerable employment while bringing the ministry team in close contact with the community. Integrated with a well-organized microcredit program, such projects can also introduce many small entrepreneurs to the free-enterprise system.

CORRUPTION

Many Great Commission businesses quickly run into corruption, a spiritual giant that debilitates many 10/40 Window nations. We read of some of these struggles in case studies 1, 8, 9, and 10. I suspect that others have encountered this hurdle in varying degrees. The Economist Intelligence Unit, which has been monitoring sixty countries for several decades, rates corruption as a bigger threat to business and the economic well-being of nations than terrorism. Corruption leads to bad government and to breakdowns in judicial systems. This often creates an environment hospitable to terrorism and racial conflicts.

Because corruption is so deeply embedded in the political and socioeconomic systems of many 10/40 Window nations, there is a strong temptation to accept it as a cultural issue that one must live with. We rationalize this capitulation, saying we have to "render to Caesar the things that are Caesar's" (Matt. 22:21), or that a "gift in secret averts anger" (Prov. 21:14). Corruption is indeed a murky issue. In Indonesia, for example, there are four broad categories of corruption:

1. An extortionate demand for a bribe comes along with a threat to create problems for the business if the bribe is not paid.
2. Along with a demand for a bribe comes an offer of service to the business to work through the bureaucracy and secure licenses and other help.
3. Help is freely given prior to the request for a gift or bribe.
4. Help is freely given and there is no demand for a bribe, but out of "gratitude" the businessman voluntarily gives a significant gift, which is accepted.

Another scenario is paying someone else to do the dirty work. For example, someone may take a stand not to pay off corrupt customs officials to clear an urgently required container. However, if this person then pays a suspiciously high service fee to a "well-connected" freight forwarder to arrange for clearance of that container, then the person has merely been spared the gory details of directly handing over the bribe.

This is not the place to go into a theological or philosophical debate on the correct interpretation of the two Bible verses above, nor on whether one can live with the last two scenarios. In fact, many 10/40 Window businessmen and women, including Christians, don't label some of these decisions and transactions as corruption, but as *guanxi,* which in China means business networking or relationship building.

However, if we understand how corruption (1) is a direct affront to our righteous God and (2) undermines and destroys nations, we know that there is no room whatsoever for compromise. Indeed, a Great Commission business run righteously in the midst of corruption has a redemptive role and will be salt and light.

OTHER ISSUES

Finding *seed capital* for Great Commission business is an interesting challenge. While there is a lot of money in a wide range of Christian organizations and foundations in the economically developed nations, little is being deployed in missions. For many Great Commission entrepreneurs, seed funding is a mirage.

Long-established Christian foundations such as Colgate, Mary Kay, ServiceMaster, and CBN, along with more recent initiatives such as Mustard Seed, Opportunity International, Tent-Makers Fellowship, Lippo, and GateWay Enterprise, are actively funding Great Commission initiatives, including Great Commission businesses. However, out in the field Great Commission entrepreneurs often need help simply producing adequate business plans and connecting with sources of funding. Many Great Commission entrepreneurs mistakenly assume that it is unspiritual to actively seek out funding with well-prepared plans and budgets.

A common blind spot is clarity on the ultimate *ownership* of the Great Commission venture. Most institutional sources of Great Commission funding would not want to fund a Great Commission entrepreneur who sees a project as his own. From the outset, those who hold the share capital in a Great Commission business need to do so only in trust, as stewards and not as owners. Such enterprises also need proper accountability structures, including boards of directors or boards of reference/advisors. All this may seem rather laborious for small businesses. However, these steps lay the foundation for healthy growth.

It is possible to *leverage on technology* to create larger enterprises. Case study 1, Infosail, case study 2, AMI, and case study 3, Galtronics, demonstrate this approach. In such cases, multinational corporations, whether for domestic or international markets, can absorb the output. Information technology outsourcing and contract manufacturing are two areas with Great Commission success stories. However, many high-tech projects in China and India have not been insulated from trauma and failure.

The case studies also illustrate the importance of business *networking*. One significant competitive advantage that a Great Commission entrepreneur can bring with him is his network of contacts, both within the target country and internationally. This business asset can provide a counterpoint to any initial weakness in local knowledge. Again, one may need to overcome spiritual reservations. Am I advocating dependence on man and not on God? I believe God majors in relationships and teaches us to be dependent on him as well as on a meaningful network of trustworthy friends. Without doubt, effective networking is a critical success factor in business, and even more so in a tough missions environment.

Another creative aspect of international networking is for the church in the traditional sending nations to see that her role in these last days may be to help equip and resource the vibrant new sending nations in Latin America as well as South Korea and China.

Equipping local people to take over the Great Commission business is a positive goal for long-term sustainability. However, this goal has to be actualized within a holistic discipling process. Timing, and depth of life-change among local people, are important. Moving too quickly could place too much temptation in front of the local leaders. They need to see that the Great Commission business is a matter of stewardship rather than ownership.

REVIEW OF THE CASE STUDIES FROM A MINISTRY PERSPECTIVE

Howard Norrish

To assess the case studies, and indeed the whole topic of kingdom enterprises, we need to identify the criteria we will use to judge ministry viability. As evangelicals, we consciously submit ourselves and our methodology to the Word of God. One of our primary motivations is fulfilling the Great Commission. Let us examine four basic questions for any business in terms of its ministry viability.

THE FIRST QUESTION

Are the basics of holistic ministry in the hearts and minds of the workers before the business is started?

A number of central teachings in Scripture underpin kingdom business. I call these the "Five Pillars": (1) the nature of vocation and calling; (2) the biblical theology of work; (3) the lordship and sovereignty of Jesus Christ; (4) the priesthood of all believers; and (5) incarnational ministry.

This basic biblical teaching provides a synthesis of work and witness, which is fundamental to ministry by kingdom entrepreneurs. We will look at these in some detail.

Vocation and Calling

One Christian writer has defined "vocation" as "the expression of one's identity and the exercise of one's gifts in a new and dynamic way to glorify God and serve his fellow beings." The Bible places great emphasis on vocation—a calling that comes to all believers from God to be his people, to live faithfully, and to declare his reign and kingdom by word and life. This is a general call to all believers (2 Tim.1:8-9; Rom. 8:28-30; Eph. 4:11). In addition, there are specific callings to individuals (Exodus 3–4; 1 Samuel 3; Isaiah 65; Jeremiah 1).

Kingdom entrepreneurs are fulfilling a valid ministry. All believers are called to ministry. All are called to witness; none are exempt from this demand. The New Testament emphasis is that we are called to the service of Jesus Christ.

There is a valid role for the fully supported missionary, youth worker, pastor, Bible teacher, and so on. It is a biblical privilege to be in these roles (1 Cor. 9:14). But, as Michael Griffith has pointed out, the call comes not so much directly from God as from the church in order that a particular role is fulfilled.

Westerners often divide our lives into the different roles we play—father, employee, citizen, football player, church member, and so forth. Our vocation is usually seen as the way we earn our living. Our spiritual calling is seen as something completely different. This dichotomization gives rise to the clergy-laity split. This split is rooted in the Greek dualism of Aristotle and Plato—the separation of the body from the spirit. Semitic biblical thinking, however, is holistic. The whole is much more important than the sum of its parts. Integration is vital in the biblical worldview.

Missions, however, tend to promote dualism. We arrange training in cross-cultural evangelism and church planting. We exhort churches to become involved with the poor, the needy, and the lost. We use phrases like, "Prepare for full-time missionary service." Much of what mission agencies promote is misleading, however. As we have already seen, all believers are called to "full-time" Christian service. Some of them are called to serve in cross-cultural settings. All believers must intentionally synthesize vocation and calling. This intentionality must be present in kingdom entrepreneurs before they start. Without it, one will take precedence over the other—to the detriment of both.

A Biblical Theology of Work

"Work is not primarily a thing one does to live, but the thing one lives to do," Dorothy Sayers observed.[1] In a survey of active churchgoers in England, researchers found that:

- 50 percent had never heard that a theology of work existed;
- most thought that work (if they had given it any thought at all) was God's punishment for our rebellion because of the Fall. Most thought there would be no work in heaven;
- a minority believed that work had nothing to do with spirituality. We work merely to survive, to pay the bills, etc.

- most churchgoers enjoyed Sundays—the sermons, the songs, the fellowship. But they saw little relevance to their work on Mondays;
- nearly everyone assumed that it was both healthy and practical to compartmentalize their lives.

Our view of the physical world often determines our view of work. If we believe the physical world is fundamentally evil, then we want no part of it. In this case, spirituality and favor with God come from withdrawing from the physical world to "holy ground," where you do not marry, you do not trade, and you live in isolation.

But Jesus taught that evil is in man (Mark 7:20). God created the world's natural resources and gave them to man for his use (Gen. 1:26, 28). After the Fall, the conditions changed, but the objective remained the same. The commission given to Adam was also given to Noah (Gen. 9:1-2). David reaffirms the commission in the Psalms (Ps. 8:3-4, 6).

Man is a spiritual and physical being put on the earth to fulfill God's purposes. One of our tasks is to control and administer the world's natural resources. By so doing, we demonstrate to some degree the nature and purposes of God. Work is God's will for us. It should make us greatly satisfied, because work allows us to fulfill part of our reason for being.

Work is not God's judgment on our fallenness. Our workplaces are not just "ponds to fish in" (to do evangelism). Sadly, many give this reason for getting into business. Such on-the-job evangelism is often at the expense of true relationships. People who view work this way look like Rambo types who view their work colleagues as potential conquests instead of as human beings who deserve our love and respect.

In his book *Decisive Issues Facing Christians Today,* John Stott gives the following rationale for work:

> Those who are trying to develop a Christian mind on work, however, turn first to creation. The Fall turned some labour into drudgery (the ground was cursed, and cultivation became possible only by toil and sweat), but work itself is a consequence of our creation in God's image. God himself is represented in Genesis 1 as a worker. Day by day . . . his creative plan unfolded. Moreover, when he saw what he had made, he pronounced it "good." He enjoyed perfect job-satisfaction. His final act of creation, before resting on the seventh day, was to create human beings, and in doing so to make them workers too. He gave them some of his own dominion over the earth and told them to exercise their creative gifts in subduing it.[2]

Work makes us more truly human. Those in "the leisured class" (those who have inherited great wealth and so don't need to work) lack work's ennoblement. Karl Marx had some concept of this—the dignity of man the worker—but his great goal was productivity, not creativity.

The climax of Creation was the Sabbath. Here God sees man not as a worker but as a rester. The Sabbath relativizes the value of work in the light of rest. Rest for what? The Sabbath was a day of worship. Our humanness and our satisfaction in work must be in good relationship not only with creation but also with our Creator. The Bible sees man as an integrated worker-worshiper. It shows worship, not work, as the summit of man's activity. It also shows that work is a vital part of what it means to be human.

When work is not linked to worship, its fallen character starts to dominate so that it becomes a means to an end and a controlling power. Work is either overestimated so that you become a workaholic, or underestimated.

By work, human beings serve the community. Our communities are interdependent. This is becoming increasingly true with globalization. The priority of work is not profit but service to the community for the common good. As believers, our ability to be salt and light in the community is vital.

In the past, the emphasis was on evangelism by winning individuals. Today, the emphasis is on multiplying churches. This reflects a growing awareness of the importance of community and the place of the church in God's plan to redeem communities and cultures. Seen in this light, work becomes a vital part in holistic ministry to the whole community, bringing "redemption lift" to that culture.

By work, we cooperate with God. Partnership with God is the pinnacle of being human. Nature is the raw material God has given us. The essence of a culture is what we do with this raw material. The Bible sees man in partnership with God—creating, conserving, cultivating, and developing the potential of nature. This is our cultural mandate. Its fullest and most elegant expression occurs in divine-human collaboration. Our business is, to some degree, a partnership between God and us. The greater the degree of partnership, the greater our satisfaction.

God's goal is that all people and all cultures should be permeated by his glory. This will come about after the gospel of the kingdom is preached in the whole world as a witness to all peoples.

Here is a good definition of work:

Work is an expenditure of energy—whether manual or mental or both—in transforming the earth, which fulfills the workers, serves the community, and glorifies God.

Biblically, we are to avoid two extremes:

- Work is a curse and we dream of a workless society.
- Work is an idol and the source of our meaning and identity.

The Bible presents work as a ministry that is the fruit of faith (1 Thess. 1:3; 2 Thess. 1:11). Work, like anything else, is meaningless apart from faith in God. It may be therapeutic (since it was given before the Fall), but it must be redeemed from vanity (Eccles. 2:17-26). Businesspeople involved in missions must have a right attitude to work so that they work cheerfully every day. They need to look beyond the task to the ultimate purpose—serving mankind and glorifying God. This attitude will change our regard for those who are unemployed and underemployed in so many restricted-access countries. Every person should have the opportunity to work. Work will enable him to fulfill himself, glorify God, and serve the community.

Christ's Lordship and Sovereignty

No area of life, no occupation, no manner of life can remain outside the claims of Jesus Christ's lordship. The Reformers wrote about what they called "particularized callings." All these callings to a particular work were equally worthy, whether one was an artist, a businessman, or a pastor. Every calling was an arena where the glory of God could be displayed.

Because Jesus is Lord, art or scientific research is as sacred as Bible study and prayer. Business and education are as holy as evangelism and Bible teaching. Each is an area where Jesus reigns and where his lordship can be affirmed, celebrated, and made known.

Christ's lordship integrates the dichotomy of the church versus the world, the sacred versus the secular. The everyday working life of the businessman involved in mission is as sacred as the evangelistic Bible study he runs.

The biblical man is a "whole" man who integrates everything under Jesus' lordship. To engineer accurately, to heal with care, to teach effectively, to farm well, to make a profit justly in business are all, in themselves, offerings of praise.

The Priesthood of All Believers

The New Testament insists on the priesthood of all believers. This reinforces the equal dignity of all believers without regard to occupation. Sadly, this emphasis was lost in the late second century through conformity to Greek and Roman organizational approaches and through applying Old Testament priesthood structures to New Testament service. Ever since, the clergy-laity divide has weakened the church by freezing the laity in huge sections of the church. If we are ever to evangelize the world, this frozen part of the church will have to be defrosted by a major infusion of redemptive energy so that tens of millions of believers are released into evangelism and discipleship. Mission-minded business is part of this movement.

One of the curses of modern evangelicalism is that most believers try to imitate—on a small scale and by part-time efforts—the work of the pastor. Believing that their business is spiritually meaningless and that the only really spiritual people are in full-time Christian work, they seek to be "part-time preachers." But this denies that the whole church is here to glorify God before an unbelieving world by living the kind of life that God intended. To do this, he gave us the powers of intellect and organization.

Because of this wrong thinking, we have a type of caste system within the church:

- high caste: martyrs, missionaries, pastors, priests, and employees of religious organizations
- middle caste: social service workers, counselors, welfare workers, health professionals, teachers, and all in education
- low caste: businessmen, carpenters, farmers, waitresses, and managers
- outcastes: salesmen, lawyers, and all who work in the media and entertainment businesses

We know that most of the main characters in the Bible were workers: cattle farmers, vineyard tenders, carpenters, businessmen, managers (of grain supplies, building projects, armies, etc.), health workers, and artists (musicians, worship leaders, and writers). God does not view any of these people as ignoble, irrelevant, or low caste. In Scripture, they are exalted by doing God's work. If we start to view ourselves as worthless and our work as irrelevant drudgery, then spirituality disappears from everyday life. The result of such thinking is that laypeople are considered useful only if:

- they give large gifts to missions;
- their jobs allow them to do a lot of "part-time preaching";
- they "net" or "spear" a lot of their colleagues and get them into the church;
- they lend their power and prestige to enhance the reputation of the pastor.

This separation of the secular from the spiritual causes:

- a privatization of our spiritual life;
- a disconnection of mission and evangelism from life;
- a separation of social action from evangelism;
- a misunderstanding of what constitutes "worldliness."

Incarnational Ministry and Business in Mission

Our great desire is that unbelievers will be able to see Jesus in all his fullness in our lives. Sadly, our Western (or foreign) culture is usually so visible to unbelievers that they have trouble seeing anything of Jesus. Incarnational ministry means more than just the living Word of God (Jesus) being clothed in flesh (ours). Jesus became flesh in a specific space/time setting. Well ahead of time, God had carefully prepared the particular cultural matrix in which Jesus was incarnated. Incarnation cannot happen in a cultural vacuum.

For Jesus, incarnation meant a human expression of his divine nature. It meant a Jewish expression of that nature—a Jewish way of life with Jewish culture and customs. It also meant subordination to a Jewish family setting. Paul sums it up succinctly: "For I tell you that Christ has become a servant of the Jews on behalf of God's truth" (Rom. 15:8, NIV). We should be able to say, "I have become a servant of the Turkmens [or some other group] on behalf of God's truth."

INCARNATIONAL WITNESS REQUIRES A SERVANT HEART

Nassim, a Muslim, listened with an open heart as I explained the gospel. When I asked why he was so open and was raising no objections, he said with deep emotion, "Years ago, my friend and I saw two nuns holding out their hands to receive money for a new Christian hospital. As we passed, my friend spat with contempt into the hands of one of the nuns. She pulled out her handkerchief and wiped off the spittle. Smiling at my friend, she said, 'All right, that was for me. Now what will you give to Jesus?'" Nassim looked up with tears in his eyes and said, "Can anyone forget love like that?"

Incarnational witness demands that our business and ministry be motivated by love. It must be a love that throws its arms around the people and the culture of the people we have come to serve. It must embrace both it and them. Nothing else will do.

Incarnational witness has a messenger in whom *agape* love has worked so deeply that personal, national, racial, cultural, and religious forms are brought into complete subjection. This will enable the messenger to envision objectively the beauty and wonder of the Holy Spirit demonstrating Jesus through him or her to the people and their culture. It is the witness of the messenger who seeks in every way possible—within the bounds of biblical ethics—to become as the hearers, so that the life of Jesus can be demonstrated in thought forms, communication forms, cultural forms, and even religious forms that are relevant and meaningful to the hearers and not likely to be misunderstood. The incarnational witness realizes that while the gospel itself offends, he or she will remove all other objectionable and foreign factors.

BASIC GUIDELINES FOR INCARNATIONAL WITNESS

- Biblical teaching, ethics, and morals are not negotiable. Changing them to conform to our host culture is not an option.
- Most of the religio-cultural forms used in English churches are not commanded in Scripture, but have been a way of containing and expressing the life of Christ in our particular cultural milieu. This is not wrong. They may be dated, but some cultural forms are necessary. The life of Christ must be expressed through a cultural context.
- The Scriptures (especially Acts 15 and Galatians) are adamant that under no circumstances should we impose our English religio-cultural forms on believers of another culture. If we insist on giving English forms along with Jesus Christ, then we elevate these forms to the level of Jesus and imply that they have saving merit. This is "another gospel"—the gospel plus English culture. Galatians condemns this as legalism. In no way can the "weak and beggarly" (Gal. 4:9, KJV) form of English Christianity add anything to the work of Jesus!
- God deliberately left a blank in the New Testament concerning almost all religio-cultural forms. This is so that the universal Lord Jesus could be expressed in and through any given culture. He can use many religio-cultural forms. Some cultures, of course, may have more possibilities than others in this respect.
- If, in its very essence, a religio-cultural form violates Scripture in ethics, morals, or because it is permeated with the demonic and cannot be cleansed, then we must abandon it. This will be true of some forms related to immorality and idolatry. But Jesus may well sanctify more than we do! Often second-generation mature

believers can evaluate and reinterpret these forms in a new context better than we can. Early European Christians turned heathen Roman temples into churches and turned heathen festivals into holy days.

- The cross-cultural communicator must carefully express the principles Jesus taught in and through the unique culture of the people. Otherwise, new disciples will naturally equate Christianity with the West—especially if the messenger is from the West.

Paul emphasized the principle of adaptation: "To the _____ I became as a _____, so that I might win the _____" (1 Cor. 9:22).

Paul gives four reasons why he became a businessman (making, selling, and repairing tents):

- He is concerned about the credibility of the message. He felt that working with his hands would gain credibility for the message. This is the major reason for starting businesses. Business enhances the believability of the gospel.
- He is concerned about identification—incarnational witness.
- He is concerned about modeling. ". . . with toil and labor we worked night and day, that we might not be a burden to any of you. . . . [and] to give you . . . an example" (2 Thess. 3:8, 9). Modeling biblical principles to new believers is crucial in church planting. They need to see that it works.
- He is concerned about reproducibility. He knows that new communities of believers must be self-supporting, self-governing, and self-propagating.

Paul's strategy worked. We follow in his footsteps.

We should ask ourselves, "If I had to leave this week, what would I leave behind?" Is what we are doing truly reproducible? Beware of just teaching prescriptive methodology. Teach principles. Local believers will then be able to apply these principles in their local cultures.

A Synthesis of Work and Witness

These biblical affirmations—the Five Pillars—allow us to celebrate business as a valid form of mission. The principles are broad enough to allow a diversity of models and a diversity of intersections between business and evangelism and business and church planting.

Business in mission requires a full synthesis by combining work with a general witness to God's glory as well as a specific witness to God's claims, motivated by the command to do evangelism and make disciples. So business is not only legitimate. It is a vehicle of witness—a model—to accompany a direct verbal witness to the redemptive work and claims of Christ.

This synthesis is important. If the business is viewed only as a platform for evangelism, governments and employees quickly figure out that deception is taking place. They learn to see believers—national and expatriate—as intruders, fakers, and sluggards.

Paul knew of this tendency. He tells new believers to

- obey their employers (Col. 3:22-25);
- be fair to employees (Col. 4:1);
- work hard so that others will respect you (1 Thess. 4:11-12);
- avoid idleness that causes unjust dependence on others (2 Thess. 3:6-15);
- be involved in productive labor that removes the temptation to steal and that equips you to share with those in need (Eph. 4:28).

By the empowerment of the Holy Spirit, businessmen and women can celebrate the fact that they are serving God and pushing forward the growth of his kingdom among unreached peoples. They will experience God's enabling just as the tabernacle builders did in Exodus 31 and 35. There we see that skills in stonecutting, carpentry, jewelry making, and tapestry were used by the Holy Spirit to create a fit dwelling place for the Most High. In New Testament terms, they were church planting! This same Holy Spirit will help us be co-creators with God in church planting movements in every unreached people group.

How Did the Case History Reporters Do?

Clearly, most of the reporters struggled with this issue. Sometimes they struggled in themselves or, in the case of Esther Hui, with their friends and churches, where they found a "caste mindset." Patrick Lai concluded that he would prefer to train new recruits rather than spend years retraining recruits who had been trained in dualistic thinking.

It is possible that non-Caucasian businesspeople have an advantage since they come from cultures that are more integrative than Western cultures. We all fight an increasing homogenization of "Christian culture" (which is essentially Western) that is spreading among believers in Asia, Africa, and Latin America.

Getting biblical holism into our businesses is vital, both as a foundation for the business and as a model to the emerging church. It appears that only a few of the basics of holistic ministry were in place before the reporters started. Most discovered the basics as their ministries developed. All appeared to have worked hard in helping their supporting constituency understand these basics. It was also hard to get newer people to understand the basics. Clem Schultz suggests that a strategy coordinator should be on the board to teach and maintain this ethos in the business. This is a good idea.

THE SECOND QUESTION

Does the business have a clear vision of its purpose in terms of a mission statement or strategic objectives?

It seems essential for a business to have not only a good business plan with a reasonable time horizon but also a good ministry plan with the same time horizon. For security reasons, the bank or government might only see the business plan. Objective consultants and advisors are probably needed to evaluate both business and ministry plans, to check their viability and integrative nature. The ministry plan must be taken as seriously as the business plan. It needs the same degree of monitoring and evaluation. If necessary, there should be course corrections to keep the business focused on its mission.

The Ministry Plan

The Abrahamic Covenant needs to be at the heart of the ministry plan, "to be a blessing to all the families" in the community (cf. Gen. 12:1-3). The goal is to be a blessing and to bring blessing. Blessing is a rich biblical word. We need to define it more carefully.

Various reporters defined "blessing" in the following ways:

[handwritten margin note: Elements of a ministry plan]

- Making money to give to Christian work locally. This is a worthy goal when the church is small and heavily dependent on foreign financial support. It is also easily measured.
- Creating employment for local believers and other local people: "Do good to all people, especially to those who belong to the family of believers" (Gal. 6:10, NIV). This is also a very worthy goal and easy to monitor.
- Transferring skills and knowledge to people (believers and nonbelievers) that will provide enhanced opportunities to find jobs—computer skills, business acumen, knowledge of English, etc. This goal is harder to measure, but still possible.

- Introducing a Christian-based value system (ethics) and showing that it helps people and the community. Proverbs 14:34 says, "Righteousness exalts a nation." Corruption impoverishes peoples. This goal is harder to measure without an initial baseline survey.
- Building trust with local people, gaining respect in the community in order to establish good relationships. This is important because the gospel runs down "corridors of trust."
- Making disciples and mentoring them. This is at the heart of the Great Commission of Matthew 28. To do it, we need a clear definition of discipleship.
- Contributing to an indigenous church planting movement in an unreached people group or a city, by providing a model that local believers can quickly and easily replicate. Very few expatriates are good evangelists. By evangelism we mean winning people to Christ and discipling them so that they go on to win others of their own people to Christ. Most people won to Christ by expatriates don't reproduce themselves. The main contribution of expatriates will be:
  - providing good models that are reproducible (the business, for example)
  - discipleship
  - leadership development

How Did the Case History Reporters Do?

All reporters had goals. Some had them at the beginning of their business. Others developed them as they went along.

Clem Schultz says that every business should have a written annual mission plan. He is right. He also says the emphasis should be church planting focused on unreached cities and people groups. This is where most businesses should focus, but the principles should apply everywhere.

The problem of corruption came up frequently. Juerg Opprecht has learned some very useful lessons in dealing with corruption and introducing Christian business ethics. Clem Schultz's suggestion of introducing training programs in business ethics is excellent.

THE THIRD QUESTION

Do the businesses have a checklist on ministry progress?

This may seem pedantic or even a new form of legalism. But airline pilots and car mechanics go through checklists. A doctor attending road accident victims automatically goes through a checklist:

A. Is the *airway* in the mouth/neck blocked?

B. Is the patient *breathing?*

C. He checks the *circulation* system for blood loss.

D. He checks for *dysfunction*—loss of a state of consciousness, confusion, etc.

E. He checks to see if the patient is *exposed*—i.e., in the middle of the road.

Checklists are useful. We all need them. Don't fly in a plane if the pilot is casual or forgetful about checklists!

Here are some useful items for reviewing our holistic ministries:

- Personnel are all spiritually accountable to a church and/or mission agency—no "Lone Rangers."
- Personnel are all committed to the team.
- The business is meeting the felt needs of the community.
- Time is given to language acquisition before people get immersed in the business.
- The business/company is people-intensive, not in terms of large numbers of employees but in giving the time and opportunity to work alongside local people.
- The skills of "intentional personal conversations" are being passed on. This usually involves natural ways of introducing redemptive elements into conversations.
- Team leaders make a clear distinction between the business manager and the ministry leader.
- There is a multinational management team.
- There is a training program for employees explaining the Christian worldview and the basis of Christian business ethics.
- The team is modeling these ethical principles every day.
- There is a regular review with each team member of the quality of his or her spirituality.
- There is regular review of how others—government officials and the community—perceive the business. Is it a blessing?
- There is a discipleship program in place that integrates work and witness.
- The team and the believing employees are encouraged to be involved in Scripture distribution in an appropriate way. How we sow the seed will vary a great deal. In many situations, it is best to use secular channels of distribution rather than direct distribution.

- There is systematic monitoring and evaluation of ministry goals. Are lessons being learned collectively and passed on? Anything that is not working should be quickly discarded. There is a can-do attitude—a belief that God has the answers to all problems.
- Guidelines are in place on how to move from one-to-one discipleship to a house church/cell group.
- All evangelism, discipleship, and church planting approaches are reviewed regularly to see if they are easily reproducible within that culture.

How Did the Case History Reporters Do?

The very fact that the reporters had to write case histories shows that they have internal checklists to evaluate the principles they are learning. Patrick Lai, Luke Wilson, Clem Schultz, and Juerg Opprecht gave what could be called checklists. Most of these are incorporated in my checklists above.

The key for successful checklists is identifying principles and not formulae, which are usually culture-bound. I was impressed that the reporters understood this and tried to report principles.

THE FOURTH QUESTION

Is there regular evaluation of the ministry?

Evaluation will usually come periodically by self-assessment. It will largely center around:

- *Effectiveness:* Is the ministry fulfilling its mission adequately?
- *Efficiency:* Is the ministry using resources, personnel, and finances well to reach the mission outcome to which it aspires?
- *Relevance:* Is the ministry relevant to its community?

How Can Effectiveness Be Measured?

- Do we all know and agree to our mission statement?
- When thinking and designing ministry programs, is a conscious link made between the mission statement/strategic objectives and the proposed program?
- Do you have quality and quantity indicators in place that capture the essence of the mission statement? Possible indicators include:

- knowledge generation and its use
- environmental changes—spiritual as well as emotional/material
- quality-of-life changes among the people you work with
- the number of people who have heard a credible witness
- the number of people coming to faith
- the existence of good collaborative arrangements with others

In development projects, a baseline study is undertaken before work begins. A modified baseline study needs to be developed for a business ministry. The Summer Institute of Linguistics usually does a six-month linguistic/social anthropological survey among a people group before sending in translators. Businessmen could add these kinds of social anthropology questions to their market research. This is what a baseline study is all about. To measure effectiveness in ethics, you must do a baseline study.

How Can Efficiency Be Measured?

The business should not only provide effective service in terms of ministry, but also cost structures appropriate to these services. Cost is not measured only in dollars. There is also the far more intangible cost of emotional and physical health. We call this member-care cost:

- Are all the team members being used to their greatest potential—in line with their abilities?
- Is optimum use being made of financial services?
- Is the administrative system providing good value?
- Are human resource systems and training programs in place to help efficiency?
- Are benchmark comparisons being made with other business-ministries?

How Can Relevance Be Measured?

No business-ministry is protected from becoming out-of-date. All businesses should be subject to closure if they become irrelevant—even if they are making money! To survive, each business-ministry must adapt to changing contexts and capacities. It must keep its mission, strategic objectives, programs, and ministry activities relevant. We need to ask:

- Are we regularly reviewing the role analysis of the team?
- Are we changing appropriately to meet changing needs?

The Motivation Behind the Business-Ministry

Keep reviewing the history of your business. Make sure new chapters are written after every major lesson learned. Get your team to read or tell these "campfire stories" regularly. Keep focusing on the mission and strategic objectives of the business-ministry. Automatic re-focusing by the team is the key to success.

Finally, each business-ministry develops an *ethos*. This is the sum of the values that the team of people aspires to: beliefs, customs, traditions, and meanings related to mission fulfillment. This is what makes each business-ministry unique. It is the ethos of the team, together with the mission, that governs the way things work. Stories about advances and setbacks illustrate important values. This living history guides how the team does things. In the military, motivation is often called high morale. It is found in all elite fighting troops. It also should be found in all kingdom businesses. Ask yourself:

- Does my company have good morale?
- Do team members have a positive attitude to change?
- Is there genuine warmth and love among the staff?
- Do we have training programs to reinforce our ethos?
- Do team members and staff feel sufficient acknowledgment and affirmation in what they do?
- Is there sufficient trust to try new things and—if necessary—to fail?
- Is there an overemphasis on control?

Other Points

Much more could be said in the evaluation of the capacity of business-ministry:

CAPACITY AREAS	COMPONENTS
1. Leadership	strategic planning, governance, structure of the ministry
2. Member Care	planning, recruiting, training, appraising, career development, crisis management, maintaining well-being of team members (spiritual, emotional, social, physical)
3. Infrastructure	communications and facilities management
4. Program management	planning, implementing, and monitoring programs and projects

| 5. Process management | problem solving, decision making, monitoring, and evaluation of the business |
| 6. Inter-business cooperation | planning, implementing, and monitoring networks and partnerships |

CONCLUSIONS

Four basic questions should be continually asked and answered by the leadership of the business:

- Are the basics of holistic ministry in the hearts and minds of the workers *before* the business is started?
- Does the business have a vision of its purpose in terms of a mission statement or strategic objectives?
- Does the business have a checklist of ministry progress?
- Is evaluation of the ministry happening regularly?

If the leadership is regularly answering these questions, then I believe the ministry will not only be viable, it will also bring glory to God and extend his kingdom. It will bless the community and will be deeply satisfying to the workers.

In one Persian Gulf country there are ten kingdom businesses. Most are just a few months old. Obviously, we could do much more to help one another. Central Asia and the Gulf have annual consultations for these enterprises. We need to see these consultations multiply throughout the creative access world. If leaders in each major location or country developed a business launch package for new kingdom businesses, we could prevent much grief and waste of time.

In major locations, kingdom businesses could come together to run "business clubs" where nonbelievers could discuss business issues and the importance of character qualities. An organization called Character First runs seminars on these issues. These seminars could be adapted for different cultures. These clubs would be invitation-only and have only about twenty to twenty-five members each. This would help smaller kingdom businesses to work in synergy to make a bigger impact.

To progress in ministry viability, we need to continue helping kingdom businesses with models and case histories. We also need to provide evaluation tools so that businesses stay on track with a strong learning and sharing ethos.

23

ADVANTAGES, DISADVANTAGES, AND LESSONS LEARNED

Randolph Case

A few main themes will frame this chapter. First, kingdom entrepreneurs enjoy some unique and powerful advantages as compared to conventional missionaries. Second, they also confront a set of disadvantages or drawbacks that create an unavoidable tension. Third, this tension stems from the paradox of being both "in business" and "about my Father's business" at the same time. Of course, it vexes the traditional missions organization as well as the traditional entrepreneurial firm; indeed, it may lie beneath the surface of all work. But kingdom entrepreneurs face the paradox head on in a way that those whose vocations appear either more "spiritual" or more "secular" may fail to do as honestly.

Fourth, herein lies the great promise of the enterprises that are the main topic of this volume. Kingdom business can, when wholeheartedly pursued, engage us consciously and daily in the impossible task of loving others at the same time as ourselves; of serving God and mammon at once; of faith and works exercised in tandem. This may leave us no choice but to seek, minute-by-minute, Christ's grace in giving away power—which is the essence of competitive advantage—in the exercise of love. This giving is the essence of the kingdom.

This chapter has two main parts. In the first, I will highlight some of the most striking advantages of kingdom entrepreneurship, gleaned from the experiences and observations of the various authors represented in this volume. Along with each advantage, I will also discuss some of the more vexing drawbacks in tension with it. The concluding section will attempt to look through these problems and opportunities to the Good News.

KINGDOM BUSINESS: ADVANTAGES AND DRAWBACKS

Kingdom Business Is Holistic

The most fundamental characteristic of kingdom entrepreneurship compared to traditional missions is its "holistic" nature. Baer (chapter 17) writes that a kingdom business is not a "shell" business with a missions center. It is both business and missions through and through. He suggests the major difference between it and the traditional work of the missionary or tentmaker is that it ministers through its for-profit operations rather than in spare time from it. Batchelder (chapter 7) considers this an opportunity for a win-win: When entrepreneurs use their God-given abilities to meet the felt needs of others, a virtuous cycle is created that both serves God's people and is economically sustainable for the long run. The same $5 that is spent for a wool scarf to keep a child warm provides a job, dignity, and an income for a widow who works in the scarf factory to feed her children. When that scarf is manufactured and that job managed according to Christian ethical principles, the business thrives. This thriving business yields profits that serve the needs of owners/investors. It also justifies their continued investment in a web of principled business relationships that both draw the lost to Christ and feed his children. As Grudem (chapter 13) might put it, the kingdom businessperson can honestly see buying and selling as "a means of loving our neighbor," ownership as a right response to God's call to subdue the earth by making it useful for us as human beings, and commerce as a natural means to share Christ.

Drawback: One risk of holism is that it may fail to make the gospel distinct enough from the normal routines of business life that it will awaken people to the revolutionary nature of Christ's prophetic message. Rundle (chapter 20) refers to David Befus of Latin America Mission, who says that if we simply make people healthier or more prosperous without telling them about the ultimate source of human satisfaction, all we've done is make them more comfortable for their journey to hell. I would add that if people see us fall prey to the same temptations as worldly business—pride, greed, lack of trust or trustworthiness—that is, if we teach a gospel we don't live, all we've done is become a stumbling block, ourselves, between them and Christ.

Kingdom Business Is Cost-effective and Efficient

The unity of effort in holism creates numerous advantages, not the least of which is increased efficiency in fulfilling the Great Commission. Cragin (chapter 15) notes that holism can help the church escape the "spare time, spare change theology" that has bifurcated the individual Christian's life and mission and undermined both his power and his witness. Not surprisingly,

Cragin computes the resources spent by the kingdom business, in dollars or man hours per person receiving witness, at one-fourth to one-half that spent by the average evangelical church or missions organization. Baer focuses on the efficiency kingdom businesses bring to the training of believers in "kingdom impact." His IDS project has taken only $150,000 in microloans to train nearly 1,000 believers in 75 new businesses around the world.

Others focus on the powerful and growing churches planted by kingdom businesses that enter a country at a dramatically lower cost than paid church planting ministries. For instance, Lai (chapter 5) tells of starting six businesses in a "closed" country for less than $10,000 each. Even though three of these failed and Lai was eventually deported for his Christian witness, the three other businesses met his internal requirement to reach profitability in eighteen months while at the same time spawning two growing churches. Thus, the net cost of starting two still-thriving churches was quite low.

Drawback: Work pursued for efficiency's sake attracts the mind and heart of the worker to means of benefit and categories of cost that are most measurable and accessible. In so doing, it may cause him to miss the "pearl of great price." Indeed, Christ would have him incur enormous cost for a pearl whose value may be neither easily measurable nor even fully accessible in this life. Watson (chapter 10) admits a demanding job in the marketplace can fail to give him much time to develop relationships with the people he wants to reach. Chan (chapter 1) describes a kingdom entrepreneur who skirts some laws in her home country that are "irrelevant, contradictory, or unreasonable. . . . To follow these rules would make tasks such as purchasing needed equipment nearly impossible . . . [or take] several years if you follow the letter of the law." Of course, obeying local laws should never supercede Christ's rule in our life, but this only highlights the point: focusing attention on measurable factors like purchasing economies and payback period in a kingdom business can distract us from kingdom priorities.

Kingdom Businesses Are Attractive, Without Deception, to Those Who May Be "Closed" to Christ

Even closed countries are typically interested in the jobs and wealth business start-ups can bring. An important benefit of kingdom business is that it can be a more honest way to bring the gospel to a "creative access" country than more clandestine efforts that use secular work as a cover for evangelism. As Lai concludes, "we came to realize that if we were to have a viable ministry, we needed a viable reason for being in the community. If we are adding value to a society in the form of education, creating jobs, bringing in capital, or enhancing people's lives, it is unlikely we will be deported for doing evangelism and church planting."

This implies a principle that runs throughout this volume. In order for the gospel to be both heard and accepted, the hearer must believe that it works, not just in the afterlife but here and now. Kingdom businesses can demonstrate the sufficiency of Christ's grace, even where there is resistance to it, because people will usually open their doors—and even their hearts—to commercial success.

Drawback: Of course, doing Christ's work in business does not always produce success in measurable financial terms. Choi (chapter 9) speaks honestly about his repeated business failures and their potentially negative effect on his ministry in Central Asia: "I had to teach [my employees] that they would not have a job if we did not meet our professional goals. They could not understand this idea." Cragin warns that most entrepreneurial start-ups fail in the first few years and that the success rate is even lower for Christian companies starting new businesses in a foreign land. Rundle has observed that a kingdom business that fails to be financially successful also typically fails as either a source of support for other ministries or as a legitimate ministry in its own right. Accordingly, William (chapter 4) has established the policy that her kingdom businesses will never accept money from either mission agencies or churches, even though she shares with them the goal of spreading the gospel in the Middle East. The reason is that "they almost always look at the business as a means to get into a country rather than as a ministry in itself." She sees that as a risk to both business and ministry success. The challenge for kingdom entrepreneurs in the face of such risk is to maintain the integrity, side-by-side, of kingdom objectives and business objectives, both sincerely pursued together. Failure to serve either effectively can seriously undermine the kingdom entrepreneur's ability to serve Christ in his work.

Kingdom Business Demonstrates a Godly Approach to Excellence

Rundle argues that the daily struggles of an effective business—meeting deadlines or satisfying customers—enable kingdom entrepreneurs to model the power of Christian discipleship to enhance personal and corporate growth. According to Grudem, these efforts are spurred on to ever-greater levels of effectiveness by business competition, which glorifies God as it helps the businessman or woman imitate his excellence. God showed us in Genesis 1 that work within the boundaries he sets is fundamentally good and that to do it right and well pleases him immensely. The great triumph of a self-sustaining, godly business, according to Batchelder, is that it creates jobs made meaningful because they produce more than they cost, and relationships made helpful because they build rather than exploit the gifts and abilities God has extended us.

Drawback: The relentless pursuit of excellent results can support flawed means and leave sinful consequences in its wake. Opprecht has observed that the importance a high-performance business gives to speed and efficiency can lead to bribery and other forms of corruption. Several of the entrepreneurs featured in this book acknowledge the need for "A" players" and "world class" organizations in order to produce excellent products and services in a challenging environment. But Grudem warns about both the destructive pride that can plague excellent performers and the jealousy and covetousness that can result in those around them. Indeed, a fundamental characteristic of business is to measure performance and allocate resources based on these measures. Unfortunately, businesses can achieve excellent financial results by measuring people and activities according to worldly standards that reward those things that best satisfy the lust of the flesh. Some of the world's most high-performing businesses are built on "excellent" systems for capitalizing on greed, vanity, one-upmanship, fear, and the like. The kingdom entrepreneur who wishes to compete successfully against these businesses risks falling prey to powerful incentives to follow their pattern in order to achieve excellent results. Indeed, the stress of a highly competitive environment can appear to justify all kinds of sins against one's competitors. And, as Watson warns, the sins that can be learned from the surrounding culture in developing countries are very different from those in developed nations. Maintaining one's faith and obedience to God in such challenging circumstances can be a constant struggle.

Kingdom Business Uses the Competitive Advantage of Talented Christians and Christian Practices to Serve the Kingdom of God

Grudem writes that inequality of possessions is fundamentally good in God's sight. In Luke 19, Jesus says to one person, "You shall have authority over ten cities," and to another, "You are to be over five cities." God gives different resources, abilities, and rewards to his people. These differences provide people with differing amounts and types of power, or "competitive advantage." This inequality is good as well, because there are many different tasks. Differing tasks bind people together to accomplish them.

The free market, by its very nature, employs power to accomplish shared goals. It deftly uses money, the currency of power, to accomplish what would not have been accomplished otherwise. Most people would agree that free-market economies have created more, accomplished more, and wielded more influence (for both good and evil) in world affairs than those based upon, for example, equality of possessions and power. When Christians with an explicit vision and calling to serve God use free enterprise, the results can be world-changing.

Drawback: What we will see if we look with a discerning eye at kingdom business is something permeating the accounts in this book but scarcely highlighted in them. Namely, kingdom businesses, like all business, are built on power differences, and the godly use of power is a capability few dare boast about. Many critics view with skepticism claims to be both "for him" and "for-profit"—profit enjoyed, by definition, because of entrenched competitive advantages over rivals, customers, suppliers, and other "competitive" entities. How can a business leader claim to love others as himself while maximizing profit at the expense of these competitors? Indeed, at the core of modern theories of business strategy is the precept that the defense of business advantage against competitors must be the chief goal of the business enterprise, or it will not survive. Later in this essay, I will call for a more hopeful perspective: that far from exploiting the power differences it enjoys, a kingdom business can use them to build loving relationships that heal the sting of power differences and employ them for both God and man.

THE PARADOX OF THE GOSPEL: IN THE WORLD
BUT NOT OF THE WORLD

The kingdom entrepreneur must navigate conflicting currents like these daily. Numerous advantages are available to kingdom businesses, but countervailing disadvantages are in tension with them. This is not merely due to the fact that, as William's Chinese saying affirms, "No needle is sharp on both ends." The tension springs from a "paradox," a self-contradictory state of affairs. It is the central paradox of the gospel, the simultaneous need to be "in the world but not of the world," the same impossible task Christ faced in the Incarnation. It is the same paradoxical struggle Jacob faced at Peniel, that of wrestling at once with the power of the flesh and the soaring Spirit of God. Like Jacob, the kingdom entrepreneur has a privileged opportunity to plunge into a conflict from which he, and the world, can emerge transformed. This opportunity carries significant risks, but I believe the new model of enterprise that emerges from the pages of this book has great promise.

Let me be more concrete. I will conclude this essay by discussing some specific strengths of entrepreneurial business management that I think are critical to the success of the "business as missions" model. These aspects are neither unique to kingdom businesses nor, certainly, are they true of all (or even most) such businesses; but they are possible for the kingdom entrepreneur in ways they are not for others. They are valuable tools for dealing with the tensions I have pointed out, for getting leverage on the paradoxical struggle to be in business and about our Father's business.

Accordingly, I suggest three areas of competence I believe we should be developing in kingdom entrepreneurship.

1. Accountability

Accounting is taught at every business school because it is the root language of business. The flaws in the accounting system that have been pointed out in recent business scandals are the exception that highlights the rule that businesses (good ones) understand and practice accountability. But many non-businesses don't. Most individuals and most government and nonprofit entities (including ministries) would benefit from better accountability systems.

We can all relate to the challenge aimed at one business leader described in this book: "You teach us a good message in the morning, but during the work day we don't see this teaching in action in your life." Two things are remarkable about this statement. First, those in the most influential positions in organizations rarely hear it, because those below them aren't willing to risk saying it. Second, the few (if any) above them—top management, absentee shareholders, board members, and so on don't see them during the workday at all.

Many full-time Christian workers are employed in organizations where accountability is not as exacting or accessible as in the for-profit business world. In some cases, a good sermon and good people skills, full pews or programs, or an inspiring newsletter at the end of the month (or year!) are the main requirements for keeping financial supporters happy. Other stakeholders—employees, board members—can be selected for their willingness to give leaders and managers a free pass to skip more demanding accountability.

This is, of course, also true in for-profit organizations, but the best ones continually fine-tune their systems for providing feedback and accountability from top to bottom in the organizational hierarchy. The kingdom business must incorporate this strength of the best entrepreneurial businesses by holding itself, and those it employs, accountable to various sources of human authority. These authorities are not only shareholders and government authorities, but also customers, peers outside the business, subordinates, and so forth. And accountability must be for "hard" results such as financial efficiency, as well as "soft" results—the unmeasurables such as witness, service, and love.

Various mechanisms can help in this task. Besides financial record keeping and reporting there are more qualitative "Management by Objective" and "Total Quality" reporting systems. Coaching and mentoring, intentional peer relationships, and "360 degree" systems for capturing anonymous feedback from subordinates, customers, and suppliers are used by premier secular organizations. I believe they are vital for the excellent kingdom business as well. Personal accountability based on a web of intentional relationships—upward, horizontal, downward—can hold the Christian businessperson accountable on a daily basis to the values and calling of God. Many of these relationships are best cultivated using the models of discipleship that our Lord and his followers presented in the New Testament and that Christians have modeled throughout the ages.

Without accountability, the kingdom entrepreneur is left with nothing but its antithesis—hypocrisy. Of the advantages of kingdom business discussed earlier in this chapter, the tension around two of these strengths— "efficiency" and "excellence"—is that our hypocrisy will inevitably cause us to abandon God's priorities in exchange for our own. This hypocrisy is characteristic of the Christian businessman who prospers in a well-run company that capitalizes on the unhealthy cravings of its customers, poor life-management skills of his employees, and gullibility (or greed) of his financial supporters—especially when he satisfies his conscience by contributing his money generously to "purer" ministries.

Obviously, accountability systems are costly to create and involve difficult measurement challenges for the entrepreneur trying to make payroll in a high stress, developing culture. The kingdom business will need help from Christian businesspeople in developed countries. This will take the form of counsel in business and leadership development as well as help in building the accountability relationships all leaders need. Some of these relationships will be with other business executives, some with educators, consultants, and the like. The conference that spawned this book is a great start in building these relationships. But it is only a first step in what I hope will be a long and powerful march.

2. Incentives

Another core strength of the entrepreneurial business model is its ability to match powerful incentives to priority objectives. Those in business may confront more realistically than others the truth that they are motivated to serve customers and bosses as well as themselves, to love their neighbor *and* themselves. The reason businesspeople do this well is that businesses skillfully use incentives—financial and non-financial—to reward some efforts and discourage others. In the best business organizations, incentives are tied skillfully to accounting/accountability systems to motivate work that all agree is vital to mutual success. Without worthwhile incentives, work becomes unreliable, unfocused, and ineffectively distributed.

A more complete discussion of the variety of incentive systems kingdom businesses need to prosper and serve God is not appropriate in this chapter. Instead, I will include two simple observations from what I feel are our authors' "best practices" concerning incentives.

First, a number of kingdom businesspeople have affirmed that they have found some "missions" objectives in their businesses to be too important to be left to the intrinsic motivation of committed Christians. That is, extrinsic incentives (like pay, profit sharing, ownership, commission, training, increased responsibility, and other benefits) often work best, even for some that are deemed "missions" objectives. For instance, even though Lai typically hires people who are supported by sending churches in developed countries, he puts their financial support in a corporate fund to finance business start-up costs. Then, he compensates these employees from business operations, based on contribution to both sets of objectives: missions objectives and business objectives. This, he feels, serves to target incentives to specific outcomes.

Second, many contributors to this book also make the opposite argument: that some objectives are spoiled by extrinsic incentives. They affirm what Michael Green (quoted by Rundle) wrote of the amateur missionaries described in Acts: "They went everywhere gossiping the gospel . . . with the conviction of those who are not paid to say that sort of thing." If love is the "greatest" tool we have in serving God, and if love "seeks not her own" (1 Corinthians 13), then some of our most important efforts will "avail nothing" if we do them for any personal incentive save the joy in serving God.

Extrinsic incentives within a kingdom business must be skillfully orchestrated—and they can never be pervasive. They need to leave room for the child of God to *give* passionately of himself, with no expectation of return, direct or indirect. Without an ethic of un-self-interested giving throughout the fabric of business relationships in a kingdom business, the pearl of great price will be lost in "business as usual." The kingdom businessperson must find a way to use competitive advantage, not first and foremost as a position to be defended, but as one from which to love and serve others by empowering them. I admit that this last is as difficult as for a rich man to enter the kingdom of God, no easier than for a camel to fit through the eye of a needle. But the challenge is, in turn, an incentive to seek grace from Christ, through whom all things are possible. It is a chance to wrestle with God, and like Jacob, to be changed by the encounter.

3. Investment

Several of the entrepreneurs in this volume operate under the incentive of agreements with external investors. Some of these investors expect market rates of return on their capital, adjusted realistically for risk, and have covenants that allow them to influence or replace management if certain performance standards are not met. Others are willing to relinquish some amount of expected return and control for the sake of expected returns to the kingdom. Both types of investors will play significant roles in kingdom entrepreneurship.

The potential benefits of external investors in kingdom business are many. As Eldred (chapter 18) and Schultz (chapter 2) have demonstrated, tapping significant Western capital sources affords kingdom businesses advantages many do not have today: (1) external accountability and support from Western businesspeople with a vested interest in business success and (2) sufficient capital and scale to be profitable and self-sufficient. Both reduce primary sources of early-stage failure in new ventures. Thus, access to "professional" capital sources limits the "downside" risk. Businesses that are sufficiently capitalized and accountable to external investors have a better chance of meeting their business objectives and supporting, rather than undermining, their missions objectives.

If external investment comes from what we might call "kingdom investors," I believe the benefits are multiplied still more. The ideal kingdom investor is a business leader with (in no particular order): (1) capital to invest, (2) desire to see lives, communities, and nations changed for Christ, and (3) a desire to give and receive counsel and accountability within a network of likeminded Christian leaders. I would like to see settings emerge in which kingdom investors can come together with kingdom entrepreneurs for mutual benefit. Kingdom entrepreneurs, as I have argued earlier, need investment capital, peer accountability relationships, and business counsel. Kingdom investors, as I have defined them, have the same needs except that they need investment *opportunities*—and a desire to see returns to the kingdom of God as well as to themselves. Building bridges between investors and entrepreneurs forms the DNA of any growing economy, and I believe it is just as vital for the growth of kingdom business in the coming years.

24

KEY CONCEPTS AND LESSONS LEARNED

Ralph A. Miller

In this age of globalization, the nations of the world need new, dynamic, God-inspired leadership to turn back the plagues of warfare, disease, famine, and spiritual darkness. Transportation technology and distribution channels have shrunk the globe to one marketplace and almost one neighborhood. Our Lord's parable of the good Samaritan, told today, might well include an African Muslim aiding an Israeli Jew who had been beaten and robbed by terrorists on an intercontinental flight.

Just as God ordained the Roman world for the rapid spread of the gospel nearly 2,000 years ago, God has ordained a global marketplace to facilitate the spread of the gospel in these pivotal times. Businesspeople have greater freedom and facility to travel the world, bringing the gospel, than at any time since Paul traveled the Roman roads.

Those who go today as tourists may have a few brief, random opportunities to witness, although that hardly rises to the Great Commission standard of "teaching them to obey everything I have commanded you" (Matt. 28:20, NIV). Those who travel as missionaries are barred from most of the neediest nations. They have no natural basis for establishing rapport with many levels of society.

However, those who travel as businesspeople, and know how to create wealth for those around them, have access to and influence with the whole globalized world of commerce. These business travelers, if they commit their money, time, and energies to the countries they visit, and leave a legacy of growing commercial activity and wealth, are well received. People at all levels of society listen to them. When they share the gospel, people usually respect rather than persecute them.

The thesis of this book is that we have entered a new paradigm in world missions. As Steven Rundle (chapter 20) says, "Globalization is turning missions on its head." God is once again using Christians to go into the marketplaces of the world, as Paul went into the *agoras* of the Roman Empire, to evangelize fellow workers and business associates.

"These things happened to them as examples and were written down as warnings for us, on whom the fulfillment of the ages has come," writes Paul in 1 Corinthians 10:11 (NIV). *On Kingdom Business* may be read in like manner by those kingdom entrepreneurs whom God has specially called for this evangelistic outreach. Both the essays and the cases have sage advice and warnings of pitfalls, and are intended to train, edify, and encourage you for sanctified and Spirit-led service.

This chapter is not intended to be a summary, but a brief discussion of some key concepts and lessons this author learned. The chapter concludes with an outline of teaching topics and resources for training the rising kingdom entrepreneur.

BUSINESS—A FORM OF WORSHIP?

From a biblical worldview, is business good or evil? Is it ordained and blessed by God, or established by Satan as part of his dominion? In chapter 13, "How Business in Itself Can Glorify God," Wayne Grudem reviews the biblical foundation for economic and business principles and practices. He sets forth the underlying biblical principles of property ownership, productivity, employment, commercial transactions, profit, money, competition, borrowing, and lending—in short, the basic principles of business. Grudem shows how these are supported by man's reflecting the image of God and carrying out his Genesis 1:28 command to "Be fruitful and multiply and fill the earth and subdue it and have dominion over . . . every living thing that moves on the earth"—a passage often referred to as the "dominion mandate."

Christians cannot be Great Commission teachers unless they are dominion mandate practitioners.[1] Without obedience to God's first command, "be fruitful and multiply and subdue the earth," God's people cannot "teach all nations to obey everything that I commanded you."

Great Commission and Dominion Mandate

In *How Now Shall We Live?* (Tyndale, 1999), Charles Colson calls the dominion mandate the "cultural mandate," saying that, having created all things, God turned over to man the task of creating the culture of all things on earth.[2] That is, we exercise dominion by conforming material things and social relationships to better serve human needs. Thus, in compliance with the "cultural mandate," we marry and create a culture of the family, we set up a business and create its culture; we form a society or government and create its culture. To glorify God, to imitate him, to prosper according to his loving desire, all of these cultures must conform to his will and his Word.

The "dominion mandate," or "cultural mandate," was not canceled when God removed Adam and Eve from the Garden because of sin. God simply allowed the consequences of sin to thwart and limit man's dominion and to make his work harder. Neither did the Great Commission (Matt. 28:19-20) nullify the dominion mandate. It only added the teaching/preaching duty to those whose lives were redeemed, those who were in obedience to God. To those who, co-laboring with God, were multiplying, subduing, and having dominion in that part of the earth that God had entrusted to them, God gave the grace to share the gospel of salvation and God's laws of life.[3]

Jesus summarized the Law with two great commandments—to love God, and to love our neighbor. It is impossible to obey the one without the other. God has given his people two great authorities and responsibilities, the dominion mandate and the Great Commission. Live according to God's purpose and then teach others to do likewise. Accept your redemption and co-labor with God, then teach others to do likewise. Like the two great commandments, these two mandates are inseparable.

In church, we hear the Great Commission preached with greater frequency than the dominion mandate. The result has been that most Christians believe the dichotomy that the ministry of "going, teaching, and preaching" is the only true calling for Christians, while multiplying, subduing, and taking dominion are, at best, secular pursuits. Thus mission agencies[4] and church mission committees[5] have despised business, the very activity that (a) can glorify God, (b) serve as example of godly life and work, and (c) provide the relationships with indigenous peoples through which material and spiritual blessings can freely flow.

"As You Are Going, Make Disciples"

One source of the prevalent attitude of the church toward business ministry versus "pure missions" may lie within the translation of the Great Commission text, Matthew 28:19. The King James and New International Versions give an unintended emphasis on *going*. The KJV says, "Go ye therefore and teach all nations." The NIV says, "Therefore go and make disciples of all nations, baptizing them . . . , teaching them to obey everything. . . ." These translations open the sentence with an imperative of the verb *to go,* giving the impression that the *going* is the thrust of the command. The original

Greek uses a different sentence structure, using a participle form of the verb to go, walk, or travel: Πορευθέντει οὖν μαθητεύσατε πάντα τὰ ἔθνη, βαπτίζοντει αὐτοὺι . . . Literally, "Therefore having gone make disciples of all nations, baptizing them. . . ."[6]

The Greek uses the imperative voice for the verb to make disciples (μαθητεύσατε)[7], rather than for the verb to go[8] (Πορευθέντει). Making disciples is clearly in the imperative mood, and is therefore the thrust of this command. The subtle difference here is that this sentence in the Greek assumes the going, while placing the emphasis on what they should be doing as they go. Jesus knew of the Jewish Diaspora and knew that his disciples would be traveling, either on business or because of persecution. The important question to him was how they were to take advantage of their circumstances for the expansion of the kingdom. The answer is Jesus' authority and control of all circumstances, which he would use for good for those who were called according to his purposes, and for the expansion of his kingdom (Matt. 28:18; Rom. 8:28).

Seen in this light, the Great Commission is fulfilled in many ways. It is a calling that puts eternal value into the traveling of the Christian backpacking kid, who wants to see the world and lingers along the way to share his faith and demonstrate kingdom principles in his work and life.[9] It is a calling to businessmen and women who are going into marketplaces anywhere in the world, into cultures that do not know Christ and his commands. All Christians are called to be in the world but not of it. They are to immerse themselves in a culture that is alien to the gospel, and, while walking there, to make disciples. In global missions, one cannot earn the right to be heard unless one participates in the culture sufficiently to feel its pain, temptations, and blessings. This can mean immersion in its economic life as an entry point into its spiritual life.

When Jesus spoke the Great Commission to his disciples, there is no evidence that he held a strategy session, sending John to Turkey and Thomas to India. He simply gave them an understanding of what activities have eternal value as they work and travel in response to circumstances and opportunities. "As you go through life, make disciples."

At Regent University, virtually all of our students go. Some go all over the world responding to amazing opportunities. Many come to us from distant shores and return there to run businesses. A small group of business leaders meets and prays weekly in Warsaw. Our Regent business school alumni have done well there and are blessing Poland as they lead various ventures. The Lord leads our alumni where he wants them. We have but to teach them to be a blessing in the work that they do, and to be always ready to tell everyone the reason for the hope that is in them (1 Pet. 3:15).

MINISTRY VERSUS BUSINESS

In holistic ministry, the two threads of business and ministry must be firmly intertwined. Like the two great commandments, they cannot be separated. James 2:14-26 makes an issue of a similar dichotomy of faith versus works. Notice, however, that faith precedes works. In the entrepreneurial endeavors cited in this book, the sequence is always faith, then sowing, then reaping. Thus, the planting of the business will precede the planting of the church. Indeed, the first fruits of the business may result in the planting of the church, if the business has been planted in righteousness.

What then are some of the ministry outcomes of a Spirit-led business? According to John Beckett, chapter 19, they reflect God's "purposes to:

- Provide a work culture that gives dignity and meaning to all who work with us, where each person is profoundly valued as an individual, and is able to express his or her God-given abilities to the fullest.
- Serve customers with genuine care and thoroughgoing excellence.
- Make integrity the standard, not just a byword. . . .
- See our work as part of a larger plan, an aspect of God's divine intent. In this context we can look for his glory and grace to be extended—right in the workplace."

When God's entrepreneurs are creating such businesses, they are indeed complying with both the dominion mandate and the Great Commission. They are creating a God-honoring culture in the sphere of control he has given them, and teaching all under their influence to obey all things that he has commanded.

In chapter 12, Peter Tsukahira says, "There may be tension between work for material gain and labor for 'heavenly treasure.'" The challenge is not how to play chameleon by alternately doing business and ministry, but to work on the business in such a Spirit-led fashion that effective ministry results. As Tsukahira says, "By the Spirit and power of Jesus' self-sacrifice working in our lives, believers can do both business and ministry effectively." We can be both missionaries and businesspeople without schizophrenia. Rundle notes, "Among the world's poorest and most oppressed peoples, a financially successful business is not only a legitimate ministry in itself, but can support other kinds of ministry. An unsuccessful business fails on both counts."

Thomas Sudyk (chapter 14) says, "A successful business needs to be based on profit. . . . Without profit, a business is just another social program distributing money from shareholders (donors) to its customers or employees." Business ministries are sustainable models for evangelization that do not depend on the ability or motivation of their sponsors to continuously contribute funds. Profitable businesses grow, leading to increased ministry. The growth of nonprofit ministries and unprofitable businesses is limited to the growth of their donor bases or new shareholder money. Growth from either source is unlikely over the long run. The dot-com stock bubble is just the latest example of this fuzzy "new economy" idea of indefinite growth without profits.

MEASURING RESULTS

In chapter 15, John Cragin applies a rigorous business measurement stick to holistic ministry. A business that is called by God and is using his resources must produce measurable results in his kingdom. Whatever is not, or cannot, be measured, will not be done consistently. Many ministry outcomes can be very difficult to quantify, but with well-thought-out goals, ways can be found to measure the results. We must also remember that the Lord can and will measure both our inputs and our outcomes. Cragin writes,

> To achieve its purpose, the business mission company must develop and invest in Great Commission efforts that are synergistic with and leveraged by the company's presence in strategically selected markets. It must set standards for evangelism and discipleship, measure results, and evaluate results per dollar invested for every sphere of influence identified in the market analysis. Company spheres of influence and the spheres of influence of each team member are specific market segments targeted for impact.

For Christian businesspeople, one of the great difficulties with measuring ministry is that they have never operated that way before. If they have never before used their business for ministry, they will have trouble integrating ministry into the other components of their business. They will particularly have trouble weighing the interaction of the ministry component in their decision making.

One Christian who has written at length on the integration of mission in business is Buck Jacobs, founder and president of the C12 Groups, a Christian CEO discipling business. In an article titled "The C12 Five Point

Alignment Matrix," [10] Jacobs describes a tool to align the five components of business so that business practices and policies will be consistent and in alignment with the mission statement. Jacobs has adapted a secular model by adding the ministry component so that it becomes an integral part of all business decision making and planning. This has helped the C12 members, people who feel the call of God to use their businesses for ministry, to keep ministry from being merely an added extra. With the mission statement as the focal point in the decision matrix, and ministry as number one of the five business components, C12 businesses are making significant progress toward the status of kingdom businesses.

CAPITAL FOR KINGDOM COMPANIES, LARGE AND SMALL

As experienced entrepreneurs know, the hardest part of a start-up or acquisition can be raising the necessary capital. God, in his wisdom, has enabled the church to employ innovative strategies to obtain the needed funds.

Consulting (chapter 2) may be a means of trading knowledge, experience, and wisdom for money, and/or influence, and/or control of aspects of the management of large businesses in the 10/40 Window. While the holistic ministry partner is interested in the ability to evangelize and disciple large numbers of people, the financial partners are interested in making money. The government, meanwhile, is interested in jobs, foreign exchange, and prestige. A joint venture company can well serve the Lord's purposes, even when owned by unbelievers in a country hostile to the gospel. But why does that surprise us when God convinced the Egyptians to donate their jewelry to their slaves! (see Ex. 12:35-36).

Ken Eldred (chapter 18) has been abundantly blessed with faith, wisdom, and humility. These character qualities enabled him to start and lead businesses, create wealth, and funnel wealth strategically into kingdom businesses. Together with loyalty to an old friend, they led him to participate in the start-up of a kingdom company designed to:

- provide employment for Christians in India
- offer attractive wages
- equip and mentor Christians in the company
- enable Christians in the company to support the local church

Eldred's ability to make money and use it wisely is just another way God uses the varied gifts of believers to serve his kingdom purposes.

There is a notion within the church that you have to lie, cheat, and steal to make a profit in business. The church needs to learn that businesses all over the world are creating wealth ethically for all of their stakeholders—customers, creditors, owners, suppliers, and employees. With wise strategic planning, careful staffing, and proper financing, companies can start and grow in most climates and take the gospel with them. For those Christians whom God has gifted in any of these areas, this is a high calling, a calling the church should be supporting.

HOLISTIC MINISTRY PRINCIPLES AND BEST PRACTICES

Principles

John Beckett's essay (chapter 19) provides foundational principles that characterize the best practices in holistic ministry, or, if you please, kingdom business. Becket says the following are ways serious Christians approach business leadership:

- the Lordship of Christ in all endeavors
- a clear sense of direction
- putting people first
- living by uncompromising integrity
- stewardship—seeing our work as a trust

Practices

Chapter 2 lists some practices learned through both negative and positive experience over the years. Great Commission companies . . .

- have strategy coordinators
- make sure that expatriates are spiritually accountable to a church or mission agency
- emphasize church planting or ministry teams, focused on cities or people groups
- have multiethnic or multinational management teams
- have not only written business plans but also annual Great Commission plans
- base employee compensation primarily on performance (not on donor support)
- must have significant export markets
- have formal employee training programs on business ethics
- screen their leadership teams before starting or expanding their businesses

Business Ministry, Relationship Building

If we see business as a predatory jungle, we might conclude that Christians would be at a disadvantage in the marketplace. But if we understand business as an arena of multiple interlocking relationships wherein all parties are interdependent and relying on unity for success, then we might expect the Christian to be an indispensable catalyst to success. Are the two great commandments of Christianity about relationships? Should a Christian, operating according to a biblical worldview, be equipped to handle conflicting relationships with wisdom? Why might a biblical worldview be more useful than a secular worldview in business? I think it is because the Bible teaches that prosperity is based on the unity created by mutual service. The secular view tends toward power and self-service, and therefore self-destructs over time.

So how do John Beckett's five principles apply to the Christian corporate leader?

The Lordship of Christ in all endeavors. If Christ has called us to lead a business, it will accomplish his purposes only if he is the source of all wisdom, provision, and guidance. He who called us to lead is also he who called other stakeholders to support us. His Spirit is the synergy and unity that provides the power for our success. His lordship unifies; all other priorities divide a company into a collection of self-seeking empire-builders.

A clear sense of direction. The first function of leadership is to set the vision around which corporate energies can coalesce. The Bible says that without a vision the people perish (Prov. 29:18). This is true of families, nations, and corporations. The vision-setting role of the leader is a role in which Spirit-filled Christian leaders should shine as they bring the mind of Christ to bear on the material and spiritual roles of their companies.

Putting people first. Many of us think that the ideal business would be one that is very profitable and has no employees. But God usually calls his leaders to lead people-intensive companies, where they can be channels for his love and guidance to his people. The stakeholders of a business, whether or not institutions represent them, are all people. The employees, the customers, the stockholders, the suppliers, and the creditors are all people with free will to continue their participation in the business endeavor or to depart. If the business stops blessing them, they depart. If they are treated unfairly, they leave. If the leader does not manage all these conflicting relationships with justice and respect, the company will be torn up by employee turnover and strikes, low sales, credit crunches, stock losses, and all the disasters executives fear. What better guide for relationships than the Bible, and what better relationship specialist than a committed Christian who can demonstrate God's love for people?

Living by uncompromising integrity. A company cannot serve as a beacon for the gospel with compromised integrity. In Jesus' day, testifying against the Pharisees, he told his followers to do what the Pharisees say but not what they do. This pious group, which should have been in the vanguard to usher in the kingdom, opposed Christ and crucified him. A kingdom company is one that God uses to usher in his kingdom. It must be in the world but not of the world. It must not be like the Pharisees, who were ultimately worldly people who looked down on the world.

Stewardship—seeing our work as a trust. The very nature of leadership of a large corporation, particularly a public corporation, is stewardship. The CEO has a fiduciary responsibility to the stakeholders. While the CEO has authority over the corporate assets, they are not his or hers to dispose of or to pilfer at will. How tragic it is to see corporate CEOs violating their trust. The Christian CEO, however, has a further stewardship responsibility to God, by whose grace he or she holds the position. The Christian CEO is obligated to accomplish God's purposes rather than selfish ones.

BLESSING A NATION THROUGH BUSINESS

Kingdom entrepreneurship involves taking Christ's multiple blessings to the ends of the earth. Jesus dispensed physical, material, and spiritual blessings. He healed, fed, raised the dead, and gave salvation to all who would hear. The kingdom minister must do no less.

What are the blessings that Third World countries seek from those who would befriend them?

- jobs for their people
- technology to raise their productivity and living standards
- innovative ideas to create wealth for their citizens
- capital to unleash their entrepreneurs' creative efforts
- exports to build foreign exchange and to finance needed imports
- respect among the world of nations

When these blessings are obviously flowing, kingdom entrepreneurs are usually welcome, even if they are evangelizing when local law or custom forbids them. Ken Crowell's companies (chapter 3) in Israel are one such example. Nations are blessed by job makers, but job takers are another matter. In the host country's eyes, job takers have no redeeming grace, and generally receive no tolerance for evangelism.

DEVELOPING NEW KINGDOM ENTREPRENEURS

As Rundle says, "kingdom entrepreneurship is a unique, highly specialized mission strategy that merits its own specialized curriculum." Rundle helps us to set that curriculum by defining the kingdom entrepreneur:

> Kingdom entrepreneurs are *authentic* businesspeople with proven competence in at least one area of business administration. They are spiritually gifted much like traditional missionaries, but are called and equipped to use those gifts in a business context. Kingdom entrepreneurs have a genuine desire to see communities of faith spring up in the spiritually driest places, and are willing to live and work in these places to make that happen. Rather than perceiving the business as a distraction from their ministry, kingdom entrepreneurs recognize it as the necessary context for their incarnational outreach. The daily struggles—meeting deadlines, satisfying customers, being victimized by corruption—are precisely the things that enable kingdom entrepreneurs to model Christian discipleship on a daily basis.

This definition speaks to the kingdom entrepreneur's spiritual gifts, his or her equipping for spiritual ministry, the cross-cultural type of places of life and work, and the type of work to be done.

With this information we should be able to tailor a screening, selection, and training process that includes the following competencies or training courses:

- evangelism and church planting
- cross-cultural training
- training in the skills of starting, financing, and operating a business
- understanding the theologies of mission, business, and their integration
- practical issues, including case studies of using business as a vehicle for cross-cultural missions
- opportunities for internships to gather experience in both business and missions

Rundle assists us by example with the syllabus of a course at Biola University.

Does the Christian higher education community have an obligation to help train new kingdom entrepreneurs? Well, if not an obligation, then certainly an opportunity.

The opportunity is for both business schools and divinity schools. Divinity schools attract many students who feel called to serve the Lord in foreign lands. They acquire skills in evangelization and church planting. As missionaries they spend much of their time itinerating to raise money, and, in-country, developing relationships strong enough to gain credibility. Their burnout rate is significant. With business training or entrepreneurial experience, these students could become self-supporting, more effective in the work of evangelism, and more comfortable in the culture.

The kingdom entrepreneur needs *both* skill sets to minister effectively. In addition to evangelism and church planting skills, he or she needs:

- the mindset of the entrepreneur (reinforced by the renewing of the mind, saturated in a biblical worldview, together with firm faith and understanding of the power of God available in the life of the believer [Rom. 8:28 and Phil. 4:13]), who always sees opportunities where others see only problems
- cross-cultural training to make him or her effective in an alien culture
- training or experience in business leadership and management
- engineering training or experience, if possible

USING THIS BOOK AS A TEXT FOR KINGDOM ENTREPRENEURSHIP

1. *Curriculum Preparation*

Rundle provides a useful syllabus with bibliography.

2. *Course Introduction, Kingdom Business as a Strategy for Evangelism*

ESSAYS:

"Preface." "How do we [show people the gospel] in the context of today's globalizing economy, in which people's felt needs center more on finding a job and attaining economic development than on investigating the claims of Christ?"

"Introduction." "Basic business techniques are critical to founding a successful kingdom business."

CASES:

Chapter 1, "Esther Hui and Infosail." Esther's business philosophy.

Chapter 2, "AMI and Great Commission Companies." "East Asian governments generally welcome foreign manufacturers, especially those with fairly large capitalization. As long as a company makes money and provides jobs for the local people, the governments will not interfere—unless it is rather openly breaking the law."

Chapter 3, "Galtronics: A Case Study in Israel." Business to establish a Christian witness in Israel. The threefold purpose of Galtronics.

Chapter 4, "Business in the Middle East." A single woman does business in the Middle East. "Business platforms also enable a demonstration of God's righteousness, in that they show that biblical ethics are realistic and enhance the dignity of human life."

SOME CRITERIA FOR ANALYZING THE CASES:

- What were the success criteria of the venture?
- What were the "kingdom accomplishments" (i.e., eternal value added, economic value added, that drew people to Christ)?
- Was there an understandable business model that met the needs of all of the stakeholders?
- Evidence of faithfulness and perseverance?
- Evidence of God's guidance? Was it a "God thing?" (Isa. 55:8-9; Prov. 3:5).
- How did they guard their hearts against greed?

CASE DISCUSSION QUESTIONS, GENERAL:

- What prior training did the entrepreneur have that helped or uniquely qualified him/her for the holistic ministry venture(s)?
- What training or education was lacking? Was the entrepreneur able to get this training or make up for the lack?
- What spiritual gifts seem to have been particularly helpful in the business and in the ministry?

- What divinely ordained meeting or circumstance do you see in the launching of this business ministry? Did the entrepreneur realize that at the time, or only later?
- What, if any, tactics has Satan used to thwart this venture? What was/is the greatest obstacle to its success?
- Is there a clear mission statement? Did the mission remain constant as the business developed?
- What factors made this business a successful tool for ministry? What did the business provide that was useful for the establishment and growth of the ministry?
- In general, what facets of business can have eternal significance? How would you measure the ministry of this business?

3. The Theology of Missions, of Business, and the Integration of the Two

ESSAYS:

Chapter 13, "How Business in Itself Can Glorify God." Those created in God's image glorify him by modeling his attributes.

Appendix B (1), "The Stewardship of Creation."

Appendix C, "Dynamics of Faith." Faith and the "R/C" ratio.

Appendix B (2), "A Call to Faithfulness."

Appendix B (3), "Taking Hold of the Life That Is Truly Life."

CASE:

Chapter 12, "The Integration of Business and Ministry." An NEC employee as well as a pastor in Japan, the author struggles with the difficulties of bridging the dichotomy between work and ministry.

4. Grounding Kingdom Business in the History of Christian Evangelism

ESSAY:

Chapter 16, "Starting Kingdom Companies: A Biblical and Historical Overview." "Expanding business ventures have been vehi-

cles of Christian skill and professionalism, God-inspired farsightedness and faith, and ethical and social concern for centuries. They
have been instrumental in impacting and transforming whole
regions, societies, and countries to the glory of God and the advancement of his kingdom."

5. Cross-cultural Business and Ministry, Outside Resources

TEXTS:

Duane Elmer, *Cross-cultural Conflict, Building Relationships for
Effective Ministry* (Downers Grove, Ill.: InterVarsity Press, 1993).

Danielle Medina Walker, et al., *Doing Business Internationally:
Participant Workbook* (Princeton, N.J.: Princeton Training
Press).

CASES:

R. T. Moran, D. O. Braaten, and J. E. Walsh, eds., *International
Business Case Studies for the Multicultural Marketplace* (Newton,
Mass.: Butterworth-Heinemann, 1994).

6. Strategic Planning for Kingdom Entrepreneurial Ministry

ESSAYS:

Chapter 14, "Strategic Considerations in Business as Mission." In a
remote Indian village, the people knew of Pepsi, but no one had ever
heard of Jesus.

Chapter 15, "The Business of Missions—the Missions of Business."
"Mission efforts must also meet the strategic effectiveness criterion
the Bible calls fruitfulness. . . . We should not waste time on fruitless
efforts."

CASES:

Chapter 6, "Business in Cambodia."

Chapter 7, "Business Among South Asian Refugees."

Chapter 8, "Business in Kyrgyzstan."

Chapter 9, "Business in Central Asia."

Chapter 10, "Business in South Asia."

Chapter 11, "Business in India."

Chapter18, "Kingdom-Based Investing" (India).

APPENDIXES

The following guidelines are simply suggestions. One needs to organize one's own presentation without being confined to the order in which these guidelines are given. The sequence of events should flow naturally in essay form. The length of the essay should be approximately 4,000-5,000 words. This means about 8-10 pages of a published book. Some essays may be shorter than this.

1. The call (a personal recounting of your motivation, preparation, and how you came to be involved in business as mission)
2. The entrepreneurial launch
    A. How you got the business started
    B. The early trials, temptations, and triumphs
3. The business plan
    A. In theory (how it was supposed to work)
    B. In practice (how it actually developed—trials and triumphs)
4. Growth of business
    A. Profitability, job creation, etc.
    B. The role the business played in advancing God's kingdom (evangelism, discipleship, teaching, empowering local believers to become economically self-sufficient, etc.)
    C. Management practices (loosely defined as human resource management, financial management, public relations, competitor relations, etc.). Note especially the incorporation of kingdom values/Christian ethics into business practice. Cite some concrete examples.
5. Evaluation
    A. Business practice
    B. Business performance
    C. Ministry effectiveness

THE STEWARDSHIP OF CREATION
C. René Padilla

I was brought up in a Christian home. My godly parents taught me that the basic law of life is love—love to God and love to one's neighbor. What was the role of material possessions, according to this approach to life? For all I remember, nothing much was ever said about it. Money was terribly scarce in our home, but the little that there was of it was carefully managed so as to cover the basic needs of our family of seven children, including education, and sometimes even to help others who had less than we did.

Anyone who has had the experience of being transplanted from one culture to another knows the (oftentimes painful) adjustments that one has to make in order to accommodate oneself to, or at least to understand, the new situation. We are cultural beings and as such are inclined to assume that the ways people, including us, feel, think, and behave in our culture are universally valid. When we are transplanted to another culture, eventually we realize that there are other ways of feeling, thinking, and behaving.

I could share with you a number of ways in which my being transplanted from Ecuador to the United States broadened my view of life and gave me a new appreciation of certain Christian values that are simply taken for granted in American culture. I still remember, for instance, how surprised I was to find out that some of my fellow students at Wheaton College who came from rather well-to-do homes were still expected by their parents to get some kind of part-time job—washing dishes or cleaning bathrooms—in order to pay a percentage of the cost of their education. That was not a part of my experience in my own culture, where such menial tasks were always reserved for servants.

On the other hand, I also remember how shocked I was when I heard people say that a person was worth so many dollars—be it $50,000, or $100,000, or $500,000, or $1 million, or whatever—depending on how much he or she owned. As time went on I learned that this way of speaking reflected an approach to life that is very much a part of the *ethos* of a deeply materialistic culture in which the value of people depends, to a large extent, not so much on who they *are* as on what they *have*. And of course, I found out that in this culture, since I had nothing, I was worth nothing.

HOW MUCH IS A PERSON WORTH?

For people who feel they are worth nothing because they have nothing, the Creation narrative in Genesis 1 has a liberating message. There, in verses 26-27 (NIV), on the sixth day of Creation,

God said: "Let us make man in our image, in our likeness, and let them rule over the fish of the sea and the birds of the air, over the livestock, over all the earth, and over all the creatures that move along the ground." So God created man in his own image, in the image of God he created him; male and female he created them.

Can there be anything more liberating for the human spirit than to know that one is made in God's image and likeness—that whether one is rich or poor, one's value is totally dependent on the fact that we all bear the image of God? We are made in the image and likeness of God—that is the most basic fact about human nature and a solid foundation for a biblical anthropology.

In practical terms, however, what does it mean to say that we are made in the image and likeness of God? In what sense can it be said that *we are like God himself?*

In the first place, the reference in verse 26 to God's image and likeness in man—male and female, as verse 27 makes clear—is immediately followed by a reference to the *human vocation in creation,* namely, to "be fruitful and increase in number; fill the earth and subdue it" (v. 28); to rule "over the fish of the sea and the birds of the air, over the livestock, over all the earth, and over all the creatures that move along the ground" (v. 26). This thought is then expanded in verses 29-30, with one more element being added to the rulership over the animal kingdom: dominion over all vegetation ("I give you every seed-bearing plant on the face of the whole earth and every tree that has fruit with seed in it. They will be yours for food. . . . I give every green plant for food.") A very clear inference is that human beings are *like* God through the exercise of stewardship of God's creation. They have been created to cooperate with God in the preservation of humankind throughout history and in the stewardship of the earth and all that is in it.

In the second place, the likeness to God is inherent to all human beings and provides the basis for the value and the dignity of every single person regardless of race or social status, nationality, or family name. Because God created man—male and female—in his image and likeness, all persons deserve to be treated like those who have been made with a God-given identity and vocation, namely, to bear God's image and to cooperate with him as stewards of his creation. A person's worth is determined not by what he or she *has* but by what he or she *is* on the basis of this identity and vocation received from God.

HOLISTIC CHRISTIAN WITNESS

This vocation as stewards of God's creation is at the very heart of what is known in theology as "the cultural mandate"—a mandate to work, to be pro-

ductive, even as God himself worked for six days and "on the seventh day
. . . rested from all his work" (Gen. 2:2, NIV). Work is, therefore, the responsibility of human beings to reflect that they are made in the image and likeness of God by caring for God's creation and transforming into *culture* that
which God created out of nothing. In all its forms—including science, technology, art, politics, economics, trade, and ecology—*culture* is largely the
result of the exercise of human stewardship over the earth.

There is no basis for the traditional dichotomy between "secular work"
and "sacred work"; between "our business" and "the Lord's business." All
our work is secular in that it relates to present-day realities in the world and
to our exercise of dominion over God's creation. At the same time, all our
work is sacred in that it has to do with our God-given vocation to cooperate
with him to fulfill his purpose for creation. "The Lord's business" cannot be
restricted to "religious" activities; it includes the totality of our lives—to the
extent to which we have integrated into our daily experience the meaning of
Paul's words, "So whether you eat or drink or whatever you do, do it all for
the glory of God" (1 Cor. 10:31, NIV).

From this perspective, the evangelistic mandate—the mandate to share
the gospel with those who do not know Jesus Christ—is inseparable from the
cultural mandate. Sharing the gospel is far more than *telling* people the good
news of Jesus the Lord and Savior for the sake of saving souls and planting
churches. Sharing the gospel is cooperating with God's purpose in Jesus
Christ to transform the totality of human life and the whole of creation so
that they may reflect his glory. This sharing takes place not only through what
we *say* but also through what we *are* and what we *do*. The synergy of being,
doing, and saying brings the evangelistic and the cultural mandates together
and makes a holistic Christian witness possible. This type of witness is to be
expected of kingdom entrepreneurs who make the stewardship of God's creation a real heart concern.

If Christian witness needs to combine the *saying* with the *being* and the
doing, Christ's witnesses are bound to face the demands of the gospel in rela-
tion to every aspect of creation and in every area of human life. Ethical questions such as the following become unavoidable:

- How can our business become economically successful without
  neglecting the ecological responsibility implied in the God-given
  vocation to take care of creation? How can production be moni-
  tored in such a way that growth is ecologically sustainable? What
  kind of practical behavior is to be expected from those who know
  that human beings are not owners but merely stewards of God's
  creation?

- How can justice and equity be properly established in our business? How can we avoid exploitation and oppression of workers, and promote good human relationships and solidarity over against individualism and unfair competition?

AGENTS OF SOCIAL CHANGE

As we have seen, work derives its meaning from the cultural mandate—it is the means through which human beings fulfill their vocation as stewards of God's creation. It is a way for them to subdue the earth in accordance with God's original ordinance.

In light of God's purpose for work as expressed in Genesis 1, seeing work as a human right—better yet, as a right to be human—is biblical. A person who can work but who is deprived of a job is prevented from satisfying basic human needs and from participating in the economic building of society. This person is also prevented from fulfilling the God-given vocation that provides the basis for human dignity.

The importance of this understanding of the lack of work can hardly be exaggerated in many a society that is affected by structural unemployment today. A case in point is Argentina, where according to the latest official figures 21.5 percent of the labor force lack work, over one half of the population of 36 million are living under the poverty line, 9 million are totally unable to satisfy their basic needs, and well over 6 million have become poor within this last year.

Much could be said about work from a political, social, and economic point of view. Both the analysis of the situation and the solutions proposed will vary according to the different outlooks of those who analyze and propose. From a theological perspective, however, the most serious damage caused by unemployment is that it robs people of the possibility of fulfilling their role as stewards of God's creation, thus depriving them of a necessary condition to affirm their human identity and self-worth.

In light of the joblessness that affects millions of people today, kingdom entrepreneurs have the opportunity to contribute toward the fulfillment of God's intention for humankind by becoming involved in the creation of work and enabling people to participate in stewardship of creation. The mark of genuine biblical evangelism—a mark that distinguishes it from proselytism—is that it takes place as an expression of true concern for individuals and communities who are not seen as "souls" to be saved but as persons who have physical, material, psychological, and spiritual needs and who are the object of God's love in Jesus Christ. As the report of the Social Concern Track at Lausanne II (Manila, June 1989) puts it:

The good news is that God has established his Kingdom of righteousness and peace through the incarnation, ministry, atoning death and resurrection of his Son, Jesus Christ. The Kingdom fulfills God's purpose in creation by bringing wholeness to humanity and all of creation. In the Kingdom people receive by grace alone a new status before God and people, a new dignity and worth as his daughters and sons, and empowerment by his Spirit to be stewards of creation and servants of one another in a new community. The Kingdom will come in its fullness in a new heaven and earth only when Jesus returns.

Those who respond to this good news who are poor in the material sense, or powerless, are empowered by the Spirit and served by other members of the Kingdom community to experience full humanity as stewards of God's creation. The non-poor who become poor-in-spirit receive a true dignity replacing false pride in riches, and are liberated to be truly human with a passion for justice for the poor. They are to trust in the power of God's Spirit which enables them to serve rather than control. They enter a new family that accepts them for what they are, rather than for their achievements in material prosperity or status. The task of evangelization among the majority of the unreached who are poor will be carried out primarily by those who are poor, with appropriate support from those economically advantaged who are poor in spirit.[1]

APPENDIX B (2)

A CALL TO FAITHFULNESS

C. René Padilla

Is it possible to both be a businessperson and be faithful to God?

At least in principle, there is no reason why people who intend to be faithful to God cannot be in business. Yet, few subjects are more relevant to kingdom entrepreneurs than faithfulness to God.

We live in a world dominated by economics and finances. Almost all of the key decisions of national governments—and that affects most people—are taken not for the common good but under the dictates of transnational financial interests. As George Soros, one of the world's wealthiest men, has put it in his analysis of *The Crisis of Global Capitalism,* in this age of what he calls the "fundamentalism of the market," universal (or social) values, such as peace, justice, and freedom have been displaced by financial values. Money has become the supreme value, not only in business but in every field of human endeavor. As a result, society is under the threat of destruction. "A society without social values," says Soros, "cannot survive, and a global society needs universal values to remain united."[1]

What does faithfulness to God mean for a kingdom entrepreneur living and working in a world dominated by the drive for material profit?

A biblical passage that can help us find an answer to this question is Deuteronomy 8:1-20, Moses' exhortation to the people of Israel as they are about to enter the Promised Land. The past, the present, and the future of Israel come within the purview of the Word of God. We will see the meaning of faithfulness to God in each historical moment.

FAITHFULNESS TO GOD IN THE PAST

Two sections of this passage—verses 2-5 and verses 14-16 (NIV)—focus on the past forty-year experience of Israel in "the vast and dreadful desert." In a way, the emphasis is not so much on Israel's faithfulness to God as on God's faithfulness to Israel, shown in his provision of food—"manna, which neither you nor your fathers had known" (v. 3; cf. v. 16)—and drink—"water out of hard rock" (v. 15). Yet God's provision is said to take place in line with God's purpose to teach Israel to depend on him, and on him alone, and to obey his commandments:

> Remember how the LORD your God led you all the way in the desert these
> forty years, to humble you and to test you in order to know what was in
> your heart, whether or not you would keep his commands. He humbled
> you, causing you to hunger and then feeding you with manna . . . to teach
> you that man does not live on bread alone but on every word that comes

from the mouth of the LORD. Your clothes did not wear out and your feet did not swell during these forty years. Know then in your heart that as a man disciplines his son, so the LORD your God disciplines you. . . .

He led you through the vast and dreadful desert, that thirsty and waterless land, with its venomous snakes and scorpions. He brought you water out of hard rock. He gave you manna to eat in the desert . . . to humble and to test you so that in the end it might go well with you (vv. 2-5, 15-16, NIV).

The underlying assumption here is that faithfulness to God is something that the people of God have to learn, and that the best place for them to learn it is the desert, in the midst of scarcity and vulnerability. This is the obverse side of the warning that appears further on, not to forget the Lord when Israel experiences prosperity in the Promised Land. Faithfulness to God requires the people's acknowledgment not only of his faithful provision but also of the purpose of his discipline—that, by being humbled, his people may learn to depend on "every word that comes from the mouth of the LORD" (v. 3). Israel is therefore exhorted to remember the way in which God tested their faithfulness to him and proved his own faithfulness to them in the past, in circumstances of extreme risk in which the only basis for hope of survival was his promise to give them "the land of promise."

FAITHFULNESS TO GOD IN THE PRESENT

What God expects of his people in the present is made quite clear at the beginning of our passage:

> Be careful to follow every command I am giving you today, so that you may live and increase and may enter and possess the land that the LORD promised on oath to your forefathers (v. 1, NIV).

The same admonition is repeated further on:

> Observe the commands of the LORD your God, walking in his ways and revering him (v. 6).

God's relationship to Israel is defined in terms of command and obedience. Israel is the people of God to the extent that God's commands, through which his will is mediated, are allowed to be the very axle of life. It is through faithfulness to God's commands that Israel derives its identity as the people of God. As Walter Brueggemann has said, "Israel's life is to be a practice of bringing every phase of its existence under the rule of Yahweh, thereby rejecting the authority and claim of any other god or any other loyalty."[2]

Clearly, the possession of "the land of promise" is conditional, and the condition is obedience to God's commands. Faithfulness to God is, so to say, the property deed that authorizes Israel to take possession of the land.

FAITHFULNESS TO GOD IN THE FUTURE

There is a sharp contrast between the past situation of Israel in the desert, described in verses 2-5 and 15b-16, and the situation that the people of God are to have in the Promised Land, described in verses 7-9 (NIV):

> For the LORD your God is bringing you into a good land—a land with streams and pools of water, with springs flowing in the valleys and hills; a land with wheat and barley, vines and fig trees, pomegranates, olive oil and honey; a land where bread will not be scarce and you will lack nothing; a land where the rocks are iron and you can dig copper out of the hills.

In "the land of promise," which is a land of abundance, the satisfaction of physical needs—food and drink—will be guaranteed; the scarcity of the desert, as well as the vulnerability and the anxiety that scarcity creates, will be over. Not only that, but Israel will also have at hand the necessary minerals to make instruments of production—iron and copper. The crossing of the Jordan will mean the entry into a gifted land that will make possible a totally different lifestyle.

There is, however, a question that Israel will have to face as it crosses the Jordan and begins to enjoy the benefits of the Promised Land—the question of faithfulness to God in the midst of plenty. During the forty-year desert sojourn, God manifested his presence with Israel, and they learned to depend on him for their survival. The danger now is that, as they cross the Jordan, they enjoy the gifts of the land but forget the Giver of the land. It is not surprising, therefore, that a large portion of our passage should be dedicated to the following warnings:

> When you have eaten and are satisfied, praise the LORD your God for the good land he has given you. Be careful that you do not forget the LORD your God, failing to observe his commands, his laws and his decrees that I am giving you this day. Otherwise, when you eat and are satisfied, when you build fine houses and settle down, and when your herds and flocks grow large and your silver and gold increase and all you have is multiplied, then your heart will become proud and you forget the LORD your God, who brought you out of Egypt, out of the land of slavery. . . .
>
> You may say to yourself, "My power and the strength of my hands have produced this wealth for me." But remember the LORD your God, for it is

he who gives you the ability to produce wealth, and so confirms his covenant, which he swore to your forefathers, as it is today (vv. 10-14, 17-18, NIV).

As the covenant people of God, Israel has received the land as a covenant gift through which God fulfills his promise to Israel's ancestors. The proper response is gratefulness. The temptation, however, will be to forget God—to take his gifts for granted, assuming that material prosperity is deserved as a mere result of hard work. The antidote to this temptation to pride is to praise God for his generosity in giving the "good land" to his people (v. 10) and to remember God's action in taking his people "out of Egypt, out of the house of slavery" (v. 14). Israel is the recipient and steward of a gift, not the producer and controller of wealth.

The exhortation to praise God and to recall his gracious liberation from slavery is accompanied by a warning concerning the sure results of not remembering:

> If you ever forget the LORD your God and follow other gods and worship and bow down to them, I testify against you today that you will surely be destroyed. Like the nations the LORD destroyed before you, so you will be destroyed for not obeying the LORD your God (vv. 19-20, NIV).

There is a close connection between Israel's faithfulness to God and God's fulfillment of his promises to Israel. God alone is the source of life for Israel. As long as Israel *remembers* God and keeps his commandments (vv. 2, 18), it can count on God's blessing in terms of possession of the land and its products (vv. 7-9, 12-13). On the other hand, if it *forgets* God (vv. 11, 19) and allows pride to take over, it will fall into idolatry and will be destroyed like other nations. When God is forgotten, self-confidence grows and leads to pride. Pride in turn results in idolatry, and idolatry ends in destruction.

GOD'S CALL TO FAITHFULNESS

What does this passage teach us about faithfulness to God? I would draw from it the following conclusions.

In the first place, if we are to be faithful to God in the midst of plenty, we have to learn to be content in the midst of scarcity. The proper attitude toward wealth and poverty is illustrated by the apostle Paul, who wrote:

> I have learned to be content whatever the circumstances. I know what it is to be in need, and I know what it is to have plenty. I have learned the secret of being content in any and every situation, whether well fed or hungry, whether living in plenty or in want. I can do everything through him who gives me strength (Phil. 4:11b-13, NIV).

Material scarcity may be used by God to teach us to depend on him, and learning to depend on him alone is essential to true Christian discipleship. To be sure, this insight may be used ideologically, as when the poor are told to accept their poverty as the will of God and nothing is done to enable them to overcome their poverty. The fact remains, however, that we all, like Israel, need to learn that "man does not live on bread alone but on every word that comes from the mouth of the LORD" (Deut. 8:3, NIV). And that is a lesson learned in the desert. The muscles of faithfulness to God are best exercised in the midst of poverty.

In the second place, faithfulness to God—unreserved commitment to him—is inseparable from obedience to his commandments. Jesus Christ himself stated that he did not come "to abolish the Law and the Prophets" but "to fulfill them" (Matt. 5:17, NIV). Accordingly, the exhortation addressed to Israel, "Observe the commands of the LORD your God, walking in his ways and revering him" (Deut. 8:6, NIV), is also addressed to us. This is not to deny the dangers of legalism, but to affirm that the practice of the will of God embodied in Jesus Christ is the acid proof of love for him. As Jesus said: "If you obey my commands, you will remain in my love, just as I have obeyed my Father's commands and remain in his love" (John 15:10, NIV).

In the third place, faithfulness to God requires that we recognize that we are not self-made persons but people in a covenant relationship to God, entirely dependent on and responsible to him. The temptation to pride is inherent to wealth. Against the claim, *"My* power and the strength of *my* hand have produced this wealth *for me"* (Deut. 8:17, NIV, emphasis added), the necessary attitude is one of praise to God for his kindness, and the recognition that it is he who gives people "the ability to produce wealth" (8:19).

Finally, faithfulness to God leads to life, while unfaithfulness to God leads to destruction. Kingdom entrepreneurs cannot dedicate themselves to creating wealth without previously clarifying in their minds the *how* and the *what for* of this task in light of the Word of God. When the means and the ends of wealth—its ways of production and its aims—are divorced from ethics, wealth becomes destructive for both individuals and communities. The creation, ownership, and distribution of wealth are not merely questions of technology, but also ethical—and spiritual—issues.

Taking Hold of the Life That Is Truly Life

C. René Padilla

Is having wealth incompatible with Christian discipleship? A straightforward interpretation of Jesus' words to the rich young man seems to imply that it is: "One thing you lack.... Go, sell everything you have and give to the poor, and you will have treasure in heaven. Then come, follow me" (Mark 10:21, NIV).

Our tendency is to minimize the importance of Jesus' demand and all too quickly to assume that his words must not be taken literally. This tendency is unwarranted and may prevent us from the kind of commitment to Jesus Christ that he expects. Let us remember his words addressed to the multitudes that were following him at a time of popularity: "[A]ny of you who does not give up *everything* he has cannot be my disciple" (Luke 14:33, NIV, emphasis added).

An obedient response to this call to radical discipleship can be seen in Habitat for Humanity International.[1] The history of this movement goes back to 1965, when Millard Fuller—a "self-made" entrepreneur who had become a millionaire at age 29—was graced to see that his wealth was destroying his health and his marriage and that he needed to redefine his priorities. Having decided to leave behind their successful business and their life of luxury and ostentation in Montgomery, Alabama, he and his wife, Linda, spent some time at the Koinonia Farm community in Americus, Georgia. This was led by Clarence Jordan, author of the "Cotton Patch" version of the New Testament. At Koinonia, Jordan and Fuller started a "partnership housing" project in which people who lacked adequate shelter were encouraged and helped to work side by side with volunteers to build simple houses which they could then own for a modest price. That was the beginning of a revolving Fund for Humanity, with money that came from the new homeowners' payments and from donations, fund-raising activities, and no-interest loans provided by supporters. The new future of Koinonia was described in an open letter in the following terms:

> What the poor need is not charity but capital, not caseworkers but coworkers. And what the rich need is a wise, honorable and just way of divesting themselves of their overabundance. The Fund for Humanity will meet both of these needs. Money for the fund will come from shared gifts by those who feel they have more than they need and from non-interest loans from those who cannot afford to make a gift but who do want to provide working capital for the disinherited. ... The fund will give away no money. It is not a handout.[2]

Fund for Humanity provided the model and the vision that, in a few years, became Habitat for Humanity International (HFHI). In 1973, Fuller, with his wife and their four children, moved to Zaire to test the model in a foreign country. Upon his return to the United States, convinced that the model was applicable all over the world, and in cooperation with a group of associates, in 1976 he launched HFHI as a nonprofit, nondenominational Christian organization dedicated "to build simple, decent, affordable houses in partnership with those in need of adequate shelter." Habitat has built more than 125,000 houses in 82 countries, including some 45,000 across the United States.

Out of the many biblical passages that could be used to show that what Fuller has called the "theology of the hammer" is rooted in the New Testament, let us consider 1 Timothy 6:3-10, 17-19. It assumes that wealth is not incompatible with Christian discipleship, but it also lays down the conditions necessary for the wealthy person to lead a life pleasing to God.

"THE LOVE OF MONEY IS A ROOT OF ALL KINDS OF EVIL" (1 TIM. 6:10)

This statement is made in the context of an apostolic warning against teachers who are propounding "false doctrines" (v. 3, NIV), "who think that godliness is a means to financial gain" (v. 5). Moved by conceit, they are preaching a "prosperity gospel" that leads people astray. The outcome of their approach, according to Paul, is predictable: "People who want to get rich fall into temptation and a trap and into many foolish and harmful desires that plunge men into ruin and destruction" (v. 9). Quite clearly, Paul has in mind specific cases that illustrate his claim, so he adds: "Some people, eager for money, have wandered from the faith and pierced themselves with many griefs" (v. 10).

The reference to religious teachers who are making religion "a means to financial gain" shows that material ambition is not restricted to businesspeople—that the temptation to greed, which according to Paul is "idolatry" (Col. 3:5, NIV), may be present among the leaders of the church. That is as true today as it was in the first century. And this possibility of corruption in the leadership of the church demands of Christians today the sensitivity that Paul consistently shows toward money questions in several of his letters.[3]

THE INSTRUCTION THE RICH NEED

Paul does not take for granted that Christians will automatically apply kingdom ethics to questions related to material wealth. On the contrary, he assumes that wealthy Christians need to be instructed on how to live so that their wealth will not become a hindrance to Christian discipleship. Paul wants them to use their wealth constructively. Consequently, he gives Timothy specific instructions that Paul's "true son in the faith" is to pass on to "those who are rich" (v. 17, NIV).

These instructions start with a reference to what may be the most common vices of the rich: pride and false hope. "Command those who are rich in the present world," he says, "not to be arrogant nor to put their hope in wealth, which is so uncertain" (v. 17). The type of arrogance that often besets the rich is well illustrated by the attitude against which Israel is warned as it is about to enter the Promised Land: "You may say to yourself, 'My power and the strength of my hand have produced this wealth for me'" (Deut. 8:17, NIV). On the other hand, the temptation of "hope in wealth, which is so uncertain" is exemplified by the attitude of the rich fool of Jesus' parable, who planned to build bigger barns to store all his grain and goods, and to say to himself, "You have plenty of good things laid up for many years. Take life easy; eat, drink and be merry" (Luke 12:19, NIV). But he did not take into account the uncertainty of wealth.

Hope in wealth, says Paul, should be replaced by "hope in God, who richly provides us with everything for our enjoyment" (1 Tim. 6:17, NIV). This exhortation evokes the one who was given to Israel as an antidote to self-centered satisfaction after entering "the land of promise": "But remember the LORD your God, for it is he who gives you the ability to produce wealth" (Deut. 8:18, NIV). A clear recognition that the whole earth belongs to God and that all humans, without exception, are totally dependent on him can keep the wealthy from putting their hope in their possessions.

First Timothy 6:18 has four commands for the rich: (1) to do good; (2) to be rich in good deeds; (3) to be generous; and (4) to be willing to share. The overlap is obvious; so is the intention, namely, to emphasize that the rich are not owners but stewards of God's gifts. This emphasis is very much in harmony with the general tenor of Scripture. Both the Old and the New Testaments assume that financial stewardship is an essential aspect of a life that is pleasing to God.

In 1 John 3:16-18, we see that sharing possessions with people in need is an unavoidable expression of love. No one who fails to share can claim to have the love of God. "Dear children," says John, "let us not love with words or tongue but with actions and in truth" (v. 18, NIV).

As Timothy commands the rich to share, he appeals not to love as a motive but to the possibility of laying up treasure "as a firm foundation for the coming age" and thus taking hold of "the life that is truly life" (1 Tim. 6:19, NIV). One is here reminded of Jesus' exhortation in Matthew 6:19-21 (NIV), the Sermon on the Mount:

> Do not store up for yourself treasures on earth, where moth and rust destroy, and where thieves break in and steal. But store up for yourselves treasures in heaven, where moth and rust do not destroy, and where thieves do not break in and steal.

Neither Jesus nor Paul defines the treasures to be stored. However, these treasures stand in sharp contrast with material possessions—"treasures on earth" (Matt. 6:19, NIV) or "wealth" (1 Tim. 6:17). While material wealth is destructible—"uncertain," according to Paul—the treasures to be coveted are everlasting and will be present in "the coming age," says Paul (v. 19). As the opening words of verse 19 in the NIV, "In this way," make clear, the way to secure these indestructible treasures is faithful obedience to the command in verse 18: "to do good, to be rich in good deeds, and to be generous and willing to share." Those who store up for themselves these treasures "take hold of the life that is truly life" (v. 19b). The only kind of life worth living is the life that has a secure future—the life that is centered in God's will.

THE GREATEST CHALLENGE TO KINGDOM ENTREPRENEURS

As we come to the end of these reflections, we go back to the question with which we started: Is the possession of wealth incompatible with Christian discipleship? In light of the Word of God, neither a negative nor a positive answer is possible without qualifications. Or, to put it in another way, both a negative and a positive answer are appropriate, depending on the intention of the people who raise the question.

For people who have not come to terms with the dangers of wealth, including the temptation to pride and false hope, the answer is, Yes, the possession of wealth is incompatible with Christian discipleship. Jesus Christ expressed that in the strongest terms when he said, "No one can serve two masters. Either he will hate the one and love the other, or he will be devoted to the one and despise the other. You cannot serve both God and Money" (Matt. 6:24, NIV). Loyalty to God excludes every other kind of loyalty, especially loyalty to the rival god—the god Money—that pretends to provide the kind of security that God alone can give.

On the other hand, for people who have put God at the very center of their lives, the answer is, No, the possession of wealth is not incompatible with, but a means to exercise, Christian discipleship. Brought into the sphere of the kingdom of God, earthly goods become an instrument to satisfy a wide variety of basic human needs—food and water, clothing and housing, education and health care—and to spread the good news of Jesus Christ around the world.

In the final analysis, the response to the question depends on the place one gives wealth in life. Single-hearted dedication to God is the one absolute requirement for Christ's disciples to take hold of the life that is truly life. The greatest challenge to kingdom entrepreneurs today, therefore, is to make quite sure that every aspect of their lives is in line with the greatest commandment: "'Love the Lord your God with all your heart and with all your soul and with all your mind.' This is the first and greatest commandment. And the second is like it: 'Love your neighbor as yourself'" (Matt. 22:37-39, NIV).

Appendix C

Dynamics of Faith

(Know—Believe—Understand: Isaiah 43:10)

Kenell J. Touryan

I. Certainty and Certitude

Two passages in Scripture put a premium on faith for the followers of Jesus Christ. In John 20:29 Jesus admonishes Thomas saying, " . . . blessed are those who have not seen and yet have believed" (NIV). Hebrews 11:6 states unambiguously, "And without faith it is impossible to please God, because anyone who comes to him must believe that he exists and that he rewards those who earnestly seek him" (NIV).

Full-time missionaries, tentmakers, and kingdom entrepreneurs have all been called to fulfill the Great Commission, an act that requires us to take our Lord at his word. We have to believe him when he says, "All authority in heaven and on earth has been given to me. . . . And surely I am with you always, to the very end of the age" (Matt. 28:18, 20, NIV). If all of this requires faith, how do we know that this faith is not mere felicitous fideism? Does faith have an objective basis? Who really is the object of that faith?

To answer these questions, we first need to characterize biblical faith. What is it? What are its theological and practical implications?

A working definition is given in Hebrews 11:1: "Faith is the substance [confirmation, gives meaning or value, the very content] of things hoped for [things in the future, not acquired, separated from the present] and the assurance [proof, evidence, certainty] of things not seen [invisible, extrasensory]" (author's translation). The first part of this definition pertains to *time* and the second to *space*. It speaks of things in the future and calls them "confirmed," thus imparting to it a nature of all-inclusive time, and presents the unseen as a factual existence, transcending physical space.

However, in an age of science and technology, the premium is placed on knowledge rather than on faith. All individuals desire to know, and know something with certainty. Philosophers define *certainty* as epistemological knowledge based on objective reasoning. Its oft-maligned cousin, *certitude*, on the other hand, is defined as subjective, psychological assurance based on faith.[1] *What is the relationship between faith and knowledge?*

A careful reading of Hebrews 11:6 reveals elements of both certainty and certitude which make knowledge and faith compatible, as we shall elaborate below. For example, "believe that he exists" (not *as if* he exists) means accepting rather than rejecting an awareness of God's objective reality—certitude that we have inherited from Adam, created in God's image, even though distorted by the Fall. The *reward* aspect, on the other hand, can be tested empirically and thus falls in the realm of certainty.

II. KNOW, BELIEVE, UNDERSTAND

Isaiah 43:10 records the following: "'You are my witnesses,' declares the LORD . . . 'so that you may *know,* and *believe* me and *understand* that I am he'" (NIV, emphasis added). If we are to understand who God is, and affirm that "Jesus Christ has come in the flesh . . ." (1 John 4:2, NIV), we can delineate a proper sequence in Isaiah 43:10. As with the apostle Paul, "faith comes from hearing the message, and the message is heard through the word of Christ" (Rom 10:17, NIV). Knowledge precedes faith. Full understanding is gained after knowledge has been obtained and faith exercised.

Knowledge and faith come in four distinct categories. The four types of knowledge are:

- we know *about* things; the I-it relationship
- we know *how*; acquired human skills
- we know *whom*; the I-thou relationship
- we know *that*; propositional knowledge, where truth statements are concepts expressed in words

The four levels of faith are:

- *fideism* or credulity—also known as blind faith
- *implicit faith*—faith based on previous experience, where a given situation is accepted without further examination (for example, that laws of regularity apply, daily; the sun rises and sets; bodies fall freely under gravity; etc.)
- *controlling faith*—also based on previous experience but involves the cognitive engagement of the mind, careful analysis, and evaluation that helps decide whether an event or a situation is in the realm of possibility or not
- *commitment faith*—leads to trust and personal involvement based on knowledge gained through each and all of the steps mentioned above

A prerequisite to understanding is faith gained through knowledge. For the Christian, knowledge comes from two sources: (1) the physical world God has created, which is his general revelation to us, and (2) Scripture, God's spoken word as his special revelation. General and special revelations taken together will energize an individual's *sensus divinitatis* and lead him to receive the message of God's love, appropriate it, and be born anew into the family of God through empowerment of the Holy Spirit. Knowledge gained through one or more of the categories noted above, followed by implicit and controlling faith, will lead the individual to commit his life to the truth as revealed in the person of Jesus Christ, and his/her mind of understanding will be opened. As Paul writes to the Ephesians, "To prepare God's people . . . in the faith and in the knowledge of the Son of God and become mature, attaining to the whole measure of the fullness of Christ" (Eph. 4:12-13, NIV).

III. FIVE EVIDENCES

For another way of demonstrating the dynamic interplay between knowledge and faith, and to better appreciate the knowledge-faith-understanding continuum, one can look at the cumulative list of evidences that, when taken *together,* provides a basis for the certainty of God's existence and his promise of rewarding those who seek him. One can identify five categories of evidences: (1) the objective reality of the physical world; (2) human nature and the moral universe; (3) evidences from history and archeological findings; (4) Scripture as God's written Word; and (5) a personal encounter with the living God through the risen Christ. Philosophers call this approach *cumulative case apologetics.* Let us explain briefly the scope of each evidence and how the five together fulfill necessary and sufficient conditions for the truth claims of Christianity.

1. *Evidences from the physical world.* The renewed emphasis on intelligent design has brought into focus several evidences from nature that have become the favored apologetic tools for some Christians but targets of attack by ontological naturalists. Among the more compelling evidences are: (a) the problem of origins (universe and life); (b) the fine-tuned nature of the universe[2]; (c) specified complexity and irreducible complexity[3]; (d) Gödel's theorem of incompleteness, applied to mathematics *and* information theory[4]; and (e) the unreasonable effectiveness of mathematics at modeling the physical world.

Each of the above has shed some new light on the possibility of finding empirical evidence for intelligent design in nature, which Hugh Ross calls the "fingerprint of God" after the manner of Psalm 8:3. However, it should be noted that the counter-attack from naturalists has been strong, pervasive, and often effective.[5] Although the above evidences collectively represent an important strand of evidence for a creator, and do strengthen the faith of the believer, they often leave the committed naturalist unimpressed. A question often asked by the ontological naturalist, as he challenges the intelligent design advocates, is how science would be done differently, if one accepts design. I believe that an appropriate answer would be that of Nobel Laureate

I. I. Rabi, who was a conservative Jew. One of his often-quoted statements goes as follows: " . . . physics filled me with awe, put me in touch with a sense of original causes. Physics brought me closer to God. That feeling stayed with me throughout my years in science. Whenever one of my students came to me with a scientific project, I asked only one question, 'Will it bring you nearer to God?'"[6] Here, Rabi does not stop at the empirical evidence of an intelligent design but, rather, identifying the intelligent designer as the Creator leads him to experience the unity between the way he can know God and the way he does his scientific work.

In my own experience with scientists in the former Soviet Union countries, paradoxically, I often meet colleagues who talk about being drawn to God while doing their research. And these are individuals who have been trained in militant atheism.

2. *Nature of human existence and the moral universe.* The issues here are the fact of human existence, the meaning of life, the complexity of self, human consciousness, the moral universe, and man's innate sense of the nouminal, among others. One of the key unresolved questions today is whether human consciousness will ever be explained from a purely naturalistic approach. Roger Penrose, for example, argues for a new physics which would approach the study of consciousness from a yet unknown angle such as quantum mechanical wave function coherence. At present consciousness transcends computation.[7] In a recent book, psychologist Jerome Kagan from Harvard breaks rank with conventional analysts and presents empirical evidence that humans are: (a) free and willful enough to do things for reasons, (b) self-conscious enough to appreciate the significance of experiences, (c) aware of long-term consequences of action, and (d) spiritual enough to be motivated to be good (not just maximizing pleasure and minimizing pain, according to the wisdom of evolutionary psychology).[8] For example, the moral imperative that leads an individual to make a leap from what is *necessary* to what one *ought* to do remains unexplained in mere naturalistic terms, as pointed out by Immanuel Kant. Although the claims of Penrose and Kagan have been strongly debated, nevertheless humans understand things and act in a way that no computer ever will.

The hierarchy of knowledge in understanding reality—the so-called supervenience theory, a bottom-up structure considered by some intelligent design proponents as being reductionist (see, for example, Teller[9])—is another approach that demonstrates that the whole is always more than the sum of its parts. The tremendous complexity inherent in the nature of human existence presents a real challenge to the naturalist, and thus represents the second strand of evidence.

3. *Evidences from history and archaeology.* If the evidences from nature point to God's fingerprint, history points to his footsteps. After all, if God created man in space and time, it is only logical that he should interact with human affairs in history. Can his footsteps be heard in human history? Here the Christian apologist raises many intriguing questions where purely naturalistic answers are inadequate. For example, religion has been found to be persistent and universal throughout human history. Every known civilization has developed religious beliefs as a key component of its culture, albeit without sufficient truth content. However, the concept of the "one true God" has appeared in diverse civilizations such as the Shang Ti (Lord of Heaven of the Chinese), Hananim (The Great One in Korea), the uncreated being Virachoca of the Inca civilization, and so forth. The longest lasting and large-scale experiment in atheism practiced by the Soviet Union and Eastern Europe was a dismal failure. After seventy years of brutal suppression, religion survived and has now become a dominant force in every country previously under the hegemony of the Soviet Union. *Could it be that reality is spiritual in origin rather than material?* Or, how does one explain in purely naturalistic terms the disappearance of powerful empires and civilizations (Babylonian, Egyptian, Roman) and the persistence of a tiny nation, Israel, persecuted relentlessly over millennia. Like the proverbial phoenix, the nation rises from its ashes after being defunct for more than 1,800 years. Finally, there is the rapid expansion of an obscure Semitic cult called "Christianity." It defeats not only a dozen well-entrenched and powerful rival cults, but the whole Roman Empire, within four centuries, without raising a sword. On the contrary, Christians were able to propagate effectively a moral vision utterly incompatible with the casual cruelty of pagan customs (Rodney Stark[10]). If such a rapid growth implies "divine nurture" and one accepts the validity of the abductive approach, it would be disingenuous not to consider the bodily resurrection of Christ that fueled such rapid growth as inference to the best explanation. In fact, if one considers *all* the data on hand, such as the empty tomb, the integrity of the followers of Christ willing to die for their cause, and the hostile atmosphere in which the Good News prevailed, the best explanation is that indeed Jesus rose bodily from the dead.

4. *Evidence from Scripture.* The arguments here are centered around the historical reliability of Scripture; its internal self-consistency; its view of nature as being contingent, created by a transcendent God; its prophetic fulfillments; and its moral imperatives set realistically within the context of an imperfect world. All the above set the Bible apart from other competing belief systems. No other religious book exposes itself to scrutiny by historians and archaeologists, who can employ extra-biblical information to verify or refute

the countless references the Bible makes to historical dates, characters, and geographic locations (see for example, Yamauchi[11]).

If evidence (3) above represents God's footsteps in history, evidence (4) is his written word—the very logos that has brought into existence all of matter, energy, and information and that which has made the world intelligible. The logos expresses speech, inward thoughts, life, light, and eventually, the materialization of all that which is intangible and inaccessible to the senses—the incarnation of the Creator in the form of his son, Jesus Christ. The logos blends the natural and supernatural into a single reality with multiple aspects that can provide the only satisfactory answers to nature's profound mysteries.

5. *Evidence from self-knowledge.* If the previous four evidences engage the mind, the fifth evidence reflects the statement of Blaise Pascal: "The heart has its reasons the mind will never know." It leads to self-evident knowledge which can become compellingly certain without being inferred from any other knowledge. Roy Clouser uses the traditional term "intuition" for such non-inferential recognition of truth.[12] Such truth is apprehended directly, non-discursively as one reflectively compares it to one's present and past experiences of self-evident beliefs.[13]

Many, if not most, scientific insights have come through the "Aha!" of intuition. One of the best-known flashes of insight is provided by Henri Poincaré. Poincaré describes first how he had intensive periods of deliberate and conscious search for what he called Fuchsian functions, but had reached an impasse. Then he describes how he left for a geologic excursion, forgetting his mathematical work. As he stepped into a bus, the solution came to him in a flash—in his words, "without anything in my former thoughts seeming to have paved the way for it."[14] Full comprehension in a single moment!

For the Christian, of course, this intuitive insight can move a step higher and come from the Holy Spirit, revealing the truth of the Incarnation into his innermost being where the knowledge *about* God leads to a personal encounter *with* the living God: a subjective experience that has its objective correlate for many to see.

If evidences (1) and (2) reveal God's fingerprint, evidence (3) his footsteps, and evidence (4) his written word, then evidence (5) reveals his heartbeat! Each evidence is *necessary,* but in itself *not sufficient.* Taken *together,* however, both conditions are fulfilled.

It should be noted that the five strands described above use the abduction method, with inference to the best explanation, and are cumulative. It would be easy to break any one of the strands or counteract any one evidence, taken by itself. But when five strands (evidences) are taken together, their strength is multiplied manifold. The five evidences cover the entire spectrum of human knowledge, from the certainty of objective realism to the certitude of personal experience, thus affirming the compatibility between knowledge and faith. An alternate representation of these five strands is an equilateral triangle. As shown in figure 1, we can represent each evidence, or a pair of related evidences, as one side of a triangle. The strength of a triangle arises from the fact that each side is supported by the other two sides. This provides a rigid geometry used to provide strength in construction. In the same manner, each evidence (or a pair of related evidences) is supported by the other set of evidences, when taken together. For example, observing intelligent design in nature (evidence 1) is further reinforced by a personal encounter with the creator (evidence 5), which in turn finds its credibility in the historical person of Jesus Christ as creator (evidence 4).[15]

Figure 1. The Triangle of Evidences

IV. THE ASTOUNDING "ALLS"

There is one more factor for the Christian apologist that provides the ultimate unifying force that brings all knowledge together, and that is the person of Jesus Christ. Unlike any other religious leader, past or present, the New Testament records a number of "alls" that speak of the sweeping claims that all of creation is under Christ's authority, and continuously infused and upheld by the power of his word:

Matthew 28:18: "Then Jesus came to them and said, 'All authority in heaven and on earth has been given to me'" (NIV).

John 1:3: "All things were made by him; and without him was not anything made that was made" (KJV).

Ephesians 1:22: "And God placed *all* things under his feet and appointed him to be head over everything for the church" (NIV).

Colossians 1:15: "He is the image of the invisible God, the firstborn over *all* creation" (NIV).

Hebrews 1:3: "The Son is the radiance of God's glory and the exact representation of his being, sustaining *all* things by his powerful word" (NIV).

The centrality of Christ in all human affairs can be best illustrated through a diagrammatic representation of the nature of man (see figure 2). The outermost ring represents the physical aspect of a human that is in touch with the physical world through the five senses. The inner circle represents his intellect, emotions, and will, which constitute his *soul*. These three are distinct faculties of an individual but are contiguous, merging to form a whole, as shown by the dotted lines[16]. The three lines intersect at a point, which can represent the *spirit* of man, where God's Spirit intersects the human spirit from *above* (a higher dimension). A point has no dimension, no substance. It only exists as lines intersect each other. The point then becomes the immaterial, intangible aspect of man, where intellect, emotion, and the will meet, yielding the *imago Dei* imprint, where the Lordship of Christ enters the individual, through the Holy Spirit, and sustains his very being.

Figure 2. The Body-Soul-Spirit Continuum

The interplay between objective knowledge and dynamic faith leads one to a more complete understanding of who God is, what he has done for humankind, and how one can establish a living relationship with him. The doubts of certitude thus lead one to the joys of certainty where he can join

Paul in affirming, "I know whom I have believed, and am persuaded [know] that he is able . . ." (2 Tim. 1:12, KJV).

V. THE ACID TEST

Of course, the interplay between knowledge and faith remains sterile unless the whole sequence is appropriated by the individual and becomes a living reality in his or her life. As with an athlete disciplining himself in preparation for the gold medal, God sends challenges to his own in the form of trials that eventually bring us to maturity in our Christian walk, transforming all knowledge into a living and dynamic faith.

One method God employs to make the knowledge-faith interplay in our lives is by confronting us with challenges that require resources far greater than we can humanly muster. Starting with the great heroes of faith in antiquity (Heb. 11:4-39), through two millennia of church history, God has often stacked the odds against his people when facing daunting challenges. We mention a few from Scripture: David facing Goliath, Gideon fighting the Medianites, Hezekiah taunted by Sennacherib, and the little boy with his brown bag amid 5,000 hungry men.

In every one of these cases, the challenges vastly exceeded the meager resources available to the individual. David with his five smooth stones and sling against a heavily armored, battle hardened Goliath. Gideon with 300 fighters against the 300,000 or so Midianite army. The boy with five loaves and two fish versus a hungry crowd of possibly over 10,000 people.

The reason God permits this great imbalance to occur is that he wants to use a quantity that he holds, the divine infinity (∞). To better picture how God reverses this inequality by using his secret quantity, let us represent the inequality by a formula $R/C \ll 1$, where R represents our limited resources and C the great challenges. For example, for Gideon, this ratio was probably 0.001 (300 divided by 300,000). The same was true for David facing Goliath. Also for King Hezekiah facing Sennacherib and the young man holding his brown bag, facing a "stadium" full of hungry people.

What God did in each of these cases, however, is *enter* the equation, *in the numerator*, with his ∞ resources. David knew from experience what God could do and indeed "the battle is the Lord's" (1 Sam. 17:37, 47). He used this knowledge, believed him, and charged the enemy. The infinity he used was the "name of the Lord Almighty" (v. 45). Any number, no matter how small, when multiplied by infinity, reverses the R/C ratio, and makes it much greater than 1.

For Gideon, the infinity was "a sword for the Lord and for Gideon" (Judg. 7:20). For the young man with the fish and loaves, it was our Lord's empowered hands, all of which reversed the ratio from very much less than one, to very much larger than one.

The following principles emerge from the above situations:

1. God does not like "nothing" or "0". After all, he created something from nothing. Multiplying "0" by "∞" yields nothing! There is no resource too insignificant for God that he cannot use it.
2. Each of us needs to yield our resources, talents, and gifts—no matter how meager—to him to multiply by his infinite power. Any number, no matter how small (but greater than "0"), when multiplied by infinity overpowers the greatest challenge in the world.
3. By taking our resources and multiplying them, God becomes our partner, albeit the senior partner, in having us face seemingly insurmountable odds. Only once in Scripture do we read that God took upon himself to bring salvation (Isa. 63:5). God's exclusive preference is to use his people as his hands and feet.

The outcome of all of this is victory over life's numerous, often-daunting challenges, but where all glory and honor go to the Triune God. This was clearly articulated by David, who gave no credit to his skilled marksmanship in downing Goliath, but rather to the name of the Lord (1 Sam. 17:45). In fact, we can join David, when he later wrote Psalm 20, declaring " . . . some trust in chariots, and some in horses, but we trust in the name of the Lord our God."

The apostle Paul expresses this inner working of God's power through his Holy Spirit by coining a new Greek word—*uper-ek-parisso*—translated in the NIV as *"immeasurably more* than we ask or think" (Eph. 3:20). The word actually means *super-extra-abundance,* an extreme state of affairs, which only the power of the indwelling Holy Spirit can bring about. Therefore, with Paul we can say with confidence, "And God is able to make all grace abound to you, so that in all things at all times, having all that you need, you will abound in every good work" (2 Cor. 9:8, NIV).

APPENDIX D

A GUIDE TO FURTHER READING

Steven L. Rundle and Patrick Lai

Kingdom entrepreneurship is a relatively new mission strategy, at least "new" in terms of the recent history of missions. It shares many things in common with tentmaking—using one's secular career as a vehicle for cross-cultural missions—but is narrower in its focus. Specifically, it involves creating businesses for the express purpose of advancing the gospel in the economically and spiritually most impoverished parts of the world. Yet, while narrow in its focus, it is obvious from the essays contained in this volume that there is also a great deal of diversity. For those wishing to learn more about this emerging field, the following bibliography is provided.

Most of what has been written on this subject uses the label "tentmaking" or "entrepreneurial tentmaking" instead of "kingdom entrepreneurship." In this bibliography we will use the terms interchangeably. Our selection process was guided by the following criteria. First, we have selected only those works that focus on businesses with a (1) cross-cultural and an (2) evangelistic purpose. This ruled out many excellent works that advocate for Christians in the marketplace more generally. We of course support the idea that Christians should reflect Christ wherever they are, home or abroad, but to include all those works would make this bibliography too unwieldy. Those who are interested in a more comprehensive list about marketplace ministry are encouraged to read *Marketplace Annotated Bibliography,* by Pete Hammond, R. Paul Stevens, and Todd Svanoe (InterVarsity Press, 2002). We made some exceptions to our cross-cultural and evangelism screens in the case of some of the theologically oriented works because we felt they were important foundations for all kingdom entrepreneurs to have. And finally, we selected only works that can be found either in journals, magazines, books, or are available on the Internet. This ruled out some very respectable papers that were published in obscure newsletters or by defunct organizations and are no longer readily available.

We have assigned codes to each article to help future researchers identify those that fall within their area of interest. Many fall into more than one category. The codes are found in brackets [ ] before the annotation, and correspond to the following categories:

[Intro]	introductory
[Theology]	the biblical basis of business in missions
[Practice]	the practice of kingdom entrepreneurship
[Ethics]	ethical issues specific to kingdom entrepreneurship

[Accountability]   accountability issues
[Preparation]   the preparation of kingdom entrepreneurs

ANNOTATED BIBLIOGRAPHY

Befus, David R. 2002. *Kingdom Business: The Ministry of Promoting Economic Development.* Miami: Latin America Mission. Available at www.lam.org.

[Practice, Theology]

Befus has a long history of involvement in the ministry of economic development. His experience includes creating and leading the early microenterprise and microfinance programs at Opportunity International, World Relief, and World Vision, teaching economic development at Westmont College, and now serving as president of Latin America Mission, an organization committed to integrating its social and evangelistic agendas. In this book, which was recently translated from Spanish, he develops five "models" that combine economic development and holistic Christian outreach. The models include: (1) "service businesses" that generate revenue to cover the cost of an affiliated local ministry, (2) "endowment businesses" which are similar to service businesses except that they support ministries in poorer, more distant locations, (3) "tentmaking businesses" which provide a platform and financial support for cross-cultural missionaries, (4) "business incubators" aimed at creating employment for church members as well as reaching specific locations for Christ, and (5) microcredit programs which use revolving funds to help the poorest of the poor start their own small-scale businesses. The strength of the book, its primary focus in fact, is on micro- and small-business development and microcredit programs. That said, this book is recommended for anyone wishing to integrate business and missions.

Chan, Kim-kwong, and Tetsunao Yamamori. 2002. *Holistic Entrepreneurs in China: A Handbook on the World Trade Organization and New Opportunities for Christians.* Pasadena, Calif.: William Carey International University Press.

[Practice]

This book is the first country-specific study of the role businesses can play in advancing the gospel in a "closed" country. Based on ten years of research and experience in China, the first half of the book looks closely at the historical, cultural, and sociopolitical dynamics of modern China. The second half gives practical examples of kingdom entrepreneurs in China. Woven throughout the book is a discussion of the implications of China's entry into the World Trade Organization. This is a refreshing book that goes beyond simply making the case that kingdom entrepreneurship and tentmaking is a good idea. While many books make that point, there has been precious little discussion of the political, cultural, and economic *context* of these businesses. It is important for scholars to start producing works that look more carefully at these issues, as they vary greatly from country to country and have a direct bearing on the success of this approach. This book is an important step in that direction. While its focus is specifically on China, the case studies will be of interest to anyone wishing to learn more about how business can be used to advance the gospel in resistant countries.

Christensen, Derek. 1997. "Training: Endurance Food for Serious Tentmakers." *International Journal of Frontier Missions* 14(3): 133-138. Available at http://www.ijfm.org.

[Preparation]

Derek Christensen is a pastor and missions scholar from Auckland, New Zealand, who has done a great deal of work in the area of tentmaker training. He argues that better training can reduce the problem of tentmaker attrition. He also identifies problems within the church's attitude about tentmaking that he believes have undermined its own efforts in this area. He stresses the importance of tentmaker character and "Christ-likeness" and is critical of attempts to take shortcuts in the training process. Christensen closes the article with a challenge to local churches to step up their training of the laity by better "equipping people for Monday morning."

Danker, William. 1971. *Profit for the Lord*. Grand Rapids, Mich.: Eerdmans. Available at: www.intent.org.

[Practice]

This is a classic and well-written book about the central role businesses played in the missionary strategy of the eighteenth- and nineteenth-century Moravians and Basel Mission Society. The book illustrates the various ways businesses were used to assist in the planting of churches and for the educational and economic benefit of new converts. Using many carefully researched case studies, Danker gives a candid appraisal of the successes and failures of these all-too-human pioneers. Perhaps the most surprising thing about the book is the striking similarities between the experiences of these pioneers and those of today's kingdom entrepreneurs. Any study of kingdom entrepreneurship would be incomplete without this book. However, the book's greatest strength is also its main weakness. Specifically, this is a very thoroughly researched, historical account of business in missions. Serious students love this book, but the less scholarly inclined find the book dry and difficult to appreciate.

English, David. 2001. "Paul's Secret: A First-Century Strategy for a Twenty-first-century World." *World Christian* 14(3): 22-26.

[Intro, Theology]

English is the executive director of Global Opportunities, an organization committed to mobilizing tentmakers. In this paper he makes a compelling argument that Paul's tentmaking was neither an access strategy nor a financial strategy. Instead, Paul worked for a living in order to model lay missions and a godly work ethic. English argues that Paul's churches spread so quickly because his converts were not exposed immediately to the professional missionary model, and therefore understood more clearly that missions is the responsibility of all Christians. This mobilization of the laity, according to English, was the power and genius of Paul's strategy.

Gibson, Dan. 1997. *Avoiding the Tentmaker Trap*. Ontario, Canada: WEC International.

[Intro]

Drawing from his personal experience, Gibson guides the reader through some of the benefits and pitfalls that may await the would-be tentmaker. Whether by design or by accident, his book lists more pitfalls than benefits. Nevertheless, the ideas are good, though not always well developed. The book also contains a resource guide in the back that lists more than 130 book titles and more than 100 addresses for further contacts and information.

Ginter, Gary. 1998. "Overcoming Resistance Through Tentmaking." In Woodberry, J. Dudley, ed. *Reaching the Resistant: Barriers and Bridges for Mission*. EMS Series 6. Pasadena, Calif.: William Carey Library, 209-218.

[Intro, Practice]

Ginter is a Chicago businessman and a leading spokesperson for the tentmaking movement. In this paper he discusses what is considered by some to be the main disadvantage of tentmaking—the apparent tradeoff between "ministry" and "work." He maintains that a tentmaker's effectiveness is critically dependent on how he or she resolves this problem. Ginter divides time into three categories: "Vocational Ministry Time," "Intentional Ministry Time," and "Serendipitous Ministry Time." The fact that all three are considered time spent in ministry shows Ginter's view that all things—

work, family, play—if done unto the Lord, are ministry of a kind. Ginter defines vocational ministry time as "the time spent serving God by serving others through your job." Intentional ministry involves planned segments of ministry time, which supplement one's vocational ministry time. Serendipitous ministry is unplanned and spontaneous opportunities that arise in everyday life. The key to successful tentmaking is the person's ability to be (1) attentive to all of these ministry opportunities, and (2) deliberate about responding to the leading of the Holy Spirit when these opportunities arise. This is a very clear and persuasive paper that should be required reading for anyone considering becoming a tentmaker.

Grenz, Stanley J. 1999. "God's Business: A Foundation for Christian Mission in the Marketplace." *Crux* 35(1): 19-25.

[Theology]

Grenz, a professor of theology and ethics, believes that treating business as a mission field is an overly narrow perspective on Christian missions. He makes the now familiar argument that businesses are intrinsically part of God's plan for the world. He also touches on some ethical questions, and the tensions that occasionally arise between what's best for the business and what's best for our missionary purpose and spiritual walk.

Hamilton, Don. 1987. *Tentmakers Speak: Practical Advice from Over 400 Missionary Tentmakers.* Duarte, Calif.: TMQ Research. Available at www.intent.org.

[Intro, Preparation]

This is a rare example of solid empirical research in the tentmaking literature. The purpose of the study was to explore the reasons for tentmakers' success or lack thereof. Hamilton conducted a survey of more than 400 tentmakers worldwide and shares the results in this very useful book. Tentmakers speak honestly about their triumphs and defeats in their work, ministry, family, and spiritual lives. He also shares their advice about preparation, what they would do over if they could, and what they feel they did right.

Hock, Ronald F. 1979. "The Workshop as a Social Setting for Paul's Missionary Preaching." *The Catholic Biblical Quarterly* 14(3): 439-450.

[Theology]

Hock is a professor of religion who has produced a number of scholarly studies of the role and context of Paul's tentmaking. In this paper he debunks the idea that Paul's preaching and working were two mutually exclusive activities. Using extra-biblical sources, and pointing to classic philosophers such as Socrates, Hock shows that it was common practice in Paul's time for the workplace to serve as the setting for theological and philosophical discourses. Thus, Hock concludes that while Paul was busy making tents, he was also busy preaching the gospel. This paper, like all of Hock's works, is persuasive and carefully argued. However, its scholarly nature makes it a difficult read for some.

Lai, Patrick. 1998. "Starting a Business in a Restricted Access Nation." *International Journal of Frontier Missions* 15(1): 41-46.

[Practice]

Lai has spent many years in Southeast Asia as an entrepreneur and church planter, and has succeeded in both areas multiple times. He is also the creator of the tentmaker portal www.OPENnetworkers.net. In this paper he offers practical advice on starting a business in less-evangelized countries. He groups countries into four economic categories; (1) developed, (2) undeveloped, (3) underdeveloped, and (4) developing, and gives some tips on what kinds of businesses might succeed in each.

Lai, Patrick. 2003. *Window Businesses: Doing Tentmaking in the 10/40 Window.* Pasadena, Calif.: William Carey International University Press.

[Intro, Practice]

This book is not only an excellent introduction to the topic of tentmaking in general, but also significantly expands the discussion Lai started in his 1998 paper (see above). In this book, Lai elaborates on topics such as (1) the training and calling of tentmakers, (2) how to research and start the most suitable business, and (3) the financial and accountability issues one must consider. This is a book that all aspiring kingdom entrepreneurs will want to read.

McLoughlin, Michael. 2000. "Back to the Future of Missions: The Case for Marketplace Ministry." *Vocatio* 1-6.

[Intro, Theology]

McLoughlin is the creator of the marketplace ministries portal www.scruples.com. His basic thesis is that "missions in the marketplace is . . . the obvious road for twenty-first century missions." Traditional missionaries, he maintains, are not well suited for ministry in the marketplace. He also argues that the word "go" in the Great Commission is more correctly translated "as you go." This changes missions from being something done overseas by other Christians to something all Christians ought to be involved in all of the time. This is a well-written article, that, while not specifically about kingdom entrepreneurship, is worth reading.

Morris, Robert. 1998. "Shrewd Yet Innocent: Thoughts on Tentmaking Integrity." *International Journal of Frontier Missions,* 15(1): 5-8. Available at http://www.ijfm.org.

[Ethics]

Morris, an experienced tentmaker, offers practical solutions to some common problems that every tentmaker faces. He begins with a discussion of the conflicting issues that may come up in a tentmaker's lifestyle, values, and witness. Morris clearly deals with the issue of bribery and what it means to tell the truth in a biblical and contextualized way. He also discusses the issue of having double and hidden agendas in work and ministry. With each topic he shares one or more biblical examples to validate his points. He concludes by rightly turning the tables on traditional missionaries and challenging some of their own double standards. This is a highly recommendable article for all tentmakers and missionaries.

Myers, Bryant. 1999. *Walking with the Poor: Principles and Practices of Tranformational Development.* Maryknoll, N.Y.: Orbis.

[Theology, Practice]

Strictly speaking, this book is about economic development. Nevertheless, the book offers one of the simplest and clearest theological arguments in favor of holistic mission, and in chapter 8 provides what is probably the best discussion of what it means, specifically, to "do" missions holistically. Unlike so many other things written about holistic mission and marketplace ministry that give little or no attention to the importance of a verbal witness, Myers places the verbal proclamation of the gospel squarely in the center of any authentic missionary effort.

Nordstrom, Dwight, and Jim Nielsen. 1998. "How Business Is Integral to Tentmaking." *International Journal of Frontier Missions* 15(1): 15-18. Available at http://www.ijfm.org.

[Practice]

Nordstrom and Nielson tell the story of three companies they started in Asia to propagate the gospel. One case tells of a company that was a great success financially but much less successful in terms of its ministry goals.

Another company was hugely successful in achieving its ministry goals but was a financial loser. The third case describes a company that was moderately successful in both areas. This article is helpful and encouraging as it is good to be reminded that achieving both financial and ministry success is not a trivial undertaking.

Norrish, Howard. 1990. "Lone Ranger: Yes or No?" *Evangelical Missions Quarterly* 26: 6-14. Available at http://www.wheaton.edu/bgc/EMIS/1990/loneranger.html

[Ethics]

Norrish addresses the question, Should tentmakers go overseas independently or in association with a mission agency? As someone who spent more than twelve years in the Middle East, both as an independent tentmaker and with a mission agency, Norrish speaks with authority on this question. He gives three advantages of being a "Lone Ranger" tentmaker. The first is image—the fact that the tentmaker is perceived by the local populace in a more positive way. The second advantage is the freedom and mobility that Lone Rangers have that others do not have. The final advantage to being a Lone Ranger is security, as the person does not have to hide or lie about their affiliation with a mission agency. Yet, despite these advantages Norrish concludes that being a Lone Ranger is unwise. He lists spiritual restoration, checks and balances, lifestyle, orientation and training, financial considerations, general support, and home church identity as reasons why tentmakers should be associated with an agency. This is a good paper about an important issue.

Reapsome, Jim. 1997. "Paul: The Nonprofessional Missionary." *Occasional Bulletin*. Available at http://www.missiology.org/EMS/bulletins/reapsome.htm.

[Intro, Theology]

Reapsome, former editor of the *Evangelical Missions Quarterly*, begins by criticizing tentmakers for their lack of training, language skills, time, church planting successes, and so on. But then he surprises the reader by challenging professional missionaries to get more involved in the secular world, even to the point of taking a job! In effect he challenges people to adopt the tentmaking approach, and points to Paul's ability to plant churches while supporting himself. He correctly notes that in many countries missionaries are perceived as people who are paid to preach. By maintaining a regular job, missionaries can overcome that perception, which is in fact precisely why the apostle Paul worked.

Rundle, Steven. 2000. "Ministry, Profits, and the Schizophrenic Tentmaker." *Evangelical Missions Quarterly* 36(3): 292-300. Available at: www.wheaton.edu/bgc/EMIS/2000/ministryprofits.html.

[Intro, Practice]

Rundle is associate professor of economics at Biola University. Pointing to some real-life examples, he claims that tentmaking entrepreneurs undermine their own missionary goals when they neglect the business and treat it as a distraction from ministry. He also briefly discusses the emergence of "Great Commission companies" and the difference between these and the more common "Christian" company.

Rundle, Steven, and Tom Steffen. 2003. *Business as Missions: Globalization and the Emerging Role of Great Commission Companies*. Downers Grove, Ill.: InterVarsity Press.

[Intro, Practice]

This book combines the insights of an economist who is actively involved with "Great Commission companies" and a highly respected missiologist who has spent many years as a church planter in Southeast Asia. The first half of the book makes the argument that globalization is not something that caught God by surprise or is out of his control. Instead, the mutually reinforcing pressures being created by globalization can be seen as God's way of bringing the *whole* church, and all of its resources, back into missions. The second half of the book is a collection of case studies of companies that were created for the exclusive purpose of bringing Good News to the less-developed and less-evangelized parts of the world.

Sherman, Doug, and William Hendricks. 1987. *Your Work Matters to God*. Colorado Springs: NavPress.

[Theology]

Many Christians believe that God has little interest in the actual widgets they make while at work. At best, they view their secular jobs as a means to an end, namely, that the ultimate purpose for holding a secular job is to share their faith at work. The widgets themselves have no intrinsic value. The authors debunk this idea in this clear, easy-to read book. They make many good points about the "sacred-secular dichotomy" and show how work is an end in itself. Though not written specifically about kingdom entrepreneurship, this is a good foundation for all kingdom entrepreneurs to have.

Siemens, Ruth E. "Why Did Paul Make Tents? A Biblical Basis for Tentmaking." GO Paper A-1 (1998). Available at: http://www.globalopps.org/materials.htm.

[Theology]

Siemens, like Christy Wilson (see page 337), is one of the early pioneers of the modern tentmaking movement. For many years she worked and witnessed in South America before founding Global Opportunities, an organization dedicated to mobilizing and equipping tentmakers. This is the most recent version of her classic paper in which she documents the role and priority of work in Paul's life and ministry during each of his missionary journeys. Drawing from Paul's own letters, Siemens gives excellent reasons for why Paul chose to work—credibility, identification, and modeling—when he had every right to request donor support instead. She also gives five reasons why Paul's example should be followed today. Siemens is especially passionate about her belief that Paul never received any donor support (except when in prison), and that authentic tentmakers today should follow that example. This narrow definition of a tentmaker is where she generates the most controversy. The paper meanders in places, and is generously seasoned with strong statements, but it never fails to stimulate a lively discussion. College students love this paper. Boring it is not.

Siemens, Ruth E. 1997. "The Tentmakers and Their Churches: Mutual Responsibility." GO Paper A-9. Available at http://www.globalopps.org.

[Accountability]

This is an excellent article containing ideas not found in other tentmaking materials about how to get home churches involved in the lives and ministry of tentmakers. The article is divided into two sections. The first section focuses on "the local church's responsibility to its tentmakers." The second section concerns "the tentmaker's responsibility to their church" and gives seven ideas for how tentmakers can build up their local church and get their church more involved in their life and work overseas.

Siemens, Ruth E. 1997. "The Tentmaker's Preparation for Work and Witness." GO Paper A-5. Available at http://www.globalopps.org.

[Preparation]

In this article, Siemens does a solid job of introducing the need for tentmakers to prepare for overseas work and ministry. As a graduate of Biola University who spent most of her career with InterVarsity Christian Fellowship ministering on the campuses of secular universities, she speaks with authority about the advantages and disadvantages of preparing for ministry at a Christian versus a secular school. Siemens ends the article by suggesting where tentmakers may go to prepare for overseas service.

Silvoso, Ed. 2002. *Anointed for Business: How Christians Can Use Their Influence in the Marketplace to Change the World*. Ventura, Calif.: Regal.

[Intro, Practice]

This is the most recent contribution in a long list of books about the impact Christians can have in the marketplace. What sets this book apart from the others is (1) its author, and (2) its emphasis on the kingdom of God. As a businessman-turned-ministry-leader, Silvoso speaks with authority about the difficulties the church is having with integrating business and missions. The emphasis seems to be on marketplace *survival*, not *transformation*. He challenges Christian business professionals to set transformation as their goal, and gives many real-life illustrations of how this happens. This is a highly recommended book for all kingdom entrepreneurs.

Stevens, Paul. 1999. *The Other Six Days: Vocation, Work, and Ministry in Biblical Perspective*. Grand Rapids, Mich.: Eerdmans.

[Theology]

Stevens is professor of applied theology at Regent College in Vancouver, Canada, and founder of the "Marketplace Theology" program there. In this book he carefully and forcefully critiques the deeply entrenched notion that the clergy are the only ones "in ministry" and the laity are those who are ministered to. He is not opposed to professional church leadership, but argues that we have in effect immobilized "average" Christians by making them feel ill-equipped and uncalled for ministry. He then presents his own view about work and how Christians in the marketplace fit within the work God is doing in the world.

Stevens, R. Paul. 2001. "The Marketplace: Mission Field or Mission?" *Crux* 37(3): 7-16.

[Theology]

Stevens begins by affirming that the marketplace is the largest and most promising mission field in the world. The workplace provides a natural relational context for ministry and vast amounts of time to let those relationships develop. Issues continually arise within the marketplace context that open the door for ministry and provide openings for sharing the gospel. However, the bulk of Stevens's paper focuses on the role of the marketplace as mission—as an intrinsic part of God's plan for the world. It participates in mission by combining talents and resources for the common good, by creating wealth and thus ministering to the world's poor, by building community, and by ministering in other ways.

Suter, H., and M. Gmur. 1997. *Business Power for God's Purpose*. VKG Publishing. Available at http://www.bpn.org.

[Intro]

This is the first real non-American work in English about tentmaking. It has a short chapter on the theological basis for Christians in the marketplace, another chapter focusing on the history of Christian missions in the marketplace, a chapter with some short case studies, a fine chapter on ethical issues, and one that considers different theological and historical views of work. This is a good introductory book, although more scholarly readers will find that the book adds little beyond what has already been written in two earlier classics, *Today's Tentmakers* (Wilson) and *Profit for the Lord* (Danker).

Swarr, S. B., and D. Nordstrom. 1999. *Transform the World: Biblical Vision and Purpose for Business*. Center for Entrepreneurship and Economic Development. http://www.ceed-uofn.org/.

[Theology, Practice]

Sharon Swarr is cofounder of the Center for Entrepreneurship and Economic Development (CEED). She and Dwight Nordstrom teamed up to write this valuable contribution to the literature. It begins with a biblical defense of business as a mission strategy, then goes into some practical issues related to the organization and management of these "Great Commission companies." Some sections of the book are not well developed, yet as a whole the book is worth reading.

Taylor, Gary. 1998. "Don't Call Me a Tentmaker." *International Journal of Frontier Missions* 15(1): 23-26.

[Practice]

Gary Taylor is founder of several multinational companies that have been used to reach difficult places for Christ. In this article, Taylor shares his personal story—his struggles and joys—in working with tentmakers who had little experience or interest in "ordinary" work. Specifically, he has "found few in the missions industry who could work in the normal secular sense of the term. It seemed very few cues remained from pre-missionary work-life to guide them into producing for their living and witnessing for their calling." Taylor clearly believes the marketplace is the key to winning the nations for Christ, yet he believes it will be real businesspeople and not missionaries or those operating under the cover of businesses who will be the most effective contributors to this task.

Wilson, J. Christy, Jr. 1979. *Today's Tentmakers*. Wheaton, Ill.: Tyndale.

[Intro]

Christy Wilson is widely recognized as the "father of the modern day tent-making movement." This book awakened the evangelical world to the opportunities and possibilities of tentmaking and has had a significant impact toward motivating professional people to believe that the unreachable are reachable through tentmaking. This book remains one of the best introductions to the topic of tentmaking.

Yamamori, Tetsunao. 1993. *Penetrating Missions' Final Frontier: A New Strategy for Unreached Peoples*. Downers Grove, Ill.: InterVarsity Press.

[Intro]

In this well-written and well-documented book, Yamamori surveys the nature and scope of the unfinished task of world missions, and gives a clear call for more tentmakers to go where traditional missionaries cannot. At the time the book was written, Yamamori was president of Food for the Hungry. His bias toward relief and development ministries is obvious, and comes through as an impassioned plea for tentmakers to serve among the poorest of the poor. This book is very similar to another one that he published in 1987, titled *God's New Envoys: A Bold Strategy for Penetrating "Closed Countries."* The statistics are now a bit dated, but the book is still well worth reading.

OTHER USEFUL RESOURCES

Baker, Dwight. 2001. "William Carey and the Business Model for Mission." Unpublished manuscript. Available at http://www.globalconnections.co.uk/pdfs/careybusinessbaker.pdf.

Burkett, Larry. 1998. *Business by the Book: The Complete Guide of Biblical Principles for the Workplace*. Nashville: Thomas Nelson.

Chewning, Richard C., John W. Eby, and Shirley J. Roels. 1990. *Business Through the Eyes of Faith*. San Francisco: Harper & Row, 1990.

Cox, John. 1997. "The Tentmaking Movement in Historical Perspective." *International Journal of Frontier Missions* 14(3): 111-117. Available at http://www.ijfm.org.

Davies, Stanley. 2001. "Business and Mission, or Business as Mission?" Available at http://www.globalconnections.co.uk/pdfs/businessandmissionreport.pdf.

English, David. 2002. "A Workable Definition? A Response to Lai's Search." Unpublished manuscript. Available at www.globalopps.org.

Ewert, Norm. 1992. "The Role of Business Enterprise in Christian Mission." *Transformation* 9: 7-14.

Guthrie, Stan. 2000. "Tentmaking." In Guthrie, Stan. *Missions in the Third Millennium: Twenty-one Key Trends for the Twenty-first Century.* Waynesboro, Ga.: Paternoster, 117-122. Available at http://www.strategicnetwork.org/index.asp?loc=kb&id=8795.

Hagan, David. 1998. "Strategic Impact Through Multiplying Modular Business," *International Journal of Frontier Missions* 15(1): 27-28, 46. Available at http://www.ijfm.org.

Hammond, Pete, R. Paul Stevens, and Todd Svanoe. 2002. *Marketplace Annotated Bibliography.* Downers Grove, Ill.: InterVarsity Press.

Lai, Patrick. 2000. "Tentmaking: In Search of a Workable Definition." Unpublished manuscript. Available at http://www.strategicnetwork.org/index.asp?loc=kb&id=9162.

Lausanne Tentmaker Statement. Available at http://www.globalopps.org/lausanne.htm.

Livingstone, Greg. 1994. "Tentmaker's Credibility." *Evangelical Missions Quarterly* 30(1): 6.

Martin, Danny. 1997. "The Place of the Local Church in Tentmaking." *International Journal of Frontier Missions* 14(3): 131-132. Available at http://www.ijfm.org.

Niles, Nathan. 2000. "Professional Tentmakers Open Doors for Ministry." *Evangelical Missions Quarterly* 36(3), 302-306. Available at http://www.wheaton.edu/bgc/EMIS/2000/proftentmakers.html.

Packer, J. I. 1990. "The Christian's Purpose in Business." In Richard C. Chewning, ed., *Biblical Principles and Business: The Practice.* Colorado Springs: NavPress, 16-25.

Rundle, Steven. 2000. "The Christian Business Scholar and the Great Commission: A Proposal for Expanding the Agenda." *Journal of Biblical Integration in Business,* 94-108. Available at http://www.cbfa.org/images/jbib/jbib_00_part1.pdf.

Schmidt, Karen. 1999. "Versatile Vocation—Using Marketplace Skills to Reach the World for Christ." *World Christian,* 31-33.

Tentmaker FAQs. Available at http://www.globalopps.org/faqs.htm.

Tsukahira, Peter. 2000. *My Father's Business.* (Self published.) http://www.ceed-uofn.org/.

Tunehag, Mats. 2001. "Business as Mission." Unpublished manuscript. Available at http://www.globalconnections.co.uk/pdfs/businessasmissiontunehag.pdf.

Wilson, J. Christy, Jr. 1997. "Successful Tentmaking Depends on Mission Agencies." *International Journal of Frontier Missions* 14(3): 141-143. Available at http://www.ijfm.org.

WEBSITES

Business Professionals Network: www.bpn.org.

CBMC: www.cbmc.com.

Center of Entrepreneurship and Economic Development: http://www.ceed-uofn.org.

Fellowship of Companies for Christ: www.fcci.org.

Global Connections: http://www.globalconnections.co.uk.

Global Opportunities: www.globalopps.org.

Intent: www.intent.org.

OPEN Networkers: www.opennetworkers.safeserver.com.

Scruples: www.scruples.org.

Strategic Network: http://www.strategicnetwork.org.

Tentmakernet: www.tentmakernet.net.

Tentmakers International Exchange: www.tieinfo.com.

NOTES

PREFACE

1. For the term "10/40 Window, see chapter 2, note 1.
2. Stan Guthrie, *Missions in the Third Millennium: Twenty-one Key Trends for the Twenty-first Century* (Waynesboro, Ga.: Paternoster, 2000), 121.
3. For examples of kingdom entrepreneurs ministering in a monocultural setting, refer to Kim-kwong Chan and Tetsunao Yamamori, *Holistic Entrepreneurs in China: A Handbook on the World Trade Organization and New Opportunities for Christians* (Pasadena, Calif.: William Carey International University Press, 2002). The case studies in this present volume, however, are all cast in a cross-cultural setting, except for the one by Kim-kwong Chan (see chapter 1) describing the work of Esther Hui in China.

CHAPTER 2: AMI AND GREAT COMMISSION COMPANIES

1. The "10/40 Window" is a somewhat arbitrary belt between 10 and 40 degrees north latitude, stretching from western Africa to Asia across the Middle East. The belt contains practically all of the world's three largest gospel-resistant population groups: Muslims, Hindus, and Buddhists. Many of the countries included in the belt do not issue visas for the missionaries. For this reason, these countries are often referred to as "restricted-access countries" or "creative-access countries," requiring creativity for entry by Christian missions.

CHAPTER 4: BUSINESS IN THE MIDDLE EAST

1. Mats Tunehag, "Earthly Profit, Heaven's Gain" (1998), available at www.iccc.net.

CHAPTER 5: CHURCH PLANTING VIA SMALL BUSINESS IN ZAZALAND

1. The names of some places, organizations, and people in this case study have been changed.
2. J. Christy Wilson, Jr., *Today's Tentmakers* (Wheaton, Ill.: Tyndale, 1985).
3. See "Tentmaking—In Search of a Workable Definition," by Patrick Lai. Available at: www.strategicnetwork.org/index.asp?loc=ko&id=9162.
4. For more on the Engel Scale, see *Perspectives on the World Christian Movement: A Reader* (Pasadena, Calif.: William Carey Library, 1981), 590-592.
5. For details, visit www.OPENNetworkers.net

CHAPTER 13: HOW BUSINESS IN ITSELF CAN GLORIFY GOD

1. All emphases in Scripture quotations in this chapter were added by the author.
2. See especially 1 Cor. 3:12-15; also Dan. 12:2; Matt. 6:10, 20-21; 19:21; Luke 6:22-23; 12:18-21, 32, 42-48; 14:13-14; 1 Cor. 3:8; 9:18; 13:3; 15:19, 29-32, 58; Gal. 6:9-10; Eph. 6:7-8; Phil. 4:17; Col. 3:23-24; 1 Tim. 6:18; Heb. 10:34, 35; 11:10, 14-16, 26, 35; 1 Pet. 1:4; 2 John 8; Rev. 11:18; 22:12; see also Matt. 5:46; 6:2-6, 16-18, 24; Luke 6:35.

CHAPTER 14: STRATEGIC CONSIDERATIONS IN BUSINESS AS MISSION

1. Source: U.S. Department of Education (*The Chronicle of Higher Education,* vol. 48, no. 1, 25).
2. 430,164 master's degrees were conferred in the 1997–1998 school year.
3. Brother Andrew, *God's Smuggler* (Grand Rapids, Mich.: Revell, 2001), 254.

CHAPTER 16: STARTING KINGDOM COMPANIES: A BIBLICAL AND HISTORICAL OVERVIEW

1. Kenneth Scott Latourette, *A History of Christianity, vol. 1 (Beginnings to 1500)* (San Francisco: Harper Collins, 1975), 21.
2. M. P. Charlesworth, *Trade Routes and Commerce of the Roman Empire* (Cambridge: Cambridge University Press, 1926), xiii.
3. Adalbert Hamman, *Die ersten Christen* (Stuttgart: Philipp Reclam, 1985), 44.
4. Ruth Tucker, *From Jerusalem to Irian Jaya: A Biographical History of Christian Missions* (Grand Rapids, Mich.: Zondervan, 1983), 25-26.
5. Charlesworth, *Trade Routes and Commerce of the Roman Empire,* 7.
6. Roland Allen, *Missionary Methods: St. Paul's or Ours?* (Grand Rapids, Mich.: Eerdmans, 1962), 14.
7. Latourette, *History of Christianity,* 75.
8. John Obert Voll, "Main Street of Eurasia," in *Aramco World* 39, no. 4 (July/August 1988), 5.
9. Ibid., 7.

10. George M. Lamsa and William Chauncey Emhardt, *The Oldest Christian People* (New York: Macmillan, 1926), 64.
11. John Stewart, *Nestorian Missionary Enterprise* (Edinburgh: T.& T. Clark, 1928), 5.
12. Hans Wilhelm Haussig, *Die Geschichte Zentralasiens und der Seidenstrasse in vorislamischer Zeit* (Darmstadt: Wissenschaftliche Buchgesellschaft, 1992), 222.
13. John Stewart, quoted in J. Christy Wilson, Jr., *Today's Tentmakers* (Wheaton, Ill.: Tyndale, 1985), 27.
14. Haussig, *Die Geschichte Zentralasiens und der Seidenstrasse in vorislamischer Zeit,* 225.
15. Ibid., 229.
16. Alvise Zorzi, *Marco Polo* (Hildesheim: Claasen Verlag, 1992).
17. Max Geiger, *Calvin, Calvinismus, Kapitalismus* (Basel: Verlag Helbing & Lichtenhahn, 1969), 240.
18. Martin Luther, quoted in Werner Lachmann, *Wirtschaft und Ethik* (Neuhausen: Hänssler, 1987), 177.
19. Richard Baxter, quoted in R. H. Tawney, *Religion and the Rise of Capitalism* (West Drayton, England: Penguin, 1938), 242.
20. Albert Helman, *Merchant, Mission and Meditation* (Paramaribo, Suriname: C. Kersten, 1968), 25-26.
21. William Danker, *Profit for the Lord* (Grand Rapids, Mich.: Eerdmans, 1971), 18.
22. Otto Uttendörfer, *Wirtschaftsgeist und Wirtschaftsorganisation Herrnhuts 1743–1800* (Herrnhut: Missionsbuchhandlung, 1926), 9.
23. Hans-Christoph Hahn, *Zinzendorf und die Herrnhuter Brüder* (Hamburg: Friedrich Wittig Verlag, 1977), 322.
24. Heinz A. Suter and Marco Gmür, *Business Power for God's Purpose* (Greng: Verlag für kulturbezogenen Gemeindebau, 1997), 89.
25. Helman, *Merchant, Mission and Meditation,* 121.
26. Wanner, Gustav Adolf, *Eduard und Wilhelm Preiswerk* (Zurich: Verein für wirtschaftshistorische Studien, 1984), 13.
27. Karl Rennstich, *Handwerker-Theologen und Industrie-Brüder als Botschafter des Friedens* (Stuttgart: Christliches Verlagshaus, 1985), 36-37.
28. Wilhelm Schlatter, *Geschichte der Basler Mission 1815–1915,* vol. 1 (Basel: Verlag der Basler Missions-Buchhandlung, 1916), 7.
29. Schlatter, *Geschichte der Basler Mission 1815–1915,* vol. 1, 24-26.
30. Rennstich, *Handwerker-Theologen und Industrie-Brüder als Botschafter des Friedens,* 42.
31. Schlatter, *Geschichte der Basler Mission 1815–1915,* vol. 1, 387-388.
32. Danker, *Profit for the Lord,* 102.
33. Gustav Adolf Wanner, *Die Basler Handelsgesellschaft AG 1859–1959* (Basel: Basler Handelsgeselschaft, 1959), 29.
34. Ibid., 51.
35. Ibid., 30.
36. Danker, *Profit for the Lord,* 103.
37. Schlatter, *Geschichte der Basler Mission 1815–1915,* vol. 2, 390.
38. Wanner, *Die Basler Handelsgesellschaft AG 1859–1959,* 216.
39. Danker, *Profit for the Lord,* 97.
40. Schlatter, *Geschichte der Basler Mission 1815–1915,* vol. 2, 162.
41. Wanner, *Die Basler Handelsgesellschaft AG 1859–1959,* 263-264.

CHAPTER 17: INTERNATIONAL DEVELOPMENT SYSTEMS: A CASE STUDY

1. A "shell business" is one that has little or no real business purpose but exists primarily as a platform for obtaining visas and having a legal presence in a country.
2. "International Development Systems" is not the actual name of the company. Since the company operates in restricted-access countries, its real identity is concealed, as are most other proper names in this chapter.
3. The Statement of Vision of International Development Systems is included as appendix 1 at the end of this chapter.
4. The IDS Project is designed to become profitable in its own right.
5. A letter of testimony from a Russian Christian involved in the Project in 2001 is included as appendix 2 at the end of this chapter.
6. A sample business plan of an IDS Project graduate is included as appendix 3 at the end of this chapter.

CHAPTER 19: TAKING FAITH TO WORK

1. Francis Schaeffer, *A Christian Manifesto* (Westchester, Ill.: Crossway, 1981), 19.

CHAPTER 20: PREPARING THE NEXT GENERATION OF KINGDOM ENTREPRENEURS

1. J. I. Packer, "The Christian's Purpose in Business," in Richard C. Chewning, ed., *Biblical Principles and Business: The Practice* (Colorado Springs: NavPress, 1990), 16-25.

2. John Green and Kevin E. Schmiesing, *The State of Economic Education in United States Seminaries* (Grand Rapids, Mich.: Acton Institute, 2001).

3. Steven Rundle, "Ministry, Profits, and the Schizophrenic Tentmaker," *Evangelical Missions Quarterly* 36, no. 3 (2000): 292-300. Available at: www.wheaton.edu/bgc/EMIS/2000/ministryprofits.html.

4. Pete Hammond, R. Paul Stevens, and Todd Svanoe, *The Marketplace Annotated Bibliography: A Christian Guide to Books on Work, Business and Vocation* (Downers Grove, Ill.: InterVarsity, 2002).

5. Don Hamilton, *Tentmakers Speak: Practical Advice from Over Four Hundred Missionary Tentmakers* (Duarte, Calif.: TMQ Research, 1987).

6. Derek Christensen, "Training: Endurance Food for Serious Tentmakers," *International Journal of Frontier Missions* 14, no. 3 (1997): 133-138.

7. Ted Ward, "Repositioning Mission Agencies for the Twenty-First Century," *International Bulletin of Missionary Research* (October 1999): 146-153.

8. William Taylor, ed., *Too Valuable to Lose: Exploring the Causes and Cures of Missionary Attrition* (Pasadena, Calif.: William Carey Library, 1997).

9. Heidi Vander Pol, *Missionary Selection, Stress, and Functioning: A Review of the Literature* (Unpublished doctoral dissertation, La Mirada, Calif.: Biola University, 1994).

10. Stanley Linquist, "A Rationale for Psychological Assessment of Missionary Candidates," *Journal of Psychology and Christianity* 2, no. 4 (1983): 10-14.

11. J. S. Black and H. B. Gregersen, "The Right Way to Manage Expats," *Harvard Business Review* (March/April 1999): 52-62.

12. Susan McGrath-Champ, Xiaohua Yang, and Georgia Chao, "Effects of Expatriate Training on Firm Performance: A Conceptual Approach," paper presented at the meetings of the Academy of International Business, in Sydney, Australia, November 16-19, 2001.

13. Joann Lublin, "Companies Use Cross-cultural Training to Help Their Employees Adjust Abroad," *The Wall Street Journal,* (August 4, 1992): B1, 6.

14. J. S. Black and M. Mendenhall, "Cross Cultural Training Effectiveness: A Review and a Theoretical Framework for Future Research," *Academy of Management Review,* 15, no. 1 (1990): 113-136; W. Britt, "Pretraining Variables in the Prediction of Missionary Success Overseas," *Journal of Psychology and Theology* 11 (1983): 203-212; D. J. Kealy and D. R. Prothroe, "The Effectiveness of Cross-cultural Training for Expatriates: An Assessment of the Literature on the Issue," *International Journal of Intercultural Relations* 20, no. 2 (1996): 141-165; E. Schubert, "A Suggested Prefield Process for Missionary Candidates," *Journal of Psychology and Theology* 27, no. 2 (1999): 87-97.

15. Sunkyu Jun, James Gentry, and Yong Hyun, "Cultural Adaptation of Business Expatriates in the Host Marketplace," *Journal of International Business Studies* 32, no. 2 (2001): 369-377.

16. Tetsunao Yamamori, *Penetrating Missions' Final Frontier: A New Strategy for Unreached Peoples* (Downers Grove, Ill.: InterVarsity, 1993), 62.

17. Black and Gregersen, "The Right Way to Manage Expats."

18. Lublin, "Companies Use Cross-cultural Training to Help Their Employees Adjust Abroad."

19. Black and Gregersen, "The Right Way to Manage Expats."

20. Patrick Lai, unpublished dissertation research, Asian Theological Seminary, Manila, 2002.

21. Rick Love, Frontiers fundraising letter, April 1999.

22. Rodney Stark, *The Rise of Christianity: How the Obscure, Marginal Jesus Movement Became the Dominant Religious Force in the Western World in a Few Centuries* (San Francisco: HarperCollins, 1996).

23. Michael Green, *Evangelism in the Early Church* (Grand Rapids, Mich.: Eerdmans, 1970), 173.

24. William Danker, *Profit for the Lord* (Grand Rapids, Mich.: Eerdmans, 1971), available at: www.intent.org.

25. Patrick Lai, "Starting a Business in a Restricted Access Nation," *International Journal of Frontier Missions* 15, no. 1 (1998): 41-46.

CHAPTER 22: REVIEW OF THE CASE STUDIES FROM A MINISTRY PERSPECTIVE

1. Dorothy Sayers, quoted in John Stott, *Decisive Issues Facing Christians Today* (Old Tappan, N.J.: Revell, 1973), 166.

2. John Stott, ibid.

CHAPTER 24: KEY CONCEPTS AND LESSONS LEARNED

1. In *How Now Shall We Live?* (Wheaton, Ill.: Tyndale, 1999), Charles Colson says, "It is our contention in this book that the Lord's cultural commission [dominion mandate] is inseparable from the great commission" (295).

2. Colson, *How Now Shall We Live?* How does a Christian worldview deal with the important subject of our daily work? Start with the dominion mandate (or, as Colson names it, the cultural mandate) in the first chapter of Genesis: "Until the sixth day, God has done the work of creation directly. But now he creates the first human beings and orders them to carry on where he leaves off: They are to reflect his image and to have dominion (Gen. 1:26). From then on, the development of the creation will be primarily social and cultural: It will be the work of humans as they obey God's command to fill and subdue the earth (Gen. 1:28). . . . Though the creation itself is 'very good,' the task of exploring and developing its powers and potentialities, the task of building a civilization, God turns over to his image bearers. 'By being fruitful they must fill it even more; by subduing it they must form it even more,' explains Al Wolters in *Creation Regained.*

"The same command is still binding on us today. Though the Fall introduced sin and evil into human history, it did not erase the cultural mandate." . . . (295).

"Christians are saved not only *from* something (sin) but also *to* something (Christ's lordship over all of life). The Christian life begins with spiritual restoration, which God works through the preaching of his Word, prayer, the sacraments, worship, and the exercise of spiritual gifts within a local church. This is the indispensable beginning, for only the redeemed person is filled with God's Spirit and can genuinely know and fulfill God's plan. But then we are meant to proceed to the restoration of all God's creation, which includes private and public virtue; individual and family life; education and community; work, politics, and law; science and medicine; literature, art, and music. This redemptive goal permeates everything we do, for there is no invisible dividing line between sacred and secular. We are to bring 'all things' under the lordship of Christ, in the home and the school, in the workshop and the corporate boardroom, on the movie screen and the concert stage, in the city council and the legislative chamber" (296).

3. The following is from my unpublished essay, "Dominion Mandate and the Great Commission":

A man who is exercising his God-given dominion mandate is working in the image of God. He serves every creature in his sphere of influence by nurturing him/her/it to its highest and most appropriate service to produce the goods, services and delights that the creator God intended for His creatures. He/she is a wealth creator in the best sense, and a blessing to his society (Prov. 31). Indeed, he is co-laboring with God because he cannot exercise leadership in this way apart from God's grace. A man who ignores his dominion mandate and will not co-labor with God is a parasite on his society. He will instinctively be shunned and suspected by others as a non-producer.

Exercising his dominion mandate presses a man closer to God and makes him aware of his inadequacies apart from God. It develops character that is admired and authority that is respected (even if it simultaneously produces persecution). It provides a man with the means to share God's abundance with others and to influence many to seek the key to and author of this abundant life. From this fruitful obedience to the dominion mandate flows the Christian's privilege of exercising the 'great commission,' which is to:

Go	the going into all the world is implied already in Gen 1:28 and 9:7. God's people are to co-labor with him wherever he calls us.
Make disciples	This is a mentoring process by setting a lifestyle example. Jesus discipled the Twelve by sharing his life with them, by showing them what he did and how, and by what power he did it.
Baptizing	Baptism confirms the faith and commitment of a disciple. It is both a sign of commitment and God's seal of redemption and adoption.
Teaching	When faith and commitment are present, real learning can begin.

4. See chapter 14, Thomas Sudyk, "Relationship with Missions."
5. See chapter 12, Peter Tsukahira, "Addressing the Dichotomy."
6. J. D. Douglas, ed., *Greek-English New Testament* (Wheaton, Ill.: Tyndale, 1990).
7. The first aorist active imperative of μαθητεύω is μαθητεύσατε. See Ray Summers, *Essentials of New Testament Greek* (Nashville, 1950 [reprint, Nashville: Broadman & Holman, 1995]), 111f., or another Greek New Testament grammar primer.
8. While this is a participle, Πορευθέντι, which sometimes is translated as an imperative, starting the sentence with the imperative *go* would seem to place the emphasis on the going rather than on the verb *making disciples.*
9. Example: God calls a young Australian on a "walkabout," passing through the United States, to get his M.B.A. at Regent University. With no resources, he takes a job and lodging with a Christian ministry. After graduation, he and a fellow alumnus form a company to serve kingdom ministries. He marries and has two sons. Wealth is created, the kingdom enhanced through obedience to the dominion

mandate and the Great Commission. God is not finished with this young man yet, but he is an example of going, trusting God, and being willing to let your light shine wherever God gives opportunity.

10. For more information on C12, or a copy of this article, go to: http://www.thec12group.com.

APPENDIX B (1): THE STEWARDSHIP OF CREATION

1. J. D. Douglas, ed., *Proclaim Christ Until He Comes (Lausanne II, 1989)* (Minneapolis: World Wide, 1990), 410.

APPENDIX B (2): A CALL TO FAITHFULNESS

1. George Soros, *La crisis del capitalismo global* (Buenos Aires: Sudamericana, 1999), 125. Translated from the Spanish by the author.

2. Walter Brueggemann, *Theology of the Old Testament: Testimony, Dispute, Advocacy* (Minneapolis: Fortress, 1997), 581.

APPENDIX B (3): TAKING HOLD OF THE LIFE THAT IS TRULY LIFE

1. Cf. Millard Fuller and Diane Scott, *Love in the Mortar Joints: The Story of Habitat for Humanity* (Clinton, N.J.: New Wine, 1980). According to former President Bill Clinton, Habitat is " . . . the most successful continuous community service project in the history of the United States. It has revolutionized the lives of thousands. . . . Millard Fuller has done as much to make the dream of homeownership a reality in our country and throughout the world as any living person" (Internet: http://www.habitat.org/how/millard.html).

2. From Internet: http://www.habitat.org/how/historytext.html.

3. Cf. Craig L. Blomberg, *Neither Poverty nor Riches: A Biblical Theology of Possessions* (Leicester: Apollos, 1999). See especially Philippians 4:10-19, a superb example of the way in which Paul combines his expression of gratitude for offerings received from the Philippian church with a clear affirmation of his freedom from self-seeking interests.

APPENDIX C: DYNAMICS OF FAITH

1. M. M. Hanna, *Crucial Questions in Apologetics* (Grand Rapids, Mich.: Baker, 1981), 80-85.

2. Peter D. Ward and Donald Brownlee, *Rare Earth* (New York: Copernicus, 2000).

3. William A. Dembski, *Intelligent Design* (Downers Grove, Ill.: InterVarsity, 1999).

4. Gregory J. Chaitin, "Gödel's Theorem and Information," *International Journal of Theoretical Physics* 21, no. 12 (1982): 941-953.

5. Cf. the Nature of Nature Conference held at the Polanyi Center, Baylor University, April 12-15, 2000 in Waco, Texas.

6. I. I. Rabi, quoted in Gerald Holton, "I. I. Rabi as Educator and Science Warrior," *Physics Today* (September 1999), 38.

7. Roger Penrose, *Shadows of the Mind: A Search for the Missing Science of Consciousness* (New York: Oxford University Press, 1996).

8. Jerome Kagan, *Three Seductive Ideas* (Cambridge, Mass.: Harvard University Press, 1989), 189-193.

9. Paul Teller, "A Poor Man's Guide to Supervenience and Determination," *Southern Journal of Philosophy* 22, Supplement (1984): 137-162.

10. Rodney Stark, *The Rise of Christianity* (San Francisco: HarperCollins, 1997), 214-215.

11. Edwin Yamauchi, *The Stones and the Scriptures* (Philadelphia and New York: Holman, 1972).

12. Roy Clouser, *Knowing with the Heart* (Downers Grove, Ill.: InterVarsity, 1999), 72.

13. Clouser gives an impressive list of thinkers who have described such non-discursive experiences: Aristotle, Aquinas, Descartes, John Locke, Leibnitz, Popper, and Plantinga. Plantinga, for example, affirms belief in God from direct perception (see *Faith and Rationality* [Notre Dame, Ind.: University of Notre Dame Press, 1983]).

14. Henri Poincaré, *The Foundations of Science*, trans. G. B. Halstead (New York: The Science Press, 1929), 388.

15. The foregoing section, "Five Evidences," is adapted from Kenell J. Touryan, "From Objective Realism to Subjective Relativism," *Journal of the American Scientific Affiliation* 53, no. 3 (September 2001): 188-193. Adapted by permission.

16. The dotted lines are drawn intentionally to sidestep the knotty issues regarding dichotomy or trichotomy. Also, the point where the three triangles—or the five evidences—meet could represent the entry point where God, through the power of his word, upholds all of reality, without contravening his physical laws.

General Index

Scripture Index